ESSAYS IN BASQUE SOCIAL ANTHROPOLOGY AND HISTORY

Edited by

William A. Douglass

Basque Studies Program Occasional Papers Series, No. 4

BASQUE STUDIES PROGRAM
University of Nevada, Reno, Nevada

Copyright 1989 by Basque Studies Program

Library of Congress Cataloging-in-Publication Data

Essays in Basque social anthropology and history / edited by William A. Douglass.
    p. cm. — (Basque Studies Program occasional papers series: no. 4)
  Includes bibliographies.
  1. Basques—Social life and customs. 2. Basques—Folklore. 3. Basques—History. I. Douglass, William A. II. Series.
GN549.B3E86   1989
306'.0899992—dc20   89-15013
                                                                             CIP
ISBN: 1-877802-02-6

TABLE OF CONTENTS

	PAGE
INTRODUCTION by William A. Douglass	**1**

PART I: BASQUE SOCIAL ANTHROPOLOGY AND FOLKLORE

ON TIME: NOTES REGARDING THE ANTHROPOLOGY OF JULIO CARO BAROJA by Jesús Azcona	**9**
SINGING DUELS AND SOCIAL SOLIDARITY: THE CASE OF THE BASQUE *CHARIVARI* by Roslyn M. Frank	**43**
BASQUE CONFLICT MANAGEMENT CHOICES by M. E. R. Nicholson	**81**
BASQUE LEGENDS IN THEIR SOCIAL CONTEXT by Elena Arana Williams	**107**
THE CURRENT STATUS OF THE ANTHROPOLOGY OF WOMEN: MODELS AND PARADIGMS by Teresa del Valle	**129**
REINVENTING BASQUE SOCIETY: CULTURAL DIFFERENCE AND THE QUEST FOR MODERNITY, 1918–1936 by Jacqueline Urla	**149**
GAC: MILITANT CARLIST ACTIVISM, 1968–1972 by Jeremy MacClancy	**177**

PART II: SOCIAL HISTORY: THE BASQUE COUNTRY AND ITS IMMIGRANT DIASPORA

AIMERY PICAUD AND THE BASQUES: SELECTIONS FROM *THE PILGRIM'S GUIDE TO SANTIAGO DE COMPOSTELA*   **189**
by Rachel Bard

BILBAO IN THE ECONOMY OF THE BASQUE COUNTRY AND NORTHWESTERN EUROPE DURING THE MODERN ERA   **215**
by Román Basurto

AN ESTIMATE OF NAVARRESE MIGRATION IN THE SECOND HALF OF THE NINETEENTH CENTURY (1879–1883)   **235**
by Angel García-Sanz Marcotegui and Alejandro Arizcun Cela

FACTORS IN THE FORMATION OF THE NEW-WORLD BASQUE EMIGRANT DIASPORA   **251**
by William A. Douglass

A WANTED MAN: THE BASQUE, EL COJO GOMEZ, IN COLOMBIA   **269**
by Kay Hummel

CALIFORNIA'S BASQUE HOTELS AND THEIR *HOTELEROS*   **297**
by Jerónima Echeverría

THE OVERLAND: THE LAST BASQUE HOTEL   **317**
by Gretchen Osa

Introduction

by

William A. Douglass

In recent years the disciplinary boundary between history and anthropology has become blurred if not quite obliterated. The reaction by some historians, most notably those of the *Annales* school, against history as the chronicle of great personages and major events coincided with the discomfort of some anthropologists with the synchronic approach of structural-functional social anthropology.

For the historian, anthropology provided a focus upon "the people" and methodological rigor in the form of models and theories, as well as a broad comparative framework which transcended the western experience. For the anthropologist, history offered a welcome means of providing the middle-range temporal depth that was regularly missing in anthropological analysis. By this I mean that it was never quite accurate to state that the standard ethnographic monograph lacked a time frame or that the discipline was insensitive to history. The most synchronic of ethnographies reflected some sense of temporal movement even if limited to cyclical processes or change within the local setting, elucidated, and therefore circumscribed, by the recollections of living actors. Furthermore, practically from its inception, anthropology elaborated grand evolutionary schemes within which to situate all human societies whether actual or extinct. The history of historians provided time frames that transcended the moment and memory of contemporaries without eliciting the whole sweep of human evolution.

Over the past two decades, then, anthropologists and historians have begun to read and invoke one another's luminaries. Thus, historians regularly cite Clifford Geertz and Mary Douglas while anthropologists reciprocate with kudos for Emmanuel Le Roy Ladurie and Carlo Ginsburg. This rapprochement is perhaps best discussed in

Bernard Cohn's (1980) seriocomic, yet seminal, description of "historyland" and "anthropologyland" that appeared in *Comparative Studies in Society and History* (a journal coedited and shared by historians and anthropologists).[1] The two intellectual "countries" trade and traffic in common ideas and concerns without quite relinquishing their individual sovereignty. Thus, it is still possible to distinguish what might be deemed "anthropological history," i.e. history informed by anthropological concerns, from "historical anthropology," i.e. anthropology with properly developed diachronic analysis.[2]

The present volume of articles, dealing with both the European homeland and emigrant diaspora of the Basques in various periods, is a prime example of the process of convergence/divergence of the two disciplines. At one level it struck me as useful to subsume essays by anthropologists with those of historians into a single volume (while seasoning the stew with a pinch of other specialists as well). Indeed, it seems to me that our historians and anthropologists might have comfortably switched topics without experiencing undue discomfort, a reflection of the converging interests of the two fields. At the same time, I suspect that had they done so the results would have been different, though not wildly so.

Part I of this collection of essays begins with Jesús Azcona's discussion of the work of Julio Caro Baroja, possibly the most controversial and enigmatic figure within twentieth-century Basque letters. In one view Caro Baroja, along with José Miguel de Barandiarán, occupies a pivotal role in the history of Basque anthropology, providing the intellectual link between nineteenth- and early twentieth-century figures like Telesforo de Aranzadi and the current generation of anthropological practitioners (which includes Azcona himself). Central to an understanding of Caro Baroja's anthropological vision is his methodology (more implicit than explicit throughout his works while varying from one to another) and his concept of time.

It is particularly appropriate to begin this volume with treatment of Julio Caro Baroja, since even prior to the promulgation of the charters of historyland and anthropologyland he held a passport from both. The nature of his loyalties and predilections in this regard is a leitmotif throughout his lengthy and amazingly prolific career. Thus he was equally as capable of proclaiming, "I am not, either by vocation or profession, a sociologist or anthropologist strictly speaking. I am, simply, a devotee of History and the Humanities who does not presume to derive from his works scientific consequences of general validity"[3] as he was of publishing a work entitled *Anthropological Disquisitions*.[4]

The following three articles of this volume deal with the issue of social conflict and its resolution in Basque society. They all manifest a distinctive blending of anthropological and historical concerns. Literary critic Roslyn Frank analyzes the nineteenth-century Basque *charivari*, treating it as a dramaturgical performance. However, rather than discussing its literary merits she examines the *charivari* as a morality play with direct social consequences, a popular extralegal mechanism for righting the social balance after perceived transgression.

Anthropologist M. E. R. Nicholson examines the alternatives available for conflict resolution in twentieth-century French Basque communities in light of the anthropological and legal literatures on disputation and mediation. She situates her argument in broad historical context by considering ways in which Basques have perceived and dealt with external threats and internal conflicts in the past.

In her article folklorist Elena Arana Williams focusses upon one line of evidence in the Basque anthropological tradition: namely, the myriad of folk tales collected over several decades by José Miguel de Barandiarán. The tales are analyzed both in terms of their internal structure and as windows upon traditional Basque world view. Like the *charivari*, they acquire moralistic overtones defining for the listener the parameters of transgression while providing a prescription for redress. The approach is consonant with the current fashion within anthropology to regard culture as a text.

The analysis of folk tales underscores the importance of females as mediators between the natural and supernatural worlds, a proper segue for Teresa del Valle's article regarding the anthropological treatment of women. As editor and coauthor of two book-length works on Basque women, del Valle courageously employs the present article as an opportunity to discuss the shortcomings of her own published research while indicating the directions that future investigations of Basque womanhood might take.

Anthropologists Jacqueline Urla and Jeremy MacClancy each address little-appreciated aspects of twentieth-century Basque nationalism. Urla analyzes the agenda of the First Basque Congress (1918) and the program of the Basque Studies Society in order to countermand the notion, current in the literature, that most of Europe's contemporary ethnonationalist movements are intrinsically traditionalist and conservative. Rather, she finds that at least some sectors of the Basque nationalist movement were, in their formative decades, modernist, and even futuristic, in orientation. They were characterized by profound confidence in the efficacy of science when applied to the resolution of social problems.

Anthropologist Jeremy MacClancy provides a welcome analysis of a largely neglected element within the recent history of political violence in the Basque Country. For the casual observer and the specialist alike, ETA has become synonymous with violent resistance to Spanish political hegemony in the Basque Country. Similarly, it is common to view Carlism as somewhat antithetical to Basque nationalism, if for no other reason than that both movements contest support on the same political turf. The present analysis of the GAC faction within Carlism underscores the complexity of twentieth-century Basque ethnonationalism defined in its broadest terms. It is also an excellent contribution to the growing literature on political violence, particularly that which deals with "terrorism."

Part II opens with historian Rachel Bard's annotated translation of Aimery Picaud's twelfth-century work, *The Pilgrim's Guide to Santiago de Compostela*, which deals with travels through the Basque Country. Bard situates the guide in both its historical and scholarly contexts. Picaud sheds early light on one of the least understood corners of medieval Europe, depicting the Basques as a barbarous and treacherous people while providing the earliest evidence of the language as reflected in a short list of vocabulary words that he transcribed.

The Basque world described by Román Basurto is markedly different. Beginning in the thirteenth century he considers the rise of the port of Bilbao, favored by its location between Atlantic and Mediterranean Europe and buoyed by maritime trade in such items as Castilian wool and Basque iron. By the sixteenth century, however, events and developments in both Europe and the Americas began to eclipse the city. Basurto provides the reader with a *longue durée* view of Bilbao's fortunes over six centuries that is worthy of a Braudel.

The article on nineteenth-century Navarrese patterns of transatlantic emigration and internal migration by Angel García-Sanz Marcotegui and Alejandro Arizcun is firmly within the recent tradition of social science history. Employing statistical data derived from censuses and other questionnaires, the authors view migration dynamics against the broader backdrop of Navarrese demographic trends, presenting a convincing argument that the relative nineteenth-century stasis in Navarra's population, when compared to national averages, is largely attributable to extensive emigration. Participation in the movement was not, however, distributed equally throughout the province, prompting the authors to construct a kind of internal regional atlas of departures and returns that will surely serve as a baseline for future refinements of our understanding of Navarrese migration patterns.

That there should be further study of Navarrese and, by extension, Basque migration is the subject of William A. Douglass's essay. Coauthor of a general work on Basque migrants, *Amerikanuak: Basques in the New World*,[5] Douglass argues that emigration is a relatively neglected subject in Basque studies. This is particularly surprising, considering that since at least the fifteenth-century transatlantic emigration and the feedback of persons, resources, and ideas from the Basque emigrant diaspora have been major factors in Old-World Basque social and economic organization. The present article discusses the theoretical concerns that inspired the argument in *Amerikanuak...* rather than its specific content and conclusions. It also surveys the current state of studies of Basque emigration, noting that relatively more is known about the activities of the migrants in their various New-World adopted settings than about the causes and consequences of their departures from the European homeland.

Kay Hummel's description of the personality and activities of a notorious Basque figure in the wilds of Colombia represents both a thematic and temporal departure. The exploits of "El Cojo Gómez" constitute a first-rate adventure story. More importantly, however, they illuminate several dimensions of a modern Basque presence in one South American nation whose influence was all out of proportion to its minuscule numbers. In documenting Gómez's activities on behalf of Allied Intelligence in World War II the article also evokes an, as yet, underdeveloped chapter in Basque history.

Our volume ends with two highly contrastive, yet complementary, views of what has often been described as the key social institution for the Basque emigrant diaspora—the ethnic boardinghouse or hotel. Jerónima Echeverría casts her historian's eye upon the hotels of California, the setting in the American West where the institution is first discernible in conjunction with the gold rush and its spin-offs. The analysis traces the California hotels in terms of their origins, spread, and evolution down to the present. A fine structural analysis of their internal organization is supplemented by a typology which distinguishes between classes of hotels according to their functions and sphere of influence.

Gretchen Osa, herself the daughter of an Elko, Nevada, hotelkeeper, effected a study of Nevada's Basque establishments. Her charming treatment, in the form of a "mood" piece inspired by the ambience of one Nevada establishment, is a wonderful reminder that both anthropology and history have humanistic roots and literary properties. Our present penchant for quantification and the quantifiable, and for couching our results in ascetic and aseptic jargon in the quest for a neutral language of objectivity can obfuscate as much as illumine. The *ongi etorri* of Marcelino and the other denizens of the Overland Hotel is as much a "welcome" to our own humanistic tradition as to a Basque establishment in one small Nevada town.

Notes

1. Bernard S. Cohn, "History and Anthropology: the State of Play," *Comparative Studies in Society and History*, vol. 22, no. 2 (April, 1980), pp. 198-221.
2. It should also be noted that both fields are currently in an extreme state of flux and that the reshaping of the two disciplines has not been without its critics. Currently, anthropology is fragmented into so many schools and approaches that it is heterodoxical to an extreme, if not downright anarchical (George E. Marcus and Michael M. J. Fischer, *Anthropology as Cultural Critique. An Experimental Moment in the Human Sciences* (Chicago and London: University of Chicago Press, 1986)). Nor is there any longer opposition to incorporating temporal awareness into anthropological analysis (of whatever stripe) whenever possible. Similarly, some historians have become extremely critical of the *Annales* school and other forms of "new" history (Gertrude Himmelfarb, *The New History and the Old. Critical Essays and Reappraisals* (Cambridge, Mass., and London: The Belknap Press of Harvard University Press, 1987); and Roger Chartier, *Cultural History* (Ithaca: Cornell University Press, 1988)). The validity of the cross-fertilization between the two disciplines has been questioned on occasion (Cf. Renato Rosaldo, "From the Door of His Tent: The Fieldworker and the Inquisitor," in James Clifford and George E. Marcus (editors), *Writing Culture* (Berkeley and Los Angeles: University of California Press, 1986), pp. 77-97). Indeed, all of this raises the thorny issue of which province of anthropologyland is informing which province of historyland and vice versa.
3. Julio Caro Baroja, *La ciudad y el campo* (Madrid: Editores Alfaguara, 1966).
4. Julio Caro Baroja and Emilio Temprano, *Disquisiciones antropológicas* (Madrid: Ediciones Istmo, 1985).
5. William A. Douglass and Jon Bilbao, *Amerikanuak: Basques in the New World* (Reno: University of Nevada Press, 1975).

PART I: Basque Social Anthropology and Folklore

On Time: Notes Regarding the Anthropology of Julio Caro Baroja

by

Jesús Azcona

The Intellectual Background of Julio Caro Baroja; Life and Works

It is not easy to summarize the intellectual profile of Julio Caro Baroja for either the Hispanic or American publics. In the Hispanic world there are few who have never heard his name, at least on television and radio programs and in newspaper articles regarding witchcraft, *Moriscos*, and the Basques. Similarly, he has published widely in the popular press on these topics as well as on contemporary Spanish life. In the years 1982 and 1983 he was himself made newsworthy in both the academic world and political circles when the city of Madrid made him a "distinguished citizen" (*hijo predilecto*) and Navarra named him an "adopted son." He also received the Prince of Asturias prize in the social sciences and was made an honorary fellow of the Royal Anthropological Institute of Great Britain and Ireland. For those most directly interested in and, indeed, personally involved in Basque nationalist politics and social problems of the Basque Country, the stands of Julio Caro Baroja elicit controversy. Nevertheless, few have read even one of his numerous works, despite the fact that many have been reissued and, one would have thought, read by his critics. Neither in the intellectual world in general nor the strictly academic one in particular are his ideas expounded and discussed. Rather, some of them are invoked occasionally to support given political postures, usually by the politicians themselves or by other interested parties.

Julio Caro Baroja is little known in North American circles, despite the fact that the first work regarding him was written in 1971 by Davydd Greenwood, an American anthropologist, and he has been in contact on several occasions with American institutions and anthropologists.

Nevertheless, the main details of his personal biography are available to all, particularly since Caro Baroja published in the book *Los Baroja* (1972) his recollections of the family through the death (in 1956) of his famed uncle Pío Baroja, and in 1981 he wrote his own short autobiography. Both previously and subsequently he has been the object of countless interviews, or his person has been profiled through his published memoirs with certain additions.[1]

Succinctly and schematically, the highlights of Julio Caro Baroja's biography are as follows. He was born in Madrid in 1914 where he received his early educational training. In 1942 he completed his doctorate in Ancient History. During this period he was in close contact with the prestigious historian H. Obermaier and the no less famed ethnologist H. Trimborn (1933-1936), as well as with a limited but renowned circle of intellectuals that met in the home of his uncle Pío, in discussion groups in cafes or at the Atheneum. These meetings took place in the years before the rebellion and military coup of General Franco.

From the war until about the early 1960s was a difficult period in every respect for Julio Caro Baroja. Some of his friends died, others were exiled or opted for "self-exile," as did his uncle Pío. In short, his accustomed academic and familial worlds collapsed. Though punctuated with difficulties, and at times requiring him to occupy posts of scant importance, this period was critical to his future development. From 1943 to 1945 he was an assistant professor in the departments of Spanish Ancient History and Dialectology at the University of Madrid. In 1944 he was named director of the Museo del Pueblo Español of Madrid and in 1947 he was made a corresponding member of the Academia de la Lengua Vasca and that of Buenas Letras in Barcelona. The post of museum director placed him in contact with American and British social anthropologists like Julian Pitt-Rivers, George M. Foster and Michael Kenny, among others. He received grants from the Wenner Gren Foundation and the British Council to continue his anthropological training. He effected fieldwork in the Saharan region of Morocco and taught anthropology at the University of Coimbra. His library research between 1936 and 1939, the new knowledge that he acquired in England and the United States and his field investigation resulted in several publications, for example, *Los pueblos del Norte de la Península Ibérica* (1943), *La vida rural vasca en Vera de Bidasoa* (1944), *Los pueblos de España. Ensayo de etnología (1946), Análisis de la cultura* (1949), *Los vascos* (1949), *Estudios saharianos* (1955), *España primitiva y romana* (1957), *Los moriscos del Reyno de Granada* (1957), *Estudios mogrebies* (1957), *Razas, pueblos y linajes* (1957) and *Vasconia* (1957). His numerous articles published throughout this period have been reissued in several volumes during the 1970s, when literature regarding Basque themes proliferated. Under the generic name of "Basque Studies," during the decade he published nine volumes of collected essays.

Between 1960 and 1975 Julio Caro Baroja continued to publish an average of half a book and more than ten articles annually. It is from this period that we have some of his most prestigious publications, including *Las brujas y su mundo* (1961), *Los judíos en la España moderna y contemporánea* (1962), *El carnaval* (1965), *La ciudad y el campo* (1966), *Vidas mágicas e inquisición* (1967), *El señor inquisidor y otras vidas por oficio* (1968), *Ensayo sobre la literatura de Cordel* (1969), *La hora navarra del XVIII* (1969), *El mito del carácter nacional. Meditaciones a contrapelo* (1970), *Inquisición, brujería y criptojudaísmo* (1970), *Etnografía histórica de Navarra* (3 volumes, 1972), *Los vascos y la historia a través de Garibay* (1972), *Semblanzas ideales* (1972) and *Los Baroja* (1972).

This period is particularly crucial to Caro Baroja's world view and conceptualization of sociocultural reality. The historicity of facts or, which is the same thing, the succession of the passage of time, is the element which appears throughout his works. Similarly, they are imbued with an awareness of the absurd dimension of life as it works towards its irreversible destiny which is death. The emphasis upon economic development by Franco's *Opus Dei* ministers converted into "archeology" much of the traditional life that Caro Baroja observed and wrote about as part of a living culture. Also, in the "inexorable" and "fatal" decade of the 1950s his father, mother and uncles Pío and Ricardo all died, leaving him with the sense that he was "now first in line for the blows of the Grim Reaper."[2] All of the foregoing affected him profoundly and sharpened his view of the world, as he himself confesses.[3]

After 1975 Julio Caro Baroja entered a period of his life characterized by considerable recognition, particularly in Spanish and Basque public circles, as well as a certain economic independence. His articles appeared with regularity in national newspapers, he taught short courses for the Consejo Superior de Investigaciones Científicas and he was named director of publications for the Institución Príncipe de Viana of Navarra and professor of philosophical anthropology at the University of the Basque Country. His publications during this period echo those of the previous one, although there is the added dimension of a concern with contemporary problems, particularly in his journalistic works and a few of his monographs. In recent years he has also demonstrated an interest in the history of anthropology, beginning with the dawn of the discipline in ancient Greek thought.

Some of his works from the period are *Las formas complejas de la vida religiosa: religión, sociedad y carácter en la España de los siglos XVI y XVII* (1978), *Una imagen del mundo perdida* (1979), *La estación del amor (fiestas populares de mayo a San Juan)* (1979), *Cuadernos de campo* (1979), *Vidas poco paralelas (con perdón de Plutarco)* (1981), *La casa en Navarra* (1982), *La aurora del pensamiento antropológico* (1983), *El estío festivo (fiestas populares de verano)* (1984), *Los fundamentos del pensamiento antropológico moderno* (1985) and *Antropología criminológica* (1986). It is during this period that many of his previously published and unpublished works regarding the Basque Country were reissued in the "Basque Studies" (Estudios Vascos) series (twelve volumes published to date). Others of his articles were reissued in *Comentarios sin fé* (1979), *Ensayos sobre la cultura popular española* (1979), *Temas castizos* (1980), *Tecnología popular española* (1983), *Paisajes y ciudades* (1984) and *Estudios ibéricos* (1985).

A simple reading of the titles of his published works underscores their abundance. It is difficult to imagine anyone equaling such a scholarly output, though Caro Baroja's life was largely free of academic posts and other occupations that might have distracted him from writing.

At present, despite his age, Julio Caro Baroja continues to work intensely, dividing his time between Madrid and Vera de Bidasoa (Navarra), once again free from the short-lived academic commitments that he made to the University of the Basque Country. No one can foresee what he may offer us next.

Julio Caro Baroja and Anthropology

The majority of Julio Caro Baroja's work has a marked ethnographic and anthropological overtone despite the fact that it usually deals with historical themes and issues. Over time this has become such a fundamental and important characteristic that familiarity with Caro Baroja's work is currently indispensable to the understanding and analysis of European peoples, as well as certain general anthropological theoretical concerns. As Davydd Greenwood observes, "his selection of theories and concepts, the sources that he employs and the themes that he investigates can serve as a model for we anthropologists; the integration of history and anthropology realized by this erudite [should serve as an example] to be explored and applied in our studies of Europe."[4] The importance of Caro Baroja's work, however, transcends Old World frontiers in that the past is a dimension of the sociocultural reality of all human groups, and it is history that has concerned and continues to concern him.

His works are equally important to the understanding and study of Basque culture. He has devoted a large part of his life and numerous publications to it. With his interest in deciphering Basque social history, his work constitutes a lengthy bridge which unites the efforts of prehistorians and archeologists with studies of contemporary Basque cultural reality. This approach is indispensable in studying the relationship between the past and the present. All three approaches are important to a full understanding of contemporary Basque culture. As Evans-Pritchard wrote, "a people's traditional history is important for the further reason that it forms part of the thought of living men and hence part of the social life which anthropologists can directly observe."[5] Or, in Caro Baroja's own words, "I do not believe that it is possible to understand mankind without taking into account its past."[6]

Nevertheless, it is difficult to classify the work of Caro Baroja in terms of either theme[7] or method. While it is certainly possible to extract certain central ideas in his work, as did Davydd Greenwood, it is equally certain that it is only possible to do so by leaving out many others. The world of folk beliefs or religious ideas and their connections with other aspects of social life has been, for example, an important theme, as underscored by Caro Baroja himself.[8] The same is true with respect to certain aspects of his methodology. The influences that he received are mingled at times with his own theoretical elaborations and personal life experiences throughout his scholarly career.

In this regard it has been repeated frequently, including by those who apparently know his work well, that Julio Caro Baroja lacks a method.[9] Indeed, his own affirmations appear to corroborate this view.[10] Clearly, it is not possible to find in his work, "a sole, clear and very elaborated methodology," but it is also true that it contains "a general orientation" a "temporal transfusion," as he himself affirms, and a methodology employing the concept of cultural cycles.[11] In my judgment this is the methodology that underlies the majority of his works, even though, as noted by Greenwood, "frequently his intentions and interpretations are so interwoven into the text that one unfamiliar with his philosophy cannot easily determine either the goals of the work or its relationship with other treatments of the same themes."[12] Nevertheless, in his earlier works, as well as in the prologues and epilogues to the reeditions of his previous publications, and in certain new publications, particularly beginning in the 1970s, we can find numerous reflections on theory and methodology. So even though they are not found in a systematic format, nor are they expounded exhaustively, they offer more than enough to discern Caro Baroja's understanding of general anthropology, as well as the presuppositions and method that underpin his own variation of it.[13]

In a theoretical and methodological sense, the space and time dimensions of sociocultural phenomena, with particular emphasis upon the latter, recur in almost obsessive fashion. Beginning in the 1970s he is particularly conscious of this and attempts to give it more definite form, particularly in two short articles whose relevance to an understanding of his concepts is underscored by Caro Baroja himself.[14] The articles in question are entitled "Cosas humanas y tiempos de ellas" (Human Facts and Their Time Dimensions) and "Mundos circundantes y contorno histórico-culturales" (Embracing Worlds and Historico-Cultural Outlines), both published in 1974. In the present work I propose to detail the progressive emergence and particular conceptualization of the time dimension in Caro Baroja's work.

His theoretical and methodological conceptualization of time, although it is close to that of culture cycles which, in fact, he employs in some of his works,[15] is more based, as he himself affirms, on the thought of nineteenth century anthropologists and historians such as Ratzel and E. Meyer.[16] It is important to understand the definition that Caro Baroja gives to cycle if we are to understand the subtle differences characteristic of the way that various intellectual schools conceive history and how they influence his thought, on the one hand, and how the thinking of Caro Baroja differs from that of his earlier teachers, such as Telesforo de Aranzadi and José Miguel de Barandiarán, on the other. For Caro Baroja, "An historical cycle is something that begins when a new development appears, which then climaxes and, subsequently, undergoes processes of decline or destruction until such time that another [cycle] with distinctive or completely different characteristics begins."[17] This definition was formulated through reflection upon developments in Vera de Bidasoa, some time after having completed his investigations there: " ... in our small and humble setting a real cycle commences at the beginning of the Modern Age and closes or is closing in inexorable fashion before our eyes. Within it there appear technical forms that supplant others, institutions are strengthened and rules are discernible. Regarding all of this there is constancy in documents of various types. But within the cycle there is also crisis, changes, transitions that must be measured and weighed."[18]

Despite the fact that the terms and analogy with the "vital cycle of mankind" suggests a certain "biologizing" of culture, such is not the case. Caro Baroja's affirmations in this regard are clear. "I have always thought that the same context is something completely distinct for different persons," he answers when questioned about the obsession of some scholars (in this case Taine), with linking the physical world with cultural life.[19] In one of his earliest and most important works he notes that, although it is important to consider the environment, it, like concepts such as "race, rationality, irrationality as sole explicators of cultural differences, are inadequate."[20] Similarly, the definition of cycle proposed by Caro Baroja differs from that employed by F. Gräbner and W. Schmidt of the *Kulterkreislehre* school of thought, as well as from that used by J. M. Barandiarán. For them the cycle or cultural circle is characterized by the *qualities* reflected in material objects, institutions and beliefs, and the culture is conceived as an indivisible structure whose parts are organically interrelated, making its constancy indisputable.[21] For Julio Caro Baroja, on the other hand, material objects, institutions and beliefs acquire priority only as expressions of forms of thought and modes of perceiving the world, and are themselves in a state of constant change. At times the change is long term, at others short term, and the rate can vary between slow and rapid. It is this which originates tensions and conflicts between men of one and another epoch. It is out of the relationship and combination of individual experience and the particular character that each culture acquires that Caro Baroja derives his conceptualizations, rather than out of atemporal essences and characteristics of the cultural creations of mankind in general (irrespective of temporal and spatial considerations).

As may be appreciated from this brief exposition we are confronted in the work of Caro Baroja with an anti-positivist and anti-essentialist view of sociocultural reality. This accounts for the constant attacks and reproaches of the work of others that are sprinkled throughout his publications.

I believe that it is not necessary to have recourse to the details of his personal life, or the fact that he failed to discharge a major academic post, or his lack of disciples, or chance which led him to read certain works and not others, or his lack of self promotion, or his basic humility (in accord with the most stereotyped opinions currently held of him), in order to understand his work and its limited impact in academic circles, although each of the above elements likely contributed. His utilization of an historical method during a lengthy period when anthropology was disposed to employ any other kind is the basis for the scant influence of his work among anthropologists both in Spain and abroad. It should not be forgotten that the deep disfavor in which the historical method fell was paralleled by the considerable prestige acquired by essentially ahistorical methodology in anthropology. In such a climate intellectual dialogue became impossible. The "near anachronism" of an author who "had managed to have an international scholarly reputation without having had an academic post and without a group of university disciples as such,"[22] can be explained by Caro Baroja's constant and extensive effort employing methods that were out of favor, in the face of unrelenting scepticism. However, once a considerable number of the anthropological "-isms" were discredited or disappeared, as were those of the anthropologists whom Caro Baroja characterized as believing they possessed "the good truth,"[23] his method was found to possess as much veracity as any other or, at the very least, addressed certain aspects of sociocultural reality that other anthropologists did not contemplate or even addressed incorrectly.

The Concept of Time

> It used to cause me considerable pain to contemplate the infinity of space; to believe that the world was interminable impressed me greatly; it saddened me to think that the day after my death space and time would continue to exist, and this despite the fact that I did not consider my life to be enviable. But when I came to realize that the ideas of space and time are spiritual necessities for us, but which have no reality; when, through Kant, I became convinced that space and time mean nothing, or at the very least that the concept we have of them cannot exist outside of ourselves, I was consoled. For me it is a reassurance to think that, just as our retinas produce colors our brain produces ideas regarding time, space and causality. Once our brain is terminated the world is extinguished. Time no longer flows; space no longer follows; there are no longer linked causes. We may suppose that a time and space continues for others. But what difference does it make if they are not ours, which is the only reality?[24]

I like to imagine Pío Baroja, who was responsible for the foregoing paragraph, taking lengthy walks, his mind aboil with the "vulgarities disguised in scientific apparatus, adorned with rhetorical concepts that simpleton professors and students accepted as prophetic visions, heard in classrooms," while he contemplated with astonishment daily fashions and sufferings, and the life and death of those who influenced him, impassioned, if somewhat stoically, with the most imaginable vital necessities, rituals and behaviors that were practically inconceivable for men who were defined as scientists.

Contemplating the customs and ideas of Basques who were born and gave birth, who toiled and were attached to a land which despite great effort scarcely provided them with their subsistence, the discourses of learned men no doubt seemed like those which Pío placed in the mouth of one of his characters, "games of prestidigitators, at times ingenious, at others vulgar, but always without any reality whether metaphysical or empirical."

Presumably, for Pío Baroja, as for many others, the infinity of time and space, rather than serving as a reflection and proof at the same time of the existence of God, as contended by the philosophical and theological scholarship of the period, became one more argument against the reality of a Supreme Being. God could not exist and create time and space as eternal while man was made mortal. A god preoccupied with the tiniest detail of cosmic engineering, in which heavenly bodies enjoyed limitless time and space, and unconcerned with mankind which suffered from the passage of time and the limitations of space did not merit divine status, or at least being mankind's deity. In order to hide such a searing injustice from the minds of men, Catholic simpletons had propagated the image of Luther and Catalina Bora contemplating cosmic time and space while lamenting the fact that they could never attain them because of their rupture with the Catholic Church.

No one doubts that time constitutes one of the fundamental dimensions in which the existence of beings and things are interwoven. Regarding it, however, anthropologists, both past and present, have reflected but little, despite making use of the concept, albeit largely in abusive fashion. They have temporalized a large part of their anthropological discourse in a manner which permits them to present the results of their research in coherent and harmonious evolutionary formats which even include time frames that evoked pleasure from the gods and the cosmic universe but which tormented Pío Baroja. The beings, things and anthropological discourse are interwoven with and in time. But with which time are we really confronted?

It is my belief that Julio Caro Baroja's reflections on temporality and spatiality as sociocultural phenomena are precisely one of his major contributions to general theory and anthropological thought in particular. Confronted with the methods of renowned schools fashionable in different periods, and with the works of those who subscribed to them, whether concerned with Basque topics or not, Julio Caro Baroja has, in a progressively firmer and more caustic manner throughout his lengthy research career, demonstrated how they have failed to deal convincingly with the temporal dimension.[25]

It is my purpose in these brief, and as yet incomplete, notes to show how, on the one hand, anthropology, in organizing its facts, constructs its own concept of time, while, on the other, I wish to discuss the sense of time that Julio Caro Baroja attributes to facts, and how from this mankind's temporality is derived.

Anthropological Time

Usually, anthropologists have found themselves trapped by a paradox and dilemma at the moment of presenting the results of their investigations. Interested in determining the origins and describing, explaining, and understanding past and present social phenomena, while discovering ultimately some sort of regularity that ties them together, anthropologists face the paradox of having to resort to the past in order to make the present intelligible and vice versa. To try to determine the past solely with the few and fragmentary bits of evidence available becomes a task that is seldom consummated satisfactorily. The pieces of the puzzle are so few and at times so ambiguous that it is only possible to interpret them, in even provisional fashion, through recourse to the present. There is a similar procedure when we seek to understand the present, which is uninterpretable without reference to the past. This is necessary not only because the present is genetically linked with the past, but also because the past forms an important component of the thinking and social life of contemporary persons. The causes and effects of an event are one thing, the role it plays in the life of a collectivity through memory and collective representations is another. Past history is found in such form enclosed in and pertaining to the present, although at the same time separated from it. Consequently, to ignore or disdain history signifies renouncing comprehension and explication of the present.[26]

Equally interested in describing and understanding social phenomena derived from different social periods and historical epochs, anthropologists are confronted with the dilemma of ascribing to them (or not) system or meaning within some sort of general framework. Failure to attribute them system or meaning is to fail to make them intelligible according to the reigning scientific canons. Conversely, to attribute to them system or meaning implies the imposition of at least a minimum sense of "order," a concept which can only be based upon a series of values of an ethical-moral nature and dependent upon a concept of mankind or the humanity that reflects it. Ignorant, in large measure, of past "order," the attributed meaning and design are only feasible in terms of present reality. Once again we are confronted with the paradox of explicating the past through the present.

The past and present interpenetrate and interrelate to such an extent that the anthropologist, in large measure, should become an historian and the historian an anthropologist. This is equally true for those who seek to reserve a certain autonomy for their field of inquiry. On the one hand, history and anthropology both belong to the field of semantics[27] and, on the other, to that of sociology.[28] Unfortunately, some would seek to maintain the distinction between anthropology and history, a posture which flies in the face of reality. This posture disqualifies them from serious consideration no matter how great their reputations. In fact their conclusions are more pertinent as raw data for an anthropological study of our own society than as conclusions regarding the societies that they purport to study.

But let us leave aside this aspect, which is simultaneously epistemological and sociological—"all epistemology that aspires to scientific meaning, that is to say, which is not tautological, becomes truly a sociology of knowledge," according to Angel Palerm.[29] Rather, let us ask instead how anthropologists and/or anthropology have resolved the paradox and dilemma delineated above.

In a synthesizing and general sense it is possible to say that there have been within anthropology antithetical and oppositional positions regarding the concept of time. There are those who opted and continue to opt for causal chains, which are eidetic or materialist, of past social phenomena with present ones. These are the several types of evolutionists or proponents of the diverse historical schools of thought. Conversely, there are those who at least theoretically renounce any type of linkage of the past with the present, restricting their analyses to contemporary reality in its many guises and interrelationships, i.e. the different functionalists and structuralists. Between the two extremes there are the few followers of the Boasian historical method for whom speculation regarding any historical sequence is premature until we have exhaustive knowledge of its detail. This is reflected in the image of Boas himself, who to the day of his death was engaged in "revising his material on the Kwakiutl, just as he had been doing sixty years earlier;"[30] just as in the words of Radcliffe-Brown for whom "the anthropologists who think of their work as a kind of historical study slip into conjecture and imagination and invest 'pseudo-historical' and 'pseudo-causal' explanations."[31] Finally, there is the posture of Tylor according to whom, "the ethnographer's business is to classify such details [the diverse cultural components] with a view to making out their distribution in geography and history and the relations which exist among them."[32] Such are some of the better known anthropological positions and affirmations regarding our initial paradox confronted by every anthropologist whether describing the present or the past.

Regarding the dilemma of attributing (or not) meaning and design to sociocultural phenomena of different historical epochs, we find identical or similar approaches. Either implicitly or explicitly in any of the methods employed in anthropological analysis, no matter how much they may differ in other regards, there is attribution of meaning and design. White notes, "Science is not merely a collection of facts and formulas. It is pre-eminently a way of dealing with experience."[33] To this we might add that every interpretation that does not spring directly from the facts themselves presupposes a conceptual and theoretical framework into which the data are integrated, with the possibility of as many interpretations as there are frames of reference or possible frames of reference. The conceptual and theoretical framework itself presupposes a definite concept of humanity which the anthropologist has formed during the course of his academic socialization and formation. Even for cultural relativists, sociocultural phenomena have meaning and value, although certainly more limited than for others, whether it be within a certain context or in the individuals' state of consciousness, as is maintained by the present defenders of counterculture and counterscience such as Castaneda and others.[34] The possible multiplicity of meanings, of values and of interpretations does not weaken what we have affirmed earlier, in fact it strengthens it.

I believe that those interpretative schemes that postulate a causal historical chain, as well as those which focus upon the interrelationships among contemporary phenomena, employ chronological order which provides them with organization and hence meaning. The difference is that for the former the present is explained by the past, whereas for the latter the present is explained by the process of becoming. When they have studied European societies, anthropologists have tended to interpret them through their past; conversely, when studying primitive societies—the so-called "peoples without histories"—at least implicitly, anthropologists have invoked the future and western history as an explanatory device: that is, the present state of reality finds its *raison d'etre* in the future when the society in question might attain the state of European ones.

The different histories of culture, as well as the explanations of contemporary culture of the several schools of thought, all utilize the diverse and multiple circumstances of primitive societies as links between the original, primitive stages of human development and the contemporary state of western society. "Savage," "primitive," "folk" or "traditional" society—independently of the terminology employed to designate particular societies throughout the academic development of anthropology—always constitute the scale or stages of an intermediate situation. Whatever cultural forms that they manifest, these societies always constitute a midpoint between what they must have been like originally and that which western societies have become. Not even Levistraussian structuralism, with its attempt to erase boundaries between societies by creating a single explicative logic for every type of sociocultural phenomenon of any society past or present, has managed to level such differences completely. Despite the fact that the unconscious model presumably functions and structures reality equally for all human beings, it is western man who has attained the highest scientific development by working with concepts rather than with symbols and signs.[35]

That which makes possible such scientific interpretive schemes, as well as the interpretation of sociocultural phenomena, is the European concept of time, just as other conceptualizations of time make possible other interpretations and sciences. Diachronic reconstructions, as well as synchronic interpretations, ultimately rest, to my mind, on a time construct which is the foundation upon which the diverse activities of individuals and collectivities transpire. There exists a beginning and an end, between the two extremes of which men and groups enter upon the scene according to a chronological order. The self-evident nature for we Europeans of this construction of temporal reality does not hold, for example, for the Hopi, to cite but one case, for whom there is no beginning or end, since the relation of simultaneity is their fundamental temporal category. While, for example, for Europeans a house and corn have their respective times of construction and growth, for the Hopi the construction of a house has neither beginning nor end and corn grows simultaneously as the house is built.[36]

The multiplicity of times and different explanations of them or, in any event, the existence of a European time concept that makes possible the formulation of an interpretative scheme and of the explication of multiple sociocultural reality, poses a series of questions that should have long since been a cause for reflection within anthropological discourse. When, how and why does a particular concept of time and history emerge that explicitly or implicitly situates certain people or collectivities within a chronology such that the most recent manifestations are explained by the negation of past ones? What does such negation imply and to whom does it apply? When, how and through what rationalizing process do primitives become the nexus or "link" in this chronology, or, which is the same, in the world of scientific knowledge? What is the significance of attributing historicity to primitive collectivities? What is the subject and at the same time the object of anthropological discourse? What is the underlying meaning of the history of culture and of one or another school's synchronic explications? And the key question is what type of human does this anthropology give us?

Precise replies to such questions go well beyond the context of the foregoing notes regarding time, as well as the anthropological work of Julio Caro Baroja. They would require a detailed study of each of the schools and orientations within anthropology, as well as analysis of each anthropologist and his works. Being conscious of the simplification in which I engage even if only referring to anthropology's utilization and, to a degree, the creation and invention of time, some of whose characteristics I have detailed, I wish to underscore how the imposition of order on culture in general, and upon primitive societies in particular, leads to the following consequences: 1) it differentiates ethically and morally certain persons and societies from others since it places them at different stages, 2) at the same time it creates an equally moral discourse regarding self-legitimating western society since it defines itself as the most perfect stage or status and, 3) it ignores and indeed disfigures the *others* by leaving out of account their time dimension.

Anthropological time, then, is time created to reaffirm western society. "Exotic" humanity only acquires rationality (from Tylor to Levi-Strauss the "philosophical savage" is invoked monotonously) through comparison with "ancient" society which, in turn, is the root of western civilization. At the same time exotic humanity continues being simply an object by means of which to objectify the essence and the nature of western man and culture. The "progressive" meaning ascribed to history and time means that the only possible intervention with the world of the primitive is in the guise of civilizing agent, which at the same time becomes an exaltation of western civilization—moral humanism never seeks to decivilize the savage world because, among other reasons, everyone continues to believe that history never marches backwards, rather that individual Europeans must become worthy of western society, the most civilized form.[37]

The passage of time is always cumulative in every context. Tylor notes, "From an ideal point of view, civilization may be looked upon as the general improvement of mankind by higher organization of the individual and of society, to the end of promoting at once man's goodness, power and happiness."[38] This Tylorian thought, whose roots are found in antiquity and whose ramifications permeate European science,[39] is made explicit in every class of evolutionary diachronic typology and implicit in synchronic analyses. Even though social phenomena have the same function and structure they are characterized by greater or lesser structural complexity. This is according to their greater or lesser "elementarity," borrowing the adjectivity of kinship and religious forms from Levi Strauss and Durkheim respectively or, for example, in accord with Radcliffe-Brown's simplicity of functional relations of certain totemic phenomena.

Anthropological time is thereby converted not solely into an epistemological category through which a certain type of society and of science is self-legitimated, rather it becomes a moral category. History is life's teacher. As Leibniz would write, "The most notable purpose of history, like that of poetry, is to teach by examples prudence and virtue, while depicting vice in such a fashion as to elicit revulsion."⁴⁰ These sentiments have been repeated often, although at times with different words, throughout recent centuries once history had usurped from religion the role of judge and exemplar of human purposes. Anthropology is history's lineal heir in this regard.

The Temporality of Things

Independently of whether I have managed to characterize adequately the anthropological solution to the paradox and dilemma facing those who wish to interpret and explicate the multiplicity and variety of sociocultural phenomena of different epochs, at the very least I believe that I have effected a simplification by virtue of presenting a synthesis and overview of the thought of a pleiad of anthropologists.

There is an undeniable tendency and pretension among analysts to totalize knowledge: we totalize the thinking of a civilization, of a people, of an epoch, of an individual, of a work, etc. If possible, this totalizing pretension is even more blatant in anthropology, becoming one of its basic characteristics and means of defining and differentiating. The lack of delimitation of anthropology's object of study was conducive to considering the holistic approach as intrinsic to the discipline. Recently Firth, in referring to the study of modern societies, wrote, "The anthropologist can be classified as a sociologist specialized in making direct small-scale, on-the-ground observations, which conserve, with respect to society and culture, a view which illustrates the totality, and which derives from the study of simple societies."⁴¹

This specificity of the anthropological focus, although still defended and practiced by many, was contested nevertheless during the profound crisis that anthropology experienced during the 1960s. The epistemological power of the paradigms that were utilized was incapable of attaining the aspired-to objective universal laws.⁴² We might add that the models used before or after were equally incapable of going beyond either essentialism (that which is ultimately achieved by Levistraussian structuralism) or a determination that is purely exterior and foreign to the symbolic realities of culture with its aleatory nature and arbitrariness, features that correspond in some fashion to human nature (which is what happens with all deterministic interpretations no matter what their stripe). In other words, what occurs is that human affairs are not so easily susceptible to schematizing and interpretation without running the risk of leaving out some of their important features. The interpretations of Mauss' "total fact" or Weber's "typical," for example, despite having constituted a major epistemological advance in their time which inspired highly significant and illuminating studies, leave out such important dimensions as subjectivity and intersubjectivity or, in the best of cases, disassociate objective factitiousness from subjective meaning, thereby violating the dual nature of cultural reality *sui generis*.[43] Similarly, in attempting to characterize in global terms human culture, past or present, analysts leave out the contextual nuances of "relations between different social sectors in a complex whole in a geographical and political setting which have a temporal dimension as well."[44] Such is the reality of all societies whether modern or primitive. It is also true of all individuals, since we can speak of multiple personal dimensions.

The social, as well as the individual, and in fact the work of an author, all possess multiple aspects that are not reducible to a single dimension without distorting the reality under investigation and analysis. Not even the work of E.B. Tylor is reducible to a single orientation, in this instance the evolutionist,[45] nor is an individual characterizable in terms of a single manner of thinking or personal identity,[46] nor may a culture be classified in sole and exclusive manner in terms of its material culture or the psychosocial orientation of its members. In this regard we might cite the well-known debate between Redfield and Lewis regarding the true character, harmonious or conflictive, of the Mexican community of Tepoztlan, and that between Benedict and Eggan over whether the culture of the Pueblo Indians was "Apollonian" (moderate, harmonious, non-conflictive and unemotive) or "Dionysian" (traumatic, violent, and repressive).[47] Similarly, there have been attempts to explain Basque culture in terms of its "Christian orientation,"[48] its roots in "a matriarchal-nativalist and communalist reality contrasted with an Indo-European patriarchal-rationalist and individualist one,"[49] or in terms of the "guideline of the disinherited."[50] Without a doubt the examples can be multiplied to correspond to the number of cultures studied, since there has long been a tendency among anthropologists to convert the people, tribe or culture studied into a kind of private reserve, estate or property.

Julio Caro Baroja is one of the few anthropologists who, for some time now, while incurring the criticism of the majority, has denounced the reductionism to which the various tendencies and schools subject sociocultural and historical reality, as well as the moralism that is latent in the exercize. In various contexts, and particularly in the prologues of his re-editions, Caro Baroja rejects all anthropological "-isms" since the establishment of the first and, relatively speaking, most important (though only due to its subsequent influence and acceptance), namely, nineteenth-century evolutionism. I consider Caro Baroja's most significant statement in this regard to be what he wrote in the prologue to his *Etnografía histórica de Navarra*. Despite its length it is worth citing the following passage:

> Practically everyone who has studied social science since the schools were first established and codified until the present day, has noted that the Moral and the Science of customs are narrowly intertwined and that strong moral and moralizing beliefs impregnate, even unconsciously, investigations with greater pretensions to objectivity. A moralist can accept as good, indeed excellent, Tertullian's sentence, according to which the soul of man is Christian by nature; although it is also necessary to recognize his capacity for sin. But what can we make of the beatitudes and, at the same time, sanctimony, simultaneously romantic and positivist, of certain sociological schools when treating the social? On the other hand what can we make of their similes, borrowed from crystallography, from pathology, from physics, etc., etc., etc.? We believe ourselves to be ethnographers or historians, as in my case; what can we make of those imagined unities and equations established by some of our predecessors with certain methodological principles that still create furor? A mature man does not shout in protest as might a younger one. Neither is he disposed to be an acolyte, another posture of the young. But he will raise lightly his hand and say to his possible listeners—Take care; take care, I say now, with the equations that get established between race, language, culture, natural region and, finally, nation. Take care in believing that through "field work," from their own sole observations, no matter how intense they may be, they are going to derive all of the elements with which to determine how a society "functions" and delineate its "structure." Take care not to confound certain types of juridical and economic organization with the "social order," and even less the "state." Take care not to mix up and confuse today with tomorrow and with yesterday.[51]

In fact that which he wrote in conclusive form when announcing his purposes and inspiration in writing *Las formas complejas de la vida religiosa* (The Complex Forms of the Religious Life)—the very title is revealing since it forces us to consider those other elementary forms of Emile Durkheim—can serve as Caro Baroja's slogan or motto. He states, "I do not wish to be a judge, but rather a painter."[52] In this regard Caro Baroja limits his brushstrokes to the negative and rejective, not even taking the trouble to obliterate completely the generally weak internal theoretical framework of that which he criticizes. How much clearer are the critical images painted on the walls of our intellectual edifices, yet we must struggle to interpret them!

This is what occurs in the case of certain anthropological theories, and particularly those referring to the Basques, which on close examination are empty.

Caro Baroja is concerned with the temporal and spatial contexts of the facts. These are the two concepts which are intimately and inextricably related and which give things their most genuine dimension or, simply, we are dealing with the dimension of things. From among the various possible modes of considering scientifically human ideas and actions, Caro Baroja opts for what might be called *situational* analysis: everything has a time and space and may only be considered within such temporal and spatial reality; to do otherwise is to extract and thereby distort reality, a misleading exercise whether effected by the ideas that a particular society holds of itself or those which historians have proposed regarding it.

I believe that this is one of the few concerns that informed his research practically from the outset when, as he himself affirms, he began his early works "cloaked in the friendship and assisted by the advice of teachers who have almost all disappeared, with the exception of Don José Miguel de Barandiarán,"[53] although it was only later that he began to make the substance and methodology of situational analysis explicit.[54] In this regard, however, it is interesting to note that even as a young man he was beginning to explore it when he demonstrated that Strabo utilized in a precise sense the notion of "culture area" with regard to the peoples of northern Iberia centuries before anthropologists constructed the notion of *Kulturkreislehre* as an heuristic and analytical device. Initially, he criticized, timidly yet accurately, the general explicative pretensions of that school while it was in its full euphoria of scientific militancy and catholicity. Caro Baroja wrote, "it is evident that the cultural historical method...has produced a certain tendency toward a mentalistic schemata and an ethnological metaphysic, and that certain of its followers do not wish 'to see what is,' as Stendhal recommended, but rather prefer that 'it be that which they pretend to see.' "[55] This criticism translated over time into a more precise attempt at theoretical elaboration and, consequently, a distancing of Caro Baroja from the teachers of the *Kulturkreislehre* school, as well as his own teachers, to the extent that they pertained to it.[56] Mediating in the dispute that took place between North American and German anthropologists regarding the greater or lesser objectivity and sciential nature of the concept of "culture area" and of "circle" and "cycle" respectively, in 1971 Caro Baroja wrote that the concept of "cycle," applied in a stricter sense than that employed first by Ratzel and then his human geographer and even historian followers, such as E. Meyer, is more useful than the purely spatial concept of "area".⁵⁷ He also gives the reasons for this affirmation by stating,

> It is because the idea of 'cycle' contains or *should contain* the following: 1) a geographical notion, *the spatial*, according to which there are human groups more interrelated than others and which live in a specific environment; that occupy, in effect, an area, 2) an historical notion, *the temporal*, according to which these groups have a determined past, one that is concrete, rather than based upon vague and specious notions that derive from a reconstructed generalized Time, as a function of ideas of evolution, mechanical diffusion, or, to the contrary, immobilism, etc., etc.; a time in which concrete events have happened, while in other places there have been other happenings: a Time in which, for example, the Arabs and the Romans lived here and there; or a Time in which neither lived due also to a concrete series of circumstances; 3) an heuristic value, according to which the notion of cycle, without being considered an absolute certainty, might lead to new discoveries and establish new working hypotheses.⁵⁸

It is above all the accentuation of the *temporal historical dimension*, as may be appreciated, which limits the construction of somewhat indiscriminate broad and general cycles, and which gives to the more modest cycles which are thereby constructed, a new character—that of the historical time of things. It is this fact which makes the causal chain between different periods and between things themselves inviolate. In other words, there is a rupture with one of the fundamental tenets of the Vienna School, that of the constancy of culture as applied, for example, by W. Schmidt and J.M. Barandiarán, respectively, to general culture and Basque culture in particular. In my opinion, it is in this sense that that which Caro Baroja has been writing repeatedly about Basque Studies these many years must be understood. It is not that Caro Baroja denies the existence of the Basques, of their language, of their customs and even of "the peculiarities of their character" (this last point, to my mind, a difficult one to demonstrate and which corresponds to a type of anthropology that is scarcely practiced today), rather that which he denies is the persistence of a uniform Basque culture over considerable geographical extent and throughout all time due to the mere fact that here and there are found a few vestiges that pertained, or rather have been attributed, to a Basque cultural cycle. He rejects the explicative reasons given for its conservation and persistence, that is, isolation or, at the very least, the lack of acculturation—referring to one of the topics most frequently invoked by anthropologists, including in past times. Similarly, he attacks the two theoretical alternatives to the historical method of the Vienna school, namely recourse to the divine act of creation or to the Bible, which some authors mention. For Caro Baroja this is sheer metaphysical theologism which is in every regard unsustainable except by means of the equally unsustainable theological insights and logics to which some who regard themselves as thinkers and anthropologists are susceptible. I repeat that it is in this regard that we should understand such affirmations by Caro Baroja as the following: "Let us set aside 'Adamism,' 'Tubalism,' and primitivism. Let us set aside 'perpetual isolation,' which easily yet treacherously explains the conservation of a language, which, without a doubt, is the most peculiar characteristic of the Basque. Because in western Europe such isolation is and has been physically impossible and the Basque Country is situated at one of the most complicated crossroads of the continent. It is not worth studying in order to repeat commonplace remarks."[59] Similarly, about the same time he said, ". . . Basque history . . . does not contain any 'abnormality' if compared to that of other western European areas and peoples. . . . which leads me to believe that all of the reasonings of an historico-cultural nature that have been proposed here and there as explanation, fail due to the deficiencies of the very method that generated them."[60]

I believe that in some regards these affirmations reflect Boasian echoes, although Boas wrote against the evolutionist pretext of finding a series of regularities grounded in similarities as a result of the uniformity of human behavior.[61] He writes in *The Aims of Anthropological Research*, "In short, the material of anthropology is such that it must be a historical science, one of the sciences the interest of which centers in the attempt to understand the individual phenomena rather than in the establishment of general laws which, on account of the complexity of the material, will be necessarily vague and, we might almost say, so self-evident that they are of little help to a real understanding."[62]

The anthropological thought of Boas, which was multidirectional given the principle of complexity which inspired it, attained during the first quarter of this century considerable international importance, particularly in two thrusts underscored by their author: that of the interrelationship between the individual and society and that of the interrelationship between the physical environment and historico-cultural contacts.[63] The tendency is blatantly *configurationalist* in the sense that the dependency and/or the interrelationship is so intimate that just as the individual can alter his own culture the latter can mold the individual by configuring his personality. Or the influence of the physical environment may be just as decisive in the configuration of culture as the capacity of culture to alter the landscape.

As I underscored elsewhere, in some of his works Caro Baroja reflects this way of thinking which, on the other hand, corresponds in many respects to that of Von Uexküll (as suggested frequently by Caro Baroja himself),[64] which has served him as a theoretical guide in his various investigations.[65]

In the anthropological thinking of Caro Baroja the accentuation of the historical temporality of things, although presumably derived ultimately from the interrelational complexity of sociocultural phenomena of which it is in turn one of the aspects, acquires, nevertheless, slowly yet constantly, increasing theoretical relevance which, to my mind, becomes simultaneously one of its most original contributions while serving as the axis upon which the greater part of Caro Baroja's work turns.

This is, without a doubt, a slow and even painful discovery. In fact it remains uncompleted, which is always the nature of knowledge and of the work of those who are capable of being surprised by what they see, think and experience. However, here and there sprinkled throughout his works, in prologues and epilogues, there are signs of both a personal preoccupation and theoretical problematic with the time dimension of things as well as of his own life.

Leaving aside the psychological time of Caro Baroja, which perhaps one day some psychologist will address utilizing what he has said in interviews and written in memoirs, thereby employing the author himself as informant (though his annotations remain inconclusive), I would now underscore one of Caro Baroja's principal thoughts regarding the temporality of things. According to him, "time is the interpretative key to existence."[66] Nevertheless, the way in which we humans measure time is one thing, time itself is quite another.

European societies, for example, have created a regulatory apparatus which derives its organizing principles from the movement of the stars, which is then codified subsequently into social time, called a calendar, with its fractioned movements measured mechanically by the clock. Other societies, like the African Barundis, structure the calendar according to the rainfall cycles, and the day principally with life rhythms and livestock products. We are dealing with two of the existing multiplicity of ways to measure time. Inspired by the radical incapacity of the individual to regulate perceptions and the successions of states of consciousness in a rational manner, the apparatus regulating temporality is generated by the group. In this sense the structure of time is arbitrary and conventional only to the group formulating the convention. There are therefore as many social times as there are distinct groups and cultures or, more accurately, as many social times as have been adopted conventionally by different groups.[67] Such is social time. Time in itself, nevertheless, only exists and is felt by virtue of things. As Lucretius (whom Caro Baroja translated and then adopted as his own) wrote, "time does not exist for itself, rather it is the things themselves which determine that meanings are distinguished in the past, present and future: no one senses time in and of itself, free from movement or repose." In contradistinction to the idealist, not to say metaphysical manner of considering time, Caro Baroja also believes that time is linked to things and that apart from them it has no absolute meaning whatsoever. It exists independently of consciousness and the perception of it held by persons. They are two distinguishable factors. Caro Baroja writes, "If we transcend the mistake originated by the notion of measuring and counting, and remain independent of all arithmetic operations, destined to determine synchronies and diachronies, we will have to think that, on the one hand, the web of relations in being, and on the other, the time dimension of artifacts must be studied in their own terms with their own methods."[68]

Consequently, for Caro Baroja, the time of things possesses objective reality: time exists not only in our minds but rather basically and primordially in the world, in things. Time is not an *a priori* of intelligence or of the mind, nor does it depend upon intuition or to any impulse of the knowing subject, rather it is a property of things, through which humans perceive temporality. It is as absurd to think that prior to the apparition of mankind the world of things didn't exist and that after we disappear they will cease to exist, as it is to think that we will continue perceiving and discovering meaning in that world after death. That which does not continue existing for us, as Pío Baroja wrote, does not cease to exist for others or, similarly, were man to disappear, it would exist for *no one* but would continue to exist. It is altogether another matter whether it is of importance to us that it exists if we cease to.[69]

Whether or not one agrees with him, such is Caro Baroja's conception, a conception which, as we all know, existed in classical antiquity. "From Democritus' atomistic conception there emerges awareness of the objective existence of space and time. Space as vacuum, within which atoms move, becomes a necessary condition of their movement. Time, while not found inextricably linked with atoms, equally exists only with respect to their movements. Space is conceived by Democritus as infinite, time as eternal. For Aristotle, too, objective space exists. Time, since it is closely linked with movement, possesses an objective foundation, this, nevertheless, with regard to 'number of movement,' doesn't exist without the soul. According to

Aristotle cosmic space is infinite, whereas time is conceived as constant and regular flux."[70] This also underlies "the conception of contemporary science, especially with regard to quantum physics and the theory of relativity." M. Bunge, for example, states "The spatiotemporal, far from existing in and of itself, is the basic design of changing objects, that is, of material things. Consequently, instead of saying that entities exist in space and in time we should say instead that space and time exist by virtue of the existence of material objects (and consequently their change). Space is the means of spatializing things, and time the means of succeeding events that happen to things (Leibniz). Consequently, if the things were to vanish then space and time would disappear as well. In sum, space and time do not have an independent existence, any more than do solidity or movement, life or death, culture or history."[71] The underlying conception, then, becomes materialist instead of idealist, dynamic rather than fixed. In one of his most recent interviews Caro Baroja tells us, "We find ourselves [in a state] of pure heraclitism: the observer changes that which he sees by his observation, that which happens, everything, and there is no longer a point of reference with which to say 'I plant myself here and will observe what happens,' rather I too am running...."[72]

It is the omission of the temporality of things, in Caro Baroja's opinion, that leads to "banality" and "vulgarity" in anthropology. The lack of clear ideas regarding the relation ascribed to "things" and the "absolute lack of investigation of time in *relation with contemporary philosophical systems*, systems which emerged about the same time as the functionalist method" are two of the reasons that lead Caro Baroja to conclude that, "philosophers from near the beginning of the century could have thought (and indeed did think) that the anthropology and sociology of their epoch contained an antiquated and withered philosophical load, that many investigators were anchored in the most vulgar position that positivism was capable of producing, or in other systems that reeked of rancidity or of something of little substance. It is evident that the new, strong, post-1900 philosophical shoots were not employed much in the work of anthropologists."[73] Among the ideas which in his judgment might have been relevant for anthropology, Caro Baroja cites the Heideggerian conception of existence—*Dasein* "not in time, but rather *by virtue* of time," the observations of the same author regarding "unauthentic" situations, and the concepts of "public time," "mundane time" and of the "surrounding world." He also mentions, as he has done in other works, Ratzel and Durkheim, and especially Simmel. The lack of taking into account the time of things has led to the creation, "more or less deliberately...of two sciences empty of historical content: two sciences that base their speculation on a notion of *original time, primitive or less primitive*, on the one hand and on the notion of *social or functional time* on the other.[74] Concretely, he is referring to evolutionism, diffusionism, and their variations, or to British social anthropology. His opinion regarding structuralism is more benevolent, "the lack of temporal precision of some investigations (of a structural character) perturb considerably the development of our findings as observers of societies, historians, ethnographers, etc."[75] Nevertheless, he believes that, "as long as we specify the concrete meaning that we give to the word 'structure,' it would seem more appropriate to combine it with historical investigation." The same is true of the structural method.[76] In his opinion, the research approach most appropriate for the study of the changing flux of things is the historical, employing certain "units of comprehension," of which the most fundamental is that of cycle, although in its reduced form, as I noted earlier. For Caro Baroja, as for Maitland and others of the last century, anthropology must continue being historical if it is to be anything. On this point he recently wrote extensively, but let us leave aside such sterile discussions, at least in the form they have taken, and consider what Caro Baroja understands for human time, that which is truly relevant for the historian and anthropologist.

Human Time

The preoccupation with and the problematic of the time of things simultaneously regard human time. The time of things and human time are two aspects of the same reality. On the one hand, things give measure to time, as we have just discussed; while, on the other, the world of perceptions, of significance and of meaning resides in things.

In human affairs these two spheres or aspects are so interwoven that in fact they become a single reality, human reality. Possibly one can say that it is the only existing reality. Any type of duality employed to analyze it, whether of an extreme Cartesian nature or in the more subtle forms of the principal modern anthropological schools, is achieved only by accentuating unilaterally one or another aspect of the reality, which signifies a distortion of it.

The fundamental unity of the world of things and of the world of perceptions and meanings is fully appreciated by Caro Baroja. To the reproaches of those who have accused him of devoting excessive attention to *material culture*, or simply of paying attention to it when others leave it out of account, he replies by invoking the fundamental unities of the two worlds and the unavoidable necessity of analyzing both if the research is to be truly *scientific*, although he doesn't use the term but rather puts it in the mouths of those who take pride in having developed "quintessential theories," a kind of "gnosis," and who, like their teachers, continued distinguishing between science and history.

Several times I have heard anthropologists and fieldwork investigators state with a peevish air that they are not interested in the 'material culture' of the area they studied; that, at best one can charge an assistant with preparing a sort of 'inventory' or 'catalogue' as an appendix to their superior speculations. Such an approach strikes me as another of the many aberrations produced by the same pedagogical methodology—an overemphasis upon disciplinary boundaries and a type of classificatory laziness. What, in a final sense, is 'material culture'? How can one speak of functionalism, of structuralism, etc. etc., without recognizing clearly that mankind's material and spiritual worlds cannot be separated during field research, nor in theoretical speculation? Because man lives, if you will, in a physical environment which is material; so are his tools, animals, plants, men and women. A supposedly pure study of technology can only be conceived as another mental aberration.[77]

Contrary to what one might think upon analyzing Caro Baroja's criticisms of the different tendencies and anthropological schools, the necessity to study material objects does not derive from the concept of totality (according to some) or of system (according to others), but rather from the indispensable importance that they acquire in mankind's cultural life in general and time construct in particular. Things and only things permit and condition the existence of the realms of perceptions and meanings, including the time dimension, although Caro Baroja himself has never "discovered and described these specific perceptible and encompassing worlds" in *systematic fashion*, he has seen the necessity of "giving their existence conscious, rational form which, at the same time, serves to invalidate so many historical logomachies—providentialist or mechanical—of those which are still proposed as 'scientific discourses,' and which are no more than an ancient mythico-magical legacy."[78] His own anthropological work is in this vein. It is also his approach in studying and analyzing "Basque themes," as he is wont to call them, during a third or more of his life. It is here that we encounter the majority of his many and diverse investigations which are conceived within a framework of "units of comprehension" or "cycles," with their diverse things and concepts, different and contradictory at one and the same time. Given the breadth of his work it is not easy to effect a systematic synthesis of it, an exercise made even more difficult by the fact that his own views have evolved, as he has written, due to the change that has transpired in the things themselves, to which he has always given "considerable proportion."[79] A good example, as I have mentioned elsewhere, is his study of Vera at *three points* in his life. "It is nothing more than a reflection of that which has happened both to the author himself and to the elements analyzed; that is, that time has forced a shift in the methodology and the results, the author's vision of the facts and the objects themselves."[80] The summation of his work remains to be done. It is my purpose in the present context to consider only the methodological and heuristic suggestions that Caro Baroja proposes for the analysis of the realm of things and of mankind's perceptions and experiencing of time.

According to Caro Baroja there is a dual problematic confronting the ethnographer: on the one hand it is necessary to classify things themselves within their own time frames while, on the other, to determine what humans who have preceded us in distinct periods characterized by other things have perceived and felt. In each epoch and in accord with occupational status each thing and each human group possesses its own time and its own respective particular perceptions. According to Caro Baroja the question is, "In what manner can an historian relate the things of times past that he studies, considering them in their own terms, in such fashion that it is the things themselves which force him to distinguish and determine what was *their own* time?" To which he answers, "I have here a problem in which the first step [towards resolution] will be to classify such things and, in sum, to ascribe to time the value of one more of their dimensions. *Not an absolute value* in which all are treated equally. We must leave aside metaphysics and realize that we are dealing with a question of method."[81] In another context he asks, "What does man see, feel, endure, savor given his distinct *perceptible worlds*, always so imprecise in their materialness?", to which he answers, "If he is a shepherd, he perceives, above all, certain significant elements, if a farmer, others. If he is a warrior and he goes from south to north he will view things differently than if as warrior he goes from north to south. Because observing men who act within the apparently immutable, one must always take into account that some can have, and do have, one blood and one religion, while others have others. Certainly, all are affected by the form of the world that surrounds them; all have economic interests to defend within it. But always given distinctive, significant elements in distinct epochs and in different generations."[82]

The interaction between both spheres, especially in what refers to "that which can be the meaning of the 'tools' as things with their *own time* acting upon present time."⁸³ poses a third problem which is "grave" in Caro Baroja's opinion, given the fact that several things "present themselves in the eyes of the observer as coexisting and related."⁸⁴ This lends to even greater complexity if we consider that these things have existed in "distinct closed and successive worlds produced by distinct and successive realities" and that "the very duration [of the things] is variable."⁸⁵

Therefore, the panorama confronting the ethnographer is intricate, contradictory and diverse. Only by forcing and, to a certain degree, distorting the reality of things is it possible to present them in a harmonious, functional and coherent light. The situation facing the ethnographer concerned with things past is even more intricate, contradictory and diverse. Only by subordinating the time of things as a function of evolution or diffusion does it become possible to organize facts temporally. Only by subtracting from things their temporality, that is, by making them atemporal metaphysically, is it possible to confuse the things of yesterday with those of today and tomorrow, as occurs so frequently in the anthropological research of Basque subjects.

The autonomy given by Caro Baroja to things themselves, with their own time frames and own perceptions at different historical moments viewed by diverse persons resolves the paradox and the dilemma confronting the historian and anthropologist in the most satisfactory manner, i.e. there exist a multiplicity of times and meanings which are always the times and meanings of certain, concrete persons; additionally, they are generally conflictive, intricate and distinctive. Each collectivity and each thing possesses its own time and meaning. Certainly, "as human beings we are at a maximum point in relation to the past," but everything changes and "things do not happen in order to be judged by posterity," nor "have they occurred with regard to a fixed 'order,' nor that they should generate other better or worse ones, nor in order for us to look for forced general laws."⁸⁶ It is impossible, then, to legitimate the present with the past or the past with the present. It is equally impossible, therefore, to make history the teacher of life, rather life informs history.

It becomes absolutely impossible to effect comparisons between epochs with differing things, times, and perceptions, as well as to establish fixed laws. Caro Baroja writes, "How is it possible to compare conceptions and relations [of time and space] of a gentle society with those of an Empire in expansion, such as the Roman, or with those of the Germanic peoples launched upon an irresistible southerly movement, or, finally, with those of the Islamized Arabs and Berbers?... The complexity of the situations in which mankind finds itself obliges us to reject every mechanical notion with regard to human behavior. In short, every interpretation which conforms to fixed laws, whether of a physical or social nature, is mechanical, and eliminates the notion of cultural change while failing to give profound and temporal significance to that which it investigates."[87]

The task is not easy or simple and, certainly, it is not exempt from a problematic that goes far beyond the pretensions of these brief observations. Caro Baroja himself is aware of this problematic. The "units of comprehension" with their own temporality, in my opinion, demand a greater theoretical elaboration and certain criteria capable of delimiting, for example, the content of time frames and the complex of phenomena analyzed. At the same time, the "scales of comprehension and the various kinds of connections" between the imminent time of a particular group and "historical time" must be stipulated. The historical burden of the vocabulary utilized by anthropology itself makes this more difficult. How do we integrate quite disparate elements such as the apparition or disappearance of certain social, cultural and human phenomena, the waxing of some and the waning of others?

The "clear and distinct temporal cycle" demands, in any event, verification by the weight of the evidence under investigation, if it may be spoken of at all. Is it possible to ascribe some sort of regularity to cultural cycles conceived thusly? That, as I affirmed earlier, is the task which remains. I believe that the effort would lead to critically important methodological and epistemological considerations for the investigation of both the present and the past.

Notes

1. J. Campos, "Julio Caro Baroja," *Insula*, vol. 14, nos. 200–201 (1963); Davydd Greenwood, "Julio Caro Baroja: sus obras e ideas," *Etnica*, no. 2 (1971), pp. 78–97; Julian Pitt-Rivers, "A Personal Memoir," *Homenaje a Julio Caro Baroja* (Madrid: CIS, 1978), pp. 887–893; R. Montero, "Un vitalista con cuentagotas," *El país semanal*, no. 71 (1978), pp. 6–9; E. L. Diaz, "Entrevista con Julio Caro Baroja," *Playboy*, no. 41 (1982), pp. 21–30.
2. Julio Caro Baroja, *Los Baroja* (Madrid: Taurus, 1972), p. 535.
3. *Homenaje a D. Julio Caro Baroja* (Madrid: Ministerio de Cultura, 1982), p. 19.
4. Davydd Greenwood, "Julio Caro Baroja: Sus obras e ideas," *Etnica*, no. 2 (1971), p. 80.
5. E. E. Evans-Pritchard, *Essays in Social Anthropology* (London: Faber and Faber, 1969), p. 51.
6. Julio Caro Baroja and E. Temprano, *Disquisiciones antropológicas* (Madrid: Istmo, 1985), p. 77.

7. Davydd Greenwood is the only one to date to have attempted a thematic exposition of Julio Caro Baroja's work. In it he discerns "some general themes which should be explored further and which can become part of the model for the anthropological study of Europe." Davydd Greenwood, "Julio Caro Baroja: Sus obras e ideas," *Etnica*, p.80. This same author compiled the first bibliography of Caro Baroja's works through 1970 arranged thematically. No one has continued this effort. Subsequently, A. Carreiro provided a chronologically ordered bibliography covering the period 1929 to 1981. *Homenaje a D. Julio Caro Baroja* (Madrid: Ministerio de Cultura, 1982), pp. 25-51. This same author provides an update through 1985 in the book *Disquisiciones antropológicas* by Julio Caro Baroja and E. Temprano, pp. 455-492.
8. Julio Caro Baroja, *Sobre la religión antigua y el calendario del pueblo vasco* (San Sebastián: Txertoa, 1980), pp. 7-9.
9. Davydd Greenwood, "Julio Caro Baroja...," p. 89; and Julio Caro Baroja and E. Temprano, *Disquisiciones antropológicas*.
10. Julio Caro Baroja, "Con D. Julio Caro Baroja. Situación actual de la antropología," *Alcoveras*, no. 0 (1982), pp. 16-18.
11. Julio Caro Baroja and E. Temprano, *Disquisiciones antropológicas*, pp. 35-36.
12. Davydd Greenwood, "Julio Caro Baroja...," p. 89.
13. Julio Caro Baroja, *De la vida rural vasca. Vera de Bidasoa* (San Sebastián: Txertoa, 1974), pp. 11-20, 349-352; Julio Caro Baroja, *Los vascos* (Madrid: Istmo, 1972), pp. 13-21, 373-384; Julio Caro Baroja, *Etnografía histórica de Navarra*, vol. 1 (1972), pp. 9-22; Julio Caro Baroja, *Etnografía histórica de Navarra*, vol. 3 (1972), pp. 457-464; Julio Caro Baroja, *Vasconia* (San Sebastián: Txertoa, 1974), pp. 7-11; and Julio Caro Baroja, *Sobre la religión...*, pp. 7-9.
14. Julio Caro Baroja, *De la vida rural vasca...*, pp. 18, 350.
15. Jesús Azcona, *Etnia y nacionalismo vasco. Una aproximación desde la antropología* (Barcelona: Anthropos, 1984), pp. 82-88.
16. Julio Caro Baroja, *De la vida rural vasca...*, p. 351, and Julio Caro Baroja, *Los pueblos del norte* (San Sebastián: Txertoa, 1973), p. 9.
17. Julio Caro Baroja and E. Temprano, *Disquisiciones antropológicas*, p. 50.
18. Julio Caro Baroja, *De la vida rural vasca...*, p. 351.
19. Julio Caro Baroja and E. Temprano, *Disquisiciones antropológicas*, p. 90.
20. Julio Caro Baroja, *Los vascos*, p. 20.

21. Jesús Azcona, "La escuela histórica de Viena y la antropología vasca," *Cuadernos de Etnología y Etnografía de Navarra*, no. 43 (1984) pp. 137-151.
22. Davydd Greenwood, "Julio Caro Baroja...," p. 90.
23. Julio Caro Baroja and E. Temprano, *Disquisiciones antropológicas*, p. 22.
24. Pío Baroja, *El árbol de la ciencia* (Madrid: Alianza, 1981), pp. 126-127.
25. Julio Caro Baroja and E. Temprano, *Disquisiciones antropológicas*, pp. 21-33.
26. E. E. Evans-Pritchard, *Essays in Social Anthropology*, pp. 51-52.
27. E. Cassirer, *An Essay on Man* (New Haven: Yale University Press, 1944), p. 195.
28. Edward H. Carr, *What is History?* (Harmondsworth: Penguin Books, 1964), p. 66.
29. Angel Palerm, *Antropología y marxismo* (México: Nueva Imagen, 1980), p. 26.
30. A. Kardiner and E. Preble, *They Studied Man* (Cleveland and New York: The World Publishing Company, 1961), p. 159.
31. A. R. Radcliffe-Brown, *Structure and Function in Primitive Society* (London: Cohen and West Ltd., 1971), p. 3.
32. E. B. Tylor, *The Origins of Culture*, vol. 1 (New York: Harper Torch Books, 1958), p. 8.
33. L. A. White, *The Science of Culture, A Study of Man and Civilization* (New York: Grove Press, 1949), p. 3.
34. Jesús Azcona, "Los movimientos religiosos en las sociedades no occidentalizadas. Las contradicciones de la colonización o la salvación blanca," *Príncipe de Viana.Suplemento de ciencias*, no. 5 (1985), pp. 157-178.
35. Claude Levi-Strauss, *La pensée sauvage* (Paris: Plon, 1969), pp. 3-47.
36. E. T. Hall, *The Silent Language* (Greenwich, Conn.: Fawcett Premier, 1959).
37. M. Duchet, *Antropología e historia en el siglo de las luces* (México: Siglo XXI, 1975).
38. E. B. Tylor, *The Origins of Culture*, vol. 1, p. 27.
39. L. Sklair, *The Sociology of Progress* (London: Routledge and Kegan Paul, 1970).
40. F. Meinecke, *El historicismo y su génesis* (México: Fondo de Cultura Económica, 1943), p. 40.
41. Translated from P. Mercier, *Ethnologie générale* (Paris: Gallimard, 1968), p. 895.

42. G. Nutini, "Sobre los conceptos de orden epistemológico y de definiciones coordinativas," in J. R. Llobera (ed.), *La antropología como ciencia* (Barcelona: Anagrama, 1975), pp. 353-371.
43. P. L. Berger and Th. Luckmann, *La construcción social de la realidad* (Buenos Aires: Amorrortu, 1983), p. 35.
44. Julio Caro Baroja, *Las formas complejas de la vida religiosa. Religión, sociedad y carácter en la España de los siglos XVI y XVII* (Madrid: Akal, 1978), p. 16.
45. P. Mercier, *Ethnologie générale*..., pp. 50-54.
46. Julio Caro Baroja, *Las formas complejas de la vida religiosa*..., p. 24.
47. I. Moreno, *Cultura y modos de producción. Una visión de la antropología desde el materialismo histórico* (Madrid: Ed. Nuestra Cultura, 1978), p. 206.
48. J. M. Barandiarán, "¿Qué es ser vasco?" in *Muga*, no. 40 (1980), pp. 14-19.
49. A. Ortiz-Osés and F. K. Mayr, *El matriarcalismo vasco* (Bilbao: Universidad de Deusto, 1980), p. 9.
50. J. Aranzadi, *Milenarismo vasco. Edad de oro, etnia y nativismo* (Madrid: Taurus, 1981), p. 530.
51. Julio Caro Baroja, *Etnografía histórica de Navarra*, vol. 1, pp. 1-10.
52. Julio Caro Baroja, *Las formas complejas de la vida religiosa*..., p. 23.
53. Julio Caro Baroja, *Sobre la religión*..., p. 7.
54. Julio Caro Baroja, *De la vida rural vasca*..., p. 19.
55. Julio Caro Baroja, *Los pueblos del norte*..., p. 30.
56. Jesús Azcona, *Etnia y nacionalismo vasco*..., pp. 32-76.
57. I find it impossible to delineate exactly the difference between the diverse conceptualizations of cultural cycle employed by Ratzel and Meyer and that utilized by Caro Baroja, given the fact that I have not utilized the originals of the former's works. The comparison I will seek to establish in the following pages is therefore between the conception of the "school" of cycles and that of Caro Baroja.
58. Julio Caro Baroja, *Etnografía histórica de Navarra*..., vol. 1, pp. 21-22.
59. Julio Caro Baroja, *Sobre la religión antigua*..., p. 8.
60. Julio Caro Baroja, *Vasconiana* (San Sebastián: Txertoa, 1974), p. 11. In writing this, Caro Baroja was presumably thinking of his teachers J. M. de Barandiarán and T. de Aranzadi who, concerned with the reconstruction of Basque culture and considering only those elements they deemed significant, linked "prehistory with the contemporary peasantry" (Julio Caro Baroja and

E. Temprano, *Disquisiciones antropológicas*..., p. 84). It should be noted that Caro Baroja always treats his teachers with great respect and admiration, despite their intellectual differences. In fact this leads him to accept as worthwhile aspects of their work which he clearly rejects in those of others. There is a significant example if we compare the original edition of *De la vida rural vasca*. *Vera de Bidasoa*, written in 1944, with the re-edition of 1974 in which Caro Baroja writes of the importance of these and other anthropologists when analyzing the household.
61. F. Boas, *Race, Language and Culture* (New York: The Free Press, 1966), pp. 270-280.
62. Ibid., p. 258.
63. Ibid., pp. 263, 458-488.
64. Julio Caro Baroja, *Los vascos*..., pp. 14-15; Julio Caro Baroja, "Cosas humanas y tiempos de ellas," in Julio Caro Baroja, *De la superstición al ateismo (meditaciones antropológicas)* (Madrid: Taurus, 1974), pp. 34-35.
65. Jesús Azcona, "La delimitación antropológica y etnológica de lo vasco y los vascos," *Cuadernos de etnología y etnografía de Navarra*, no. 40 (1982), pp. 783-785; and Jesús Azcona, *Etnia y nacionalismo vasco* (Barcelona: Anthropos, 1984), p. 76.
66. Julio Caro Baroja, "El tiempo en antropología," *Revista de Occidente*, No. 2 (1980), p. 36.
67. J. Ziegler, "Les temps social des sociétés industrielles et des sociétés émergentes," ms. (Varna: AIS, VII Congreso Mundial, 1970).
68. Julio Caro Baroja, "El tiempo en antropología," p. 37.
69. Davydd Greenwood ("Julio Caro Baroja: Sus obras...," p. 91) as well as E. Temprano (Julio Caro Baroja and E. Temprano, *Disquisiciones antropológicas*, p. 44) underscore the influence of Pío Baroja in the work of Julio Caro Baroja. However, regarding the concepts of time and space there exist clear differences between them. When asked precisely about the Kantian conceptions of time and space Caro Baroja answers, "I have an empirical concept rather than a metaphysical and absolute idea of space and time. I believe that space and time, in any investigation, are not givens." Ibid., p. 44.
70. G. Klaus and M. Buhr, *Philosophisches Wörterbuch* (Leipzig: VEB Bibliographisches Institut, 1975), p. 1013.
71. M. Bunge, *Materialismo y ciencia* (Barcelona: Ariel, 1981), p. 39.
72. "Con D. Julio Caro Baroja. Situación actual de la antropología," *Alcoveras*, no. 0 (1982), p. 18.
73. Julio Caro Baroja, "El tiempo en antropología," pp. 30-31.

74. Julio Caro Baroja, *Etnografía histórica de Navarra*, vol. 3, p. 460.
75. Julio Caro Baroja, "Cosas humanas...," in Julio Caro Baroja, *De la superstición al ateismo*..., p. 23.
76. In Caro Baroja's thought regarding structuralism there is not only a change of opinion in recent years, but rather, in my opinion, a simplification as well. By generalizing and underscoring its relationship only with history or science, he reduces structuralism to a stereotype or, in his own terminology, to one of the "commonplaces." The same may be said of the majority of his affirmations regarding the other schools of thought. Julio Caro Baroja, *Etnografía histórica de Navarra*, vol. 3, p. 463; and Julio Caro Baroja and E. Temprano, *Disquisiciones antropológicas*, pp. 28–34, 93–136.
77. Julio Caro Baroja, "Mundos circundantes y contornos histórico-culturales," in Julio Caro Baroja, *De la superstición*..., p. 57.
78. Ibid., p. 35.
79. Julio Caro Baroja, *Vasconiana*..., p. 19.
80. Jesús Azcona, "La delimitación antropológica...," p. 785.
81. Julio Caro Baroja, "Cosas humanas y tiempos...," p. 22.
82. Julio Caro Baroja, "Mundos circundantes y contornos...," p. 32.
83. Julio Caro Baroja, "El tiempo en antropología," p. 36.
84. Julio Caro Baroja, "Cosas humanas y tiempos...," p. 22.
85. Julio Caro Baroja, "El tiempo en antropología," p. 37.
86. Julio Caro Baroja, "Cosas humanas y tiempos...," pp. 19, 27.
87. Julio Caro Baroja, "Mundos circundantes y contornos...," pp. 42, 49.

Singing Duels and Social Solidarity: The Case of the Basque *Charivari*

by

Roslyn M. Frank

Modern analysts argue that the Basque poetic duel characteristic of *bertsolaritza* contests is either a modern phenomenon or that it has mythic origins.[1] The *charivari* is relegated to the realm of folklore. An alternative interpretation is that these social forms are derived from the archaic dramatic mock trials which developed as a political response to the incorporation of previously autonomous communities into state systems and the process of class formation. This interpretation of the Basque data unifies a group of otherwise disparate social-artistic phenomena and suggests the social and historic reasons for their evolution into contemporary forms.

The initial focus of this interpretation will be an analysis of the disputing processes of the French Basque provinces of Lapurdi, Nafarroa Behera, and Zuberoa as they are manifested in the *charivari*, a type of mock folk trial. In addition, the disputing processes found in several structural variants of the public *charivari* will also be considered. The specific examples cited cover a period from approximately 1815 to the 1930s, although references to earlier and later versions of these disputing processes will also be utilized.

In recent years a substantial number of cross-cultural case studies have been published concerning disputing processes at the village level in Western and non-Western cultures; however, no such case studies have been undertaken of Basque ethnographic data from this perspective.[2] The theoretical model used here will be the analysis of disputing processes developed in the pioneering work of Nader:

> The study of dispute settlement focuses on only one of the many functions of law. As a topic it crosscuts a segment of the law domain by incorporating a particular type of settlement—

judicial process—into the broader domain—dispute settlement, which perforce leads us to dwell on problems of law in culture and society. The consideration of judicial process as one point of the continuum of the broader category of public forms of dispute settlement leads us to considerations of an anthropological nature in trying to explain process, use, and function of various dispute settling mechanisms as they relate to the presence or absence of a judicial process.[3]

The first sections of the study will examine the general characteristics of these mock trials in order to establish their taxonomy, their structural morphology, and the disputing processes of conflict resolution embedded in them. The second section will be dedicated to the examination of the disputing processes of a specific trial, that of Turrut-Arrosa, which took place around 1815 in the Basque village of Sara. The final section will investigate the role of the *bertsolari* improviser in these trials. The analysis will move in inverse chronological order, from an examination of the twentieth-century variants back to the nineteenth-century one of Turrut-Arrosa. This approach will reveal the way in which the structural components of the mock trial have been modified over a period of nearly two centuries. Finally, these structural components will be related to their contemporary counterparts, and considered with respect to modern *bertsolaritza* debates.

All societies have developed procedures that can be called into operation when trouble arises, when an infraction of societal norms occurs or is perceived to occur. Basque society is no exception for the disputing processes found in these mock trials, and their structural variants, have played a central role in conflict resolution at the village level for many centuries. In considering the disputing processes present in a given society, there are four basic types of case materials available to the anthropologist of law: observed cases, cases taken from recorded materials, memory cases, and hypothetical cases.[4] Obviously, the preferred type would be that which is directly observed and recorded by a trained field worker and the least reliable that of the hypothetical case. Since the data under analysis here primarily concern past cases, the main sources of reference will be taken from recorded materials, i.e., those recorded directly by Basque observers and memory cases. This material in turn will be supplemented by evidence drawn from other pertinent documents, as well as from fieldwork conducted in the Basque Country.

Before beginning a detailed analysis of the *charivari* and its variants, a few explanatory remarks are necessary to clarify the terminology used. While previous studies have frequently employed the terms *karrosa*, *asto-lasterka*, and *tobera-mustrak* as if they referred to different entities, all are in fact merely regional variants of nearly identical phenomena. For that reason the more encompassing generic term *charivari* will be utilized when speaking of the overall phenomenon itself. The term *public charivari* will be used when referring to the pan-village daytime performances and the expression *nighttime charivari* when making reference to the *galarrotsa*, *tzintzarrotsa*, and *tobera* variants.[5] The disputing processes of conflict resolution embedded in the *charivari* have also been grafted onto other activities and ritual behaviors which at first glance would not reveal explicit structural linkages to the folk trials.

In order to establish the overall taxonomy of the mock trials, and particularly the significance of Turrut-Arrosa's case, Iribarren's description of the twentieth-century *karrosa* variant of Valcarlos will be first analyzed.[6] As will be seen, Turrut-Arrosa's mock trial forms part of an elaborate ritual custom referred to by Iribarren as a *karrosa*, a public theatrical performance aimed at public disgrace of those involved. In the town of Valcarlos, near Roncesvalles, *karrosas* were performed until the year 1930, and for this reason the variant of this town will serve as a model in order to determine the general characteristics of the phenomena so that later the structural components of these mock trials can be compared to those of Turrut-Arrosa.

According to Iribarren, the *karrosa* was invoked in the case of repeated intoxication, public disturbances, attempted rape or assault of a woman, offenses against marital or parental authority, husband and wife beating, and other offenses against societal norms. When such an action took place, the *karrosa* was organized and its celebration was announced in Valcarlos and in the neighboring villages of Garazi, in the valley of Saint-Jean Pied de Port on the French side of the frontier.[7] The news of the forthcoming *karrosa* was received by the villagers with great enthusiasm. On the day designated for the celebration of the festival the villagers went about forming the tribunal and electing the people who were to play the principal roles in the mock trial, attempting to choose individuals for each role who were the most physically different from the person they were going to imitate. Just as in the *Commedia dell'Arte* the characters were always the same, consisting of the following cast: *yuyia*, "judge and accuser"; *grefierra*, "secretary"; *kridia*, "lawyer for the defense"; *apeza*, "parish priest"; *bereterrak*, "priest's helpers"; *kurriera*, "courier on horseback"; and *bertsolari*, "improviser." Each one of these dressed up with the costumes and accoutrements appropriate to his role: the judge in a top hat, with a long beard, eyeglasses, and a large book; the secretary with spectacles and an enormous goose-quill pen; the defense lawyer with a toga, beard, and a roll of paper in his hand; and the priest who would wear a robe loaned to him by the regular parish priest.

While the cast of characters was being chosen those who were to perform the role of the injured party and the accused were also designated. Here again the choice was dictated by the desire to find individuals who were comic counterparts, and they were attired in such a way that it was easy to see they were in fact caricatures. For example, the last *karrosa*, which took place in Valcarlos in 1930, was organized because a young woman had been attacked by a young man. She called on her sister for aid and the latter, who was ironing at the time, came with the hot iron in her hand and gave the attacker a blow, burning his face. In the mock trial the person playing the role of the attacker had painted on his face the mark of the iron. The actor was so ridiculous his very presence on stage made the audience burst into laughter.

After everyone was properly disguised the tribunal and the couple came in and took their places on the raised stage in the middle of the plaza. Along with the judicial authorities the village dancers came and, before the proceedings began, would execute a dance about the stage. After the dance was finished the trial started. The order of the events in the trial was rigidly structured. First, the judge read the charges against the accused from his book. He exaggerated them in a humorous way, accentuating his speech with apostrophes and gesticulations. Next, he invited the parties involved to reenact the crime.

In order for the reenactment of the crime to be realized with greater accuracy at times the actual physical surroundings of the crime were reconstructed. For example, in a *karrosa* celebrated in 1885, after the husband and wife of the house of Pedrota had had a violent fight while working in their cornfield, the organizers of the trial arranged a pseudocornfield at the back of the stage. In an earlier *karrosa*, organized to chastise a woman who had given her husband a beating in the kitchen, the kitchen itself was reproduced on the stage.

The characters playing the role of the accused always attempted to reproduce the event in the most comic and exaggerated manner. In the case of the previously cited *karrosa* against the house of Pedrota one of the real protagonists, the woman, watched the spectacle from the window of the house of Txotxoa. While the actors were reproducing the beating she had given her husband, the real husband-beater gestured to those on stage, indicating that the beating was not being reproduced to her liking, i.e., that the actors were not imitating the event as it had occurred.

After the crime had been reenacted, the next step was the interrogation of the witnesses who filed before the tribunal. In giving their testimony they brought out all the "dirty clothes" of the accused, including those of the most intimate nature. The *bertsolari* would improvise jokes and allusive songs after each witness had spoken. Next, the lawyer for the defense stood up and performed. The individual playing this role attempted to fake a defense, for in reality he endeavored with his speech to complicate even further the situation of the accused with arguments and clarifications that implicated the victim with new charges and crimes, all of which was marvelously entertaining to the audience.

Finally, the priest intervened in order to clarify the case. The intervention of the priest is significant since he is nowhere present in Turrut-Arrosa's trial. According to Iribarren, in the *karrosa* of Valcarlos, the priest would always attempt to find ways of excusing the accused. The tribunal, in turn, accepted the priest's suggestion and the accused promised to mend his ways. Then the priest blessed the accused and the trial was terminated with the judge reading his verdict. However, since the dancers played a role in the ceremony, a break was created in the trial so that they could dance. The actual significance of the specific dances executed has been lost, but the purpose of the performance is clear. Under the pretext of needing a new proof or more information, the judge would order the courier to go on horseback in search of it. While the courier was gone the dancers performed and when he returned the case was reopened. At this point, when the judge was to pronounce his verdict, a live cat tied to the end of a pole was brought into the square and, after having been drenched with gasoline or another type of flammable liquid, was set on fire. After the trial was completed the audience would join in the dancing and when the festivities terminated, "the neighbors would go home commenting on the spectacle ... pleased that they had fulfilled their duties as citizens."[8]

The specific events surrounding the celebration of the last *karrosa* in Valcarlos in 1930 emphasize the changing norms of the region and the fact that a century earlier Turrut-Arrosa's trial was celebrated in a markedly different atmosphere. The last *karrosa* came about because of the attempted rape of the young woman previously mentioned who sought the aid of her sister.

> Once the celebration was announced, the Civil Governor intervened because of the petitions of the two sisters. He prohibited the event. However, the citizens of Valcarlos were not to be swayed and they simply moved the celebration to the next town of Arneguy, located across the bridge in France. That afternoon there were only two people left in Valcarlos, the mayor and the parish priest, for all the rest had gone to Arneguy. The Civil

Governor called out the Spanish police who watched the spectacle from the international bridge, and in the evening when the organizers of the *karrosa* came back across the bridge they were arrested at the request of the Civil Governor, who fined them for their disobedience.[9]

According to Iribarren, a *karrosa* has not been celebrated in the town of Valcarlos since 1930, even though there have been occasions which would have called for one.[10] Nevertheless, in other parts of Nafarroa Behera, Zuberoa, and Lapurdi, the celebration of the open-air mock trials has persisted.[11] For instance, in Saint Jean Pied de Port, they are celebrated at great expense with considerable sums invested in the costumes of the actors. Given the difficulties and expense they do not take place frequently.

The twentieth-century versions of the *karrosa* represent a blend of several legal procedures. At one level the entire phenomenon is framed as a trial, but with a dramatic reenactment of the alleged crime. Additionally, the testimony of the witnesses and other procedures of the discovery process are not aimed primarily at determining the *truth*. A precise rendering of the events under examination does not appear to be the principal goal, given that all parties involved exaggerate claims and introduce extraneous and even false testimony and accusations. Also, although the structural components present include the intervention of lawyers, as well as a judge and tribunal, i.e., third parties (fictitiously) empowered to adjudicate the case and consequently to reach a decision as to the guilt or innocence of the accused, in actuality, the disputing process in all cases cited functions on the basis of the legal procedure of *mediation* rather than *adjudication* because the judge is not authorized to enforce the verdict. As Iribarren states, the priest's intervention is "always to find a formula for settlement."[12]

Focusing on this aspect of the process, the twentieth-century procedure employed is that of mediation, traditionally defined as a situation in which a third party intervenes in the dispute. However, if the principals are defined as the two parties in apparent conflict, e.g., the husband and wife, the young woman and her assailant, etc., neither solicits the aid nor intervention of the mediators. An alternate interpretation would convert the villagers themselves into the offended party who presses the case for mediation.

For instance, in the dispute of 1930, it is evident that the two sisters involved in the events did not favor holding the trial. Nor is there evidence the parties involved directly in the perceived disputes intervened to bring about the performance. However, this point cannot be ascertained definitely, since it is not clear in other cases whether or not, prior to active disputation, the offended party did or did not speak to members of the community concerning the grievance and the possible means of resolving it. What is clear from historical records is that over the centuries both the legal authorities in France and Spain, as well as some of the parties implicated, objected vehemently to the performances. These objections were eventually enacted into a multitude of ordinances and decrees intended to punish those organizing and performing the mock trials.[13]

The alleged crimes of the parties brought to trial reveal that they fall into the category of private and criminal complaints which in some societies may not be filed in court unless the injured party has first undertaken an attempt at reconciliation with the offending party at the local level.[14] Included in the list of actions here would be breach of the peace, e.g., public intoxication, bodily injury, domestic violence, offenses against marital or parental authority, and attempted rape.

Cross-cultural studies of the disputing process demonstrate that mediation is institutionalized in some agent of reconciliation. The mayor, priest, or other authorized community figure holds a hearing asking each party to state his side of the dispute. The mediator's role is to act as a conciliator in order to get the parties back together and to negotiate a settlement rather than to try to find fault. His purpose is to point out the rights and wrongs, the strengths and weaknesses in each position, and to suggest a compromise, hence mitigating the long-range effects that might occur were the dispute allowed to escalate. Therefore, he may coax the parties with logic, condemn them for their obstinacy and unreasonableness, or shame them for their intransigence. To bring about a reconciliation of their differences he might cite prior friendship, common economic interests, or suggest that the village welfare would be better served by their reconciliation.[15]

Even though the *charivariak* operated outside the regular legal framework, this fact does not negate the efficacy of this Basque disputing process as a functional reconciliation mechanism for the resolution and mitigation of conflict at the village level, even when the entire performance was in fact a legal fiction, a farcical reenactment of the crime, and a comic parody of the mediation procedures.

Having examined the structural morphology and disputing processes employed in the *karrosa* variant of the public *charivari*, two additional variants need to be mentioned, the *asto-lasterka* and the *tobera-mustrak*. In Nafarroa Behera the *asto-lasterka* "donkey-race," a structural variant of the Lapurdin and Zuberoan *karrosa*, is found. The performance of the *asto-lasterka* does not differ significantly from the *karrosa* with the exception that the accused may be brought to the square on a donkey.[16] The name assigned to this performance is obviously connected to the earlier Greek and Roman *charivari* parades where the accused arrived astride a donkey.[17]

A third variant called the *tobera-mustrak* is found in Zuberoa and Nafarroa Behera and includes the performance of the mock trial as described by Iribarren. However, this variant is much more complex and often has a larger number of participants. Depending on the size of the village, the number of performers (main characters, peripheral ones, dancers, and musicians) may vary from twenty to eighty. The specific structural components of the *tobera-mustrak* will be analyzed later.

Before turning to Turrut-Arrosa's trial, the nighttime variant of the *charivari* will be considered. This variant, quite similar to the *shivaree*, has been the most extensively investigated form of the *charivari* in other parts of Europe. The structural components of the Basque nighttime *charivari*, referred to alternately as *galarrotsa*, *tzintzarrotsa*, and *tobera*, are brought into play in the case of marriages not in accord with societal norms, such as one between an elderly widower and a young woman, an older woman and a young man, or a local resident with an outsider. When such a situation arose, a nighttime *charivari* would be organized by the young people of the village, often with the participation of members of adjoining ones. A *bertsolari* improviser would be contacted who, along with the young people and their noisemakers, would proceed to the offender's house where they would initiate the *charivari*. A single *bertsolari* would sing out the alleged crimes of the accused in improvised couplets and the group would respond after each with its instruments. These couplets, which were taken up and repeated in chorus by the group, fall into two categories: traditional ones and those composed expressly for the case in question. Each night these proceedings were repeated with all the accompanying din of the musical instruments until either the couple would pay a retribution in wine or money or until the marriage took place, although even then the *charivari* might not be terminated.[18]

Among the musical instruments employed—pots and pans, bells removed from all the livestock, the *thupina-utsu*, a type of stringed drum, and the *adar-turrutak*, cow horns—the latter are of particular interest. The use of these cow-horn trumpets in the mocking ceremonies appears to have given rise to two expressions in Basque: *adarra jo* "to mock," literally, "to play the horn," and *turrut egin* "to mock" from *turrut*, an onomatopoeic word. The *charivari* horning also generated other types of semantic structures, such as the term *turrut* applied as a nickname to the individual "horned." For example, the main character in the case to be studied in the next section was nicknamed *Turrut-Arrosa*, "Horned Arrosa."[19] According to Michel, in Zuberoa a widower would never attempt to get married in the daytime, but rather only under the cover of darkness so as to escape the *charivari*. However, even this tactic often proved futile as there would be a nighttime *charivari*. This time with the musicians and the *bertsolari* in the lead, the retinue would follow the couple to the church where they continued to sing out their objections. In Nafarroa Behera the proceedings were finalized when a live cat, wrapped in straw and carried on a pole, was set on fire. The *charivari* participants then followed the newly married couple back again to their house. Nevertheless, the case did not necessarily terminate there and the nighttime *charivari* could continue for many nights or transform into a daytime mock trial in which two lawyer *bertsolariak* were contracted, one to plead the case of the young people and the other that of the accused.[20]

Having examined the general characteristics of the *charivari*, the specific case of Turrut-Arrosa, in which nighttime *charivariak* are followed by an elaborate mock trial involving the people from several different villages, may now be analyzed. The source for this case study is a manuscript of the Reverend Wentworth Webster (1828–1907), who lived for about forty years in the Basque Country, primarily in the village of Sara in Lapurdi, after having served as the pastor for the Anglican congregation in Biarritz. To this day the principal source for Basque folk tales in English is Webster's *Basque Legends* (1877). While examining his original manuscripts and papers, housed in the Municipal Library in Bayonne, Charles Videgain encountered an unpublished description of a *charivari* collected by Webster. The French text of this document, along with various couplets in Basque, was published by Videgain in 1974. It is this manuscript that will form the basis of analysis for Turrut-Arrosa's trial and punishment.

Although the names of many of Webster's Basque informants are indicated in the listing he made of his papers, he did not include an entry for the *charivari* of Sara. However, he does indicate that the other materials which he translated into English for his *Basque Legends* were collected from 1873–1875, and that the majority of the tales were "dictated by Mme. Bellevue" of Saint-Jean-de-Luz. It may be assumed the text of the *charivari* was collected at the same time and in a similar way from Mme. Bellevue herself, or from another Basque informant, and that the manuscript refers to events which took place in Sara around 1815.[21] The text of the manuscript is as follows:

Sixty years ago an individual nicknamed Turrut-Arrosa, son and master of the Arrosa house, was going to marry for the fourth time. The first three wives had died in childbirth and in spite of his advanced age he was going to marry a fourth. All the young people of Sara decided to use all the customary mockeries against him. Every night the young people gathered about the Arrosa house to play their horns (*adar-turrutak*), and even the young people of Saint-Pée and Souraide frequently came to play their instruments.

After Turrut-Arrosa had married his fourth wife, the young people of Sara decided that a public *charivari* would be made against him, no matter what the expenses that would be incurred by the proper celebration of such a festival.

When the day came, all the square of Sara was overflowing with people; the young people who had gotten ready in the quarter of Ichtilarte descended from that quarter and came to the middle of the square. A drum major named Jean Louis Mikeleperitz marched at the head; then came the mass of the troupe, surrounding the newly married couple (who represented Turrut-Arrosa and his wife).

In the square the stage had been constructed where Piarres Adame, a famous improviser from Sara, was. A tribunal had been constituted which was to judge Turrut-Arrosa. That tribunal had a courier on horseback who was to bring it the documents. The courier was late. The president [of the tribunal] sent another horseman who fell in front of the Sorhotenea house, and then Piarres Adame made up this couplet to him:

Yaun yuyeak igorri du Kurrier berria
Ustez eta izanen den lehengoa baino hobia
Sorhoteneko atean dago zalditik eroria.

[Sir judge sent for a new courier,
Believing he would be better than the first
He's there in front of the door of Sorhotenea's house,
having fallen from his horse.]

The tribunal condemned Turrut-Arrosa to be castrated; the preparations were made to carry out the sentence; the castrator was Piarres Urtte who came forward with his instrument, with water and salt. The victim (one named Urchoko) was placed on a table in spite of his resistance; in the midst of his screams and moans he was castrated, and into the square were thrown the testicles of a young calf as if they had been those of Turrut-

Arrosa. Undoubtedly, it was then when Piarres Adame made up this couplet:

> Berriz gertatzen bada okasione horretan
> Bizirik ehortzi beharko dik teilariako errekan
> Eta besta eder bat egin yaun horren ohoretan.

> [If it happens again on that occasion
> He will have to be buried alive in the Teilaria River
> And in that man's honor another fine festival will be made.]

As the wife of Turrut was pregnant, she pretended to be having labor pains, and Latapie, the doctor of Saint-Pée, was summoned. The latter gave aid to the patient who gave birth to a cat.

That unfortunate animal suffered all the punishments of the world trying to escape from the crowd, and then Piarres Adame made up these other verses:

> Latapie yaunak ederki
> Nola futre sakerdi
> Gizon gibel zurien andrerik
> Ez ditake ongi erdi.

> [Sir Latapie has done well
> How on earth could she give birth?
> A yellow-livered man's wife
> Can't successfully give birth.][22]

At this juncture the procedures of conflict resolution embedded in Turrut-Arrosa's public *charivari* can be analyzed. A disputing process is composed of at least three distinct phases or stages: the *grievance* or *preconflict* stage, i.e., the genesis of the conflict; the *conflict* stage; and finally the phase of *active dispute settlement*. A final and often neglected stage concerns the *social consequences* following settlement. The grievance or preconflict stage refers to a circumstance or condition which one person or a group perceives to be unjust. This stage is characterized by the perception of a person or group that the rights of one party are being infringed, interfered with, or denied by another party. At this point the grievance may be escalated through confrontation to the conflict stage.[23]

In the case of Turrut-Arrosa, the prehistory of the dispute is based on the fact his first three wives had died in childbirth and his advanced age notwithstanding, an element emphasized by the teller, he is still going to remarry. Although the advanced age of one of the parties wishing to contract marriage is consistently a salient factor in triggering the performance of a nighttime charivari, the death in childbirth of a former wife or wives has not been emphasized as a possible causative factor in previous studies of this phenomenon. Nonetheless, given the fact that the performance was utilized particularly against widowers, it might be assumed the previous wife might have died in childbirth, at least in some cases.[24] The relevance of this observation to the case in question will become more apparent later.

In the disputing process the disagreement enters the conflict state if the aggrieved party opts for confrontation by communicating feelings of injustice to the offending party. At this point both parties become aware of disagreement. In the case of Turrut-Arrosa this state is characterized by the participation of the offended group, the young people of Sara, who perceive their societal norms as being violated. Since Turrut-Arrosa persisted in his desire to remarry, the nighttime *charivari* is organized and performed repeatedly, not only by the townspeople of Sara, but also by those of two neighboring towns (Saint-Pée and Souraide). Through their intervention the matter becomes public and the conflict escalates to the dispute stage in which the sanctions become public disgrace and shame. At this juncture in the disputing process there is no mention of the alternative procedure by which the offending party could resolve the conflict through retribution, i.e., by paying a sum of money or giving a quantity of wine to the offended party, those engaging in the public denunciation. In other words, the mode of negotiation is negated. Turrut-Arrosa does not choose to mitigate the conflict by deciding not to marry, nor does he reach any other mutually acceptable resolution of the matter in dispute; rather he proceeds with the action which has been publicly condemned.

Essentially, the difference between the negotiated settlement, which apparently may have still been possible in the earlier stage of this conflict, and the alternate mode of settlement through adjudication, resides in the presence or absence of an authorized third party, a person or group who becomes actively involved in the disagreement. As Gulliver observes: "no dispute exists unless and until the right claimant, or someone on his behalf, actively raises the initial disagreement from the level of dyadic argument into the public arena, with the express intention of doing something about the desired claims."[25] The choice to escalate the conflict to the level of a dispute and to utilize adjudication, implies the presence of an adjudicator with a certain degree of authority whose judgment is in some sense binding. Whereas in the nighttime *charivari* no adjudicator is present, in the daytime one a full tribunal with a judge and lawyers is brought into play as the disputing process moves from the conflict stage into that of active dispute settlement.

An additional factor entering into any decision to escalate the conflict to the level of dispute is the cost dimension. Only in the case where the offense is considered by the offended party to be of sufficient importance and gravity would a decision to escalate the conflict occur. In the case of Turrut-Arrosa, the cost dimension is clearly apparent in the text, for the young people of Sara decide to organize a public *charivari*, "no matter what the expenses that would be incurred by the proper celebration. . . . "[26] Besides the concrete financial outlays incurred in the preparation of the public *charivari*, another aspect of the cost dimension is the time expended by the townspeople in order to organize such an elaborate performance. Once again the choice to hold the public *charivari* implies that the violation was felt to be sufficiently serious to justify such expenditures of time and money.

In general, disputing processes have multiple functions, for they can serve to educate, indoctrinate, punish, and harass, as well as provide entertainment. They are also fundamental in the maintenance of the status quo and in the integration of communities through the reinforcement of societal norms. The public *charivari* performed in Sara undoubtedly fulfilled all of these functions, not only for this community but also for the surrounding villages which directly participated in the proceedings either as actors, dancers, or as members of the audience.

The analysis of Turrut-Arrosa's trial and punishment is complicated by the fact that both are themselves fictional, particularly the castration and birthing episodes. Although the events are dressed as fiction, their objective referents were obviously understood by those present and the fiction still served to publicly chastise the offender. In this sense, the fictionalized events were still operative as mechanisms of social control and, therefore, should not be viewed as simply "farce" or "spectacle."

The fictional framing of the disputing process also obscures the precise nature of the relationship of these fictionalized events to Basque societal norms, since the norms being violated are implicitly rather than explicitly expressed in the disputing process employed. However, Turrut-Arrosa's case, as well as previous nighttime and public *charivaris* which took place in the Basque Country, both before and after this individual case, may be viewed as part of a long-term "extended case" begun many years or centuries earlier, with consequences that continued to affect social relations within the group under study. This approach allows the "trouble case," a case that repeatedly surfaces over a long period of time, to become an arena in which various structural principles are brought into play.[27] Thus utilized, the individual cases become a diagnostic tool for they function: 1) to pinpoint a stress point in the social structure of the community, 2) to illustrate an issue the people involved perceived to be conflict-engendering, and 3) to focus on the way this conflict was structured in the society.

The considerable number of condemnations of the nighttime and public *charivari* by legal authorities of this region indicates their frequency and the fact that the state clearly disapproved of their performance. Thus, there existed two conflicting sets of societal norms, one which gave rise repeatedly to their enactment and another which attempted to suppress them.[28]

Considering the Turrut-Arrosa events as part of an "extended case" spanning many centuries and focusing on a specific conflict-engendering issue gives rise to the question of the relationship of the mock trial and mock punishment to earlier methods used in resolving the same conflict. The question may be stated as follows: were the fictional events acted out here once based on a reenactment of real events? In other words, is the fiction based on a previous reality or was a fictional reenactment of the trial and punishment always the mechanism by which social control was effected?

Although the answer to this question is complicated, as will be seen in the following sections, it is clear that historically another level of fictionalization of real events did take place in the disputing processes, for in many regions of the French Basque Country the pressure of state legal sanctions led to the eventual condemnation of even the mock trials and punishments. When this occurred, another level of dramatic encapsulation took place: the accused parties ceased to have specific names and became stereotypes. When the *charivari* was then performed it was in fact a performance of a mock performance, one which might be viewed as a fiction imitating another fiction. These stereotyped farces reproduced as fiction the nighttime *charivari* and its escalation into a mock trial. Even the threats and condemnations of the officials were woven into the dramatic narrative. In actuality, these farces or secondary fictions were probably performed regularly to chastise real community members under the guise of the farce.

This fictional encapsulation can be seen in farces such as *Malkus et Malkulina* in which a widower wishing to remarry is threatened with the performance of a *charivari*; *Saturne et Venus* in which a mayor, when asked to stop the performance of the encapsulated *charivari*, states he knows of no law disallowing it; or *Rocquillard et Arieder* in which a mayor appears representing the legal authorities and threatens the fictional organizers with punishment.²⁹

The incorporation of real events into the fictionalized farcical version points to a significant and constant element which occurs over and over again in the evolution of the Basque *charivari*. When confronted with an opposing set of societal norms, one which precluded an overt presentation of the events, the Basques still managed to preserve the condemned structures by inserting them in a disguised manner into a supposedly fictional context. The real performance of the mock trial and punishment became fictionalized, and the real condemnations themselves were even incorporated at the level of fiction into the new "play." Thus, the Basque people utilized the mechanism of fictionalization to avoid the actual condemnation of the *charivari* and, therefore, were still able to perform it, since the authorities would have viewed the *charivaris* as art, not reality. In this way the normative messages embedded in the farces still continued to operate as vehicles of social control.³⁰

Veyrin has also commented on other variants of this mechanism of fictionalization:

> Since it was impossible to obtain permission to overtly perform the *charivari* they employed the pretext of a *cavalcade* which is composed essentially of the same elements as the *Santibate*, plus a large number of miscellaneous personages (*zirtzilak*), dressed in tattered clothes, who entertain the audience with their comic actions. The parade lasts an entire afternoon because of the many interludes of dances that precede and interrupt the trial proceedings: pleadings, debates, condemnation and execution of the guilty parties. . . . During the second half of the nineteenth century, the authorities, in effect, forbade those representations which, under the guise of fantasy, mocked too crudely their victims. A vain measure of the Basques, always astute when it comes to doing what they want, were content to announce irreproachable legendary or hagiographic pieces in which they inserted, in a rather haphazard manner, the forbidden fruit. Sometimes . . . [the *charivari*] was presented in its entirety at the beginning of the performance. More frequently, the scenes [of the *charivari*] were disseminated throughout the rustic tragedy, in such inextricable confusion that only those spectators who were aware of what was happening could follow the plot. Finally, other times the more subtle authors were able to fuse somewhat the two subjects in such a way that the farce appeared to be a vague parody of the serious piece.³¹

Writing in 1959, Alford gives concrete examples of this encapsulation mechanism:

> In the Soule province a Pastorale is allowed by the Prèfet whose authority is necessary for an outdoor theatre temporarily filling the *place*—but a *Charivari* is not. So they interpolate a *Charivari* scene amongst those of the Pastorale, without change of costume. One sees Sara, Abraham's wife, suddenly turn into the husband-beating woman, or Charlemagne into the much harried elderly widower to be punished. The Epilogue announces in traditional manner "You have heard our Tragedy" although the audience has been rocking with Rabelaisian laughter. The Gascon police are quite unconscious of the changes of character.[32]

This mechanism of fictional encapsulation of real events suggests that earlier trials and punishments, once part of the traditional legal processes of the Basque people, may also have become fictionalized and incorporated into the structures of disputing processes such as those found in Turrut-Arrosa's case. Although a detailed study of the historical nature of the trial procedures employed in Turrut-Arrosa's case will not be attempted here, a close examination of his punishment reveals it has two stages: first, his castration, brought about apparently because he was perceived as having caused the deaths of his previous wives in childbirth and, second, the threat of further punishment, that of being buried alive in the river. As will be seen, the reasons leading to his punishment may not have been specifically that he wanted to remarry but rather that he may have been perceived as unfit for procreative functions and, consequently, guilty of parricide.

For Turrut-Arrosa to be perceived as the perpetrator of his wives' deaths in childbirth the difficulties of the births must be attributed in some way to him. This hypothesis is suggested, although not fully substantiated, by data collected in this region concerning folk concepts of procreation and fertility, older men being viewed as undergoing male menopause and becoming unfit for procreation, as well as for other male activities.[33] The employment of castration in Turrut-Arrosa's case implies it may once have been a means of rendering unhealthy, "yellow-livered" males incapable of reproduction.[34] Although data on this particular mode of fertility control is limited, some fifty years before Turrut-Arrosa's trial, the Cortes of Navarra, the governing body of this Basque province, became preoccupied because of the zeal with which its castrators were exercising their profession on human subjects. In 1765 this concern was translated into action by the Cortes in Law 68, which was then forwarded to King Charles for approval on March 10, 1766.[35] Turrut-Arrosa's punishment involved both castration and the threat of being buried alive in a river. The latter was in fact a common medieval punishment, specifically in cases of parricide, and continued to be practiced in this region into the nineteenth century, even though by this time the offender was hanged prior to being immersed. With respect to the linkage between castration and live burial, there is a curious Basque saying included in Oihenart's collection of 1657 which states: *Emaztearen gaizes xikira sedina adarregui ehorz sedin*, "Let the one who has been castrated because of crimes against his wife be buried with horns."[36] The use of the subjunctive as well as the overall syntactic structure of the saying suggests its language may reflect a fragmented version of a legal admonition which still formed part of popular speech in Oihenart's time in the middle of the seventeenth century. The saying is subject to several interpretations. However, it states quite clearly the offender in question, in addition to being castrated, is to be buried with horns, the horns mentioned being reminiscent of the *adar-turrutak* which were played in the *charivari* and in cases of parricide to publicly shame the offender while he was being paraded about on a donkey. In cases of parricide the ritualized usage of the instruments in the Basque Country was still prevalent in the nineteenth century.[37] Therefore, Turrut-Arrosa's mock punishment appears to be an encapsulated fictional rendering of earlier legal norms.

It might be noted that, in parts of Europe from the early Middle Ages until at least the seventeenth century, castration was a relatively common method of controlling those individuals whose antisocial behavior was considered detrimental to society, and its application was certainly not limited simply to controlling potential or real sexual offenders.[38] In the Basque Country itself, particularly Navarra, castration was obviously viewed in a far different light by Turrut-Arrosa's audience than it is today, given that there castration was still a much-sought remedy for hernias and ruptures until at least the early part of the nineteenth century.[39]

The final structural element in the informant's rendition of Turrut-Arrosa's trial and punishment is the appearance of the cat in the mock birthing scene. Of all the actors, only the *bertsolari* and doctor are not fictitious. The real doctor is the woman actress who gives birth to a cat which is subsequently thrown to the audience, just as in the pseudocastration where the audience was given the calf's testicles as a visible proof of the actions being carried out on stage. According to the informant's words, the audience also attempted to bring harm to the animal.

The symbolism of the cat can be interpreted on several different levels. According to one contemporary Basque informant interviewed concerning this ritual, the cat must have been black and was meant to symbolize a deformed or dead fetus, a miscarriage.[40] The closing words of the *bertsolari* Piarres Adame, which accompany this part of the ritual, would appear to substantiate this idea: "Mr. Latapie [the doctor from Saint-Pée] has done well; how on earth could she give birth; a yellow-livered man's wife cannot successfully give birth."[41] In this interpretation the cat has a very specific objective referent, a dead fetus.

The symbolism of the cat is also found as a recurring structural element in other *charivariak* of the same period and later, where it is burned alive on a pole after having been wrapped in straw and doused with a flammable liquid. Given that another highly feared symbolic hexing of the future offspring of unpopular marriages was the tying of knots, the cat sacrifice may have functioned in a similar manner.[42] This interpretation would cause the cat to become a magical means of impeding the future fertility of the couple. Furthermore, it may have been intended to symbolize the past infertility of the widower and/or death in childbirth of a previous wife or her offspring.

At another level the cat-birthing scene would seem superfluous as a hexing mechanism, given Turrut-Arrosa's previous symbolic castration. Perhaps the cat ritual functioned as a magical impediment to procreation, whereas his castration would have been a more concrete and prosaic means of achieving the same goal.

In summary, the precise symbolism of the cat-birthing scene cannot be determined, especially in light of the fact the cat sacrifice was also a final element in the performance of mock trials which did not necessarily involve cases of remarriage. For this reason, the birthing scene may be a variant of the cat sacrifice, and the audience's attempt to bring harm to it may be explained by the fact that in other performances of the same period the cat would have been set on fire. Although the cat's symbolism is unclear, it undoubtedly is an archaic magical element inherited from earlier stages of the disputing process.

Before concluding this section, another permutation of the structures of the public *charivari* needs to be addressed. As has been indicated previously, when faced with opposition, the Basque solution was to disguise the *charivari* by inserting it into the *charivari* farces or by integrating it into performances of apparently innocuous legendary or hagiographic folk dramas. Another method of fictional encapsulation was that of grafting the *charivari* structures onto the villagewide Carnival activities called *cavalcades* or *parades* in French.

These activities, named *Santibate* in Nafarroa Behera and *maskaradak* in Zuberoa, include many of the same characters found in the *charivaris* and are structurally very similar to the more elaborate *tobera-mustrak* variant of the *charivari*. Alford has commented on this striking similarity: "When the *Cavalcades* go out for Carnival dancing they are called *Santibate*, i.e., Carnival. When they go out for *tobera mustrak* . . . [they are] a show or play in punishment or derision of some village bad behavior. . . . The Carnival (spring-rite) elements have become mixed with the punishment-play elements. . . ."[43] Caro Baroja has also observed this fusion of structural elements.[44] However, neither author seems aware of the fact that this fusion may also be a response to earlier condemnations of overt performances of the *charivaris*, condemnations which did not initially outlaw their performance, but rather attempted to regulate and limit them to a specific time period, that of Carnival, a period when they could be performed without penalty.[45]

This may also explain in part the striking similarities between certain characters found in the Zuberoan *maskaradak* and those found typically in the *charivaris* discussed here. For example, it may shed light on the presence of the cat, a character called *Gathia* according to Hérelle and *Gathuzain* "cat keeper" by Alford, who carries the *sorgin guraizeak* "witch's scissors" in its hands. These "witch's scissors" complement the instruments carried by the castrators who castrate the main character of the *maskaradak*, the *zamalzain* horseman, and then throw his pseudotesticles into the air. In modern-day performances these now take on the more civilized form of two burnt corks or potatoes rather than that of calf's testicles, as occurred in Turrut-Arrosa's mock castration.[46]

The *zamalzain* hobby-horse character, whose origins are probably linked to much earlier symbolic stratas of ritual death and resurrection, is found throughout Europe, particularly as part of the cast of characters in the Morris dances. In the Zuberoan *maskaradak* its immediate symbolic referent may be found in the structural elements inherited from the *charivaris* as well as from the *asto-lasterka* variants where the accused was paraded about on a horse or donkey prior to his condemnation. This interpretation of the symbolic referent of the main character, the castrated *zamalzain*, is reinforced by the fact that in the north of England a parallel development of the accused character has occurred in a *charivari* variant called "Riding the Stang," for a stang is a pole and it is astride this artificial hobby-horse steed the culprit must ride.[47]

An interpretation which would allow for the individual riding a horse, donkey, or a structural homologue—a pole, a hobby-horse, etc.—to be the real target of the punishment would explain the presence of another character found in Turrut-Arrosa's trial and the *tobera-mustrak* variant of the daytime *charivari* described by Duvoisin: the courier or *huissier* who appears mounted on horseback or a donkey. He is a "stylized character, very lively, generally donned with a great cocked hat and dressed, as the ancient buffoons, in pants with each leg of a different color."[48] According to Duvoisin, this character is killed and resurrected in the midst of the *charivari* proceedings: "The courier will be accused of lying or of another type of crime by one of the lawyers. The judge condemns him to death; he flees; the guards pursue him shooting. He ends up being decapitated in the square, but he comes back to life."[49] At an earlier stage in the performance he is thrown from his mount after being harassed by other characters, an incident that recalls the fall taken by the courier horseman in Turrut-Arrosa's trial, as well as the harassment of the *zamalzain* hobby-horse character of the Zuberoan *maskaradak*.

In Duvoisin's description of the final resolution of the *toberamustrak* the judge condemns the accused to death. However, this death sentence is precluded by a reprieve brought at the very last minute from the king, and consequently the accused is saved from punishment. If a displacement of the symbolic axis has occurred, then the verdict is carried out, however, not on the individual directly accused of the crime, but rather on his symbolic counterpart, the individual on horseback, who, in turn, at another level, would have been perceived by the audience as the accused himself given that he was mounted, a traditional and recognized symbol of ignominy.

In summary, Webster's informant provides an example of a public *charivari* whose structural components suggest that the multitude of undocumented *charivariak* of this period and earlier periods may contain information which would explain their condemnation by the non-Basque-speaking legal authorities of the region. These authorities may well have suspected the Basques were somehow managing to outwit them, and through fictional encapsulation and other mechanisms of displacement were still accomplishing their intended goals. These condemnations may also be explained by the fact that frequent targets of these trials were not only members of the Basque-speaking community itself, but also legal institutions and authorities who were perceived as attempting to oppress or otherwise coerce the Basque people into modes of conduct which they rejected. Often one of the functions of the *charivaris*, although disguised and obscured by the Basque language and other mechanisms of fictional encapsulation, was that of social and political protest against those forces emanating both from within the Basque-speaking community and from without it, whose goal was the suppression of the Basque normative systems.

Finally, the role of the *bertsolari* in the disputing process may be analyzed. Although in recent years a substantial number of studies has appeared dedicated to the Basque *bertsolari* improvisers and their artistic production, little attention has been paid to their social and political role. As Azurmendi has recently pointed out, these studies have been characterized by two major directions: one that would establish *bertsolaritza* as a modern phenomenon, originating around 1800, and another that would attribute to it essentially mythical origins, maintaining that it has been a component of Basque culture since time immemorial.[50] The majority of these works define *bertsolaritza* primarily from the point of view of "oral literature." This definition of the phenomenon has influenced the direction of present investigations, limiting them primarily to an analysis of the phenomenon as "literature" and, therefore, inevitably imposing upon them models of investigation appropriate to the examination of literary works. Consequently, little attention has been given to the social context and origins of the phenomenon, i.e., the specific social functions it has traditionally fulfilled within Basque society. The following section concerning the *bertsolari*'s role in Basque disputing processes will provide an alternate avenue of investigation which will raise several fundamental questions related to the structural components of modern *bertsolaritza* debates.

In the disputing processes studied here the *bertsolari* improviser plays a central role, for his presence is found in all the examples cited. In all cases he functions to reinforce the societal norms by means of his comic-satiric improvisations. The *bertsolari*, therefore, has traditionally acted to reinforce the notion of *community* and to serve as a vehicle through which members of the Basque community are defined as insiders and outsiders, an outsider being an individual who functions outside the community's normative system. The singer and his verses act here as integrative forces, for they ostracize the rule breaker.

Additionally, in the case of the public *charivari*, the improviser clearly mediates between the audience and the events taking place on stage, contributing yet another level to the legal proceedings, since his verses, which are addressed to the public, allow him to comment on the action in a manner similar to a Greek chorus. Through his dialogue with the audience, its presence is recognized and integrated into the performance, and the audience is converted into an active participant.

Finally, as Webster's informant demonstrates in the narration of Turrut-Arrosa's trial, the *bertsolari*'s verses were memorized by members of the audience and, as mnemotechnic devices, they were repeated for decades in the retelling of the events. For instance, in Turrut-Arrosa's text, after some sixty years had passed, the teller was still weaving Piarres Adame's couplets into the narrative. Hence, through the vehicle of poetry and song, the normative messages encoded into Turrut-Arrosa's *charivari* transcended the specific timeframe of the event itself and continued to shame the offender and to reinforce the societal norms in question for many generations.

That the *bertsolari*'s role was not limited merely to commenting on the actions on stage is revealed in Duvoisin's (1841) detailed comments. In his discussion of the components of the public mock trials of this period he states that after the judge and two lawyers have taken their seats behind three tables on the stage, the *bertsolari* takes his place in front of them to the left of the magistrates. Silence is ordered and the *bertsolari* begins to sing, improvising his verses to the melody played by the musicians. He announces the subject of the trial to the public in a half-comic, half-serious manner. In the last couplet he indicates which lawyer is to begin, therefore assigning to him the role of prosecutor. He rises and begins singing his improvised accusation on behalf of the victim. However, in his couplets he not only pleads the case but also attacks his foil, the defendant's attorney, who, in turn, must sing his own improvised couplets to defend himself and the accused. This singing contest is frequently interrupted by the vociferous applause and laughter of the audience, and rapidly becomes a general and often satiric and ribald commentary on the vices in question. The debate between the lawyers is broken by interludes of dance performances and the antics of the buffoons and other characters. After these breaks the lawyers begin anew.[51] Although Duvoisin does not mention whether the resumption of the debate also included a change in the melody and rhyme scheme of the improvised verses, such a conclusion might follow from the structures found in modern-day *bertsolaritza* contests.

Within the disputing process, the two lawyers must also be classified as *bertsolariak*, having functions equally as important as those of the *bertsolari* who opens and closes the legal proceedings. According to Duvoisin, in 1841 the *bertsolari* lawyers were still being contracted by the organizers and apprised of the details of the case in question prior to the public trial. These *bertsolari* lawyers were highly respected by the Basque-speaking populace: "There exists in the country a certain number of these sorts of lawyers, whose reputation, once established, affords them the consideration that elsewhere is given by wealth, and their company is very sought after."[52]

The striking structural parallels between the public *charivari*'s improvised legal proceedings and modern-day *bertsolaritza* debates gives rise to the hypothesis that modern contests are structurally linked to earlier disputing processes which included improvised singing duels between two *bertsolari* lawyers. Such a conclusion would imply that the specific social context of the earlier disputing processes, which once gave form and meaning to the two lawyers' improvised verses, has been lost, i.e., the fact that a particular individual and/or vice was being brought to trial for judgment. Nevertheless, the previous social functions are still partially operative today in the modern *bertsolaritza* contests, for these frequently contain mordant comic satires of vices, particularly those judged to be of a political or ideological nature, and veiled indictments of individuals or institutions whose actions appear to violate contemporary societal norms.

In these instances, the improvised couplets sung by the two contestants represent a debate, a process of disputation which reflects and dramatizes two opposing points of view on a contemporary issue often of fundamental importance to the Basque-speaking audience. This debate process contains a verbal reenactment in the form of an improvised verse dialogue of the event or vice being satirized. Here each singer attempts to defend his own position against the attacks of his opponent, while at the same time continuing to develop the story line of the event being narrated. In this way modern *bertsolaritza* debates continue to function as a mechanism for defining Basque value systems and ideology as well as a vehicle for ostracizing those who act as outsiders, i.e., those who disobey the implicit and evolving normative system of the Basque people, a system which the *bertsolaritza* contests themselves also constantly serve to redefine and modify.

The presence of the singing lawyers in the public *charivari* may also shed light on the social origins of the debate form of modern *bertsolaritza*. In 1841 Duvoisin indicates the public mock trials were already falling into disuse, implying that they were even more popular at an earlier date. Viewed historically, in the course of time the outer frame of the disputing process appears to have fallen away leaving only the singing-debate tradition which then continued to function as a part of the village festivities, but separate from the *charivari* trials, while the trials themselves were also becoming less and less frequent. The *bertsolari* lawyers continued to be contracted by the villagers for such festive occasions, and vices were exposed and satirized by the performers in their contests. Yet, with the passage of time, the legal nature of the proceedings became increasingly obscured.

Although within the fully structured *charivari*, the judge and tribunal awarded a judgment to the winning *bertsolari* lawyer, i.e., either to the prosecution or the defense, in later stages the awards were given to the *bertsolari* himself solely on the basis of his performance rather than on the merits of the case he was pleading. An alternate interpretation of the fully structured performance would be that the earlier judgment was also rendered primarily on the basis of the superior pleading of one of the two lawyers, i.e., on the ingeniousness of his defense, his verbal ability, and his skills of improvisation, all being characteristics of fundamental importance to any modern-day lawyer. Once the singing contest became dislodged from the prior legal process, the abilities of the *bertsolari* came to be judged in constantly more aesthetic terms, a process which is still continuing as Basque literary critics now fervently discuss the intricacies of *bertsolaritza* meter and rhyme, metaphor and simile. The displacement of the disputing processes and the introduction of a primarily "poetic" focus were undoubtedly fostered by the *juegos florales*, started by M. D'Abbadie in 1853 in the north Basque Country, and in the south in 1879.[53]

This interpretation casts doubt upon the school of thought which would date the origins of modern *bertsolaritza* only from the beginning of the nineteenth century. Duvoisin's commentary of 1841 lends credence to the beliefs that these singing contests were far more popular at an earlier date and that they may have been an integral and essential component of the traditional Basque disputing processes. It would follow, then, that the repeated condemnations of the public *charivari* could provide a means of determining the antiquity of the trials as well as the *bertsolaritza* debates embedded in them. Given that in his monumental study of the *charivari* Peignot (1833) traces these condemnations back into the Middle Ages, the *bertsolari*'s role in them may, in fact, date from such an early period.[54]

This line of argument would suggest modern-day *bertsolaritza* contests may be linked to Basque conflict-resolution processes and legal proceedings of great antiquity. However, it does not imply singing contests between two individuals did not occur in a variety of settings outside the formal structures of the trials, but rather that only those singers who had previously gained experience and expertise in numerous singing duels would have been sufficiently respected and revered so as to have been chosen to defend as legal bards in the folk trials.

In the Basque Country today there still exists the popular belief that any individual accused by another in improvised *bertsolari* couplets can only defend himself against his accuser through the vehicle of poetry, i.e., by using the traditional *bertsolari* forms. Failure to respond in kind to the accusations is considered a violation of the norms of *bertsolaritza* debate and, furthermore, a sign that the individual accused lacks one of the qualities of being a true ethnic Basque speaker, the ability to compose as a *bertsolari*. If the accused chooses to defend himself and attack his accuser by another means, for example, in prose, or if he has another defend him in his place, he is considered to have lost status within the Basque-speaking community.

Within the context of the various disputing processes presently identified in ethnographic studies, the Basque singing duels as a means of conflict resolution at the village level do not represent a unique phenomenon, for they are also found as a central component in the disputing process of the Iglulik Eskimo culture. Just as in Eskimo society, Basque singing duels were and are a traditional means of gaining prestige and respect among one's peers.[55] For instance, among the rural Basque-speaking populace there still exists the belief that great *bertsolari* singers possess special powers of vision which allow them to improvise and perceive reality at levels not achieved by average mortals. As one informant indicated, "The great *bertsolari* has eyes that look inward where he sees his visions."[56] This rural Basque belief system, which attributes nearly shamanistic powers to the *bertsolari*, may explain the resistance on the part of some Basque speakers to modern attempts to reduce *bertsolaritza* to a mere art form with a set of artistic techniques that can be "learned" by anyone.[57]

In the Basque Country both the *charivari* performance and the *bertsolari* singing-debate traditions have continued as vital elements of Basque culture into the twentieth century. In the adjoining regions both traditions have lost status, the former being retained as a sporadic vehicle of protest among the rural lower classes and the urban proletariat while the latter singing-debate tradition has essentially disappeared as a viable element within the disputing processes of the popular classes. The retention by the Basque of the elements which appear to be connected to similar disputing processes found earlier in the adjacent areas leads to a series of questions concerning the underlying factors which permitted the Basque people to maintain and foster what, from the point of view of the rest of this region, would be archaic disputing processes.

Although a thorough examination of the myriad of socioeconomic, sociocultural, and sociolinguistic factors which operated in this evolution would far exceed the limits of this brief exploration, there are several fundamental points which may be outlined. The major role played by the Basque singing duels and the two *bertsolari* lawyers in the *charivari* performances suggests that significant structural parallels may exist in the disputing processes of adjoining areas of the Pyrenees and Provence where *charivari* performances were also repeatedly condemned. Although scholars have often written of these *charivaris* as mere "folk custom" or as a quaint form of "popular justice," looking at them primarily as mechanisms for publicly shaming or otherwise punishing those entering a second marriage or violating marital authority, it is clear that under the rubric of *charivari* lurked a myriad of folk trials and related protests of a highly political nature. A *charivari* performance was not infrequently the prelude to a major popular uprising against the authorities who had just been the disguised or not-so-disguised target of the *charivari* trial.[58]

These repeated condemnations demonstrate the existence of two conflicting sets of societal norms, one reflecting the interests of the authorities, i.e., the upper-class power elites, and the other the interests of the lower classes. During the Middle Ages and later the role played by lower-class singer improvisers as popular advocates would certainly have contributed to them being viewed with great animosity by members of the nobility and power elites, for the lawyer improvisers would have represented a major ideological threat. At the same time, the lower classes would have viewed them in quite a different light, since in the folk trials and related forms of popular protest organized by these lower classes the singer improviser's participation would have been of fundamental importance. Just as the courtly poets and singers functioned to reproduce the ideology of this class, these lower-class advocate singers would have been powerful tools in the maintenance of "community" and "class" identity. The verses composed by the singer improvisers and repeatedly sung by the lower classes would have been vital agents for the dissemination of information concerning the perceived "crimes" which were committed by the upper-class "outsiders" against the normative systems of the lower classes.

During the course of several centuries in the adjoining regions the constant condemnation and devaluation of the lower-class improvisers appear to have undermined the respect paid them by the populace, and in this way the lower classes would slowly come to be deprived of one of their major apparatuses of power. The singer's function as advocate in the disputing processes of the lower classes would, therefore, also explain in part the repeated condemnations found in these regions of the wandering minstrels who worked and identified with the popular classes. There they would have acted on behalf of the populace, articulating and defending its normative system and acting to reproduce its ideology, just as the Basque *bertsolari* lawyers have continued to do even though they, too, have been repeatedly chastised, threatened, and punished by those acting on behalf of an upper-class value system.

The socioeconomic patterns of conflict articulated in the condemnations also appear to have functioned to create class divisions between the singers themselves, some of whom moved into the orbit of the upper classes where they were publicly praised and lauded for their "poetic" abilities while, at the same time, they were tacitly being recognized for their role as effective spokespersons for the value system of the upper classes. For example, during the Middle Ages there was an ongoing polemic concerning the proper classification of minstrels and related performers. This debate, carried out by the upper classes and their spokespersons, allowed those working in this profession to be ranked from highest to lowest and, consequently, those whose merits were judged lowest and basest were the most ostracized and condemned by the political and religious elites, even though the minstrels' anger was much feared by the aristocracy, a situation which gave rise to the continuous giving of lavish gifts and prizes to these important members of the medieval press corps.[59]

At the same time, outside the Basque Country, an upper-class "literary" culture was beginning to flourish among the noble classes. This literary culture would eventually serve to block the illiterate lower-class singer improviser's access to upper-class culture. These lower-class illiterates would be replaced by the *troubadour* poets who, because they were already literate, a fact that indicates they had also already moved somewhat upwards on the social ladder, were esteemed within the context of this newly literate environment for their ability to write down their compositions rather than for their ability to compose them on the spot.

During the Renaissance, outside the Basque-speaking region, the force of poetic language came to be harnessed to the needs of the state, needs that included the eventual imposition of a unified and dominant nation-state language. While poetry continued to have a social function, as it did in the Middle Ages, the content of that function did not remain the same because the social, economic, and political structures that defined poetry had changed. The literate poet's dependence on his upper-class patrons, the social relations that existed between him and his audience, gave "Renaissance poetry the power to carry out a host of new functions that might be summed up in the phrase 'public relations'."[60]

Poetry was regarded as an inculcator of civic virtue as defined by the dominant class, a source of financial support and means of procuring a comfortable job for the writer, as well as a form of social protection and instrument of socialization. Poems were conceived as a vehicle for influence-peddling and a means of accomplishing specific social tasks through the careful manufacturing of consent. Authors of Renaissance defenses of art present poetry in exactly this way. Poetry was valued primarily for what it could do, and especially for what it could do for the aristocracy it served.[61]

This set of sociocultural factors may be contrasted to those operating in the Basque Country where only in the last twenty years has there been a real "literary" interest in *bertsolaritza* poetry. Therefore, until quite recently the entire phenomenon has been in the hands of the lower-class rural Basques who were generally totally illiterate in their own language.[62] Only in recent times have individuals who are literate in Basque come to play a major role in the evolution of *bertsolaritza* debates. In fact, until the sixteenth century there was no "literary" tradition whatsoever in the Basque language, for it wasn't until 1545 that the first book was published in Basque. Actually, until the nineteenth century, Basque "culture" continued to be transmitted and maintained almost exclusively by oral tradition. In terms of a literary poetic tradition it was not until essentially the twentieth century that a rich tradition of written poetry began to flourish. Therefore, the class divisions implicit in the evolution of a high literary culture in the adjoining regions simply did not emerge among Basque speakers. Since among the Basque-speaking populace a literary elitist culture did not develop during the Middle Ages and Renaissance, there was no possibility for the "poetic" aspects of Basque disputing processes to become absorbed as "literature" into the culture of a literate upper class.

This sociocultural situation was directly influenced by sociolinguistic factors. Historically, the Basque Country has been characterized by a linguistic situation of extreme diglossia, with bilingualism existing only among the upper classes who served, until quite recently, as the only linguistic bridge between the lower-class Basque-speaking populace and the power elites of the two adjoining nation-states, France and Spain. Therefore, only those *bertsolariak* who had already acquired a knowledge of one of the nation-state languages, and great facility in it, could have moved into the orbit of the upper-class non-Basque-speaking elites, which occurred particularly in the case of the singer improvisers who went to work in the court of Navarra, although some of them may have been composing in Basque.[63]

These sociolinguistic factors, as well as the mechanisms of fictional encapsulation outlined earlier, may explain why in the Basque Country the voices of the *bertsolari* lawyers were not stifled at an earlier date. The sociolinguistic situation found in other regions of this area may have allowed the pressures of the apparatuses of power exercised by the upper classes to more readily divide the singers into two camps and to extinguish the voices of those who functioned on behalf of the lower classes. In the Basque Country this was more difficult because the lower-class monolingual Basque speakers were linguistically isolated from these pressures.[64] Also, in many cases the upper-class authorities were monolingual and simply did not fully understand what was being articulated by the lower-class Basque-speaking *bertsolari* advocates, just as today the modern *bertsolaritza* contests are incomprehensible to the French- or Spanish-speaking populaces of this region and, therefore, from their point of view represent only a marginal cultural phenomenon which often passes unnoticed within the context of the dominant French and Spanish cultures. It should be remembered that Basque is a non-Indo-European language and, therefore, is totally incomprehensible to a speaker of a Romance language.[65]

Although the singing debates which still survive in the Basque Country today appear to have been lost in the adjoining areas of the Pyrenees and Provence, during the Middle Ages there is ample evidence that improvised verbal confrontations between two singers were a common vehicle for barbed satires and social protest. These medieval debates are classified into three major types which parallel the structures of *bertsolaritza* debates: the *tenso*, in which two singers freely discussed a given subject, each taking the point of view which seemed good to him; the *joc-partitz* or *partimen*, in which the challenger proposed a theme, indicated two opposed attitudes towards it, and gave his opponent his choice of maintaining one or the other; and the *débat* or *disputoison*, a controversy put into the mouths of two types or personified abstractions, each of which pleaded the cause of its own superiority, while in the end the decision was often referred to a judge.[66]

During the Middle Ages these variants frequently degenerated into vapid literary exercises performed by hired singers and musicians whose task it was to amuse the wealthy. Nonetheless, for several centuries among the popular classes these improvised debates continued to be utilized as powerful mechanisms of political and social protest. The Basque mock trials and singing duels would represent a structural continuation of these earlier forms of protest and social control. While in the adjoining regions these debate structures eventually were absorbed as "literature" into the culture of the upper classes, in the Basque Country this process of absorption did not take place and, as an integral part of Basque disputing processes, they have continued to exist almost exclusively in the hands of the lower-class Basque-speaking populace.[67]

Before concluding this study, the etymology of the term *charivari* needs to be mentioned. Although nearly all theories concerning the etymology of this term trace its origins to southwestern France, it is clear that even in the Middle Ages the meaning of the word was not clearly understood by French-speaking commentators. The term had no specific meaning in French, a fact that seems to be underscored by the appearance of a myriad of phonological variants. After dedicating some thirty-five pages to a review of these variants and their supposed etymologies, Peignot concludes: "C'est une marque qui la véritable [etymology of the word] n'est pas connue."[68]

An alternate etymological approach might derive the term from an indigenous language of the same zone, such as from the Basque term *echevarri* or *echavarri* (from *etxe-berri/barri*), "new house," a common last name in Basque and a direct reference to setting up a new household, or a marriage, this being the earliest focal point for the celebration of a *charivari*, either to sanction the marriage or to condemn it.[69] Hence, the meaning of the word in Basque is intimately linked to actual causative factors which gave rise to the performance of the *charivari*. Phonologically, the two terms are essentially identical since there are ample examples of the Basque last name becoming *Chavarri*, *Chavier*, *Xavier*, etc., in which the initial *e* is lost and the trilled *r* becomes reduced. This would have produced a form such as **chavari*, quite similar to Peignot's Bas-Langeudoc variant *chavaric* and, with the retention of the second *e*, a dialectical variant **chevari* from *echevarri* would have resulted, which could be linked to the forms *chivaree* or *shivaree* found in English.[70]

In summary, the present study of the taxonomy, structural morphology, and disputing processes of conflict resolution embedded in the *charivari* trials and their structural variants demonstrate the complex and multifaceted nature of the modifications which have occurred over many centuries. In addition, the Basque data suggest that a similar evolution of the structural component of the *charivari* may also have taken place in the adjoining regions, although at a much earlier date. This interpretation, based only on structural similarities, would be even stronger if, for instance, the etymological origin of the term *charivari* could be traced back to a source within the Basque language itself.

The structural similarities noted here between the two sets of data would be further reinforced by semantic linkages indicating that some level of lexical borrowing occurred between the two language groups, i.e., the Basque and Romance groups, in which the Basque term was used in order to name a similar preexisting structure. Or it may indicate the functioning of some other type of cultural diffusion which would have contributed to transmission of the Basque term and its assignment, already by the early Middle Ages, to similar activities found in the societies of the adjoining non-Basque-speaking regions. Detailed study of the process and problems of this semantic and/or cultural diffusion of the term will shed even further light on the origins and evolution of the *charivari* in the Basque Country and the rest of Europe.

In conclusion, the Basque data presented in this study—the public *charivari*, its structural variants, as well as the singing duels of the lawyer bards—should be viewed as forming part of a larger social and historical pattern. In such fashion the whole cultural complex may be considered to reflect strategies of resistance and reaction to the attempts made to transfer control of public discourse and the disputing process from local communities to state mechanisms. This interpretation of the Basque data unifies the disparate social-artistic phenomena. The resultant cognitive framework redefines the singing duels and the *charivari* so that they no longer need to be characterized as isolated modern devices nor as mythical or folkloric survivals. In this new interpretation they become concrete representations of social solidarity.[71]

Notes

1. Joxe Azurmendi, "Bertsolaritzaren estudiorako," *Jakin*, nos. 14–15 (1980), pp. 139–164.
2. Cf. Laura Nader, Klaus F. Koch, and Bruce Cox, "The Ethnography of Law: A Bibliographical Survey," *Current Anthropology*, vol. 3, no. 7, (June 1966), pp. 267–294; and Laura Nader (ed.), *Law in Culture and Society* (Chicago: Aldine Publishing House, 1969), pp. 419–438.
3. Laura Nader (ed.), *Law in Culture...* , p. 10; Cf. also Laura Nader and Harry F. Todd, Jr., *The Disputing Process. Law in Ten Societies* (New York: Columbia University Press, 1978); and P. H. Gulliver, "Case Studies of Law in Non-Western Societies," in Laura Nader (ed.), *Law in Culture...* , pp. 11–68.
4. Laura Nader and Harry F. Todd, Jr., *The Disputing Process...* , pp. 1–40; and Laura Nader, *Law in Culture...* , pp. 1–10.
5. The term *galarrotsa*, "bell noise," comes from *gale/gare*, a variant of *joale/joare*, "bell" and *otsa* "noise" and *tzintzarrotsa* from *tzintzarri* "bell" and *otsa* "noise." The term *tobera* is used to refer to a nighttime *charivari* and to the more elaborate daytime performances called *tobera-mustrak*. However, its other meanings link it directly to yet another ritual, also referred to as *tobera*, suggesting that all the rituals were named using the same word because of functional and structural linkages existing between them. The latter-mentioned ritual clearly derives its name from the musical instrument played, the *tobera*, a metal or wooden bar, which along with the *bertsolari* improviser, other musicians and villagers, form part of a nighttime ritual sanctioning of approved weddings. The nomenclature implies the nighttime *charivari*, and its daytime continuation, which ridicule

and condemn unapproved weddings, are the structural inversions or parodies of the ritual sanctioning. Cf. Manuel Lecuona, "Las toberas," *Euskalerriaren alde*, vol. 10 (1920), pp. 41–55; and J. A. de Donostia, "Apuntes de folklore vasco. Toberas," *Revista internacional de estudios vascos*, vol. 15 (1924), pp. 1–18.
6. José M. Iribarren, "Costumbres de Valcarlos," *Historias y costumbres* (Pamplona: Príncipe de Viana, 1956), pp. 220–235. Iribarren links the term *karrosa* to the Spanish word *carroza*. However, it is more likely that *karrosa* is a prevarication of *galarrotsa* "bell noise" which in turn would connect it directly to the nighttime *charivari* by the same name, just as the term *tobera* is found for both nighttime and daytime versions. From *galarrotsa* would have come *kalarrotsa* and by folk etymology, *karrosa*. For the purposes of clarity, in this paper *karrosa* has been used to distinguish the daytime public *charivari* from its nighttime variants, even though the two words are in all probability the same.
7. Cf. Francisque Michel, *Le Pays Basque* (Paris: Librairie de Firmin Didot Frères, Fils et Cie, 1857), p. 59, for a description of the curious voting procedure employed to determine whether the mock trial should be held.
8. José M. Iribarren, "Costumbres de Valcarlos," p. 224.
9. Ibid.
10. Ibid.
11. Cf. Violet Alford, "Rough Music or *charivari*," *Folklore*, vol. 70 (1959), pp. 505–518; Jean Ithurriague, "La littérature populaire," in Gaëtan Bernoville, Michel Etcheverry, Jean Ithurriague, and Philippe Veyrin, *Visages du Pays Basque* (Paris: Editions des Horizons de France, 1942), pp. 164–167; Testis, "Tobera munstra 1973 [a Saint-Etienne-de Baigorry], *Gure Herria*, vol. 43 (1973), pp. 123–127; and Philippe Veyrin, *Les basques de Labourd, de Soule et de Basse-Navarre. Leur histoire et leurs traditions*, (Grenoble: Arthaud, 1955), pp. 282–287.
12. José M. Iribarren, "Costumbres de Valcarlos," p. 223.
13. Cf. Natalie Zemon Davis, *Society and Culture in Early Modern France* (Stanford, California: Stanford University Press, 1975), pp. 97–123; 296–309; G. Hérelle, "Les charivaris nocturnes dans le pays basque français," *Revista internacional de estudios vascos*, vol. 15 (1924), pp. 505–522; L. Peitit de Julleville, *Históire de théâtre en France. Les comediens en France au Moyen Age* (Paris: L. Cerf, 1885); Henri Lalou, "Des charivaris et de leur repression dans le midi de la France," *Revue des Pyrénées*, vol. 16 (1904), pp. 493–514; Claude Noirot, *L'Origine des masque,*

mommeries, bernez, et revennez es iours gras de caresme prenant, menez sur l'asne à rebours et charivary. Le Iugement des anciens Peres et philosophes sur le subiect des masquarades, le tout extrait du livre de la Mommerie de Claude Noirot, Iuge en mairarie de Lengres (Jean Chauveau Lengres, 1609), reprinted and edited by C. Leber, *Collection des meilleurs dissertations... relatifs a l'histoire de France*, vol. 9 (Paris: 1838); G. Peignot, *Histoire morale, civile, politique et literaire de charivari. Depuis son origine vers le IVe siècle* (Turgon: Druillat, 1833).
14. Harry F. Todd, Jr., "Litigous Marginals: Character and Disputing in a Bavarian Village," in Laura Nader and Harry F. Todd, Jr., *The Disputing Process...*, pp. 107–121.
15. Ibid.
16. José M. Iribarren, "Costumbres de Valcarlos," p. 224.
17. Cf. Violet Alford, "Rough Music or *Charivari*," and "The Hobbyhorse and Other Animal Masks," *Folklore*, vol. 79 (1968), pp. 122–134; Natalie Zemon Davis, *Society and Culture...*; Francisque Michel, *Le Pays Basque*, pp. 65–68.
18. Cf. G. Hérelle, "Les charivaris nocturnes..."; Violet Alford, "Rough Music or *Charivari*"; J. M. Satrustegi, *Euskaldunen Seksu Bideak* (Oñati: Jakin, 1975), pp. 91–96.
19. The use of cow horns as primary instruments in the nighttime *charivari* and the *asto-lasterka* variant may explain the semiotic transfer of the cow horn to the "mocked" one, the one who has been "horned" by these musical instruments of public disgrace.
20. Francisque Michel, *Le Pays Basque*, p. 57.
21. Cf. Charles Videgain, "Quelques contes basques tirés du manuscrit Webster," *Fontes Linguae Vasconum Studia et Documenta*, vol. 6, no. 18 (Pamplona, 1974), pp. 453–464.
22. Ibid., pp. 463–464. Cf. Philippe Veyrin, *Les basques de Labourd...*, p. 213; J. M. Lasagabaster, "Euskal-Nobelaren Gizarte-Kondairaren Oinarriak," *Euskal Linguistika eta Literatura Bide Berriak* (Bilbo: Deustuko Unibertsitateko Argitarazioak, 1981) p. 357, for a discussion of a short work called *Piarres Adame, Saratarraren zenbait historio* (Pau: Garet, 1888), apparently based on the life of this famous *bertsolari* and written by another native of Sara, Jean Baptiste Elissanburu. (New edition, Donostia: Elkar, 1982; the new edition also includes P. Iturralde, *Murtuts eta Bertxe...* [sic].
23. Laura Nader and Harry F. Todd, Jr., *The Disputing Process...*, pp. 14–17.

24. Cf. Natalie Zemon Davis, *Society and Culture...*, p. 301, footnote 37, for a discussion of the way in which "the *charivari* expresses to some extent a concern with the dead spouse."
25. P. H. Gulliver, "Case Studies of Law...," p. 14.
26. Charles Videgain, "Quelques contes basques...," pp. 463–464.
27. Laura Nader and Harry F. Todd, Jr., *The Disputing Process...*, pp. 5–8.
28. G. Hérelle, "Les *charivaris* nocturnes...."
29. Ibid., p. 508.
30. A major area of investigation lies in analyzing the way in which this type of mechanism functioned within the framework of the more encompassing instrument of the *pase foral*, which the Basque people invoked repeatedly in order to be able to maintain their ethnicity and normative systems while still apparently "obeying" the laws imposed upon them by entities within the two political units of France and Spain. The Basque *pase foral* formula, *se obedece, pero no se cumple*, was a mechanism of Basque legal behavior which allowed them to achieve their own goals by complying with the "letter of the law" but not with its intent.
31. Philippe Veyrin, *Les basques de Labourd...*, pp. 286–287.
32. Violet Alford, "Rough Music or *Charivari*," p. 513.
33. Cf. Sandra Ott, "Aristotle among the Basques: The 'Cheese Analogy' of Conception," *Man*, vol. 14 (1980), pp. 699–711; J. M. Satrustegi, *Euskaldunen Seksu Bideak*.
34. José M. Iribarren, "Pícaros, truhanes y capuceros," *Historias y costumbres* (Pamplona: Príncipe de Viana, 1956), p. 243.
35. José M. Iribarren, "Crimen y castigo de Chanforrín," *Historias y costumbres* (Pamplona: Príncipe de Viana, 1956), pp. 53–76.
36. Cf. C. C. Uhlenbeck, "The Basque Names for Woman," *A Grammatical Miscellany Offered to O. Jespersen* (Copenhagen: G. Allen & Unwin Ltd., 1930), p. 422. For a discussion of the legal term *gaizes* cf. Bonifacio de Echegaray, "Algunas voces vascas usadas en el Fuero General de Navarra," *Euskera*, vol. 8, nos. 1–2 (1927), pp. 54–56.
37. Cf. José M. Iribarren, "Crimen y castigo...," pp. 53–76.
38. Camilo José Cela, *Diccionario secreto*, second edition (Madrid: Alianza Editorial, 1975), pp. 279–289.
39. José M. Iribarren, "Pícaros, truhanes y capuceros," pp. 242–243.
40. My thanks to Txomin Arratibel of Ezkio, Guipúzcoa, for this information.
41. Charles Videgain, "Quelques contes basque...," p. 464. The phrase *Latapie yaunak ederki* employs the common grammatical suppression of the verb, here that governed by the ergative

noun *yaunak*. For the understood verb, I supplied "done" even though it might also be rendered as "acted" or "knows." The phrase *Nola futre sakerdi* is obviously a spelling error and the phrase was really *Nola futre, dezake erdi* with the woman being the understood ergative subject. For the sake of clarity in English, *gibel zuri* "white-liver(ed)" has been translated as "yellow-livered."

42. Cf. G. Hérelle, "Les *charivaris* nocturnes...," p. 508, note 2; and p. 513; Violet Alford, "The Cat Saint," *Folklore*, vol. 52 (1941), pp. 161–183, for a discussion of the possible influence of a cat saint. The linkage of cats to the *charivari* also is found in the *cencerrada* of Spain, cf. Miguel de Cervantes, *Don Quijote de la Mancha*, part 2, vol. 46 (Mexico: Editorial Porrua, 1977), pp. 510–512.

43. Violet Alford, "The Springtime Bear in the Pyrenees," *Folklore*, vol. 41 (1930), p. 266; cf. also Violet Alford, "Ensayo sobre los orígenes de las mascaradas de Zuberoa," *Revista internacional de estudios vascos*, vol. 22 (1931), pp. 373–396; Juan Antonio Urbeltz, *Dantzak* (Bilbao: Grijelmo, S. A., 1978), pp. 216–230.

44. "La asociación de las comparsas y máscaras de invierno con la representación satírica del tipo '*charivari*' debe obedecer a un nexo íntimo que se les encontraba, a una similitud en su '*función*' originaria," in Julio Caro Baroja, *El Carnaval (Analisis histórico-cultural)* (Madrid: Taurus, 1965), p. 194.

45. G. Hérelle, "Les *charivaris* nocturnes...," p. 506. In other parts of Europe it was common for the *charivari* and related ceremonies to be regulated so that they coincided with other fixed pagan and/or Christian festivities. Cf. Jacques Le Goff and Jean-Claude Schmitt, *Le Charivari. Actes de la table ronde organisée a Paris (25–27 avril 1977) par l'Ecole des Hautes Etudes en Sciences Sociales et le Centre National de la Recherche Scientifique* (Paris: Mouton Editeur, 1981), pp. 177–264.

46. Violet Alford, "Les mascarades souletins en 1914 et aujourd'hui," *Eusko Jakintza*, vol. 3 (1949), p. 380, records the following variant: "La castration fut présentée gravement et comme un acte rituel. Une souris et un oiseau furent mis en liberté simultanément comme signe que l'act était accompli, au lieu des deux bouchons jetés en l'air, saisis aussitôt et grignotés par les Noirs [a second set of actors which parodies the first]." The mouse and bird are indeed strange symbolic homologues.

47. Violet Alford, "Rough Music or *Charivari*," p. 508.
48. Philippe Veyrin, *Les basques de Labourd...*, p. 286.
49. Jean Duvoisin, "Comédies des basques," *Album Pyrenéen. Revue Bearnaise. Littérature. Sciences. Beaux Arts. Agriculture*, vol.

2 (Pau: 1841),pp. 210–211; cf. also Francisque Michel, *Le Pays Basque*, pp. 55–66.
50. Joxe Azurmendi, "Bertsolaritzaren estudiorako," pp. 139–164.
51. Jean Duvoisin, "Comédies des basques," pp. 210–211.
52. Ibid.; cf. Francisque Michel, *Le Pays Basque*, pp. 59–60.
53. According to some, it was hoped that these "poetic" contests, based on those found in Provence and Catalunya, would bring about a renaissance of Basque "poetry" and, consequently, Basque "culture," erudite poetry being viewed as a sign of high culture. It was thought that the contests might create a break with the popular *bertsolari* forms which were understood to be low culture and folkloric from an upper-class point of view. In the end, the preexisting traditional *bertsolari* forms prevailed and imposed their unique stamp upon the development of Basque poetry. Cf. Gabriel Aresti, *Obras completas*, vol. 1, and *Poesía*, vol. 1, Luís Haranburu, ed. (Donostia: Kriselu, 1976), pp. 14–35.
54. G. Peignot, *Histoire morale, civile...* , pp. 57–144; cf. also Claude Noirot, *L'Origine des masque....*
55. Cf. N. H. H. Graburn, "Eskimo Law in Light of Self- and Group-Interest," *Law and Society Review*, vol. 4, no. 1 (1969), pp. 45–60; Knud Rasmussen, "Intellectual Culture of the Iglulik Eskimos," *Report of the Fifth Thule Expedition 1921–24*, vol. 7, no. 1 (1929), pp. 227–244. This does not imply that in other contemporary cultures improvised singing has not played a role in disputing processes. Cf. M. Gluckman, "Gossip and Scandal," *Current Anthropology*, vol. 4, no. 3 (1963), pp. 307–316; Melville J. Herskovits, *Life in a Haitian Valley* (New York: Knopf, 1937); Albert B. Lord, *The Singer of Tales* (New York: Atheneum, 1965).
56. I am endebted to Iñaki Hernández, a son of a famous *bertsolari*, as well as to many other Basque speakers for these observations.
57. Cf. Lanean Elkar, "Santutxuko bertsolari-eskola," *Jakin*, vols. 17–18 (1981), pp. 165–179.
58. Cf. Violet Alford, "Rough Music or *Charivari*"; Charles Tilly, "Collective Violence in Nineteenth-Century French Cities (Public lecture, Reed College, February 1968) cited in Natalie Zemon Davis, *Society and Culture...* ; G. Peignot, *Histoire morale, civile...* ; P. Larousse, *Grand dictionnaire universel du XIXe siècle*, vol. 3 (Paris: Administration du Grand Dictionnaire Universel, 1865), pp. 995–996. A modern proof of the highly political connotations of the *charivari* is the French political journal *Le Charivari*, founded in 1832, to satirize the government of Louis-Philippe. Cf. P. Larousse, *Grand dictionnaire...* , p. 996.

59. Cf. Ramón Menéndez Pidal, *Poesía juglaresca y juglares* (Madrid: Espasa-Calpe, S. A., 1962), pp. 44–77; E. K. Chambers, *The Medieval Stage*, vol. 1 (Oxford: Clarendon Press, 1903), pp. 22–86.
60. Jane P. Tompkins, "The Reader in History. The Changing Shape of Literary Response," *Reader-Response Criticism from Formalism to Post-Structuralism* (Baltimore and London: Johns Hopkins University Press, 1981), p. 208.
61. Ibid.
62. Cf. Juan Mari Lecuona, "Bertsolariak historian," *Jakin*, vols. 14–15 (1980), pp. 6–16. Today of some 600,000 Basque speakers, only about 25 percent, or 150,000, are fully literate in their own language. Of the total population of the Basque Country, only about 5 percent of the populace is considered fully literate in Basque.
63. Ramón Menéndez Pidal, *Poesía juglaresca y juglares*, p. 77; Joxe Azurmendi, "Bertsolaritzaren estudiorako," pp. 153–158.
64. In the Basque Country other types of pressures undermined the prestige of the female *bertsolariak* who were far more numerous at an earlier date. "These women composed poems of an infinite number of stanzas and sang them to audiences. . . . " Rodney Gallop, *A Book of the Basques* (Reno: University of Nevada Press, 1970 [1930]), p. 135. Cf. also Joxe Azurmendi, "Bertsolaritzaren estudiorako," p. 148; Ramón Menéndez Pidal, *Poesía juglaresca y juglares*, pp. 49, 59; Joseph Nogaret, *Petite histoire du Pays Basque français* (Paris: Libraire Ancienne Honoré Champion, 1923), p. 85.
65. The sociolinguistic factors operating in the Basque case are particularly interesting since it is well known that the minstrel tradition in the rest of Europe contributed to bringing about linguistic standardization and borrowings. Cf. Ramón Menéndez Pidal, *Poesía juglaresca y juglares*, pp. 76–77.
66. E. K. Chambers, *The Medieval Stage*, pp. 78–80; John Rutherford, *The Troubadours: Their Loves and their Lyrics; with Remarks on their Influence, Social and Literary* (London: Smith, Elder, and Company, 1873), pp. 44–65. Obviously, these literary forms have a mixed genealogy, drawing from Greek, Roman and Arabic literary traditions as well as from indigenous European bardic sources.
67. In the Basque Country only in the last twenty years has there been a real "literary" interest in *bertsolaritza*. Therefore, until quite recently the entire phenomenon was in the hands of the lower-class Basques who were generally totally illiterate in their own language. Only in the past few decades have individuals who are literate in Basque come to play a major role in the evolution of *bertsolaritza*. Cf. Juan Mari Lecuona, "Bertsolariak

historian"; Antonio Zavala, *Bosquejo de historia del bertsolarismo* (San Sebastián: Editorial Auñamendi, 1964).
68. G. Peignot, *Histoire morale, civile*... , p. 43.
69. Cf. note 4 concerning the *toberak*.
70. The form *charivari* would have evolved from **chavari* and Bas-Langeudoc forms, e.g., *chavari(k)*, through the process of phonetic reduplication. Cf. G. Peignot, *Histoire morale, civile*... , p. 16.
71. Cf. Christian Desplat, *Charivaris en Gascogne. La "Morale des Peuples" du XVIe au XXe siècle* (Nancy, France: Bibliothèque Berger-Levrault, 1982) and Henry Rey-Flaud, *Le charivari. Les rituels fondamentaux de la sexualité* (Paris: Payrot, 1985).

Basque Conflict Management Choices

by

M.E.R. Nicholson

Introduction

Although much has been recorded about the long history of Basque written law, little has been reported about modern Basque legal behavior. Merely listing articles on the Basque *fors* and *fueros*, or charters, of the seven provinces, takes eighteen pages in the *Eusko-Bibliographia*.[1] This wealth of literature concentrates on complexities of substance and formalities of procedure, leaving largely unexplored the dimension of everyday conflict management. The following discussion, based on the writer's 1980 and 1983 interviews in southwestern France, attempts to fill part of this lacuna in the record of Basque culture and society.

The international coverage by the popular press of Basque political extremism creates the impression that violence is the only Basque conflict management method. This writer's research documents that such is not the case. Although Basques do tend to meet external threats to their independence with physical aggression, they respond to internal conflict in a variety of ways, often seeking voluntary third-party intervention. That is, they have a bimodal conflict management pattern with a clear distinction drawn between the intercultural and intracultural arenas.

Mediation is the preferred process, or mode, by which today's French Basques manage local-level conflict. Goyheneche's *Le Pays Basque*, a comprehensive historical account of northern *Euskalerria*, or homeland of the Basques, indicates the depth of the cultural roots of mediation.[2] That such a preference can be traced back to at least the twelfth century is not surprising. The consensual nature of mediation makes it highly appropriate for a society where a tradition of representative government still survives in the valleywide communal land associations.

The use of mediation among Europe's most ancient people has theoretical significance for the analysis of third-party intervention. Viable mediation among a population for centuries part of a major nation challenges the assumption of some theorists that mediation is appropriate primarily for nonindustrialized, Third World societies.[3] Moreover, the Basque reliance on the notary suggests that intercultural mediators may offer a valuable concrete focus for investigating the dynamics of ethnicity maintenance.[4]

Intercultural Basque Conflict Management

Worldwide coverage of Basque fatality-causing intercultural confrontations has made the public aware that Europe's oldest ethnic group can be as violent as the residents of Northern Ireland or Lebanon. Press accounts periodically highlight the murder and mayhem created by the most militant members of the Basque separatist organization, ETA, or Basque Homeland and Freedom. Few, if any, nonacademic publications explain that the relatively selective assassinations occur mainly in Spain and are largely directed at government officials known to be responsible for the post-Franco arrest, torture and death of eight hundred Basques.[5] While some less sensational observers assert that support for the ETA actually is more limited than the organization claims,[6] other serious students of the subject disagree. They note that "many Basque Nationalist Party members are closet supporters" of ETA actions, that the ETA limits its numbers in order to remain "mobile and cellular," and that the ETA's overt electoral arm, the Herri Batasuna party, is a factor in the electoral arena.[7]

Whatever the exact dimensions of the ETA or whatever the degree of lethal support for Basque nationalism on either side of the Pyrenees, Basque mortal methods of coping with intercultural conflict have a long-documented history. This is not surprising considering the severe external challenges to the independent Basque spirit and strong sense of cultural superiority which are rooted in their pride in their immeasurably ancient culture.[8] In defense of their socio-cultural rights through the centuries Basques have responded repeatedly with a "militant protectiveness of their territory."[9] For example, during the fourth century A.D. Basques took advantage of Roman weakness to "raid villages and pillage villas."[10] Roman fortifications from this era indicate that "Basque militarism" probably was "organized on a wide scale."[11]

In subsequent centuries the Basques "belligerently" resisted the Visigoths, Muslims and Franks.[12] Basques south of the Pyrenees engaged in "incessant" armed hostilities with the Visigoths, while their transmontane counterparts ambushed alien travelers and made surprise attacks on Frankish settlements on the plains of the Adour.[13] Twice in fifty years—778 and 842—the Basques attacked Frankish armies in the Roncesvalles Pass.[14] Intermittent hostilities with the Arabs south of the Pyrenees were paralleled to the north, until 982, by intermittent fighting with Norman raiders.[15] The later stream of pilgrims passing through the Pyrenees on its way to Compostela constituted another type of invasion and resulted in reactions which led a twelfth-century foreign writer to claim that the Basques were " . . . expert in all violences, fierce and savage. . . . "[16]

Active hostility to the presence and pressure of non-Basques has not abated since divisive incorporation of *Euskalerria* into the emerging Spanish and French states. Basques south of the Pyrenees fought in the Carlist Wars of the last century and the Spanish Civil War of the 1930s. Northern Basques launched a "private war against the irresistible tide of centralization" after the 1610 Edict of Union with France.[17] Residents of the Labourd and Soule areas marched on government offices, organized strikes or boycotts, and participated in riots, while natives of Basse Navarre fought for their legal rights as a *Pays d'Etat*, or special legal subdivision, via maneuvers in the French national court system.[18] Their descendants, after the 1789 Revolution, launched a "war of ruse and tenacity,"[19] which continues even today, against Republican demands for equal division of all inheritance. Many Basques proudly explained to the writer how generations of Basque notaries have aided clients in circumventing the letter of this particular national law which directly challenges the Basque tradition of single heir inheritance.

Intracultural Conflict Management

The very pride, toughness, and obstinacy[20] that provide strength against external encroachment have the unfortunate potential to rend the internal socio-cultural fabric. Indeed, this happened in the fifteenth century when a rivalry between branches of the Basque royal house of the kingdom of Navarra developed into "one of the bloodiest civil wars in Spanish history."[21] Goyheneche suggests that the Beaumont-Gramont factionalism may have reflected ancient, underlying clan divisions of the originally pastoral Basques.[22] These had been held in check under less disruptive circumstances. The intracultural dichotomy created among Basques by the Spanish Civil War of the 1930s does recall the fifteenth-century situation.[23] The distinguishing factor between the two situations of widespread unsettled political conditions lies in the increased role and influence of external power in the form of the Spanish state.

Despite these tragic episodes, the Basques differ from many of their southern European neighbors whose seemingly perpetual local feuding results from their competitive, hierarchical, and honor-oriented cultural pattern.[24] Since cultural survival is a prime goal,[25] the Basques channel intracultural combative energy into institutionalized contests. These include dance groups, sports teams, and even poet-singers, *bertsolariak*, who represent different communities, valleys, or even regions across the international frontier. In addition, communities organize endurance matches of various types, including *la force basque* in France, which allow the male participants to demonstrate *indarra*, or physical strength, which is admired along with *sendoatsuna*, or one's strength of character.[26]

These diversions, which provide a "safety valve," do not serve to unify the local entity in any lasting manner. The independent Basque spirit persists, often offering resistance to local government. Some villages only function in a minimally adequate administrative fashion,[27] while others face citizen resistance to normal communal responsibilities.[28] A few become paralyzed by factionalism which may combine ideological and generational differences.[29] Some such situations are manifestations of long-term local cleavages, whereas others merely may be temporary aberrations. One interviewee suggested that the periodic bifurcations of one village were due to the necessity of presenting two electoral slates.

Whether fundamentally or artificially divided, members of quarreling political contingents are bound by the general Basque standard of restrained behavior at the neighborhood and village levels. The expectation of controlled behavior governs in even the most contentious local circumstances. For example, Bidart makes the following observation of a highly heated controversy over a building project in his natal village north of the Pyrenees: " . . . confrontation has rarely taken place during a [village] council meeting. . . . One avoids, thus, as much as possible open and interpersonal confrontation in such a public place as the town hall." (translation by this writer)[30] Douglass confirms the prevalence of such Basque behavioral control in neighborhoods and villages south of the Pyrenees.[31] In addition, Gallop indicates such "reserve" extends to intercultural contacts which occur on an individual basis; that is, Basques generally demonstrate restraint rather than aggression in person-to-person contacts with "foreigners."[32]

The negative evaluation of contentiousness is evident in *euskara*, or the Basque language. For example, two terms for "a dispute" have combative connotations. *Aharra*, alternatively *aharri*, means "ram," evoking the image of traditional ovine head-butting contests, while *mokoka* also means "blows of a bird's beak." The negative connotation of other words is expressed in terms of human behavior. *Kasaila*, or "quarrel," also expresses "the cry of children," while *kalapita*, or "dispute," also translates as "chatterbox" and "talebearer." The root of *liskadura*, or "quarrel" and "dispute," also serves as the base for "combat." In addition, the related verb *liskatu*, or "to quarrel," also expresses "to get wet and become slippery."[33]

This negative perspective carries over into the attitude of the average person toward discussion of conflict. Many Basques, at least initially, are unwilling to offer examples of "disputes" or "quarrels." Those who were most reticent had rarely left their region. In contrast, Basques who had been away for years generally were more willing to discuss past and present conflicts. However, one older non-legal mediator who had spent a decade in the United States did not use these terms, but spoke instead about "problems" which he claimed Basques prefer to "keep to themselves."

Even the word "problem" was unacceptable to one woman who began by flatly denying that there were any "disputes" in her town. She only acknowledged the existence of intra-Basque conflict after the writer inquired about the translation in *euskara* for "to hold a grudge." Then she admitted that Basques frequently hold grudges against members of their families or neighbors. She did not volunteer any examples, but did comment that she had tried to counsel a friend who had marital "difficulties."

In contrast, one resident of twenty years, who was born elsewhere and who still feels an outsider, had no compunction about describing neighborhood disputes, even to naming the participants. This person alleges that many Basques are quarrelsome because of their insistence upon being considered the equal of their neighbors: "Each person jealously guards his individual rights." Unlike the Mediterranean concept of honor, which habitually leads to feuds, the Basque concept of personal rights normally leads to other conflict management choices.

Conflict Management Choices[34]

This reality of clashes between prideful individuals has generated the Basques' pragmatic recognition that intracultural compromises are necessary for group survival. Thus, antagonists are encouraged to come to mutually acceptable arrangements which will eliminate, or at least contain, disruptive interaction. This attitude is evident in *hautsi-mautsi*, one of the Basque nouns for "compromise" and "arrangement." *Mautsi* comes from *moixtu* or *motztu*, a verb meaning to "cut short," "abridge," "curtail" or "shrink," while *hautsi* denotes "breaking" or "transgressing."[35]

An emphasis on reweaving the torn social fabric appears in *antolabide*, another noun meaning "compromise." It literally means "road repair," formed from *antolatu*, the verb "to repair," and *bide*, the noun for "road."[36] *Argitu* provides an additional linguistic clue to the general Basque conflict management perspective.[37] It means both "to resolve," in the sense of finding a solution to a problem, and "to explain" or "to enlighten." It is related to the noun *argi*, denoting "light," "candle" and "clear."[38]

Much of this rational, pragmatic attitude pervades intracultural Basque choices for handling grievances as well as the disputes into which they may escalate. The chart shown below compares and contrasts the etic, or external, with the emic, or internal. The first column presents the tripartite analytical construct which pervades the theoretical literature on disputing and conflict management.[39] Choices are listed in terms of the number of active "sides." Thus, a unilateral process, or "mode," is conducted by only the aggrieved party, whereas a bilateral method involves both the disputants, and a trilateral alternative incorporates a third party. The second column offers a visual representation of the Basque conflict management choices to demonstrate the differences from the theorists' paradigm.

Chart 1: *Theoretical Conflict Management Choices*

Theoretical Categories	Basque Perceptions	
Unilateral	**Individual**	
"Lumping"	"Lumping"	Grudge-holding
Avoidance/exiting	Avoidance	
—	Departure	
Self-help	Self-help	
Coercion	Coercion	
Bilateral	**Mutual**	
—	Verbal Competition	
Duel	—	
Feud	—	
War	—	
Negotiation	*Antolabide*	
Trilateral		
Mediation	*Arartekotasun/Bitartekotasun*	
Arbitration		
Adjudication	**Supplemental**	
	Adjudication	

Unilateral or Independent Choices

The first set of choices involves the independent or individual options of an aggrieved party. As the phrase "lumping it" suggests, an aggrieved may choose to handle conflict by doing nothing at all. Another course involves "avoidance," also called "exiting," which involves the aggrieved party's limiting or withdrawing completely from the situation or relationship creating conflict. According to such lawyers as Felstiner, the avoidance tactic cannot be commonly used in "technically simple poor societies" because the disputants in a small-scale society would experience too high a cost socially and psychologically.[40] Anyone familiar with a Basque community, however, is likely to question Felstiner's assumption. Certainly Basques themselves admit that some conflict situations lead to avoidance patterns between neighbors or relatives. Several Basques felt that avoidance has decreased recently due to the feasibility of taking court action since legal aid is provided by the government, unions, and other associations. Two persons independently commented that one today does not have to accept "being pushed around," whether one chooses to file a court case or only to threaten to sue as a lever against an opponent.

Sometimes "lumping" or avoidance is merely a stage in "grudge-holding." Grudges, some lasting decades, are reported by Basques, as well as non-Basques, as being fairly common. The social breaches and omissions which initiate grudges vary, but one frequent cause is disagreement over boundaries of agricultural holdings. Sometimes the aggrieved party eventually resorts to other modes of conflict management, often with compensation and/or vengeance as a motive.

More than one interviewee advanced the opinion that grudge-holding is less extensive today than in the years prior to World War II. This individual explained that rural people now have the means to "circulate more" and, therefore, are less likely to be consumed by concern over boundaries or other arguments with neighbors or family members. Another person suggested that the greater degree of information now available in both urban and rural locales helps potential disputants find constructive alternatives. One such recent alternative has been the government-sponsored *conciliateur* program available at the canton level since 1978.

Long before the development of modern legal aid, the Basques had—and still have—another option generally not considered by Felstiner and rarely discussed by other theorists. "Departure," which entails physically leaving the social setting, may have been, and may continue to be, a viable choice for the Basques as well as for other peoples.[41] Douglass has suggested that one of the reasons behind

Basque emigration through the centuries undoubtedly was unresolvable family conflicts for which avoidance was as impossible as Felstiner has assumed.[42]

The conflict management choice of "self-help" includes a whole range of actions from writing a letter of complaint to physical self-defense against an attacker. In contrast, "coercion" is the aggressive use of or threat to use force. Coercion can take the form of physical, psychological, religious, or magic-related tactics. Some "guerrilla" or "terrorist" actions which classified etically as coercion may be considered emically as legitimate self-help.

In most local-level circumstances, however, Basques do not physically assault those with whom they disagree, although a few aggrieved persons do handle certain disputes by attacking the property of the aggriever. For example, an argument over boundary lines simmered for nearly twenty years while A waited until certain trees, which neighbor B unwittingly had planted on A's property, were full grown before chopping them down in the presence of B who was still unaware of his past error.[43] In another town Q, a man considered particularly quarrelsome by his neighbors, discovered one morning that his prize ram had had its front teeth mysteriously extracted during the night. This occurred just before an important livestock competition in which, as neighbors were well aware, the ram would have been entered had it remained a perfect specimen.

The extent to which coercion is chosen is difficult to assess because of the very nature of the topic. Until evidence indicates otherwise, the hypothesis is that physical coercion is infrequent. Interviews provide one instance which may have involved a brief use of intimidation, although the success of the aggrieved party may have been due entirely to the element of surprise. Immediately upon discovering that a tree on his property had been cut down and removed, irate farmer F drove to the workyard of carpenter C. Without any comment, F swiftly loaded into his truck some freshly cut planks, which he observed were all that remained of his tree. The carpenter, who had bought the tree from one of F's neighbors, had no chance to take any countermeasures before F left.

The decline in use of economic and/or social pressure or intimidation is suggested by comments about "the little man" no longer letting himself be "pushed around." Certainly psychological pressure against those thought to violate social norms was crucial to the custom of *charivaris* described by Frank elsewhere in this volume. Past use of religious or magical coercion seems apparent in many sorcery accusations and confessions of alleged witches reported in historical accounts.[44] The researcher has yet to ask about current manifestations as means of conflict management.

Bilateral or Mutual Choices

In the second section of Chart 1 "verbal competition" is a new category suggested for further investigation. Considering the Basque channeling of competition into periodic contests between villages and their dislike of public confrontations, this choice is unlikely to have been, or to occur today as, a real alternative unless undertaken in a ritualized format. The Basque tradition of extemporaneous song competitions between poets, or *bertsolariak*, alternatively *pertsolariak*, may be a more genteel descendant of an ancient form of song duel conducted in the Basques' pastoral or early agricultural past.[45]

The next three conflict management modes are not characteristic of current Basque intracultural conflict management at the local level. The general concept of a "duel" is the direct confrontation of two persons in a single physically violent episode. In contrast, in a "feud" more than one party may participate on each side, and the repeated exchanges of hostilities may not be conducted face to face. The Haize-Garbia French-Basque dictionary has no entry for "duel."[46] Under "vendetta," the French word for "feud," the same volume lists *mendekio* which appears also under "vengeance." *Mendekio* is translated in the Basque-French volume only as "vengeance," or retaliation for an alleged wrong.[47] Although interviewees mentioned self-help acts of vengeance, no one described a situation which etically would be considered feud. Neither did any data suggest that "war," a multiparticipant escalation of feud, is a current local conflict management response in southwestern France.

For legal anthropological theorists such as Nader and Todd "negotiation," or the process of settling conflict by discussion, refers only to bilateral discussions.[48] Gulliver suggests that negotiation can include "mediation," or the use of an intermediary whose role is primarily advisory.[49] An accepted subtype of mediation is "conciliation," which involves the intermediary's working with one side at a time, rather than with both together. In etic terms "arbitration" is a stronger version of "mediation" because both sides have agreed beforehand to accept the intermediary's decision. These categories are not meaningful to the Basques who equate "negotiation" with "conciliation" and "arbitration" as processes used for achieving compromise.

"Negotiation" is translated in *euskara* as *antolabide*, the word mentioned earlier as meaning "road repair" and "compromise."[50] This same word also expresses "conciliation" and "arbitration."[51] Some slight distinction, which may be only a matter of dialect, is made between "negotiator" and "arbitrator." The former is *antolamenduketa ibili*, or literally "the person repairing the comings and goings."[52] The latter is *antolatzaile*, or "repairer," literally "repair agent," since *-tzaile* (also *-tzale*) is the suffix for "agent of."[53] Negotiation may come to be recognized eventually as a separate process because of labor-management relations between Basques and non-Basques. As Arno suggests, the "control communication" exerted by non-Basque management in intercultural disputing situations may come to affect the structural relationship of Basque disputants enough to establish a new pattern as a conflict management choice.[54]

The fact that the process of "adjudication" cannot be expressed in pure Basque, but only through derivatives of Latin,[55] suggests that such third-party intervention was unknown until after the Romans arrived in the Basque area in the third century B.C. Even after two millennia in which adjudication has gained a strong following in many places in Europe and abroad, the French Basques have not turned in significant numbers to this mode of conflict management. Although a few individuals claim that Basques increasingly are going to court, the general opinion of those interviewed is that Basques do not choose adjudication more now than in the past. A lawyer specifically denied that Basque adjudication has increased in the last twenty or thirty years. One notary commented that he often is asked to put an arbitration clause in a contract since people express a determination to avoid going to court. Such a clause allows the parties involved to specify a mutual friend, or to each pick a friend who then, together with his counterpart, can choose an intervenor should a future disagreement arise.

Another notary and several individuals without legal training remarked that the residents of northern *Euskalerria* share the view expressed by many other Frenchmen that, "A bad decision outside of court is better than a good court decision." They went on to explain that one reason for this view has been the Basque unfamiliarity with and/or dislike of the alien legal concepts applied in the national courts. The use of the French language and the court costs have been other negative factors. An added impediment for rural Basques has been the need to travel to the coast except for a short period in this century when a civil tribunal was open in St. Palais. During those years rural disputants allegedly did file more suits, but the total number still was modest, since the negative language and financial factors still existed.

Several Basques, however, noted that one type of dispute is being taken to court at a somewhat higher rate than before. A number of Basques mentioned that some younger married couples are filing divorce cases now, whereas in the past incompatible spouses either stayed together or just separated. One notary, however, commented that this appears to be part of a national trend, rather than merely a local development. This same man and another colleague remarked that such a change, like a slight rise in court cases involving land, may be partly the result of the national government's introduction of financial aid for civil suits about ten years ago. They thought this also was a factor in a surge of boundary cases originating in one rural town earlier in this decade.

In addition, some disputes are filed primarily for tactical reasons. These may be resolved before trial by mediation undertaken by the lawyers for both parties. For example, an aggrieved party who knows that his dispute does not have the support or sympathy of fellow villagers may not wish to ask a local mediator to intervene. This was true of a recent neighborhood noise complaint openly discussed by villagers as unreasonable. Speaking in general terms, one man with political experience suggested that filing a court case may be the way today's disputant can temper the "malevolence" of a more powerful local opponent. A merchant confirmed this opinion, asserting that "the younger generation will not allow itself to be pushed around as its parents were." He also noted that even the threat of going to court is an effective way to show resistance to an opponent who may have anticipated unimpeded manipulation of his fellow villager.

Mediation and Mediators

While *antolabide* expresses etic conflict management processes ranging from negotiation to arbitration, *euskara* recognizes "mediation" by words based on a separate root. The root translates "midline" or "mean" as in the sense of midpoint between two extremes.[56] It is used with the suffix *-tasun*, for "manner" or "quality," to create both *arartekotasun* and *bitartekotasun* which translate as "mediation."[57] It also is the basis for *ararteko* and *biarteko*, both translating as "mediator." The prefix *ar-* may come from *ara* for "measure" or "standard," creating "measure midpoint" or "mean standard." The prefix *bi-*, which represents "two" and requires an intervening consonant for pronunciation purposes, emphasizes the position between two opposites.

Basque cultural patterns encourage mediation for all types of interaction at all social levels. This was true for the powerful as well as the peasant in the past. It is true today in the rural French setting or in the complex management-worker situation of Basque cooperatives in industrialized Mondragon in Spain.[58] The consensual nature of mediation is congruent with the traditional social pattern of autonomous entities with decisions achieved by consensus at periodic local assemblies of all household heads and at annual valleywide meetings of locally-elected representatives.[59] Its origins so ancient that they are unrecorded, this representative pattern continued throughout the Middle Ages despite the ennoblement of some families and the development of some degree of social stratification.[60] It continues today in terms of the valleywide communal land associations.

Modern Basques take their disputes to a variety of mediators as they reportedly have been doing since the end of the twelfth century. Historical records mention the intervention of well-known individuals such as Sancho the Strong, Basque King of Navarra in 1196, and one of his successors, Carlos II in 1385.[61] Also reported as mediators are bishops in 1297 and 1660. On at least one occasion a high-placed non-Basque was used as a mediator. In 1256 Gaston de Bearn helped reconcile the two powerful men contending for the rule of the province of Soule when the seneschal of Henry III of England fought to oust a viscount deemed rebellious because he had sworn allegiance to the Basque king of Navarra rather than to the non-Basque monarch. French *intendants* and Spanish *corregidores*, who represented their respective rulers in later centuries, sometimes mediated disputes between villages or valleys.[62] In addition, through several centuries various French and Spanish monarchs sent envoys to a series of Basque Pyrenean boundary mediation sessions. Indeed, legal historian Descheemaeker lauds the Basque management of boundary conflict as "a rare example of continuity, wisdom and fidelity to a pacific ideal."[63] This gives an interesting perspective on a people better known for the sanguinary aspects of their past.

Chart 2: *Mediators in Terms of Basque Social Dimensions*

Type of Mediator	Family	Neighborhood	Village	Valley	Extra-Basque
Family Member/Friend	X	X			
Gizonak	X	X	X		
Clergy	X	X	X		
Doctor	X				
Mayor	X	X	X	X	
Rental Agent					X
Teacher	X		X		
Conciliateur	X	X			X
Notary	X	X	X	X	X
Lawyer	X				X
Policeman					X

Today a variety of Basque mediators handles current disputes in the family, in the neighborhood, at the village or valley levels, and in contexts involving non-Basques. Chart I indicates, in terms of these social dimensions, the range of mediators—from individuals with whom disputants have a personal relationship to those valued for their broader experience and/or their special knowledge.[64] An example of the first category of mediator is the only identified female mediator who helpfully intervened in a series of family disputes in the 1950s. Ott tells how a friend of a groom-to-be intervened to reduce tensions because the household of the bride-to-be disapproved of her spousal choice.[65]

Basques from all walks of life report that prior to World War II many Basques asked for conflict management assistance from one of those local elders called *les sages* in French and *gizonak* in Basque. The *euskara* term literally means "men" but conceptually refers to those who, in traditional terms, are knowledgeable, wise, and adept at arranging compromises.[66] While many younger Basques cannot remember or identify any *gizonak*, some of the middle-aged can recall the activities of such intervenors. All ages agree that few, if any, *gizonak* still perform their traditional function.

Fortunately, this writer met a dapper and gentlemanly octogenarian who had served as such a local mediator. A soldier in the French army during World War I, Manex enjoyed talking about his years in the United States in the 1920s, but did not mention his conflict management experiences until identified by his daughter-in-law as a former mediator. Because of modesty, typical Basque reticence, or the sheer passage of time, he claimed he could not recall specific disputes that he had handled. He did admit that he had "helped people with problems" after his return to southwestern France up to World War II. Most frequently, he averred, he had listened to "everyday problems" over a glass of wine at a local bar and "just talked with everyone about working things out."

Manex's greater experience of the world, along with his improved economic status after his years of sheepherding in Wyoming, may have marked him as a suitable intervenor even though he was only in his thirties when he returned. His acceptance as a mediator when still a relatively young man suggests that perhaps some *gizonak* normally were drawn from among those men who returned to *Euskalerria* after earning their fortune or after having learned how to deal with more complex situations. If this is so, then one reason for the decline of this intervenor might have been the increasing level of sophistication of villagers as a whole due to the number of Basques who saw service in World War II, in Indochina and in Algeria, followed by more young people going away for work or study in the large French cities.

Such an increase in "worldliness" also may be one of the factors responsible for the parallel decline in the frequency with which priests and schoolmasters are used as mediators. That is, the priest and the schoolmaster may be asked less frequently to intervene because they no longer stand out as more educated and experienced. Another important factor in terms of the priest's role is the effect of two centuries of strong, steady French anticlericism, specifically mentioned by Basques themselves as eroding the priest's public image. This national attitude gradually has influenced urban and more educated rural Basques. In contrast, many of their Spanish coethics still see the priest as an important intervenor.[67]

Other factors may contribute to create change or at least the impression of change. Some Basques north of the Pyrenees suggest that the decline of the cleric as mediator has accelerated within the past fifteen years as priests have become more vocal on political issues. One priest pointed out that by taking a public stand his colleagues in essence have undercut their credibility as neutral intermediaries. A teacher who takes an overt political position also may have fewer disputants seeking out his assistance.

Nevertheless, what Basques and other observers have noticed may be less a significant alteration in the pattern of conflict management choice than a shift in the proportion of mediators available for the number of disputes which arise. Two different phenomena, however, appear to be responsible for modifying the mediator-dispute balance. As the number of clerics has declined, particularly in the last two decades, each priest has had to cover two to four small parishes. Thus, each potential mediator has been available in each locale for a smaller number of hours than his nonperipatetic predecessor. Not being present full time also means less familiarity with the intricate relationships within each village and perhaps less acceptance as an insider. In contrast, the number of teaching personnel has increased substantially since the beginning of this century. This expansion of potential mediators may have had a "diluting" effect; that is, more teachers now may handle one or two disputes, whereas prior to World War I or even World War II one or two teachers might have been asked to intervene in more cases in the same time period. Further investigation is needed to confirm both aspects of this hypothesis.

When first interviewed, one cleric commented that he had no mediations in perhaps ten years and that he knew of no colleague who had recent cases. In a subsequent conversation, however, he reported that a colleague had just mentioned being in the process of mediating a family dispute. Several interviewees referred to a priest's having acted more as a facilitator than a mediator in a dispute between a group of Basque entrepreneurs and a large non-Basque commercial enterprise. Further research is needed to ascertain what distinguishes those curés who are asked to assist from those who are not. Since the religious position with its substantial degree of education no longer seems a sufficient qualification, individual personality traits or specific knowledge and experience may be deciding factors.

Doctors and mayors are among the mediators still asked to intervene because their knowledge of the disputants is seen as being combined with a neutral or objective position with regard to the matter in contention. For instance, a doctor mentioned his frequent role as a middleman in terms of difficult family situations where a disinterested opinion is helpful. One mayor sought to resolve a conflict between neighbors whose own friends and associates had been unable to find an acceptable compromise. Other mayors have tried, albeit with only moderate success, to reconcile competing hunting associations, two neighboring villages, and a rebellious village with its valleywide communal land association. The frustrations and failures of mayors indicate one of the limits of mediation between groups or corporate entities at the valley and intravalley levels. Here, as at the village level, the disputants have proceeded to court or at least have threatened to do so. Most, if not all, of such subsequent court decisions have been in favor of the disputant seeking to uphold traditional Basque practices rather than for the plaintiff who asks that a new pattern be recognized as legal.

Basques speak of seeking mediators on the basis of particular expertise, but ethnic affiliation also is important, if not paramount. When asked who might serve as a mediator, a few Basques included the *gendarme*, or national policeman, because of his technical legal knowledge. That no specific examples were provided is not surprising. Not only are policemen seen as a repressive aspect of the national government, but in southwestern France they are not Basque since the policy is to not assign anyone to his natal area. In contrast, a Basque rental agent told of having interceded in a number of disputes between landlords and tenants, particularly when the former were Basque and the latter non-Basques.

Basque lawyers comment that their clients often request mediation. This is especially appropriate in intracultural cases, but also is a part of certain civil law situations where French laws mandate pretrial arbitration.[68] Basque clients generally expect postfiling mediation efforts, so that many intra-Basque cases are settled before coming to trial. The extent to which Basque-non-Basque cases proceed to trial is yet to be investigated, as is the question of the circumstances in which a Basque disputant might hire a non-Basque lawyer.

Among the mediators sought for wider knowledge and broader perspective, one formerly established type of intervenor has disappeared, while another has been created within the past decade. The former was the *juge de paix*, or justice of the peace, who was an active part of the national judicial system earlier in this century. A local resident, he attracted a certain number of Basque disputants because of his understanding of Basque customs and his regular appearance, on circuit, at each town hall. The official role began to be curtailed in the late 1920s, and after World War II the jurisdiction was restricted further. The position was abolished entirely in the Basque area in 1958, reducing the alternatives available until the 1978 introduction of the *conciliateur*.

This addition to the range of available mediators is a volunteer appointed by the judicial branch of the government to his own canton as was the policy for the justice of the peace. A retired male without legal training who has been recommended by a town council, this intervenor may be a former businessman, a civil servant, or a teacher who is willing to be available at the canton headquarters for a minimum of specified hours. This new intervenor handles minor civil conflicts in even a more informal fashion than did the justice of the peace. This writer's study of six *conciliateurs* reveals that they heard more family and neighborhood disputes than rental, debt, or damage cases. The mediator's background and personality were as important as his flexibility with regard to his availability in influencing the frequency with which Basques have taken advantage of this choice.

Of the range of Basque intervenors, the notary appears to be the most important in southwestern France. When the writer asked a cross-section of Basques about who helped handle conflicts or disputes, each person gave the notary as a first answer. When asked specifically about mediators, each person immediately mentioned the notary. Lay persons and those with legal training agreed that the notary serves the greatest number of disputants for the widest variety of cases. The notary functions in terms of all social dimensions as indicated in Chart 2. Indeed, each *notaire*, or notary, who was interviewed stressed that he handles all types of disputes, not just ones in the legal realm where he is officially responsible for drawing up and recording all contracts, including wills. As a Basque living in the canton where he practices, each notary is familiar with neighborhood, village, and valley problems. In addition, at least a third of the current notaries purchased their practice from a relative, usually a father, so that the relationship with the community often involves a special sense of continuity.

One notary clearly expressed his sense of responsibility by saying, "Mediation is my métier." Another notary added that he had the right under national law to "arrange compromises" in many civil disputes.[69] A third notary agreed that he was bound by both tradition and law to mediate. When queried about any referrals to other types of intervenors, this man noted that he preferred to wait, giving the parties time to come to a clearer perspective. Moreover, he admitted, a referral would be an admission of failure. Thus, the notary's public image and self-image are that of an expert who arranges compromises which will insure that the Basque disputants do not have to seek further help, especially outside the Basque community.

Part of the Basque notary's intervention involves Basque-non-Basque mediation, particularly in terms of their dealings with the state which he officially represents under a lifetime contract. One major aspect of the notary's intercultural role was intensified after the Revolution of 1789 because the republican government adopted a policy of equal division of inheritance. This directly threatened the culturally central Basque practice of single-heir inheritance.[70] Consequently, the notary's legal knowledge was essential in assisting his clients in their "war of ruse and tenacity" to meet the letter, but not the spirit, of the national inheritance policy throughout the nineteenth century.[71] The notary continues this crucial role today, although the specific terms of the national law have been modified to favor slightly the heir who remains on productive agricultural land.[72]

The notary's intercultural mediation role, however, was not a new development. Although this function probably did expand in response to the centralization pressures of the emerging French state, the notary began mediating between Basques and non-Basques once the position of *notaire* emerged in the 1200s. At that time the effects of the Albigensian crusade, in conjunction with the increasing influence of a money economy, swept legalists, clerics, and the bourgeoisie into power.[73] Basque notaries, like their counterparts in other regions, have served to preserve the traditions of their individual locales since the Middle Ages.[74] The legal charters of the three northern provinces of *Euskalerria* specified that notaries be from the local community and know the Basque language.[75] These charters were ratified by successive monarchs, English and French, from the 1100s until each province's union with France, after which they were respected as local law until the Revolution of 1789.

Significance of the Basque Preference for Mediation

The long Basque tradition of mediation suggests the hypothesis that intercultural mediation may be a useful aspect of an ethnic population's efforts to resist assimilation. Whatever its limitations either for individual or group disputants, mediation offers a less dangerous and more flexible approach than other conflict management modes. The "dark side" of mediation is less dangerous for an ethnic group than the more destructive potential of either unilateral or bilateral modes. By its very nature mediation does not risk a strong negative reaction, which is crucial at the intercultural level since an ethnic group generally is the weaker party.

An uneven dialogue may not be fair, just, or satisfying, but it is less likely to result in the destruction of the weaker participant than other modes. Only in some countries, and only recently, has adjudication offered a hopeful alternative for a limited number of ethnic peoples. French Basques have had good reason to doubt the benefits of French adjudication controlled by the same national administrations that abolished ancient Basque written law and, until recent years, implemented measures to eradicate the Basque language.

Moreover, unlike adjudication, mediation requires no complex or corporate mechanisms. It does not need trained personnel for intracultural or intercultural use. As a result, an individual mediator can be selected in terms of the substance of the dispute, the circumstances of the disputants, and the tactics of the opponent. Besides this day-to-day flexibility, mediation as a mode can change more quickly to reflect alterations in either internal or external circumstances. For example, the number of and background of mediators have altered over the years. Basque disputants in this century have turned more frequently to persons with greater knowledge of the non-Basque world as it increasingly has impinged on their activities. The survival of Basque culture up to and through the twentieth century suggests that intercultural mediation has long been a basic and consistent, albeit fluid, conflict management strategy of Basque society for several millennia. Such flexibility in conflict management may be a desirable, possibly requisite, characteristic of any ethnic people whose basic aim is cultural survival.

The Basque conflict management preference for mediation challenges the views of American theorists who claim that mediation is not appropriate or suitable for a complex, industrialized society.[76] Felstiner asserts that disputants in such "Technologically Complex Rich Societies" rely on avoidance/exiting and adjudication, whereas disputants in "Technologically Simple Poor Societies" choose mediation because they cannot afford the social cost of avoidance/exiting in a face-to-face society.[77] The Basque pattern challenges these assumptions which lie at the heart of the ten-year argument against mediation alternatives which have burgeoned recently in the United States and western Europe. On one hand, Basque use of avoidance/exiting, as well as "lumping" and departure, in small rural communities does not fit the assumed conflict management profile of a simple, non-industrialized society. On the other hand, Basque reliance on mediation does not fit the assumed conflict management profile of a complex, industrialized society.[78] Clearly the Basque data demonstrate the insufficiency of this particular dichotomy conceived as it is without considering the many ethnic societies, such as at least nineteen in Europe, that still survive within industrialized states.[79]

This case study of Basque conflict management indicates that the mediation mode may be an element of the oppositional process by which "persistent peoples" resist state-coordinated pressures to assimilate.[80] This writer suggests that reliance on intercultural mediation avoids the greater risks inherent in the use of other conflict management modes. Compromise also offers a greater opportunity to preserve some crucial symbolic customs. Furthermore, the presence of one or more intercultural mediators provides a concrete way for an ethnic group to deal with the nonethnic world with the least possible attrition of central values.

The intercultural mediator is one tangible aid for insuring the survival of the intangible, but crucial, ethnic cultural core despite changes which affect the group's nature or membership. One example is the Basque notary in terms of his role in the preservation of single-heir inheritance by obeying the letter, but not the spirit, of the national law. The Basque notary illustrates how an intercultural mediator can assist in circumventing the intrusions of the state. In doing so he participates in the oppositional process by which an ethnic group protects itself. Another influential intercultural mediator is the politician who mobilizes supporters in terms of ethnic nationalism in order to fight the intrusions of the welfare state.[81]

The Basque reliance on intercultural mediators suggests another hypothesis with even broader theoretical implications. Intercultural individuals, like the notary, who represent both an ethnic group and its encompassing state, may act in terms of both the processes of regularization and the processes of situational adjustment. These intertwined sets of processes are described by Moore as constantly operating between societal entities whether between ethnic groups, or between an ethnic or non-ethnic group and its encompassing state.[82] Systematic, long-term observation of intercultural mediators may provide documentation of how these two processes work in terms of persistent peoples. Such data would allow the development and testing of hypotheses about the actual interaction of a macro-politico-economic system with its constituent parts.

Summary and Conclusion

This case study of Basque conflict management in southwestern France begins to fill a lacuna in the record of Basque behavior. A review of the data on the Basques indicates a bimodal pattern. History-writing non-Basques have reported amply on sanguinary Basque reactions to external oppression, while interviews of Basques at the local level have indicated a range of more temperate responses to internal contention. Coercion has been the dominant intercultural mode, while mediation has been the prevalent intracultural one. Both these choices grow out of Basque pride in their ancient heritage and their determination to endure as an ethnic entity. Their desire to maintain their independence has generated their strong action as a group against continual external oppression by other groups, whether Roman or bureaucratic. Their desire to protect their cultural core has compelled their compromising as individuals to contain internal contention natural among prideful, obstinate coethnics.

This major pattern has a minor, intermittent complement. In the intercultural context the alternative is mediation used during periods of relative peace. In the intracultural context the alternative is civil war arising during periods of widespread political unrest. Such scholars as Goyheneche and Descheemaeker record instances of intercultural mediation during times of relative political calm.

The data discussed earlier demonstrate that Basques use a variety of processes with mediation prevalent, central, and crucial. Unilateral or independent modes are common, whereas bilateral processes appear infrequently. The use of verbal competition, however, merits further study considering the Basque *bertsolari*, or poet-singer, tradition. Similarly, the use of negotiation, as etically defined, needs closer scrutiny in light of its role in labor-management disputes.

Basques prefer to avoid the trilateral, or, as they view it, supplemental, process of adjudication because it is controlled by the French state which has a long history of antagonism to Basque law and language. Some disputants do file court cases, particularly in divorce disputes, in part because financial aid for the needy now is available for civil suits. The threat of filing and of going to court is used as a strategic move, especially against a more powerful opponent. Nevertheless, Basque lawyers to whom coethnics turn to initiate suits have not observed any sizeable trend toward adjudication.

Basques consider mediation a more appropriate internal approach because it is a mutual and nonadversarial process. Its existence documented since the 1100s, mediation appears to have been an important choice since the emergence of the position of the notary who now is its prime practitioner. The Basque notary functions in all local-level social dimensions and is the most widely used intercultural mediator. Other intervenors, who serve more restricted dispute processing roles, range from the helpful family member to the coethnic lawyer. Ad hoc neighborhood mediators, or *gizonak*, no longer appear to function, but such new intervenors as rental agents and the nationally appointed *conciliateur*, a retired local resident, have emerged. After the notary, the mayor has the widest intervention scope, but perhaps the least success in terms of arranging a satisfactory compromise. The failure of mediation at the valley or supravalley level reflects the growing competition for scarce resources. Such failure also indicates the increasing degree of the Basque spirit of independence and, thus, of a less controlled approach to contention, as the conflict arena becomes more removed from the crucial social center.

Mediation is particularly suitable for an ethnic entity valuing its independence but needing to contain internal contention which might destroy the group. Mediation provides the flexibility needed by a people who have persisted by constantly adapting to changing circumstances.[83] It requires no political apparatus and no full-time specialists. Its personnel alter naturally over time as circumstances change. Its procedures vary as particular conditions demand. Indeed, mediation is the matrix for Basque intracultural conflict management, binding together the range of mutual modes.

The preceding conflict management investigation of Europe's oldest unassimilated ethnic population contributes to the advancement of theory in four distinct ways. First, the contrast between etic categories and emic perceptions indicates some of the limitations inherent in using an abstract construct. Second, discussion of the actual, rather than ideal, role of mediation and of specific mediators demonstrates the weakness of the dichotomous ideal-type approach and assumptions of theorists Felstiner and Merry. Third, consideration of the range of Basque choices affords an opportunity to develop reality-based hypotheses about socio-cultural dynamics. While some hypotheses are limited to particular Basque conflict management modes, others relate to the role of the intercultural mediator in terms of the interaction of an ethnic group with its encompassing state. Fourth, this case study suggests that systematic investigation of intercultural mediators may offer one means of documenting the processes of regularization and the processes of situational adjustments occurring between a state and its constituent parts. This, in turn, could provide a data-based foundation for the construction of theory which reflects multifaceted reality.

Notes

1. Jon Bilbao, *Eusko-Bibliographia*, vols. 1–8 (San Sebastián: Editorial Auñamendi, 1970).
2. Eugène Goyheneche, *Le Pays Basque: Soule, Labourd, Basse-Navarre* (Pau: Société Nouvelle d'Editions Régionales et de Diffusion, 1979).

3. W. L. F. Felstiner, "Influence of Social Organization on Dispute Processing," *Law and Society Review*, vol. 9, no. 1 (1974), pp. 63–94; and Sally Engle Merry, "The Social Organization of Mediation in Nonindustrial Societies: Implications for Informal Community Justice in America," in R. L. Abel, ed., *The Politics of Informal Justice*, vol. 2 (New York: Academic Press, 1982).
4. E. H. Spicer, "Persistent Cultural Systems: A Comparative Study of Identity Systems That Can Adapt to Contrasting Environments," *Science*, vol. 174, pp. 795–800; and *The Yaquis: A Cultural History* (Tucson: University of Arizona Press, 1980); G. P. Castile and Gilbert Kushner, eds., *Persistent Peoples: Cultural Enclaves in Perspective* (Tucson: University of Arizona Press, 1981); and A. P. Royce, *Ethnic Identity: Strategies of Diversity* (Bloomington: University of Indiana Press, 1982).
5. Anonymous, personal communication from an American living in Spain (1981).
6. R. MacKay, "Torture in Spain," *San Francisco Examiner*, May 17, 1981, p. A13; and J. Monahan, "Spain Steps Up Antiterror Fight," *Christian Science Monitor*, April 23, 1981, pp. 1, 12.
7. William A. Douglass, personal communication (1985).
8. Rodney Gallop, *A Book of the Basques* (Reno: University of Nevada Press, 1970), pp. 44–68.
9. Rachel Bard, *Navarra, the Durable Kingdom* (Reno: University of Nevada Press, 1982), p. 9.
10. Eugène Goyheneche, *Le Pays Basque . . .*, p. 54.
11. William A. Douglass and Jon Bilbao, *Amerikanuak: Basques in the New World* (Reno: University of Nevada Press, 1975), pp. 21–24.
12. Rachel Bard, *Navarra . . .*, pp. 13–14.
13. Eugène Goyheneche, *Le Pays Basque . . .*, pp. 56–57.
14. William A. Douglass and Jon Bilbao, *Amerikanuak . . .*, pp. 41–44.
15. Philippe Veyrin, *Les basques*, fifth edition (Paris: Arthaud, 1975), p. 98.
16. Pierre Laffitte and Pierre Charritton, "Le caractère des basques" in J. Haritschelhar, ed., *Etre basque* (Toulouse: Edition Privat, 1983), p. 111.
17. Rachel Bard, *Navarra . . .*, p. 83.
18. Eugène Goyheneche, *Le Pays Basque . . .*, pp. 264–282; 297–302.
19. Pierre Lhande, *Autour d'un foyer basque: récits et idées* (Paris: Nouvelle Libraire Nationale, 1908), p. 29.
20. Pierre Laffitte and Pierre Charritton, "Le caractère des Basques," p. 110.
21. Rachel Bard, *Navarra . . .*, pp. 78–79.
22. Eugène Goyheneche, *Le Pays Basque . . .*, p. 195.

23. Pierre Laffitte and Pierre Charritton, "Le caractère des Basques," p. 110.
24. Sandra Ott, *An Ethnographic Study of a French Basque Mountain Community*, Ph.D. dissertation (Oxford University, 1978), pp. 280–283.
25. Rodney Gallop, *A Book of the Basques*, pp. 63–64, 68.
26. William A. Douglass and Jon Bilbao, *Amerikanuak* . . . , p. 407.
27. William A. Douglass, interview (Reno, Nevada, August 11, 1979).
28. Rodney Gallop, *A Book of the Basques*, p. 63.
29. Pierre Bidart, *Pouvoir politique à Baigorri, village basque* (Bayonne: Editions Ipar, 1977).
30. Ibid., p. 200.
31. William A. Douglass, personal communication (1981).
32. Rodney Gallop, *A Book of the Basques*, pp. 63–64.
33. Haize-Garbia, *Dictionnaire basque pour tous*, vol. 1 (Hendaye: Editions Edili et Haize-Garbia, 1972), pp. 3, 100, 103, 122, 136.
34. Unless otherwise indicated, examples come from the writer's own research.
35. The three variations are due to lack of orthographic standardization (Haize-Garbia, *Dictionnaire basque* . . . , vol. 1, p. x).
36. Haize-Garbia, *Dictionnaire basque pour tous*, vol. 2 (Hendaye: Editions Edili et Haize-Garbia, 1975), p. 102; and Haize-Garbia, *Dictionnaire basque* . . . , vol. 1, pp. 7, 23.
37. The variation *arkitu* exists due to "g"-"k" interchangeability. (Haize-Garbia, *Dictionnaire basque* . . . , vol. 2, p. viii).
38. Haize-Garbia, *Dictionnaire basque* . . . , vol. 1, p. 9; and Haize-Garbia, *Dictionnaire basque* . . . , vol. 2, p. 517.
39. See specifically Laura Nader and H. F. Todd, Jr., (eds.) "Introduction," in *The Disputing Process—Law in Ten Societies* (New York: Academic Press, 1978), pp. 9–11.
40. W. L. F. Felstiner, "Influence of Social Organization . . . ," and "Avoidance as Dispute Processing: An Elaboration," *Law and Society Review*, vol. 9, no. 4 (1975), pp. 695–706.
41. This alternative is open to the Sukuma of north-central Tanzania. Interviewees there commonly claimed that many residents of the most recently settled district were either witches or angry disputants from the four more-established Sukuma areas. Irrevocable departure in the form of suicide also has been reported for both the Basques and the Sukuma as a possible but infrequent alternative. M. E. R. Nicholson, *Legal Change among the Sukuma of Tanzania*, Ph.D. dissertation, University of Minnesota, 1968.
42. William A. Douglass, personal communication (1981).
43. William A. Douglass, interview (Reno, Nevada, August 11, 1979).

44. Julio Caro Baroja, *The World of the Witches* (Chicago: University of Chicago Press, 1973).
45. Haize-Garbia, *Dictionnaire basque*..., vol. 1, p. 166. Analogous situations include the Eskimo song duel and political songs at Sukuma dance contests.
46. Haize-Garbia, *Dictionnaire basque*..., vol. 2.
47. Haize-Garbia, *Dictionnaire basque*..., vol. 1, p. 132.
48. Laura Nader and H. F. Todd, Jr., "Introduction," in *The Disputing Process*....
49. P. H. Gulliver, *Disputes and Negotiations* (New York: Academic Press, 1979).
50. Haize-Garbia, *Dictionnaire basque*..., vol. 2, p. 401.
51. Haize-Garbia, *Dictionnaire basque*..., vol. 1, p. 2.
52. Haize-Garbia, *Dictionnaire basque*..., vol. 2, p. 401.
53. Haize-Garbia, *Dictionnaire basque*..., vol. 1, p. 7.
54. Andrew Arno, "Structural Communication and Control Communication: An Interactionist Perspective on Legal and Customary Procedures for Conflict Management," *American Anthropologist*, vol. 87, no. 1 (1985), pp. 40–55.
55. Haize-Garbia, *Dictionnaire basque*..., vol. 2, p. 7.
56. Haize-Garbia, *Dictionnaire basque*..., vol. 1, p. 10.
57. Ibid., pp. 11, 23, 25.
58. D. J. Greenwood, personal communication (1980).
59. Eugène Goyheneche, *Le Pays Basque*..., pp. 143–145.
60. Manex Goyhenetche, *Pays Basque nord: un peuple colonisé* (Bayonne: Editions Elkar, 1979), p. 45. Goyhenetche contends that "feudalism was unknown in the Basque homeland, but Ourliac affirms only that the peoples of southern France successfully resisted the full development of feudalism because of well-established egalitarian social systems." Paul Ourliac, "Les coutumes de sud-ouest de la France," and "L'espirit du droit méridional," in *Etudes d'histoire du droit medieval* (Paris: Editions A. et J. Picard, 1979).
61. Eugène Goyheneche, *Le Pays Basque*..., pp. 133, 199.
62. Pierre Bidart, *Pouvoir politique*..., pp. 61–62; and D. J. Greenwood, personal communication (1980).
63. J. Descheemaeker, "Une frontière féodale au XXe siècle," *Pyrénées, vol. 12 (1952), p. 9.*
64. For a comparison of the range of Basque mediators with that in nine other societies, see M. E. R. Nicholson, "Modern Mediator in Cross-cultural Perspective," *Windsor Yearbook of Access to Justice*, vol. 3, pp. 204–227.
65. Sandra Ott, *An Ethnographic Study*..., p. 87.

66. Sandra Ott, *An Ethnographic Study* . . . ; and William A. Douglass, interview (Reno, Nevada, August 11, 1979).
67. William A. Douglass, interview (Reno, Nevada, August 11, 1979).
68. E. Balme, "Compromis et sentence arbitrale," *Juris-classeur notarial*, no. 1/5202 (1968).
69. Ibid.
70. Iban Bilbao, interview (Reno, Nevada, August 12, 1979).
71. Pierre Lhande, *Autour d'un foyer basque* . . . , p. 29.
72. Maite Lafourcade and Jean Etcheverry-Ainchart, "La transmission juridique de la maison basque," in *Etxea ou la maison basque. Les cahiers de culture basque*, no. 1 (St. Jean-Luz: Association Lauburu, 1979).
73. Paul Ourliac, "Troubadours et juristes," in *Etudes d'histoire* . . . .
74. "Notary," in *The New Encyclopedia Britannica: Micropaedia*, vol. 7 (1979), p. 46; and Paul Ourliac, "La crise des droits locaux et leur survivance a l'époque moderne," in *Etudes de Droit et d'Histoire* (Paris: Editions A. et J. Picard, 1980).
75. Eugène Goyheneche, *Le Pays Basque* . . . , p. 143.
76. W. L. F. Felstiner, "Influence of Social Organization . . . "; W. L. F. Felstiner and L. A. Williams, *Community Mediation in Dorchester, Mass.* (Washington, D.C.: Department of Justice, 1980); and Sally Engle Merry, "The Social Organization of Mediation . . . . "
77. W. L. F. Felstiner, "Influence of Social Organization . . . . "
78. For details on an American mediation program which challenges other Felstiner assumptions, see M. E. R. Nicholson, "Modern Mediator . . . . "
79. Guy Heraud, *L'Europe des ethnies*, 2nd edition (Paris: Presses d'Europe, 1974).
80. E. H. Spicer, "Persistent Cultural Systems . . . " and *The Yaquis* . . . ; G. P. Castile and Gilbert Kushner, eds., *Persistent Peoples* . . . ; and A. P. Royce, *Ethnic Identity* . . . .
81. Regarding the Welsh, see R. G. Fox, C. H. Aull, and L. F. Cimino, "Ethnic Nationalism and the Welfare State," in C. F. Keyes, ed., *Ethnic Change* (Seattle: University of Washington Press, 1981).
82. Sally Falk Moore, *Law as Process: An Anthropological Approach* (Boston: Routledge, Kegan Paul, 1978).
83. Pierre Laffitte and Pierre Charritton, "Le caractère des basques," p. 123.

Basque Legends in Their Social Context

by

Elena Arana Williams

Introduction

The most comprehensive collections of Basque narrative did not appear until the 1920s, but they have the added value both of being extensive and of being directed by native scholars, who had thorough knowledge of the language and the society.[1] These are *Euskalerriaren Yakintza* (Popular Knowledge of the Basque People) by R. M. de Azkue, a Catholic priest and scholar of Basque language and verbal art, and the scholarly journal *Eusko-Folklore* which, under the guidance of J. M. de Barandiarán, another Catholic priest, published almost exclusively mythological narratives in the issues from 1921 to 1946.

Azkue was familiar with some of the theoretical issues of folklore at the time. In his introduction he speaks of the classification of tales, but acknowledges that this problem was not resolved and presented innumerable difficulties. As a linguist, Azkue hints at comparing Basque stories to those of other countries, specifically the area of the Caucasus and the Baltic Sea, following the comparative model of other linguists at the time. The merit of his collection resides in the impressive range of materials it covers: from every genre of oral folklore to items of historic and ethnographic significance to the researcher today.

Barandiarán, on the other hand, was trained as an anthropologist and can be credited with shifting the interest in Basque myth and legends from linguistic to anthropological circles. The central concerns of anthropology in the 1860s had been prehistoric archaeology, the study of physical types of mankind, and comparative philology.[2]

Prehistoric archaeology and the study of the Basque physical type were Barandiarán's consuming interests. He pursued them in the earlier part of a professional career that extends from the 1920s to the present. Often during his archaeological digs, Barandiarán collected a great number of mythical legends from shepherds and other country people. Encouraged by cave paintings and other artifacts he found during his expeditions, Barandiarán attempted to integrate Basque mythology into his studies of prehistoric archaeology, in the first scientific attempt to integrate Basque folklore, anthropology and ethnology.

Barandiarán was influenced early in his career by an evolutionary approach to anthropology. For evolutionary anthropologists, as man evolved from primitive to civilized, customs and beliefs of the lower stages were gradually rejected, while some persisted as peripheral modes of thought and expression. These were the survivals of folklore that could be found among the peasants. Barandiarán saw mythology as the key to reconstruct an ancient system of Basque religion, a goal that he later admitted was ultimately impossible to attain due to the fragmentary nature of the data. The interest in Basque mythological narrative was thus abandoned in the 1940s, victim of the limitations of the survivalist approach.

From that time to the present the contents of *Eusko-Folklore* switched to accommodate the results of exhaustive ethnological questionnaires. While other genres of folklore attracted the attention of oral literary scholars, the study of legends suffered from their identification with myth, which in turn suffered from identification with religion and prehistory. Today we are aware of the limitations of the term "myth" and know that it should be used loosely. A current and general definition of the term defines it as "a unifying concept which enables scholars to talk about narratives and other forms which make up the body of 'assumed knowledge' a given society has about the universe, the natural and the supernatural worlds, and man's place in the totality."[3]

In Basque narrative it is the frequent presence of supernatural beings that gives stories their mythical quality. In their effort to investigate a prehistoric religion, Barandiarán and others perhaps dwelt too much on the antiquity and origins surrounding these supernatural creatures, disregarding the fact that the stories also contain many modern elements contemporary to the time of their telling. Combining the old and the new, these stories were being told because their meaning was still of social importance to the community. A better understanding is possible if one views them through the general conditions, beliefs, and ideology of the culture.

It is with this idea in mind that I will approach a group of stories, part of the vast collection gathered by Barandiarán, an invaluable collection because of his integrity and respect for the material. In this paper I will look at those tales which concern a class of supernatural beings known in the culture as *laminak* or *lamiak*. When gender is ascribed to them, *laminak* are invariably female. Their most salient female feature is their long mane of hair that hangs loosely and can reach down to the waist. Their physical appearance, however, varies widely, depending mostly on their role in the particular story: from young and beautiful to ageless or repulsive. At times their appearance is of no importance and they are simply not described in the story. *Laminak* never appear totally human. Even in those cases where they are said to have a female figure this is qualified by the fact that their feet are webbed like a duck's (in stories told in the interior villages), or else their lower body resembles that of a fish (in those told closer to the coast).

The knowledge about *laminak* is transmitted in a number of ways: as *dits*, legends, and even through curses or threats in verse form. Most commonly, the *laminak* appear in short, direct stories with succinct moral messages. From the most minimal narrative unit to longer, more complex stories, all these different forms of verbal art focus on a specific cluster of themes concerning human beings and their existence in society. The narratives constitute a frame of reference within which questions of human nature—mostly explorations of human frailties—transpire, and are represented among themselves and with the *laminak*.

These encounters mirror social interactions experienced in the daily life of the community, and they raise issues of social importance, ranging from matters of reciprocity and general adult responsibilities to the dangers surrounding love and marriage. The *laminak* stories constitute a metaphor of the difficulties surrounding human relationships, set in a particular Basque context and reflecting strong cultural values. In the interplay between the familiar and the supernatural, the factual and the ideal, they are able simultaneously to present a formal image of abstract cultural principles while becoming a vehicle for social communication.

My intention in this paper is to look for correspondence between the situations present in the narrative and other cultural activities, beliefs, and social conditions. My goal will be to establish some coherence between the meaning of the stories and their cultural setting. This is essentially the method of structuralism, which can be particularly useful to move from written texts into cultural analysis. But most importantly, it is the abundant ethnographic information that exists in Basque scholarship that will ultimately provide the evidence, as structuralist and symbolic analysis can be most fruitful only when grounded in ethnographic data. As Mary Douglas has said, the scholar's task is to understand enough of the background of the myth to be able to construct its range of reference for its native audience.[4]

The Individual and Society

The first story addresses the problems of lying and of individual greed, a problem that is in direct contrast to powerful Basque ideals of honesty and mutual assistance. Text A concerns the consequences of not living up to these ideals.

Text A

Laminak were similar to witches and spent their time on or lived on the river banks.

So that no one would see them, if anyone approached they would dive into the water.

They made a living from negation; if a farmer thought he had twenty measures of wheat growing in his field and if someone asked him how many he thought he had and he answered sixteen, subsequently (even though he might have had fourteen or eighteen, or even twenty), because of the lie he had told, the *laminak* would take four away from him. That is, they appropriated the difference between what he had declared and what he expected to obtain.[5]

The basic structure of this story rests on the opposition between truth and falsehood, which in turn belongs to the larger domain of social conduct. Conduct of the self towards others is the responsibility of the individual in society. In this story, as in others of similar structure, the issue of individual greed and the consequences of lying are brought out into the open. An individual who lies allows the negative side of his nature to determine his behavior. Motivated by personal greed, he commits a transgression against the ideal social order of the community. The *laminak* are then brought in to mediate this conflict, and are ideally suited to fulfill this role as mediators between human nature and social order. *Laminak* occupy a position halfway between nature and culture, retaining something of that duality. They are close to nature in their make-up (they are half fish and dive into the water at the approach of humans), and yet they possess the power to restore social order by reversing the intended effects of the lie.

The ideals of the reciprocity and mutual assistance among neighbors in Basque society have been noted by various scholars of Basque culture (Barandiarán, Caro Baroja, Douglass, and Ott among others).

Reciprocity involves the exchange of different types of goods and services. When an individual lies about the amount of his possessions, he is in fact refusing to participate honestly in a system of exchange and cooperation. The *laminak*, with their power to punish automatically, reverse the effects of greed by depriving hoarders of their goods. Compromise is achieved and balance is restored to the group.

In Basque mythology, the "living off negation" is the power to take possessions from those who deny they have them. This power is attributed not only to *laminak* but also to Mari, another related supernatural being. Barandiarán says that if a shepherd, for example, hides the fact that he has 100 sheep, so as not to help a neighbor in need by stating a false number, or inflates the total because of false pride, he mysteriously loses the number that he had tried to hide or to add, and these appear later at Mari's place of residence. These animals provide the sustenance for Mari and her kin. It is also said that these supernatural beings live off the affirmative and the negative (*Ezagaz eta baigaz bizi omen da*), from what human beings deliberately hide or add to their actual possessions.

This strong concern with hiding the truth regarding material possessions is handled in all cases in the same direct manner. In anthropological terms the punishment can be seen as a rite of reversal. The main functionalist view of such rites is that they symbolically express underlying and normally suppressed conflicts within the society. Accordingly, they constitute a mechanism by which the pressures engendered by social conflict may be vented without allowing the conflict to become fully overt and thereby threaten the survival of the society.[6]

With regard to Basque rural society, ethnographers have pointed out the remarkable absence of overt conflict in issues of mutual assistance among neighbors. It is difficult, of course, to assess the degrees of conflict that might in fact exist in a community that demands honesty in the disclosure of one's true material worth. The widespread concern over this topic in legend certainly implies that the issue is much in people's minds. The stories can function at several overlapping levels: they can allow people to explore the boundaries of appropriate and inappropriate behavior by pointing out the difficulties of living up to the ideals; they can be used to externalize real underlying conflict, by functioning as a warning or even threat of punishment; and in some cases they may actually fulfill their cautionary role and prevent conflict from occurring or spreading.

The decisive action of taking the goods away certainly contains a built-in deterrent for disorderly behavior. The punishment itself is not excessive—it simply reverses the intended wrong. According to the society's ideals, honesty and cooperation result in the mutual benefit of both parties and should be enough to counter the drive of the heart's passions. But the stories are evidence of people's weaknesses in that respect. Through the figure of the *laminak* (and Mari) they elevate the values of honesty and sharing to a suprasocietal level, i.e., to the supernatural and its powers. By relying ultimately on these powers they add greater authority to the social rules.

Text B elaborates on the issue of material goods.

Text B
In the famous cave of Balzola (Dima) there lived some young ladies that the shepherds often saw brushing their hair while sitting on the rocks. They had sheets and towels of very good quality. People would ask them: "Where do you get such good sheets?" And they answered: "From those who say they don't have them."

These young ladies would come down to go to the dances, and there they covered their feet (which resembled those of chickens), so that people would not notice they were *laminak*.[7]

While the tone of the story in Text A was somewhat didactic, the point being to illustrate the punishment inflicted upon those who lie, the tone of Text B is more casual. It simply states, in a matter-of-fact manner, that people do hide the truth regarding their possessions. After all, that is how the *laminak* accumulate their alleged vast riches. The information in Text B puts the *laminak* in an almost worldly female domain of young ladies who possessed beautiful linens. The implicit meaning, however, is basically the same as that of Text A. Here, sheets and towels fill the role of the wheat in the previous text. Items of linen such as sheets and towels were highly desirable objects for the rural household, figuring prominently in contracts of marriage as part of the bride's dowry. In other variants of these stories, the function is filled by apples, sheep, and other equally desirable objects. While linens or apples may be seen more as luxuries than as basics, wheat and sheep were necessary for the survival of the group, and often determined the difference between hunger or well-being, illness or health. Altogether, the general availability and the willingness to assist others with these goods could determine to a great extent the viability of the community.

Mary Douglas has said that the function of myth is to portray the contradictions in the basic premises of the culture.[8] The ideals of reciprocity and mutual assistance in Basque society express a fundamental egalitarian supposition. Egalitarianism as a cultural norm among Basques has been noted by various scholars. And yet the culture also regards favorably the attainment of wealth. Wealth in itself is an ambiguous force because of its power both to nourish and to destroy, to create community and to disrupt relationships. In these stories it is not the possession of goods itself that is censured; it is the lying about them that legitimates gossip and criticism. In the stories people can recognize indirectly what is difficult to admit openly but is nevertheless clear to all—that the ideal is not attainable, or at least egalitarianism, mutual aid, and the pursuit of wealth are difficult to balance.

In contrast to the negative issue of hoarding goods, there is another type of story that conveys the message that all is well when humans and *laminak* cooperate with each other as good neighbors should.

Text C
In the old days they used to leave cornbread overnight on the table at home.

Then the *laminak* of Gaztelu would come at night to work in the fields of that house and they would eat that bread.[9]

There are various examples in the literature of this type of positive interaction, where generosity and cooperation bring peace and prosperity. Text D illustrates clearly opposite norms of behavior:

Text D
The people of Bazterretxe, every night before they went to bed, left in the corner near the fire, along with a bowl of milk, some toasted cornbread crumbs and pieces of leftover salt pork on the skillet.

When they were sound asleep, the *laminak* would come down the chimney and slurp, slurp, would make themselves comfortable eating everything next to the fire. Afterwards, silently they went back up the chimney.

The next day the people of Bazterretxe would find their fields fertilized, their trenches cleaned, the soil plowed, and the cornfields weeded.

One night, they went to bed after forgetting to put next to the fire the bowl of milk, the leftovers of salt pork, and the cornbread crumbs, and the *laminak*, offended, moved to another neighborhood, far, very far away, and they never came back to work for Bazterretxe.[10]

In this story there is an implicit agreement between the *laminak* and the people of Bazterretxe—not a written contract, but a pact binding the two parties to mutual aid and cooperation. The agreement is broken by the lack of responsibility of the inhabitants of Bazterretxe who bring unto themselves the negative consequences of their failure to fulfill their obligation toward the *laminak*, who in this case were their friends and helpers.

In Text A we were told that *laminak* are just like witches, in Text B they were described as beautiful young ladies, and in their role as "helpers" in Texts C and D they are often described as supernatural beings of very small size. This last image is somewhat similar to a class of fairies of Northern European folklore. All these variant forms attributed to the *laminak* are due in part to the complex nature of mythology itself. The products of different belief systems layer upon each other and in time create a multiplicity of forms. These images can be used selectively by the tellers to fit the particulars of each case. People in every society make a selection from the vast number of topics that exist in folklore to the elements that are most meaningful in expressing their cultural experience.

In Basque mythological tales it is common to find overlapping and cross-references among the attributes and powers of *laminak*, witches, and other supernatural female agents. What distinguishes *laminak*—especially from Mari—however, is that theirs is not an arbitrary, evil abuse of power.[11] They are brought in more as mediators, helping humans to reflect on their actions. *Laminak* are spirits of the forest, spirits of nature, sometimes attractive and even benevolent beings, not particularly evil in and of themselves. It is the people in these stories who bring unhappiness upon themselves with their own actions.

Text E

There lived *laminak* on the hilltop of Mondarrain. There was an underground passage from Mondarrain to the house of Eiheraxarre (in the town of Espelette).

At night a *lamina* would come to Eiheraxarre asking for flour. She met the housewife there who was spinning every night, and she would demand flour to make fritters.

And the woman would give it to her.

Finally, tired of this, the woman told her husband what was happening.

So, the husband stayed up one night spinning and put some grease in a skillet on the stove. Then, when the *lamina* arrived, she told the man: "Last night you were spinning *firin-firin* (finely) and tonight *furdulun-furdulun* (coarsely). What's your name?"

"Me, myself," said the man, and presently threw the hot grease into the *lamina*'s face.

The *lamina* went back to Mondarrain crying, and her friends asked her: "Who did that to you?" and she answered: "Me, myself." "Then, if you've done it yourself, there is nothing we can do."[12]

In this story, a *lamina*'s disorderly behavior determines the outcome of the plot. *Laminak* are often close to humans, and their actions as well can have negative and positive consequences. Personal responsibility and the place of the individual in the community are the key concerns.

The *laminaks'* power, their capacity to punish or reward, resides in their marginal state of being. They are ambiguous creatures, not totally of this world. They are neither human nor animal, yet partake of both. They inhabit hard-to-define places, transitory in nature, such as caves and rivers, crossroads and bridges. They are often seen on the boundaries of such places, such as the rocks that exist at the entrance of caves or on the river banks. They sit and linger there, as if waiting for humans to test their strengths, uncover their weaknesses, and direct them in the right way, revealing human nature to itself.

In Text B we are told how *laminak* in their role as beautiful young ladies often attended dances and how they covered their feet so as not to be discovered. Village dances were publicly sanctioned events where young people would meet freely and where romances began that could eventually lead to marriage. Young people from isolated farms would attend a number of these dances in neighboring towns. If a young man saw a girl he liked, he might try to dance the last piece with her so as to be able to walk her back home at night.[13] It is in this context that the presence of *laminak* becomes appropriate, since *laminak* are known at times to have used their considerable female charms to entice young men.

Love and Marriage

Text F

A young man from a farm in Garagartza (Mondragon) hiked up the mountain daily where he took his sheep to pasture. A *lamina*, who looked like a young woman, dressed in gold, came out of the cave where she lived, met the shepherd one day, and proposed marriage to him.

The young man came back from the mountain and discussed the case with his mother. She gave him this advice: look at the feet of the woman of the mountain. When the shepherd went back to meet the young woman, he saw her sitting on a mountain goat, brushing her hair, and he noticed that her feet resembled those of a goose. Because of this he decided not to marry her. But later he got sick and died. The *lamina* came to his funeral, but did not pass through the door of the church in Garagartza.[14]

The naming of the neighborhood and place the event transpires makes stories such as this one more tangible. In contrast to the specificity of place, the details of the encounter between the young man and the *lamina* are left to the imagination—full of implications but devoid of explanation.

The tales of young men in love with *laminak* are never sexually explicit—European tales hardly ever are—but they do present a scenario of seduction. The trademarks of the *laminak* in their seductive role arise from two complementary sources: their possession of vast riches (they are dressed in gold) and the sensual manner in which they present themselves, especially in their leisurely brushing of their long manes of hair. In this image of the *lamina*, wealth and physical attraction are symbolically merged, presenting a formidable test of fortitude for the young men involved.

This fantastic female imagery contrasts sharply with reality on both counts. First, gold as a symbol of wealth or material well-being was virtually inaccessible to young and old alike. Work did not produce cash; it was mostly based on a system of exchange of goods. Gold may also represent access to the independence which poverty denied young people. Second, young Basque women around the turn of the century did not present themselves with loose, long hair. By early adolescence, shortly after their first communion, girls would braid their hair or have it wrapped at the nape. As an informant put it: "By that time, they had reached the age to gather their hair."[15] In Basque folklore there are stories in which female vanity and laziness are illustrated by the excessive preoccupation of adolescent girls with hair brushing. This transgression can be the cause of harsh parental punishment.[16] The image of the *lamina*, her unrestrained sexuality symbolized by her flowing hair, is in direct opposition to the parental attempt to control their daughters' sexuality by insisting that they gather their hair tightly.[17]

And yet, it is not sexual contact itself that is being censured in these stories. We know that, despite parental attempts to control the sexuality of young people, sexual activity did take place and illegitimate children were neither unusual nor cause for excessive punishment. Affairs were subject to gossip and verbal criticism, but that was in general the full extent of the censure. It is the ideal of marriage, rather than just sexuality, that is the object of this type of story. There is something incongruous and unreal as well about a *lamina* (a creature of nature) coming out and proposing marriage (a social institution) in such a straightforward manner.

Marriage, as a strong social institution in Basque society, involved not just the couple but it had far-reaching consequences for the two households involved and was therefore regulated by the parents according to various rules and constraints. It is those young men who fell for a *lamina*, allowing themselves to be talked into a marriage situation outside the societal framework, who suffered gravely the consequences of their passion. Even in Text G, a humorous variant, the young man still meets his death.

Text G

The boy from Korrione went to Kobaundi (the large cave) of the Kobate mountain.

There he found a *lamina*; she was a beautiful woman, more beautiful than the Christians of this area.

This *lamina* promised to marry him, under one condition: he had to guess her age.

The boy asked for the help of a woman in the neighborhood. The woman told him she would find out for him.

This woman went to Kobaundi. She placed herself facing the cave with her rear end, bent her head and looked back from between her legs.

The *lamina* came out and, frightened, exclaimed: "I'm one hundred and five years old, but I've never seen anything like that!"

The woman then told the boy: "That woman is one hundred and five years old."

The boy then told the *lamina*: "You are one hundred and five years old."

The *lamina* then agreed to marry him.

The boy told his mother.

The boy's mother told him to look at the *lamina*'s feet. He did and the *lamina*'s feet were like those of a duck. This boy got frightened and ill. Later he died.[18]

The young men in these stories are in an ambiguous relation to society, at the stage between boyhood and adulthood when they are capable of performing a large number of tasks and labor for the benefit of the family group and yet have not acquired full adult responsibilities. In rural Basque society marriage was the most important rite of passage into the world of adults, giving people the maximum prestige and authority that they could obtain. People, who after reaching a certain age were not married, were often the object of jokes and even ridicule.[19]

Young men in love with *laminak* are postured dangerously with respect to the females of their world. They are torn between the attraction of a *lamina*, a beautiful but vain creature who is in direct contrast to the socially approved choice of a modest, hard-working woman capable of continuing the family line, improving the *baserria* (farm-home) and producing acceptable offspring. Opposing the *lamina* here is the authority of the mother, who is presented as the only one with the clarity of mind and the knowledge to make him see his mistake and warn him of the danger involved. The power inherent in the idea of unavoidable sorrow and ultimate death that afflict the young men illustrates the gravity of their mistake.

Ethnographers tell us that a man's choice of marriage partner is important enough that it alone can decide his eligibility as heir of the farm. A marriage disapproved by the parents was enough to disqualify him from inheriting the familial patrimony.[20] Parents looked for marriages of interest that were often based on economic factors, including those among near relatives or among people with wide differences in age. The marriage of an old, rich uncle and a young niece was not unusual, and when it occurred the parents often chose the girl as the heiress of the property.

The centrality of the home in Basque culture and the importance of the indivisible *baserria* have received considerable attention from scholars. It is in light of this situation that the choice of a marriage partner demands extreme caution. In rural Basque households it was expected that the young heir and his wife would live with the parents for a good part of their lives, until the deaths of the latter. Under these circumstances, the authority of the mother in controlling the young man's choice for her future daughter-in-law acquired special significance.

These stories illustrate how uncontrolled sexual attraction, a dangerous part of a young man's nature, can lead him to a disastrous choice of marriage partner. In previous texts we have seen how the ideal of reciprocal action springs from an egalitarian supposition among adults; here, in the relationship among parents and children, we see the hierarchical structure of the society.

Women and Laminak

The interactions between women and *laminak* underscore the difficulty humans have in dealing with their own nature. They bring up those frailties that preclude people from living up to ideals in themselves and in their relationships with others.

Text H
In the cave of Oleta in Lekeitio there were *laminak* in the old days. The informant's great grandmother, who was a midwife,

was once asked to come and help a *lamina* in labor. (As was told to him by his grandmother.) After the delivery, the *laminak* invited the midwife to stay and eat supper with them. The bread they served was of extraordinary white quality and it caught the attention of the midwife. Very carefully, she hid a piece of it in order to take it home and show her family. But when she finished eating the midwife found that she could not get up from the table. The *laminak* understood that the reason was that she had taken a piece of bread without their permission and asked her to put it back on the table.

She did that and then the *laminak* gave her an entire loaf for her family.[21]

This story depicts the very common situation of a woman assisting her neighbors in childbirth. The *laminak* once again are placed in a worldly domain, where they behave appropriately when faced with the event of childbirth. As is customary, they invite the midwife to have supper with them as part of their payment and sign of appreciation for her efforts. In return, the woman, driven by her curiosity and desire to possess an item of "superior quality," behaves in a socially inappropriate manner. The *laminak* in this particular case are quite magnanimous and choose to overlook her indiscretion.

The structure of this interaction is parallel to those stories of males who, driven by greed, try to cheat their neighbors. While men are often motivated by greed or lust, women's offenses take the form of multiple small transgressions. These social problems crop up repeatedly in the narrative, the underlying tension being how to control one's nature in order to live at peace with one's self and one's neighbors.

Text I

On the rocks of Aizpuru lived some *laminak*. One of them went into labor and they brought the woman of Yoane as a midwife.

At the *laminak*'s home everything was made out of gold.

When the woman finished her work, they asked her how much they owed her.

She told them she wanted a carding comb.

They gave her one made out of gold, asking her not to look back on her way home.

The *laminak* then accompanied her on her way, while playing music.

Entering her home, with one leg out and the other one in, (the woman) looked back, and then the *laminak* angrily took half of her carding comb back.

They say that with the other half they built Yoanea.²²

In this story the woman was not able to contain her curiosity, which drives her to disregard the only request of the generous *laminak*. Because of her lack of restraint, the woman brings upon herself the loss of half of her reward.

By contrast, in the next story a friendly *lamina* gives a woman a lesson on how not to be deceived by false appearances. The woman follows her advice and is amply rewarded for being trustworthy and decisive.

Text J
Once a *lamina* was about to go into labor.

She sent one of her friends to call a woman from town who was a midwife.

On their way there, the (*lamina*) friend told the midwife: "As you finish your work, they'll ask you to choose between two pots, one with gold at the top and the other one with ashes on the surface. Choose the one with the ashes, because that will be the one with gold."

"Yes, of course!" (the woman answered).

The midwife acted accordingly, and everything turned out as the *lamina* had promised.²³

In the relationship between women and *laminak* there is one particular case that demands special attention. The times women are most seriously threatened by *laminak* are when they take and attempt to keep the object that has most value for the *laminak*: their comb. The importance of the comb in these stories is a logical extension of that foremost characteristic of *laminak*: their hair. The *laminak's* hair is a symbol of their natural power, their femaleness and their sexuality. The symbolic value of the hair is directed through the ever-present comb (an object of culture) towards cultural ends. The motif of a supernatural female grooming her hair with a comb—a gold comb—is the most frequent commonplace in Basque folklore of the supernatural. According to one of Barandiarán's informants: "At sunrise they (*laminak*) came out of the river and sat on the bank next to it to comb their long, curled, beautiful hair. This was their most frequent occupation."²⁴ When somebody approached the area, however, the *laminak* hurriedly jumped into the water, which explains how they forgot to take their combs with them and abandoned them on the site.

A woman passing by would see the comb and take it home with her. Later, a *lamina* would approach her house to demand with threats to get her comb back. This is the background for a series of threats or curses in verse form that are widely known throughout the country. The *laminak*, acting carelessly, lose their most treasured possession, and women, taking advantage of the situation, take the comb home intending to keep it for themselves.

Here are a few examples of some of those threats:

Ceanuri: Lambreabe'ko etzanderea
Ekasu nire orrasie
Espabe egingo dot sure arkasie.

Lady of Lambreabe
Give me my comb.
If not I'll (ruin) your offspring.

Elorrio: Joxepinaxi,
Nun don nire orrasi?
Emoten ezpostan nire orrasi,
Nik kendukonat iri bizi.

Joxepinasi,
Where is my comb?
If you don't give me my comb
I'll take your life.

Amorebieta: Ah, neska!
Nun dire nire orraska?

Ah, girl!
Where is my comb?

Ataun: Andra Geazi,
Ekatzu nere orrasi;
Bestela galduko ittut
Zure ondorengo azkazi.

Lady Grace,
Give me back my comb;
If not I'll destroy
Your future offspring.

Oyarzun: Matxine'ko neskamea,
Ekatzu nere orrazea.
Bestela emango dinat
Ere biziko ezurretako onazea.

> Girl servant of Matxine,
> Give me back my comb.
> If not I'll give you
> Pain in your bones for the rest of your life.²⁵

Women who steal the *laminak*'s combs are involved in a power struggle. In their quest for a power that is inaccessible to them, by virtue of their being human, women expose themselves to open-ended threats, full of ambivalence and danger. The *laminak* stories show that the actions of human beings contain the seeds for order and disorder; by stealing the comb women provoke the anger of the *laminak* who have the power both to create and destroy. Death and suffering, as well as their opposites of fertility and sexuality, are an integral part of nature. They are vital issues whose implications tend to be felt more strongly in the home, the realm that the culture has assigned mainly to women. Although there are a few instances of men stealing objects from the *laminak*, the bulk of the struggle with the comb is centered on women.

Along with their preoccupation with their hair and combs, *laminak* are close to women in other respects as well. *Laminak* are often seen doing the laundry or weaving, and generally are involved in many traditional female occupations. As we have seen, they require the expertise of women in events such as childbirth. The boundaries between female home life and that of *laminak* are blurred in this special affinity of their mutual concerns. All those occupations such as washing, brushing, weaving, or assisting in childbirth help transform nature into culture: controlling hair, avoiding dirt, transforming flax into fabric, and socializing children. But the power of *laminak*, as illustrated in the stories, goes beyond domestic tasks to enforce cultural values and arbitrate community life. While there is no doubt that the influence of women also extends beyond the domestic realm, there is no public form of expression of that notion, except by inference in the narrative, through their identification with *laminak*.

Most expressive forms of rural Basque culture, such as dance, games, the *bertsolariak* or even music are predominantly male-oriented activities. It is only in mythical narrative that female images acquire special importance. The telling of these stories generally took place in familiar surroundings, at home in the evenings or in close neighborhood gatherings as part of general conversation. The content of the stories, with its everyday concerns, reflects that environment. This type of private context contrasts sharply with the very public performance of the male-centered events.

In this case folklore reflected the social organization of Basque society, which was similar to most known societies of the world, with men controlling the public sphere of activity and women's lives limited to the family and home. However, the special characteristics of the family home in Basque culture, and the major role of the woman in it, accorded Basque women special status in contrast to those in neighboring Mediterranean cultures. Barandiarán says that significant aspects of religion in Basque society took place at home, where the woman acted as minister of a sort of "domestic cult." By this he meant that women were in charge of the enactment of rituals concerning worship of the ancestors, blessing the members of the family once a year, and instructing all on duties towards the elders and on their obligations to the neighborhood.[26]

The rituals concerning previous inhabitants of the home, entrusted to women, had far-reaching implications that transcended immediate domestic concerns. On the spiritual side they protected family continuity, and economically they determined the impartible transmission of property. In time the Basque house had acquired an identity of its own; this identity was signified by a house name that served to identify all members of a domestic group. People in the community identified each other through their house names instead of through individual surnames. Basque women, often heirs and mistresses in their own right, were known for their "effrontery" and were also notorious as witches.[27] The audacity attributed to Basque women helps to explain their power struggle with *laminak* over possession of the comb. Societies that define women as lacking legitimate public authority have no way of acknowledging the reality of female power. The powerful woman is often considered a witch.[28]

Conclusion

Mary Douglas has said that the vital issues in culture are how to organize other people and oneself in relation to them, how to control turbulent youth, how to soothe disgruntled neighbors, how to gain one's rights, how to prevent usurpation of authority, or how to justify it. To serve these practical ends all kinds of beliefs in the omniscience and omnipotence of the environment are called into play. If social life in a particular community has settled down into any sort of constant form, social problems tend to crop up in the same areas of tension or strife. And so as part of the machinery for resolving them, beliefs about automatic punishment, destiny, ghostly vengeance and witchcraft crystallize in the institutions.[29] The stories about *laminak* are only part of a larger body of mythological narratives that deal with some of those same concerns underscored by Douglas.

They are all issues that concern both men and women in their day-to-day lives and, aside from their social function, the stories also have a metaphysical bent—reflecting on human nature, its limitations and consequences for a peaceful community life. Some stories are funny and some are sad, but they all deal with issues that don't go away. The stories are part of a communal effort to create a better environment for all, constantly exploring values as part of an ongoing culture-building process.

What sets apart these stories from other forms of Basque folklore is that those issues are explored here through female mediators. Further study, including analysis of other supernatural beings such as the contrasts between *laminak* and Mari on the one hand and the cult to the Virgin Mother on the other, so important in Basque culture, is necessary to probe the fabric of Basque secular and religious myth, and can illuminate aspects of culture that are not as easily accessible by other means.

Informants gave Barandiarán two main reasons for the disappearance of *laminak* from the Basque Country. First was the growth of Eibar, a town where arms were manufactured. Second, *laminak* disappeared after chapels were built in areas where they used to live, places where people now attend regular religious ceremonies. It is consistent with their role that wise creatures such as *laminak* would choose to leave an area noted for the manufacture of artifacts of destruction. Just as important, the moral secular system that they represented was co-opted by an institutionalized church and educational system.

Notes

1. Julio Caro Baroja (Madrid: Ediciones Istmo, 1971) gives a good bibliography of previous collections in *Los vascos*, pp. 292–293. The French-Basque collections, such as J. F. Cerquand's *Legendes et recits populaires du pays basque* (Pau: L. Ribaud, 1875); Wentworth Webster's *Basque Legends* (London, 1879); and Julien Vinson's *Le Folklore du pays basque* (Paris: Maisonneuve, 1883) are cited as the most reliable. It is important to remember here that during the nineteenth century, a number of writings on myth and legend often suffered from romantic and nationalistic excesses.
2. See "Arnold, Tylor and the Uses of Invention" in George W. Stocking, Jr., *Race, Culture and Evolution. Essays in the His-*

tory of Anthropology (Chicago: The University of Chicago Press. Phoenix Ed., 1982), pp. 69-90.
3. W. A. Lessa and E. Z. Vogt, *Reader in Comparative Religion. An Anthropological Approach* (New York: Harper and Row, 1979), p. 188. The term myth is a convenient label for an enormous variety of narrative styles, contents, forms and functions. Lessa and Vogt emphasize the notion that significant statements about myth should be context conscious.
4. Mary Douglas, *Implicit Meanings. Essays in Anthropology* (London, Henley, Boston: Routledge and Kegan Paul, 1978), p. 169.
5. J. M. Barandiarán, *Obras completas*, vol. 2 (Bilbao: La Gran Enciclopedia Vasca, 1973), p. 421.
6. Anthony F. C. Wallace, *Religion: An Anthropological View* (New York: Random House, 1966), pp. 203-205.
7. J. M. Barandiarán, *Obras completas*, vol. 2, p. 36.
8. Mary Douglas, *Implicit Meanings...*, p. 156.
9. Ibid., p. 454.
10. Ibid., p. 456.
11. In Basque mythology, Mari is the "queen" of the underworld. She has the power to destroy, not only individuals but entire communities, by causing violent hailstorms and ruining harvests, all without any apparent significant reason. She encapsulates all the fury of nature.
12. J. M. Barandiarán, *Obras completas*, vol. 2, p. 437.
13. This explanation came from the biography of a carpenter in the town of Betelu in Navarra. There this practice was called *neskalauntza*. The information was gathered by a group of ethnographers working for *Cuadernos de etnología y etnografía de Navarra*, vol. 38, pp. 209-302.
14. J. M. Barandiarán, *Obras completas*, vol. 2, p. 194.
15. This information comes from an article dealing with rituals of adolescent girls in Arrayoz, Navarra. (*Cuadernos de etnología y etnografía de Navarra*, vol. 39, pp. 473-487.) This type of material is scarce in Basque scholarship and should be very important to reveal aspects of the female-centered mythology.
16. The motif of excessive hair brushing of adolescent girls is present mostly in the cycle of stories concerning Mari's origins. They are not part of the *laminak* cycle, but are closely related to it. here is one of the variants:
    In a farm in Zegama there was a couple who had a daughter. She was in the habit of combing her hair every night, spending long hours on this task. This is why her mother was forced often to grab the comb from her, and send her to bed, until one time, tired of scolding her, she cursed her this way:

"May the lightning take you." The young girl rapidly changed in color, her hair seemed to be in flames, and she instantly disappeared. In those days, there was a shepherd tending sheep near the cave of Aitzkorri. He was sitting next to the cave one day when he saw coming out of it a mysterious creature in the shape of a human skeleton (it was the dame of Aketegui) who told him: "If you weren't wearing the medallion of the Virgin Mary, I would devour you." Then (the creature) told him how she was condemned to live in that cave because of her mother's curse, and asked him to make this publicly known in town. J. M. Barandiarán, *Obras completas*, vol. 1 (Bilbao: La Gran Enciclopedia Vasca, 1971), p. 282.
17. The significance of hair in society has received considerable attention in anthropology. Margaret Williamson, in her article "Powhatan Hair" in *Man* (N. S.), vol. 14, 1980, gives a good bibliography on the subject. There is E. R. Leach, "Magical Hair," in *Journal of the Royal Anthropological Institute*, vol. 88 (1958), pp. 147–164; C. R. Hallpike, "Social Hair," in *Man* (N. S.), vol. 4, (1969), pp. 256 – 264; P. Hershman, "Hair, Sex, and Dirt," in *Man* (N. S.), vol. 9 (1974), pp. 275-298; M. D. M. Derret, "Religious Hair," in *Man* (N. S.), vol. 8, (1973) pp. 100–103; Raymond Firth, "Hair as Private Asset and Public Symbol," in *Symbols, Public and Private* (Ithaca: Cornell University Press, 1975), pp. 262-298; Terence S. Turner, "Tchrikin: a Central Brazilian Tribe and Its Symbolic Language of Bodily Adornment," in *Natural History*, vol. 78, no. 8 (1969), pp. 50-70; and Mary Douglas, *Natural Symbols* (New York: Pantheon Books, 1970).
18. J. M. Barandiarán, *Obras completas*, vol. 2, p. 446.
19. Julio Caro Baroja, *Los vascos* (Madrid: Ediciones Istmo, 1971), p. 245.
20. Julio Caro Baroja, *Estudios vascos*, vol. 7 (San Sebastián: Editorial Txertoa, 1976), p. 128.
21. J. M. Barandiarán, *Obras completas*, vol. 2, p. 202.
22. Ibid., p. 449.
23. Ibid., p. 451.
24. Ibid., p. 426.
25. Ibid., p. 431.
26. J. M. Barandiarán, *Obras completas*, vol. 1, p. 365.
27. Natalie Davis, *The Return of Martin Guerre* (Cambridge, Mass., and London, England: Harvard University Press, 1983), p. 32.
28. Witchcraft in Basque society has been treated by Julio Caro Baroja in *The World of the Witches* (Chicago: The University of Chicago Press, 1964) and most recently by Gustav Henningson in *The*

Witches' Advocate: Basque Witchcraft and the Spanish Inquisition (1609–1614) (Reno: University of Nevada Press, 1980).
29. Mary Douglas, *Purity and Danger* (London, Henley, Boston: Routledge and Kegan Paul, 1978), p. 91.

The Current Status of the Anthropology of Women: Models and Paradigms[1]

by

Teresa del Valle

I. Theoretical Presuppositions

Systems analysis in the study of gender relations is gaining considerable importance, not only in anthropology but in history[2] and geography as well.[3] Its attraction seems to lie in its broad scope and the possibility that it affords of transcending analytical categories and designations by means of a certain capacity for interpretation and explication. It provides a theoretical and methodological option that should continue to be amplified and refined. It is in this vein that the present article examines the following question: To what degree does consideration of gender as a cultural system further our knowledge of the bases and forms in which an asymmetrical division between men and women operates? In this manner, utilizing the results of research I have conducted on various aspects of Basque culture, it is possible to incorporate new elements into the analysis which represents a theoretical advance.

Traditionally, and in accord with the binary system proposed by Levi-Strauss, the identity of women is elaborated in reference to that of men. This prompts us to maintain the stereotypes of the closed categories man/woman, even when it is understood that the former embraces all varieties of manhood and the latter those of womanhood, when frequently the designations are not stated in such terms. In the majority of treatments of the subject the dominant view of the male category in contradistinction to its female counterpart leads to simplification which supports the idea of a commonality shared by women, rather than the variability that the category glosses over. At the same time, the female category embraces collectivities as disparate as an association of prolife women and their feminist foes. Both become fused together under the same epigraph. In the case of men, to the contrary, there is less reference to a generic classification since it is common to discriminate male variation according to type of employment, formal and informal affiliations, and means of garnering social prestige, to cite but a few distinguishing factors.

If, on the one hand, we follow the definition of cultural constructs and on the other, social structure and its contextualization in time, it is possible to attain a "systems approach" which is to be desired until such time that we have a better dynamic term for expressing interactional and contextual aspects.

The view of gender as cultural construct is rooted in the field of symbolic anthropology where certain of its principal characteristics are evident: the priority that is given to an interpretation derived from a dialectic between concrete data and explicative scheme; the centrality of the symbol that embraces the different dimensions as well as the distinct factors that can influence its reading such as the place in which it appears, the moment, the form of the reading—whether it is individual or collective, the importance of context. Such a view is based upon the affirmation of a human capacity to manipulate symbolic categories, a key attribute when we consider the factors that intervene most directly in the formation of gender constructs. It is through this capacity that we can perceive how symbolic systems become simultaneously condition and consequence of the social interaction.

The efficacy of the symbol consists on the one hand in its interior quality (interpretative) which is capable of emerging from a private to a public situation. The power of symbols resides in this conjunction of the interior and the exterior, of the microcosms and the macrocosms, accompanied by an element of uncertainty, ambiguity, and creativity.[4] It is for these reasons that it is so critical to consider how a culture (or subculture) is elaborated or, in the present case, how it signifies what it means to be a man or a woman. Into such expression enters that which is affirmed as well as the various grades of that which is excluded. At the same time, it is here that we encounter the power of such systems composed of premises, norms, positive and negative attributes, and the reason why they permeate so completely, giving rise to various kinds of readings or interpretations. The symbolic capacity to produce as well as to interpret, to read, to signify is admirable, but when it is given priority from one angle alone—the masculine viewpoint—it is unilateral and excluding.

Central to the focus of gender is the differentiation between sex and gender. The former includes all that refers to the biological while the latter encompasses the cultural interpretation of sex (for example, the establishment of differences based upon anatomical categories) and all that is incorporated into the definition of what constitutes the spectrum that runs from femaleness to maleness. There is a general aspect that is applicable to all the experiences or visions of gender, which is that all cultures create, perceive, and recreate the fact that the human species is sexually differentiated, but that the specific contents reflect great variability from culture to culture and, within each, according to specific historic, religious, economic, and political contexts. It is also implicit that cultural constructs of gender, while they may embrace the entire man-woman spectrum, have been generated more from the viewpoint of the male experience than from that of its female counterpart. At the same time the attention that is given in the focus to symbols and meanings is relevant, as is that directed at the vehicles of transmission, such as language, rituals, space, and nonverbal expressions, to cite a few.

In this conceptualization, the definition that I use for cultural constructs refers to the complex of statements, predicates, meanings, and interpretations elaborated from a perspective that gives them a certain coherence, in such fashion that they appear as points of reference for a particular people. Within the range of human cultural constructs this article deals with those addressing the fact that the species is sexually differentiated.

In the analysis of gender it is possible to emphasize the subtlety that may exist in the utilization of cultural categories presented as derivatives or products of the biological, since this may give them more weight than if they were exclusively cultural. Thus the elaboration of stereotypes of mood states of women based upon menstruation, pregnancy, and menopause are held deeply and are therefore more persistent than those which derive from the perception of process. As an example of the latter we can cite the stereotype that women are more realistic than men, as has been stated in several studies, as a result of certain characteristics that appear in the socialization processes.[5] Consequently, it is important to discover the connections that are established with nature. These tend to be produced by means of symbols derived possibly from the human body, or from vital processes: menstruation, birth, death. At times they derive from the components that form part of such phenomena and experiences. Also, they may result from the connection with natural elements: the agricultural cycle, seeds, roots, flowering trees, ripe fruits.

The subtlety that is evident in the manipulation of nature reaffirms the cultural and constitutes at the same time expressions of new cultural forms. Its success resides in the transmission of a whole series of experiences of interrelations, of fluxes, of energies that have evocative power to establish connections, even where they are lacking, simply by means of the evocation that moves them.

At the same time it is important to pay attention to the creation of stereotypes, a definition of which might be: characteristics that are applied in a fixed mode as representative of a person, a group, a collectivity. In regarding gender as a complex of ideas, it is possible to perceive its activation in the manner in which the society classifies its roles and constructs its stereotypes. Thus it is necessary to note that each sex is attributed determined roles which, in the majority of instances, are congruent with the preconceived ideas that are held regarding men and women. For example, the dichotomized roles of male salaried workers/female housewives are often sustained by the perception of men as adventurers, oriented towards the exterior, with public projection, whereas women are perceived as private, defensive of the interior and of closed spaces, and preoccupied with minutiae and intranscendental matters.

The objective of gender stereotypes is that it should appear natural that men are better endowed for certain roles. At the same time the stereotypes function through the existence of oppositions: male/female (the one is seen as the exclusion of the other). In order to perceive all of the above it is necessary to pay attention to expressions, to language. Thus, the European concept of the aggressive/logical/problem-solving male, oriented to success/ambition, may serve for certain situations. In others there may appear the passionate/dominating/changeable man, if what is desired is to highlight the daring and uncontrollable forces in male nature. In opposition there is the passive/clinging/tender/sweet/consoling woman, which tells us much about this society's concepts regarding human nature insofar as it is manifested as maleness or femaleness.

In considering stereotypes it is important to distinguish them from attributes. The stereotype may be the fixation of an attribute and its employment goes beyond its scope and context. For example, a characteristic attributed to Basque women is that of being clean, something which is valued. However, presenting her as always obsessed with house cleaning and with clean laundry, and making this an element in her competition with other women, is to stereotype an attribute and convert it into a fixed characteristic of all Basque women that is charged with pejorative connotations. The stereotype, as something that is fixed and with multiple associations, is converted into a limiting element which in many cases frustrates the attempt to go beyond it to consider the true essence of a person or group. Additionally, it is often easier to invoke a stereotype because it economizes, it saves us from the bother of having to employ other processes of assignation, discernment, and search.

Stereotypes provide forms with which to perceive sex; they are not rules or norms but they can have a normative effect. By hearing that women are diligent, responsible, and clean it is possible to act in accord with the stereotypes due to the force of the social pressure that they themselves exert.

II. Methodological Exposition and Revision

This analysis is based principally on two approaches espoused by Sherry B. Ortner and Harriet Whitehead in *Sexual Meanings, the Cultural Construction of Gender and Sexuality*.[6] The first is a culturalist orientation and the second more sociological in nature. I will describe the first and emphasize the second in order to expound in the third and fourth parts of this article some points derived from a critical consideration of both approaches.

The culturalist focus contends that a concrete gender symbol, such as the seed or bee, must be understood by considering the place that it occupies in a wider system of symbols, meanings, and beliefs. Thus, it is necessary to go beyond the symbol itself, or of the associations that it might have with the masculine or feminine, in order to examine it within a broader system of the symbols, beliefs, classifications, and premises. It then becomes possible to determine how symbols are reflected in the events of social life, in behavior, in the interactions, and in socialization. In this focus the methodological emphasis is upon concentrating on the internal logic of symbols and upon the structural relations that exist among them. It implies the search for the orientations, the premises, the categories that are established and which sustain other aspects and beliefs. An example would be the study that Stanley Brandes conducted in the Andalusian town of San Blas.[7]

Brandes works with popular symbols such as the goat and the snake, which in this area are identified with the feminine sex instead of with the masculine one, as is the case with these symbols in other cultures. Similarly, the lamb, symbol of gentleness in other cultural contexts, is here related to masculinity. There is a series of positive and negative attributes, reinforced by powerful religious beliefs, associated with each of the symbols. At the same time they deal with bodily substances and the origin of corporal strength that resides in male semen, but which is a limited resource that must be protected from the unbounded sexual appetite of women. There dominates a fear that the woman may rob a man of his strength or destroy a family's honor in satisfying her sexual appetite with other men outside of marriage. The attributes of femaleness reside in the blood and may be transmitted, conferring upon women a capacity which forces a man to be ever vigilant that his wife and daughters do not stray from the proper path. At the same time, men constantly should be wary against feminine attacks.

Brandes' sources of data for the analysis are the beliefs regarding reproduction, the body, that which is sacred and profane, that which is pure or contaminated, and that which gives rise to gender-differentiated relations between men and women. Consequently, the author operates at the level of beliefs in which the symbols are contextualized. From there he formulates cultural constructions regarding sex in its strict biological sense, of its function, the origin of the sexual hierarchy, the association of the woman with the home, the female/male roles, husband/wife, and of the behavioral expectations over time: youth, maturity, old age.

Although the analysis of symbolic contents abounds in Brandes' approach, it ultimately remains up in the air for lack of contextualization through examination of the relationship that exists among the persons who elaborate, live, and give meaning to the symbols. Everything is viewed as the cultural expression of a rural society, the framework of whose reality is woven together by internal and external kinship ties and grounded in various activities that are characteristic of a mixed economy. Thus, while there is emphasis upon symbols, to what degree are we able to contextualize them in the cultural universe (leaving aside their relation to key aspects of the lives of the persons who are the protagonists of the study)?

The second approach presented by Ortner and Whitehead presupposes that certain types of social orders tend to generate, through the logic of their functioning, particular classes of cultural perceptions of sex and of the male/female experience. In other more traditional studies the cultural traits have been treated as reflections of primary structures—lineages, castes, classes—and as serving to reinforce such structures. In this approach the analysis focuses upon the actresses/actors who as a consequence of the social context in which they operate, and of their participation in relationships organized in a particular fashion, determine that sex, sexuality, that which it means to be woman or man, appear with their own meaning that may only be understood through the interpretations provided by the participants themselves. Consequently, the emphasis is upon the formal characteristics of the structure and the forms in which the participants, acting within these structures, configure their perceptions of the world, of nature, of themselves, and social relations. The importance is in the ways in which these persons behave, interpret their own roles, and in the context which they attribute to such performance. In this view the conceptualization of sex and the cultural constructions regarding what it means to be male or female emerge from the various strategies for action, or from the analysis of behaviors resulting from the society's social, economic, and political organization. An example of this approach is provided by the Maasai people of Africa for whom the process of evolving from a man into an autonomous elder depends in part upon the acquisition of wives and cattle. In this cultural context a man's transition period from that of propertyless to propertied person is ritualized and has important significance. From the analytical viewpoint of how the actors live, it is this transition process in which the Maasai concept of masculinity is constructed and elaborated.

In this approach the analytical method consists in showing how the participants operate or act in terms of certain institutional norms or rules of the game in which the world tends to be made up of "natural," inevitable appearances. Thus the "spell" of the Maasai warriors may be understood as an aspect or trait of the "common sentiment" of a world view, such as it appears to the actors who participate in social relations organized in particular ways and through the interpretations of them made by the actors/actresses themselves. It is obvious that the process is circular. The very structure of the social relationships (forms of interaction, ritual forms, exchanges) is molded by, and crystalizes in, the cultural concepts that the social dynamics have inspired.

In the analysis of this focus issues abound, such as the selection of those certain aspects of social relations which have the greatest influence in the formation of gender systems. Those which are proposed include: (1) kinship and marriage, (2) prestige structures, and (3) kinship and marriage as a function of prestige structures.

The importance given to systems of prestige, or "social honor," rests fundamentally upon the notion that prestige embraces different qualities and is allocated differentially among persons and groups within a society. Thus, the "prestige structures" refer to the gradations which result from concrete social evaluation and the conditions that are created for the reproduction and transmission of the system and of the statuses within it.

It is difficult to define the ways in which such statuses are established, inasmuch as they derive from the evaluations that others make of a particular person and the social esteem that is accorded such determinations. A status group is comprised of a number of persons who share the same circumstance and who, in turn, are aware of their commonalities. The sources of prestige, both for persons and groups, are relatively few and direct, encompassing: control of material resources (including human labor), political skill, practical personal talent, kinship and marital ties, and connections with the wealthy and powerful. Prestige systems are rarely a simple and direct reflection of material wealth; rather, other elements enter into consideration.

The means of attainment of status are either ascribed, as would be the case with kinship ties, or acquired, as personal triumphs, or derived from other personal qualities. They always appear in conjunction with, or as expressions of, symbolic associations and beliefs that order human behavior according to patterns of deference and condescension, of respect and disparagement, and, in many instances, of command and obedience. Such beliefs and symbolic associations may be regarded as the legitimating ideology.

The importance of the relationship between prestige structures and gender systems rests primarily upon the fact that gender systems *are* themselves prestige structures. The extent to which greater or lesser weight is given to sexual differentiation varies from society to society. While it may be a basic contention, as often happens in simple societies where age and sex are organizing principles, in others it is not as important. Nevertheless, it may be noted that in every society studied to date maleness and femaleness constitute two assignations with different values that result in a greater emphasis upon the primacy or importance of men. Secondly, the prestige structures have a notable symbolic consistency. This may be seen in oppositions and meanings: the strong opposed to the weak; the informed in opposition to the ignorant. At the level of meanings a prestige structure can be invoked metaphorically to support another. For example, in the Basque case the value of children within marriage is invoked to underscore the responsibility of the woman in the transmission of the Basque language within the family. Similarly, it is possible to evoke a disparaged structure, such as prostitution, in order to emphasize the importance of premarital virginity. Thirdly, gender systems appear as means whereby the action of attainment, maintenance, and development of masculine prestige is articulated in terms of the structural relation between the sexes. The relationships between man and woman in all of their manifestations (sexual division of labor, marriage, consanguinity) are designed to contribute principally to male prestige viewed from the perspective of the male actor.

Consequently, in general men compete in terms of statuses that can be identified in terms of categories of roles which in many cases are exclusively in the male domain (warrior, fighter, politician, worker), whereas for women the crux of the definition lies in those categories based upon relationships between men and women (mother, wife, fiancée, sister, girlfriend).

Neither of our original foci—the culturalist and the more sociological orientation—are exclusive; rather, they represent distinct methodological emphases within the broader effort of interpreting and analyzing gender as a cultural system. In both, the point of departure is the presupposition that woman-man/sex-reproduction constitute a series of symbolic constructs irrespective of the "natural bases" upon which they rest. Consequently, in investigating such matters one begins with the question of the meaning of sex and gender as symbols within concrete cultural contexts. Then the analysis proceeds by searching for and demonstrating the contexts in which the constructs "have meaning," whether the broadest possible context in the complex of symbols themselves, as we have seen in the case of Brandes' work, or a particular set of social relationships, as is apparent in other analyses.[8] In the latter example the emphasis is upon the actors, deriving from context the relation between social structure and symbolic systems. Of the two approaches, the latter would seem to be the most encompassing and complex, although within certain limitations. In this regard I would propose several steps that need to be taken. They derive from the work that I have completed with Basque culture and that which I am currently conducting, dealing with sociocultural space and its relation with gender systems.

III. The Extension of Generative Structures of the Construction of Gender

A. Other Structures to Consider

Apropos to the foregoing discussion, in addition to social relations that have been mentioned as generators and molders of the construction of gender, I would add the following: rituals, games, competitions; socialization processes; and spatial structuring.

The reason for considering rituals, games, and competitions stems from their very symbolic capacity; it rests on the fact that the criterion of sexual differentiation is employed as an element in delimiting who may participate and who is to be excluded. In all of this there is a wealth of symbolism which frequently reflects generic meanings. We can cite examples: marriage rituals in which men and women participate, initiation rites (in general exclusively for one or the other sex), games of strength (generally for males),[9] competitions in which external qualities (beauty, grace) are valued and which reaffirm the attributes of subordination and acquiescence (feminine in general).

The importance of socialization processes is directly related to the initial acquisition of the value judgments attributed to prestige structures. It is necessary to be aware of the structures that inform a differentiated view of the world in which women function, of the space that corresponds to it, of their potential or lack thereof to launch initiatives, and of the kinds of relevant symbolic referents. In short, it facilitates understanding of the source of attitudes regarding women which would seem to marginate them a priori. This is, for example, reflected in the common reticence of women to participate in public spheres, contexts in which there is a lack of traditional identifications or role connections with those that most frequently define women, such as mother and spouse. Similarly, women often appear as mediators or representatives of other people's positions, acting out a preassigned role, rather than as proponents or defenders of their own causes. It is necessary to understand the suppression or silencing of women with regard to their own initiatives, ruptures with the past, new strategies.

It is at this point that importance of the socialization process comes into play since it regards, at both the individual and collective levels, the ways in which a society constructs and transmits its identities and roles. At the same time socialization is related to kinship structures and marriage, and the ties that both have with the means of acquiring prestige.

In an earlier article I proposed five aspects to keep in mind while analyzing socialization in order to determine "to what extent the differential socialization experience can explain partially the reticence of women to assume more responsibilities."[10] Stated differently, socialization may explain the extent to which a woman is programmed to *not* exercise power. The aspects include: (1) different expectations for women, both with respect to daily life and future projects, (2) criteria for a sexual division of labor within the home, (3) both limiting and expansive experience in the assignation or utilization of physical space through both work and play, (4) the principal interests of women as they are manifested in conversations whereby girls are identified differently than boys, and (5) the influence of maternal presence and paternal absence in the configuration of roles and models.

Within all of the above we need to be sensitive to whether or not there is differential socialization within the single-parent versus the two-parent household. Included in the first category would be the household headed by a widow, an unwed mother, or a previously married woman (whether separated, divorced or abandoned). In such contexts we should determine if the woman's experience as head of a household has a direct and positive influence as role model for her daughter(s). Conversely, the woman may feel that her domestic group is incomplete and transmit such to her daughter, thereby negatively undermining the latter's self-esteem.

It might be suggested that the figure of the absent father acts as a symbolic referent that obfuscates recognition of the mother's contribution in his stead. In any event, in the case of single-parent families or domestic groups, in which the mother is the focal point without symbolic reference to the absent father, the daughters and sons (but particularly the former) project notable autonomous expectations and life projects, and are more disposed to assume tasks that imply decision-making capacity with corresponding responsibilities.

The manner in which space is structured both expresses and encompasses gender-based differentiations and their interrelations with other factors, such as economic ones, and, within these, the division of labor. At the same time it is intimately related to social prestige and symbolic referents. I plan to develop this point more fully in future publications since it is now the central concern of my research.

B. References to Context

To the second of the two approaches that we have considered I would add the necessity of historical, religious, and political contextualization. This becomes relevant when we pay attention to the emergence of new cultural constructs, and in particular when we study these within or as related to political systems with nationalist overtones. In the Basque case, for example, whether considering the model of womanhood that seems to be generally accepted or whether examining the real-life experiences of women inserted into actual peripheral political groups, one must take into account the impact and transformative power of the ideological elements that are found implicitly or explicitly in the gender system. The symbols, signs, and attributes of the system derive in many instances from the particular experiences of the diverse nationalist/patriotic tendencies.

In the above I believe that reference to context is fundamental. What is required is to take a further step and identify those contexts which are particularly significant when attempting to recognize structures for the analysis of cultural constructs. For present purposes, and with the expectation of being able to introduce additional ones as the analysis proceeds, the structures that I regard as most relevant are: the historical, religious, economic, and political contexts. Nevertheless, there remains the challenge of devising a methodology for linking the centrality of the actress/actor, the structures to which I previously alluded, to these contexts.

A problem to resolve is that of understanding on the one hand the centrality of the actress/actor and how she/he perceives the direct and indirect manifestations of the various contexts. For example, in the economic context we need to understand to what degree the present economic recession in the Basque Country creates contrasting views regarding salaried employment versus involvement in the domestic sphere, or, conversely, whether "submerged" employment, in which many women are involved, is perceived as a compromise, falling somewhere between the employment and domestic spheres, but with no further critical ramifications or implications.

One part of the approach is to allow the actors themselves to provide the perceptions, expressions, and interpretations. It is that which they communicate to us most directly in their own discourses, either in replying directly to the investigator's questions or in the verbal and nonverbal expressions, songs, dress, use and disuse of space, posters, pamphlets, and artistic expression, to cite but a few.

Another dimension which must be taken into account is those aspects noted by the investigation that appear to be unconnected but which serve either to contextualize the discourse or to provide new interpretations of it. In this respect data derived from political speeches or from advertisements in the media may be manifestations of the importance of the contexts to which I alluded earlier. At the moment of analysis such differentiated data can serve as connectors, contrasters, and inspirations of new interpretations when compared with what is seemingly expressed by the actors themselves.

In addition to the investigation of dominant constructions (of which kinship and marriage systems are particularly important) I propose that we focus upon structures from which there may emerge subversive, alternative constructs out of which new value systems may be created. In this regard the areas to examine through the actresses/actors are those related to the marginal and with elements of change. At times it may be that a particular complex is not as yet regarded as "marginal" because it has yet to acquire sufficient weight or to pose a threat. Here we are dealing with "new spaces" in which there are new forms of interaction, role expressions, and alternative prestige systems. In the sphere of gender, a Basque example might be the novelty that results in changes in the status of a married couple such as temporary and permanent separation, or divorce. Others might regard the categories of women that we will consider below. The same may be said of the importance of alternative rituals such as the new forms of socialization, some of which emerge from necessity, and others as elaborations of creative projects.

IV. The Centrality of the Marginal for Extending the Vision of the Elaboration of Gender

It seems to me that in general the focus that emphasizes cultural constructs of gender in the study of women represents an advance over previous approaches, an improvement which allows us to go beyond restrictive analytical categories to get at interpretations of gender that correspond to actual archetypal or dominant actresses. I arrived at this conclusion through reflection on the one hand, and by evaluating the results of a previously published study I conducted with a team, *Mujer vasca. Imagen y realidad*[11] (Basque Woman. Image and Reality) on the other. In this work there is an elaborate model of the Basque woman's value system; indeed it is suggested that values—premises, norms, and attributes—are primary in the construction of gender. The danger is that, treated thusly, the definition of the system of values can then be used to stereotype an entire population without allowing for change or alternative systems. It can become the standard by which all behavior is measured in terms of what is regarded normal and, consequently, to stigmatize those persons who deviate from the preferred model behavior.

The model of the values of the Basque woman that appears in Figure One was elaborated by studying three generations of females selected from rural, coastal, and urban contexts. In delimiting value premises we began with the most general, "the world is conceived as a series of individualized elements in conjunctive harmony," which hypothetically applies equally to men and women. The following generalization was that "each sex has different and complementary purposes" in order to then enter the female realm: "The woman is defined in terms of them." It is this last premise which penetrates most directly the gender-differentiated weighting of the concrete life circumstances of the woman and the obstacles to change that she confronts daily.

Moving beyond the premises to the realm of important activities there is priority accorded to the domestic and familial spheres; her most valued relations regard the family and the attributes by which a woman defines herself are, in order of declining importance: good mother, cleanly person, and hard worker.

Keeping this in mind we find that the general orientation within the system as presented supports the centrality of the woman within the domestic sphere, of her position as axis of the family, of her role as both supporter and mediator. All of this is in perfect agreement with the premise, "the woman is defined in terms of others." This implies that all of her actions and orientations that are directed at finding her own satisfaction and self-realization in other people's happiness will receive strong support, not only because she will feel that she is responding to the expectations of others but because the reinforcement will come from several sources and she will sense sufficient social approval and support. What's more, she can expect other persons, like her siblings, parents, spouse, companions, friends, bosses, and fellow workers, to demand such behavior of her. In the act itself she will receive her compensation, and this will at the same time reinforce the continual reproduction of behaviors supported by such values.

Figure One: *Schematic Representation of the Value Structure of the Basque Woman*

```
The world is conceived as a series of individualized elements in conjunctive harmony.
                                    │
Each sex has different and complementary purposes.
                                    │
The woman is defined in terms of others.
                                    │
        ┌───────────────────────────┴───────────────────────────┐
   DIRECTIVES/NORMS                                         ATTRIBUTES
        │                                                       │
   ┌────┼────────────────┐                          ┌────────────┴────────┐
ACTIVITIES          RELATIONS                   POSITIVES             NEGATIVES
```

ACTIVITIES
- Domestic activity takes priority
  - Proper space
  - Responsibility
  - Organization
- Salaried activity which is subsidiary to the male's and to the domestic sphere
  - Relationships
  - Independence
  - Salary

RELATIONS
- Within affective relations, one's family ties are prioritized:
  1. children
  2. husband
  3. other relatives
  4. friends
  - Mutual aid
  - Security
  - Unity
  - Harmony
  - Continuity
  - Achievement
- Sexual relations between a married couple are meant exclusively to reinforce family unity and harmony
  - Communication
  - Security
  - Fidelity
  - Exclusivity

POSITIVES
- Good mother
- Cleanly
- Hardworking
- Intelligent
- Sociable
- Good appearance

NEGATIVES
- Idler
- Dirty
- Irresponsible

From all this there emerge certain questions. What has entered into the construction of this system of values? To what life model of the Basque woman does it correspond? What is the model that is most conducive to self-realization for a woman operating according to such a value system? With what life model system, with which situations, and with what life projects will such a value system conflict? Other complementary questions would be: why does a woman maintain the life models that correspond to such a system? What are the life models that the corresponding men should have? Can we derive the latter by considering the model that defines the woman?

All such questions were outside the methodology followed in the previous work. Although it embraced a broad frame of reference the focus was exclusively on women according to their age, work circumstances, civil state, language use, and place of residence. Furthermore, it is probable that a repetition of the study would render similar results since it addressed what might be called the generality of the Basque woman and the principal and most utilized contexts in which it is evident. Nevertheless, the collection of further data, during which I have been sensitive to minority variants, now allows me to compose a list of female categories derived in large part from the Basque population, but which in my judgment remain outside the value system that we considered previously. This leads me to underscore the importance that our analytical categories acquire in the course of an investigation and the limitations they can impose upon us if they continue to be applied systematically without any further reflection. Further, we may even through such application incorporate into the analysis cultural constructs that derive from our investigation rather than from the study population.

In regarding the value system presented in our model of Basque women, it is interesting to consider where to situate the following persons:

—the lesbian woman
—the autonomous single woman
—the autonomous single woman with children
—the autonomous woman (separated/divorced) with life goals that exclude children
—the autonomous woman (separated/divorced) with life goals that involve future custody of children
—the autonomous woman (separated/divorced) who exercises rights of visitation with children
—the single woman with an adopted son or daughter
—the lesbian woman who lives with another

—the lesbian woman who lives with another and who has an adopted son/daughter
—the single lesbian mother who lives with another woman
—the nun
—the celibate secular missionary

As may be appreciated, the definition of these women is related to several factors such as: (1) sexual preference (celibacy, heterosexuality, lesbianism, bisexuality, transexuality, transvestism), (2) civil state (single or married), and (3) manners of exercising maternity (real or social).

In reviewing the data from our previous study I realize that many of these categories were glossed over in the larger depiction of the Basque woman; others were treated as possible exceptions since the study focused upon only certain variables. In short, these categories were small percentagewise and were regarded as discrepant voices that served to delineate contrasts or to demonstrate that not everyone was in agreement regarding certain matters. Nevertheless, it is one thing to consider the percentages to be small with respect to the general pattern and quite another to focus upon the individuals who comprise these distinct categories, regarding them as the focus of study rather than as marginal. In this event they may be viewed as possible avenues of change, of proposals, of different values, and of alternative lifestyles.

With the above I wish to emphasize that, in the majority of cases, the value system that is generally accepted is that which corresponds to what the society regards as ideal or most acceptable, which then equals what is "normal." In depicting such a system and determining its supports it is likely that all other behaviors constitute or fall into the category of abnormality, of marginality. Its influence may well extend beyond the definition of abnormality, of marginality as a social concept; rather, it may even cause health practitioners to consider persons manifesting such behavior as abnormal, marginal deviates.

It is for this reason that I have emphasized the need to focus critically upon the construction of gender concepts based upon the affirmation that sex is an ascribed characteristic in favor of an alternative view that, "even that which is given may be changed, even that which is given may be interpreted." If we begin a gender study with population census data we find only a binomial division man/woman based upon the existence of genetic, biological, and genital characteristics. Nevertheless, everyday experience tells us that the psychological identity of an individual may or may not be consonant with such definition, giving rise to new categories which, according to the degree to which they differ from the binomial view, are regarded as deviations. The variability in the cultural constructs of gender that are elaborated in each culture may be expressed in terms of the degrees of concordance and dissonance that are present between such categorizations and one based upon a strictly biological model.

Taking into account all the possibilities, a cultural view as the focus for the formation of gender systems provides a broader approach with which to address health issues and psychological problems of females, as well as those of males. It supposes an openness to variability which then obviates the danger of assigning persons to rigid and immutable categories, bound by some notion of what is natural when in fact we are dealing with a cultural phenomenon. We must also remember that the elaboration of gender constructs is influenced by history, by economic context, and by ideologies.

A woman internalizes from birth—through color symbols, toys, activities, norms that are imposed upon her, images to which she is subjected—the conviction that gender constructs are based upon biological factors. Similarly, she incorporates the behaviors that are expected of her—to be supportive, to seek her own realization through others, to take on as her own others' agendas, to respond instead of initiate—all of which are regarded as natural instead of as forms that have been created and recreated within the dominantly cultural category of "woman." The female identity is just as fluid and subject to change as its male counterpart. It is an invention, a product of distinct social groupings acting in accord with a certain value system. To move from that which "comes to us as a given" to that "which we have been constructing," supposes a qualitative leap, but which in the long run can lead to results which can be quantified.

Changes in the value systems are critical if there are to be improvements in the woman's quality of life. I propose that we must pay close attention in our research to marginal situations given that changes tend to emerge more from marginality than from circumstances regarded as normal. That is to say, if we wish to be sensitive to emerging elements one of our concerns would be the identification and study of marginality. We must focus upon women who are transcending ordinary circumstances, those regarded as normal, and who venture to look for new solutions. Many of them experience dislocation due to the insecurity of the experimenting process itself and the lack of references and models.

That which I now propose is of fundamental importance to the study of new gender constructs originated by women themselves and which may best be perceived by female investigators, since I believe that the new values and new alternative forms are not going to come out of groupings regarded by society as normal and healthy. Rather, the new forms are likely to derive from problematic and uncertain situations. Consequently, our focus should shift toward those groupings which are experiencing doubts, anxiety, discontinuities. Thus, the new values (or countervalues) may best be studied by examining the challenges posed by women who separate from their spouses (either temporarily or permanently), groupings of single mothers, collectivities of lesbian women, of feminists, widows who handle grief positively, and of the new forms of female associates and social networks that are established. In my opinion it is often the role of the investigator to discern which areas of study can contribute new understandings, such as the questioning of the creation of categories, systems of classification created in the present instance by the anthropological discipline, which lead to fixed interpretations. In broaching more broadly defined studies which transcend limiting categories, such as analyses of the marginal, abnormal, subversive, and concentrating our central focus upon these, we may begin to understand life forms whose content is surprising both in terms of novelty and freshness.

Notes

1. I wish to acknowledge the stimulating suggestions offered by Virginia Maquieira and Verena Stolcke in the discussion following presentation of this paper during VII Jornadas de Investigación Interdisciplinar session entitled "Women and Men in the Formation of Western Thought" held at the Autonomous University of Madrid, March 10–11, 1988.
2. M. Navarro, "El androcentrismo en la historia: la mujer como sujeto invisible," II World Basque Congress (Paper given in the session on Women and Social Reality). Donostia-San Sebastián, October 5–8, 1987.
3. Janice Monk and M. Dolores García-Ramón, "Geografía feminista: una perspectiva internacional," *Documents d'anàlisi geogràfica*, no. 10 (1987), pp. 147–157.
4. Joseba Zulaika, "Problemática teórica actual de la antropología simbólica," Ponencia presentada en el III Congreso de Antropología, Simposium de Antropología Simbólica, Donostia, 23–27 de abril de 1984.
5. Teresa del Valle, "La mujer en la sociedad y cultura vasca. Temas, problemas a explorar e hipótesis esbozadas," en Teresa del Valle, Carmen Larrañaga, Carmen Pérez, Begoña Arregui, y Lourdes Méndez, *La mujer y la palabra* (San Sebastián: La Primitiva Casa Baroja, 1987), pp. 145–155.

6. Sherry B. Ortner and Harriet Whitehead, "Introduction; Accounting for Sexual Meanings," in Sherry B. Ortner and Harriet Whitehead (eds.), *Sexual Meanings. The Cultural Construction of Gender and Sexuality* (Cambridge: Cambridge University Press, 1981), pp. 1–27.
7. Stanley Brandes, "Like Wounded Stags: Male Sexual Ideology in an Andalusian Town," in Sherry B. Ortner and Harriet Whitehead (eds.), *Sexual Meanings...* , pp. 216–239.
8. Sherry B. Ortner and Harriet Whitehead, "Introduction; Accounting for Sexual Meanings," p. 106.
9. The study of the ritualization of strength is particularly pertinent for the construction of gender in Basque culture. Teresa del Valle, "La mujer... ," pp. 137–145.
10. Ibid., p. 154.
11. Teresa del Valle et al., *Mujer vasca. Imagen y realidad* (Barcelona: Editorial Anthropos, 1985).

Reinventing Basque Society: Cultural Difference and the Quest for Modernity, 1918-1936

by

Jacqueline Urla

At the close of World War I, a spirit of optimism and energetic reform in both social and economic life spread across Western Europe. In France, England, Italy, and Germany in the twenties and thirties a "New Man" and a "New Woman" that would build the future out of the ruins of the war seemed to be close on the horizon. New standards of speed and efficiency were possible through the scientific management of work, and countries from all sides of the political spectrum expressed enthusiasm for Henry Ford's "Americanist" plan which promised increased productivity without social conflict. This was a time in which the liberal laissez-faire social politics gave way to active intervention into previously untouched areas of the social fabric as part of a firm belief in the possibility of creating a new, more rational social order.

South of the Pyrenees, Spain was generally seen as somewhat marginal, not fully in step with the drive towards social modernization and reform that pervaded much of the rest of Europe in the interwar years. Reeling from the loss of Cuba in 1898, a moral as well as financial disaster, slow to industrialize, with a still strong Catholic Church, and a regime in chronic political crisis, Spain was indeed lagging behind its sister nations. Spain, that is, but not the Basque Provinces nor Catalonia.

In Spain, the modernizing impulse came as much or more from the "periphery" than from the political center. There were of course beacons of progressive thought and intellectual exchange in Madrid, exemplified by the Institución Libre de Enseñanza and the Junta para la Ampliación de Estudios Históricos e Investigaciones Científicas (Committee for the Extension of Historical Studies and Scientific Research) founded in 1907, but for the most part, a powerful antipositivist

Catholic hierarchy had rendered the appearance of the modern social sciences in Spain tardy and tenuous.

By the beginning of the twentieth century, we find the appearance of several scientific societies in conjunction with the emergence of vital nationalist movements in what are often called the "historic nationalities" of Catalonia, the Basque Country, and Galicia: the Institut d'Estudis Catalans (1907), the Sociedad de Estudios Vascos or Eusko Ikaskuntza (1918), and the Seminario de Estudos Galegos (1923).

These scientific societies were responsible for importing new currents of thought and techniques of social reform into their respective countries and for fostering a rich and creative artistic and cultural life which was simultaneously modern and specific. Relegated to the backwater of "regional studies," there is little historiography of these institutions, the relationship between them and with other scientific societies in Europe, and their contribution to social and cultural life in Spain.

The Sociedad de Estudios Vascos, or Basque Studies Society, is best remembered for its role in preparing the first Basque Statute of Autonomy, a document of obvious significance in the history of Basque politics. It is perhaps less known that the Society's aims were indeed much broader. Likening itself to the eighteenth-century Real Sociedad Vascongada de Amigos del País, which had been a vehicle for the introduction of Enlightenment rationality into Spain, the Basque Studies Society sought to rationalize Basque studies and society, bringing them out of an era of "obscure provincialisms," applying to them the latest theories of the scientific world.[1]

The members of the Society were the furthest thing imaginable from the provincial, close-minded collectors of archaic customs and picturesque traditions that we associate with antiquarian societies. Doctors, lawyers, anthropologists, architects, philologists, they saw themselves as artisans of a new society which, while retaining its cultural distinctiveness, would also be reformed to meet the new norms of what constituted a healthy population and social order. Being Basque and being modern were not seen as contradictory. Rather, the preservation of Basque cultural identity came to be seen as analogous to other questions of social welfare (urban housing, public hygiene, safety in the workplace) that were being identified as problems which required techniques of social intervention.

In what follows, I will examine some of the ways in which the two problematics of "the social" and "cultural differences" are related in the projects and goals of the Basque Studies Society between 1918 and the start of the Spanish Civil War. By "problematic" I refer to the way in which the social order and the cultural order are conceived, the problems which they present, and the types of responses or solutions that are devised to resolve them. I will argue that the twenties constitutes a critical moment in which the logic and methods of social planning are transposed to and reshape the strategies of Basque cultural resistance.

Reconstructing Basque Society

At the end of the war, the Basque Country, or rather the part of it located along the Vizcayan and Guipuzcoan coast next to France, was rapidly becoming a modern industrial society. Economically, these provinces were substantially wealthier and further advanced on the path of industrialization than the rest of Spain, which remained predominantly agrarian. Already by the late nineteenth century, we find prospering Basque shipping, metallurgical, paper, and banking industries. Spain's neutrality during the Great War provided a moment of brilliant expansion for Basque industries, as their products enjoyed high prices and little competition throughout Europe.[2]

Historians have shown that this growth brought with it a number of critical social transformations and conflicts as well. While the Basque countryside remained a traditional peasant economy, the cities witnessed a large population influx as hundreds of poor, landless laborers migrated from the Spanish interior to industrial jobs in Bilbao and the ports of Guipuzcoa. A host of environmental and economic problems began to plague Bilbao, the center of Basque industrial growth. In addition, the largely immigrant working class was becoming increasingly organized and militant in the emerging socialist and anarchist labor movement gaining force throughout Spain. Iron and steel workers in Bilbao organized the first labor strike in Spain in 1890, and again in 1903. These were met with violent and repressive martial law which temporarily quelled the movement, but did nothing to resolve the sources of the conflict.

Alongside the processes of industrialization and class differentiation that were taking place in the late nineteenth and early twentieth centuries, a new political force was discernible, Basque nationalism. Debate between scholars over the causes for the emergence of this "late peripheral nationalism" has generally stressed two principal factors: class conflict and insufficient or weak formation of the Spanish state. More recently, Douglass has made an interesting argument that colonization may also have contributed to the debilitation of Spain's internal state-building.[3]

Until their defeat in the second Carlist War in the 1870s, the Basque provinces had enjoyed a great deal of administrative autonomy under a unique system of contracts between regional and central authorities called *fueros*, or foral laws. These laws, codified in the fourteenth and fifteenth centuries, were the product of customary privileges accorded to Basque towns (*villas*) and provinces by the Spanish crown in the course of the Middle Ages as a means of securing their military cooperation in defending the northeast border against invasion. Such contracts were prevalent throughout medieval Europe, but unlike France, where administrative centralization was set into place under the Jacobin influence at the time of the French Revolution, in Spain, the *fueros* persisted well into the late nineteenth century. Under these agreements, Basques were exempt from the basic obligations of citizenship—military service and taxation—and provincial assemblies were able to veto the king's edicts if they were seen to violate the rights guaranteed by the contracts.

Even after these laws were abolished in 1876, Basque provincial governments still retained special economic privileges through a set of agreements called *conciertos económicos*. While Basques now had to serve in the national army, observe the same laws, and the customs barriers were permanently established along what is now the Spanish national border, the provinces had greater control over the collection and payment of taxes to the central government than any other region of Spain. These privileges helped promote the expansion of Basque industry in the late 1800s.[4] Juan Linz[5] has argued that the political, social, and cultural pluralism that was fostered by these regional contracts is responsible for the failure to construct a sense of Spanish national identity. It is certainly the case that this long-standing tradition of administrative independence, coupled with their cultural and linguistic differences, was invoked by Basque nationalists as a historical precedent legitimizing their claim to autonomy from the central government.

While some Western social scientists have looked at Basque nationalism as a consequence of broader problems within Spanish nation-building, other social and economic historians have leaned more towards explanations based on factors of internal class conflict. The expansion of economic growth encouraged by the *conciertos económicos*, the influx of British foreign investment, and World War I led to the consolidation of a wealthy Basque capitalist class which looked to the central government for protectionist policies, welcomed the abolition of the *fueros*, and had no interest in preserving Basque localism. As this economic elite grew in power, it became differentiated from the urban Basque middle and petty bourgeoisie—the small business owners, artisans, civil servants, and professionals—who found themselves caught between the financial and manufacturing giants, with whom they could not compete, and the increasingly militant working class. This class directly experienced the effects of the social problems and labor conflicts that prevailed in the urban centers. They saw the steps toward political centralization eroding their local political power and the protective tariffs benefitting the large capitalists, but hurting their own smaller businesses and commerce. Basque nationalism is consequently widely regarded as the political response of this economically threatened class to the rapid social transformation and limited political power which it faced at the end of the nineteenth century.

As has been shown in the excellent work of Antonio Elorza[6] and Jean-Claude Larronde,[7] Basque nationalist ideology, first formulated in the 1890s by Sabino Arana y Goiri, the son of a Vizcayan industrialist, was highly conservative and religious. It proclaimed Basques to be a separate race plagued by contamination from foreign workers and abandoned by its hispanicized, capitalistic oligarchy. Nineteenth-century nationalism condemned the cities and industries as the corruptor of authentic Basque values and idealized the rural life of farmers, *baserritarrak*. Despite this emotional evocation of the symbols of rural life, Basque nationalism, writes Marianne Heiberg, "was an ideology constructed by urbanites to deal with urban problems."[8] Marxist historians, in particular, have shown how the nationalist assertion of a common "racial" identity served both to repudiate the hispanicized oligarchy's claim to power as well as to split the working class movement along ethnic lines, thereby thwarting attempts to build a broad-based socialist movement.[9] The Basque Nationalist Party (P.N.V.) was formed in 1895 and had only a very small following in the urban centers. Over time, its strongly traditional social values, Catholicism, and antiurban, anti-industrialization stance attracted the support of the conservative rural farmers.[10] With the end of World War I, nationalist leaders hoped that the newly formed League of Nations would endorse their claim to sovereignty. This international support was not forthcoming, but Basque nationalism continued to gain in electoral support after 1917. By 1933, the Basque Nationalist Party alone captured 30–40 percent of the vote throughout the Basque provinces, and several other leftist nationalist parties had emerged onto the political stage as well.[11]

It was in this climate of economic prosperity, growing patriotic fervor, and social and political transformation that the Basque Studies Society was formed. Basque studies already had a long tradition by the time the Society was created. As in many other parts of Europe, archeology, ethnography, and folklore studies, as well as numerous cultural associations, were in existence by the second half of the nineteenth century. Publications like *Euskal Herria* (1880–1936) and regular Basque cultural festivals testified to the growing interest in Basque studies. Luís de Eleizalde, an organizer of the first Congress in 1918, described the climate as one in which there is no area or field of study that is not being carefully explored in order to discover that which is due to the Basque 'genius' in the political and social institutions, in history, plastic arts, music, literature, and in the sciences.[12]

One has the impression of a whole society in a state of cultural paroxysm, turning itself inside out to discover the peculiar markers of its identity. While the organizers of the first Congress praised such efforts, they believed the time had come to bring these disparate cultural and scholarly societies under some kind of single organizing agency. This was to be the Basque Studies Society, created out of the first Congress, which would henceforth play the role of "unifying and directing the renaissance of our culture."[13] The aim of the Society went beyond simply coordinating research; it hoped to promote a more rigorous scientific methodology and pragmatic orientation in these studies. The time had come, said organizers, "for this people to study its grandiose past and brilliant present in the light of science, with the purpose of improving the future."[14] In short, Basque studies was to become a science.

The ethos of the Basque Studies Society was one of progress and reform. The participants fit closely the description Robert Clark has given of the "second generation" of the industrial boom which came to fill the ranks of the new Nationalist movement:

These were the men who handled the increasingly complex administrative and information network generated by industrialization. They were lawyers and doctors, journalists and teachers, artists, composers and writers, the providers of services, such as transportation, communication, design and planning.[15]

Most of the men and women in the Society did support some form of Basque nationalism or autonomy, and several played important roles in the writing of the Statute of Autonomy. But as their work at the congresses reveals, few shared in the rigid traditionalism of Aranist nationalism. There was no rejection of modernization, but rather a strong desire to embrace it and utilize what it had to offer to benefit Basque society.

The desire of this sector of the Basque intelligentsia to integrate nationalism with universal modern ideas was reflected in *Hermes* (1917–1922), one of the most important cultural magazines published in Bilbao. In *Hermes*, writes Juan Pablo Fusi, we find not nostalgia, but

an innovative image of the Basque Country as a dynamic, industrial, urban, and modern region, thereby implicitly rejecting the identification of the Basque Country with provincial traditionalisms, idyllic rural landscapes, and innocent and naive legends so frequent in the regionalist "mannerist" [literary style] of the nineteenth century and in the Basque literature of the twentieth century.[16]

The detailed chronicle of the first Congress in 1918 reveals an exuberant group of participants who viewed themselves as a vital crossroads in the history of their country, and who were hardly able to contain the thrill they felt at seeing themselves taking the future of their society into their own hands. This was no small event; a host of dignitaries including the King of Spain, Alfonse XIII, came to address the crowd which had assembled in numbers far surpassing the original expectations of the organizers.

The question the founders asked themselves was not only "Who are we?" but "Who *should* we be?" It was very clear from the start of the first Congress in 1918 that the inquiry into the origins and forms of Basque society and history was paired with a deep commitment to its *renovación*, its "renewal." *Renovación* was, after all, the dominant theme in most of the writings of the Spanish intellectuals known as the *Generación del '98*. Miguel de Unamuno, a native Basque, may have joined with these Spanish regenerationists, convinced that the "New Man" could not be a "Basque Man."[17] But this is precisely what the Basque Studies Society was attempting to do.

Not only did the participants of the Congress view themselves as shaping their destiny, *they also believed it was absolutely essential that they do so*. Rapid social and economic changes were perceived as a threat to both the continuity of Basque identity and to the social order. On the one hand, scholars and scientists felt themselves to be racing against time to document the essential characteristics of a fading identity. The continuity of a distinctive Basque personality could no longer be assumed; something urgent had to be done in order that "we Basques can continue being ourselves" (*los vascos sigamos siendo nosotros mismos*).[18] On the other, it appeared self-evident that Basques were confronted with pressing social questions—pollution, congestion, workers' strikes, and disease—and the assembled scholars and professionals wasted no time in looking for ways to alleviate these problems. In both the social and the cultural domains, deliberate intervention seemed to be necessary and vital.

To save Basques, one had to first "know" them, to constitute them as an object of scientific inquiry. The Society began turning the analytical techniques of the human sciences upon Basque society and culture, dividing up their studies into six fields: race, language, history, art, education, and social and political systems. Each section had a director, and each organized general lectures to be delivered at the congresses by specialists in their field. In addition, there were also short courses and smaller sessions provided. The first congress was the broadest in scope, addressing all of the six fields. The four following congresses were devoted to special themes, mostly related to questions in education: Education and Socio-economic Questions (1920), Language and Education (1922), Vocational Training (1926), Popular Art (1930), Natural Sciences (primarily medicine) (1934, not published). The work of each section, which continued throughout the year, was to identify what was peculiarly Basque, indicate new areas of research, and provide a list of recommendations for applications of the findings to the improvement of society. All of this was to be done, as members constantly reiterated in almost every lecture, with the utmost scientific rigor. Eventually, it was hoped that the Society would become the first public Basque university with the various sections becoming regular disciplines. In this way, the Basque Studies Society hoped to promote and regulate the production of knowledge in a rational fashion and produce the intellectuals, professionals, and administrators who would be able to govern society once autonomy was obtained.

Leoncio de Urabayen, geographer and founding member of the Basque Studies Society, described the status of intellectual life in the Basque Country in the following way:

> We must be very clear about this. We are in bad shape. We have become accustomed to compare ourselves with backward countries and thus think we occupy a good spot in the world of civilized peoples. This is not so. And it will never be so as long as we commit the grave Spanish error of not knowing what is going on in the world.[19]

Urabayen called upon the progressive intellectual elite to look to the centers of research in Europe and the United States for knowledge of the latest theoretical and practical advances being made in the social and biological sciences. Although unwilling to surrender to a purely secular positivism, the Basque Studies Society consciously cultivated an international scientific orientation like that which inspired the *Junta para la Ampliación*. Throughout the articles of the congresses, one finds frequent references to foreign conferences and research as Basque scholars sought to incorporate the findings and methods of new disciplines, universalistic in scope, into the production of the particular—Basque society. Members were sent to international congresses, critical meeting grounds for exchanging information in the late nineteenth and early twentieth centuries, and formal relations were established with major European and American libraries and academic institutions. Students were sent to study abroad in France,

Germany, England, Belgium, and Switzerland and brought back reports on the latest techniques in pedagogy, archeology, horticulture, fishing, cooperatives, and the rational organization of work. In this respect, the Society operated as both a promoter of Basque cultural studies and somewhat as a laboratory for the study of modern techniques of social management.

The Basque Society's enthusiasm for social engineering is not nearly as extreme or utopian as that which inspired Italian and German fascist experiments in the twenties and thirties. The predominant influence is Le Play and his followers at the Musée Sociale in Paris (1894). What I want to point out is that this growing concern with health of the social body coincides with a new approach to the question of cultural preservation. If one looks at the writings of nationalists like Sabino Arana, one sees that Basqueness was a question of ancestry; being Basque was a birthright, traced by one's genealogy and symbolized by one's last name. One could be more or less Basque depending on the "purity" of one's blood, measured strictly by the number of Basque surnames one possessed.[20] Arana viewed the problem of ensuring Basque continuity as one of protecting Basques from contamination by the *maketos*, the Spanish immigrants who were flooding to the industries in his native Bilbao. Whereas for Arana the key to protecting an endangered Basque identity was isolation, the scientists of the Basque Studies Society advocated intervention. If Basques had survived into the modern age lacking an awareness of the need to take measures to cultivate their culture, it was a "pure miracle," said Congress organizer Luís de Eleizalde. The message that the Congress delivered to the audience was that continuity could no longer be assured without the deliberate planning of their future.

The projects and areas of study of the Society spanned numerous fields. In what follows I have singled out three areas of concern: race, social insurance, and language. The choice of these subjects is not arbitrary; they are the topics which continually reappear in the course of the Society's eighteen years of existence. I will consider how the participants problematized their field of study and the kinds of practical recommendations that were suggested. The juxtaposition of these disparate projects within a single institution is historically unusual and, I believe, enlightening by helping to make visible an underlying common rationality. In each of these areas, the organizing metaphor is a physiological one: that of a diseased body which must be restored to health. Although each area had its own peculiar understanding of what health meant and how to achieve it, there is a striking parallel between them: they all reveal a belief that regulation and scientific study would help to attain both a healthier, more productive society, as well as an enduring culture.

Regenerating the Race: The Healthy Body

The section of the congress devoted to "race" beautifully exemplifies the continuity between the goals of cultural preservation and social intervention. In this section, anthropologists and doctors worked side by side at the task of documenting Basques as a physical type and as a medical population. At the turn of the century, anthropology was understood as the study of the anatomical and physical characteristics of the different "races." As a result, a great portion of anthropology consisted of measuring and recording cranial diameters, nose length, facial structure, eye color, and body type—what we would today call "anthropometry." The collection of this data, together with a growing inventory of material culture, customary practices and folklore collected through ethnography, archeological data, and linguistics were regarded as contributing to the description of Basques as "a perfectly distinct ethnic type that has perpetuated itself in its territory since the neolithic era . . . until today."[21] Anthropology emerged at the turn of the century as an experimental science which would lay to rest the long-standing debates over the origin of the Basques and their relationship to Iberians and other European peoples. Invested with the authority of the positive sciences, anthropology seemed to provide the chance of finally determining the status of Basques through its irrefutable "facts."

Interest in anthropology was by no means restricted to Basque scholars. Anthropological societies were already in existence in London, Paris, and the United States. In Spain, the Royal Society of Moral and Political Sciences conducted a massive ethnographic survey in the first years of the twentieth century. There is no doubt, however, that the interest in anthropology in the Basque Country was especially acute given the legitimation it provided for the nationalist political project. So connected were the nationalist and anthropological discourses that one observer was prompted to remind his colleagues that "anthropological laboratories are not the ones in charge of dispensing to peoples certification of the right to exist as a nation."[22]

However, the anthropologists repeatedly emphasized their autonomy from ideological interests. Their science, they argued, would henceforth establish Basques for what they are, and not what others want them to be (*los vascos son lo que son, y no lo que se quiere que sean*).[23] This position cut both ways: on the one hand, it rejected the dominant Spanish culture's definition of Basques as a marginal, barbaric, or incomplete culture. But it also simultaneously sought to detach the debate from popular discourse and amateur investigators and restrict the authority to determine Basqueness to a select group of experts. What Basques *were* became something to be determined by scientists. Nationalist political interests, of course, did not disappear from anthropology, but the debate over who and what is a Basque became framed as a scientific discourse constrained by its logic and conceptual categories. Mastery over this discourse or, at a minimum, invocation of anthropological findings, became an essential rhetorical tool in the dispute over Basque political and cultural rights.

Few sciences have received as much popular interest or played as definitive a role in transforming Basque identity into an object of scientific inquiry as anthropology. The concerns of Basque anthropologists in the twenties did not stop with establishing and describing the existence of a biologically and culturally distinct Basque. In their recommendations at the end of the congress, anthropologists expressed concern for the future vitality of the race. Here, doctors were called upon to take part in identifying the potential threats to public health in order to propose means to combat them. Pointing to statistics on the incidence of disease, madness, idiocy, epilepsy, deafness, and "precocious criminality," anthropologists warned that these were the signs of a progressive degeneration of the race.

Throughout the years of the Basque Society's existence, sanitation or public hygiene was a recurring prominent concern of anthropologists, doctors, urban planners, and local administrators. Indeed, the largest number of professional organizations to join the Society were from veterinary, medical and public health professions. Improving public hygiene was a key issue at the Assembly on Municipal Administration held in 1919, and at least half of the last Congress on the Natural Sciences (Bilbao, 1934) was devoted to health and medicine.[24] After the first congress, it became clear that a separate medical or public health section was needed to handle the work which lay ahead. However, their common origin is telling and helps to highlight the early shared concerns of eugenics and public health.

These new and threatening problems called for programs of reform, new means of collecting information, and increased surveillance over behavior. Numerous recommendations for action were made in great detail at the end of the first congress. Among these were control over alcohol consumption, supervision of tavern hygiene and ventilation, the creation of open-air playgrounds, school lunchrooms, convalescent homes or hospitals for the isolation of the sick, health inspection, and health insurance. The prevention of health problems, especially tuberculosis and venereal disease, mandated extensive intervention into public institutions and social practices. Doctors discussed, for example, the health implications of child and female labor laws, or the quality of worker housing and factory hygiene.[25] The proposals for reform reflect the prevailing beliefs in nineteenth-century criminology and sociology that physical or medical pathologies were causally related to states of moral degeneracy. The equation between the immoral, the dangerous, and the unhealthy pervaded the thinking of the society doctors and social reformers. Such thinking led doctors and anthropologists to call for surveillance and regulation of previously private practices, including childbirth, wet nursing, and even the choice of marriage partners, on the grounds that these had important medical consequences not only for the individual, but for society as well.

In order to produce a healthy population, doctors and anthropologists believed it was essential to collect vast quantities of statistical information related to health. As noted, it was the availability of records on the incidence of diseases which first allowed anthropologists to speak of the physical degeneration of the race as a quantifiable problem. Throughout the first congress, and those that followed, researchers called for the improvement of the quantity and quality of statistical information, which would permit an ever more precise description of the social body. In order to achieve this, teachers, doctors, the military, and local clergy were called upon to cooperate in the gathering and sharing of statistics on disease and health conditions in their communities. The records of the parish priest, which had long been the primary source for information on fertility and mortality rates, were now seen as too limited in scope. The emergence of mass education and compulsory military service in the nineteenth century gave anthropologists and doctors new opportunities for gathering medical data. Participants in the congress spoke excitedly of the medical exam accompanying conscription as facilitating the analysis of an enormous body of physical data heretofore impossible to obtain. Here were the medical histories, cranial dimensions, eye color, and body types of every young Basque man undergoing examination. The anthropologists wasted no time in calling for the legal right to have access to this information. Doctors also recommended the creation of a *cartilla higiénica*, or "medical identification card," which would allow for the long-term tracking and comparison of individual medical histories, thereby greatly expanding the potential for the analysis of social health patterns.

Finally, the medical gaze was also directed at the schools. Schools, like the army, became critical sites for collecting medical information, as well as vital instruments for the supervision and reform of unhealthy practices before they became habitual. Health inspectors and annual medical exams were required in order to "watch over the health of the students, the hygiene of the neighborhood, and the future of the race, and to carry out that campaign so necessary against tuberculosis and alcoholism that can only be realized through the joint action of the Doctor and the Schoolteacher."[26] In virtually every area of social reform undertaken by the Basque Studies Society, it was strongly believed that reform of social practices, in order to be successful, could not just proceed from above, that is, through law and a corps of inspectors (preferably local teachers, priests, or functionaries). Individuals had to be enlisted in the process of their own reform. Education was thus a central strategy for improving social welfare by having people identify and stop "undesirable" practices where they were believed to originate: in the home and, especially, in the mind.

> A well-directed education constitutes an excellent means of moral strengthening capable of correcting deficient hereditary dispositions. It enlightens the individual as to the risks and dangers to which he exposes himself by taking up wayward habits as well as the advantages of an honest and temperate life.[27]

Primary schools were the best tools because they were able to influence as yet malleable children. The society spent time giving courses to schoolteachers, local functionaries, and social workers on how to detect problems and instruct children and mothers in hygienic practices. Organizers knew that schools would not be enough. "We must ensure that the cultural effort reach the furthest corner of the country."[28] To that end, popular conferences open to the pubic on a variety of topics, from domestic economy, sexual hygiene, alcoholism, new agricultural techniques, etc., were employed as a strategy for intervening into everyday practices. In his address on education in 1922, Leoncio Urabayen encouraged the Society to involve local residents in this process, sending them the written materials and slides ahead of time so that they could give these conferences themselves. "For this, we need only follow the example of the Parisian 'Société Nationale des Conférences Populaires.' " If these conferences could be organized during annual holiday, said Urabayen, it was even better; in this way

> the fairs would acquire a more noble character, and would correct the natural tendency toward amusement that brings the participants to the fair, channeling this desire for festivity toward healthy diversions. Educational meetings would keep the men away from the taverns and would thus benefit them considerably even if for no other reason than this.[29]

The discourse of the anthropologist/doctor had important effects on two levels: (1) that of individual Basque identity, whose biological and cultural features were being specified; and (2) the level of the social body or population that was described in terms of particular patterns of behavior and incidence of disease.

At the level of individual identity the result of this anthropological discourse was to constitute a standard or "typical" Basque. Physical anthropology made it such that one could point to a number of biological traits which were presumed to define and demonstrate Basqueness. Similarly, ethnographers, archeologists, and folklorists produced a cultural dimension to Basque identity, for instance, the prehistoric dolmen, the farmhouse (*baserri*), dances, music (the *txistu* or flute), the art of *bertsolaritza* (oral poetry), and so on. This repertoire of popular culture was first collected with the latest technology in film and recording and then actively promoted by the Society which worked directly with local town councils to organize displays and courses for teachers of traditional Basque culture.[30] These cultural features, almost all of which were drawn from rural life, together with the physical characteristics of the "Basque" head or nose and, subsequently, blood type, have become canonized as the "true" or "authentic" elements of Basque identity. Their legacy survives as the general frame of reference for most discussions of who or what it means to be a Basque.[31]

The effects of this discourse and programs for reform at the level of the population may be less noticeable to us today, living as we do in a world that takes the concept of population and sociological analysis for granted. In the name of the health of the race, doctors and anthropologists were defining a new object of study and setting the stage for investigation and deep intervention into personal habits and social practices. We have seen that this relied heavily on the development of the state's bureaucratic institutions—the school, the army, hospitals—as well as the Church, for both the collection of statistical data and the implementation of reform. Thus, while the cultural and physical features of the Basque "race" were being analyzed and reported in the pages of popular folklore journals, like *Euskal Erria* or the more academic *Revista Internacional de Estudios Vascos*, and displayed in the ethnographic museum of San Sebastián, the investigation into disease patterns and prophylactic programs was leading to the emergence of Basques as a medicalized social body. This new understanding of Basques was located not in the museum, but in the documents and reports of doctors, administrators, and health inspectors; those who were actually carrying out programs of surveillance and reform.

Social Insurance: The Healthy Society

If for anthropologists health regarded the physical body, for Basque social scientists it referred to a stable and harmonious social system. Indeed, the two projects of public hygiene and social stability were seen as intimately interwoven. In the context of rapid social change, class differentiation, and labor strikes, it is not surprising that the theme of social stability should have earned the attention of the Basque Studies Congress. While some of the strategies for attaining social harmony called for a strengthening of rural institutions, the majority of interest was focused on resolving urban social problems and, in particular, improving the living and working conditions of the working classes. Writers often invoked the rural Basque Land as the fountain of a healthy and uncontaminated Basque culture and consequently lamented the rural exodus. However, even though the cities were the source of the greatest threat to social stability, a return to the land was not deemed a viable alternative. "Perhaps," as one said, "it is harder to be a good urbanite than to be a good farmer,"[32] but the solution lay not in leaving the cities, but in better and more plans for social intervention.

Most of the members of the Basque Studies Society were professionals of nationalist or pro-Basque tendencies and strongly Catholic. Many were concerned with the growing disparity between the "haves and have-nots," but none considered a proletarian revolution to be a viable solution. On the whole, Catholic reformism (e.g. cooperativism, mutual aid societies) was preferred to socialism, which was perceived as antireligious and anti-Basque.

For the most part, the Society shied away from taking a political stand on the ongoing social confrontation or directly addressing issues of class antagonism, or "the social question" as it was more commonly referred to. Instead, it focused its attention on methods of improving the living and working conditions of the working classes through two principal strategies: hygiene, as we have seen, and social insurance. Several papers were produced on the topic of social insurance at the first congress, and by the second in 1920, interest was such that an entire section was dedicated to it. The section was divided into subsections on insurance for different social groups: schoolchildren, military personnel, invalids, orphans, widows. Insurance was further broken down into different types: retirement pensions, illness, accident, old age, unemployment, etc.

Unlike the more divisive issue of agrarian reform, social insurance, like measures aimed at public health, seemed to occupy a relatively neutral space. The society approached this as a primarily scientific and technical issue, part of the necessary and inevitable rationalization of society that was taking place throughout Europe, rather than as a political task. Elsewhere, notably in Germany, France, and England, steps toward instituting social security and insurance had been initiated since at least Bismarck's reign. Spain was somewhat slower to move on this issue, but child labor laws began to appear by the 1850s, and in 1883 the Commission for Social Reforms was established to study questions relating to the welfare of the working classes. The first two decades of the century, just prior to the creation of the Basque Studies Society, were active ones for Spanish social legislation—beginning in 1900 with two laws introduced by Dato, one pertaining to work accidents, and the other to conditions of employment for women and children, and ending with passage of the eight-hour workday act in 1919. During this period, the two most important administrative organs for social legislation were established: the *Instituto de Reformas Sociales* in 1903, "a veritable laboratory of social legislation," and one year later, the *Instituto Nacional de Previsión*, created with the purpose of establishing a national social security system.

The Basque Studies Society's interest in social legislation and insurance was thus part of a much larger phenomenon taking place in Spain and throughout Europe in reaction to industrialization. Perhaps, if the Spanish bourgeoisie had been stronger and the landed interests weaker, the state might have been more committed to applying its laws more rigorously. As it was, the ineffectiveness of the state apparatus, together with the Basque interest in maintaining administrative autonomy, led Society member José Posse y Villelga in 1920 to propose the creation of an autonomous *Instituto Social Vasco* to identify the needs for, and direct the planning of, a social security system, understood broadly, for the four Basque provinces in Spain.

My interest in the Society's concern with insurance is not in how it relates to the struggle for autonomy or class conflict, but rather with the conception of society and the actuarial rationality which it reflects. This rationality, I believe, is one which is increasingly applied to other areas of social life, and to the problem of Basque cultural identity in particular.

Lecturing to the first congress on the subject of retirement pensions, Miguel Fernández Dans explained that the building block of all insurance schemes is the notion of *previsión*, or "foresight."

> *Previsión* is defined as the disposition of the will to consider future events as if they were realities, and being aware of them and the contingencies that may accompany these events impels the will to make the necessary efforts to avoid or resolve them,

or otherwise attenuate those consequences which may be harmful. As one can see, the objective of *previsión* is determined by the course of future events and the possible risks which these may entail for human life.[33]

The author stresses that foresight, in contrast to divination and other "primitive" methods of predicting the future, is based upon a knowledge of the laws that govern social behavior. *Previsión* is thus a science which, together with hygiene, its "twin sister," constitutes "preventative sciences [which] derive their basic principles from past events which, when transformed into numbers, we know as 'statistics.' "[34]

As this statement indicates, essential to actuarial programs and rationality was the development of statistical sociology. This involves breaking down the population into quantifiable segments, according to economic or other *a priori* criteria (e.g. class, place of birth, age, etc.) and correlating this with other types of behavior (e.g. the incidence of death, accidents, violent crimes, etc.). These correlations are examined for statistical patterns or regularities on the basis of which predictions of future trends are made. In this way, social programs based on statistics are seen to be "scientific" rather than subjective. Statistics, however, are not simply "uncovering" facts of social behavior; they are actively constructing a new way of understanding human practices as patterned behavior to which are assigned certain risk factors. Statistics have the effect of "normalization"; the individual is known in terms of how he or she compares to a statistical norm.[35] The following excerpt from a discussion on work hazard insurance illustrates the manner in which a statistical classification system is imposed upon social phenomena.

> If we wish to lay down the rules for a workers' accident insurance, it is indispensable that we constitute them [accidents] in precise statistics, so that via an orderly classification by jobs and a methodical grouping of the accidents by the nature and gravity of the lesions produced, it will be easy to determine the risk to which the worker's life is exposed.[36]

The collection of statistics was not simply a matter of scientific curiosity; it was seen as essential to effective social reform. Trying to carry out social or economic reform without this knowledge was likened to trying to prescribe medicine without first performing a diagnosis. The statistician, argued society sociologist José de Orueta, was analogous to the medical examiner:

> Just as the principle *noscete ipsum* has ben recognized as appropriate for individual health such that to know oneself well, the individual needs to weigh himself, measure his pulse and take

his temperature, know the amount of his nutritional intake and the analysis of his blood and its residue—in sum, *know oneself through numbers*—the same has to necessarily apply to collective health, and with even greater reason, since it is only numbers that can give representation and measurement of the actual vitality of a people.[37]

Thus, the goal of a healthy and stable society became a mandate for a particular type of knowledge—statistical sociology. With numbers, said Orueta to his colleagues, "one has science, not mere opinions."[38]

Numbers were becoming increasingly available in the course of the nineteenth century. The first major work on a national level was Madoz's *Diccionario geográfico-estadístico-histórico de España y sus posesiones de ultramar* (1845–50). This work went beyond documentation of wealth and population numbers to include data on crime, language, and customs. In 1856, the *Comisión General de Estadística* was created and began publishing two years later the *Anuario Estadístico de España*. The special economic arrangements of the *conciertos económicos* of 1878 obliged the Basque provinces to account for their wealth and taxes and to publish a Bulletin of Municipal Statistics which provided a large amount of data on education, suicides, savings, accidents, fires, police, jails, and so forth. In addition, we have seen that doctors were attempting to utilize the army and the schools as tools for gathering data on the physical health of the population. In 1920, the Basque Studies Society proposed the creation of a Social Institute which would be responsible for collecting and compiling statistical data for the four provinces. Contact was established with the *Instituto Geográfico y Estadístico de Madrid* and the project was approved in 1921, though never realized.

Describing the social body in terms of statistics was thus the first step in accomplishing the aims of *previsión*. The second step was to change behavior. In reading the articles on the need for insurance and savings banks, we find the sociologists and economists did not have in mind pure risk management. The latter, which appears to be a somewhat later evolution in actuarial thinking, entails the construction of models of social behavior for planners to predict, avoid, or otherwise attempt to minimize the effects of potential risks. In such models, the individual is virtually irrelevant, whereas in the vision of the Basque Studies Society reformers, individuals had to be drawn into the process of reform. Foresight was seen as a way of living and reflecting upon one's behavior, a process in which the population needed to be educated. José Posse y Villelga, a social Catholic reformer, argued that this would not be difficult for Basques since the basic principles of *previsión* could be found in certain traditional forms of fishing and farming cooperatives (*cofradías* and *hermandades*).[39] As one owner of a livestock insurance company put it, the interests of the insurance agent and the Basqueophile (*amante guardador de costumbres vascos*) were not only compatible, they were complementary.[40] Once identified, this "natural" predilection toward foresight had to become conscious and deliberate.

Savings banks were regarded as one of the first ways of building and strengthening the new "social virtue" of foresight. Their purpose was not, like that of mutual aid societies, simply to accumulate funds for future needs, but, like the role of schools in public hygiene, they were to transform social habits and practices. The creation of a new mentality, in addition to policies, was seen as vital because, as in the case of public health, coercion and legal injunctions alone were not considered capable of achieving the type of profound social transformation envisioned. Posse y Villelga spoke of this transformation as a battle in which rebellion or nostalgia for traditional practices had to be overcome by demonstrating the greater rationality of this new set of priorities and way of living. The youth were identified as the best place to start:

> Savings banks should concentrate their activity on the still-forming generations more so than those already formed. The latter are contaminated by social and economic vices that conspire against the practice of saving. The former are free of prejudice and exempt from disturbing inclinations. A constant and direct guidance should be exercised over them in order to shape their will toward foresight, carrying out a task of spiritual formation from which the elements ready to practice insurance in its diverse forms will be obtained.[41]

The objective was not adherence to law, as I have said, but to convince individuals to assume an actuarial way of looking at their own behavior, choosing courses of action in terms of social patterns and potential risks.

We have usually understood insurance and social security as part of the socio-economic strategies by which modern welfare states seek to compensate for the contradictions generated by the advancement of capitalism. Certainly this is one possible way of interpreting the interest in insurance at this stage in the industrial boom of the Basque Country. However, it is worth noting that to the participants in the Basque Studies Congresses, the development of insurance and foresight was not simply a means of staving off worker unrest. As Ewald has suggested in his exhaustive study of welfare politics in France, the rationale of insurance constituted a new political "imaginaire," a new way of thinking about society. *Previsión*, or foresight, was hailed as the "barometer of civilization,"[42] a motor of progress leading nations on the path of well-being, grandeur, and moral and economic advancement. Members advocated applying the principles of insurance to other areas of social life, including the restoration of cultural identity. The logic of this rationality was based upon a vision of society as an entity amenable to administrative regulation. This regulation, different from liberal juridical models of law based on the notion of individual rights, is based on populational norms and is aimed, not at protecting rights, but at shaping and managing social habits and their risks. The principal strategy of insurance is not policing, but planning.

Language Restoration: The Emergence of Planning

In some ways, the Basque attempt to preserve their language, *euskera*, may seem at odds with the picture I am presenting of progressive rationalization of society. This was certainly the opinion of André Meillet, a leading comparative linguist of the period. Writing at the end of the Great War, Meillet viewed the multiplicity of languages as irrational and contrary to the progress of universal culture.

One of the new features of the modern world is that rationality tends to replace irrationality. Undoubtedly languages do not lend themselves to "taylorization" as easily as do industrial enterprises. But the local "patois" are dying just as surely as the small artisans are disappearing in the face of assembly-line mass production.

As they become aware of their power over language, the citizens of this new world which they believe to be emerging out of the blood and ruins, without tyranny over any nation, and by the free but unanimous choice of individuals, social groups, and peoples, will know how to reshape the current linguistic anarchy toward the discipline which tomorrow's universal civilization will begin to impose.[43]

Philologists and educators of the Basque Studies Society were far from agreeing upon the rationality of linguistic homogenization; the section on language was the most widely attended of the first congress and efforts to promote the language received the greatest proportion of the Society's monies. Yet at another level Meillet and the Basques did agree. Both shared a vision of language as *social* practice, something which not only could, but ought to be, shaped according to new social groupings and social interests. The tactics of language reform and preservation, which had been of concern to Basques for at least two centuries, were reformulated during the twenties. At this time, reformers became concerned not simply with the corpus, but with altering the social status and habitual use of the Basque language. It is this interest in status planning which is at the heart of the Basque language movement today.

Basque is the only pre-Indo-European language which managed to survive linguistic Romanicization; however, it has been gradually losing geographic territory. Since the eighteenth century, documents show that Spanish was already the predominant language spoken in the cities and, despite a long tradition of relative administrative autonomy, Basque was not widely used for administrative purposes.

It is common to look at modern efforts to combat the decline of Basque as part of a long tradition of defenses of the Basque language which accompanies the emergence of a Basque national consciousness. Yet such a view, I believe, distracts our attention from changes in the way in which language practices are problematized and, consequently, changes in the strategies for their reform. We find efforts to legitimize, purify, or otherwise reform the Basque language at least as early as the eighteenth century. The first of these emerges in the first half of the eighteenth century in the form of grammars, dictionaries,[44] and apologies[45] in direct response to the creation of the Spanish Language Academy, the appearance of the first authoritative dictionary of the Spanish language in 1726, and the writings of philologists who portrayed Basque as a crude vernacular unsuited for the expression of higher intellectual pursuits. The aim of this early work was to demonstrate that Basque had a logical grammar and sufficient lexicon comparable to Latin, and thus was as capable of complex and poetic expression as any other romance-derived language, perhaps more so. This project continued throughout the nineteenth century when, with the appearance of nationalism, the concern shifted away from proving parity to establishing linguistic difference by purifying Basque of Spanish expressions in keeping with the desire to establish Basques as radically different people from Spanish.

By the early part of the twentieth century, Basque language reform was of considerable popular interest. More than a few individuals tried their hand at suggesting new theories, etymologies, and reforms. This was a period abounding with projects that "dreamed with ingenuous and limitless optimism of a language that would come out of the laboratory fully pressed, renewed, and rebuilt, with a new orthography, new vocabulary, new syntax, new declensions, [and] new conjugations."[46] In keeping with its general orientation, the Basque Studies Society sought to rationalize and professionalize language studies. Its first action was to create a Language Academy,

Euskaltzaindia (1919), which would oversee and set the guidelines for a scientific linguistics. The "truth" of the language was to be told by experts who were guided not by their "passions" but by the rigors of scientific method and objective facts. As we saw in the study of the Basque "race," and also in the sociological study of the "social question," the concerns of the linguistic section were descriptive and prescriptive: to effect a complete and rigorous study of the language as a system (e.g. its syntax, grammatical rules, phonology, etc.) and to develop methods of the recuperation of its use. As Idoia Estornes observes, "It was not simply a question of dissecting and analyzing the language on the operating table, but also of returning it to health and life after being wounded by policies—local and/or national—of persecution or abandonment."[47]

Two of the most important programmatic pieces were Luís de Eleizalde's "Methodology for the Restoration of Basque" (1919),[48] and Julio Urquijo's "International Language and National Languages" (1919).[49] Eleizalde identified two basic goals of restoration: (1) to make Basque a vehicle of collective life and (2) to modernize Basque in order that it become a language of science and "high" culture, rather than simply a language of folklore or religious catechism. In both of these aims, we find a shift of tremendous importance in the object of language reform. Unlike previous defenses and prescriptive grammars of Basque, which were concerned with its internal logic or origin, what was now being brought into focus more clearly was the question of *usage*: who speaks Basque, when, and where became the subject of study and reform. Eleizalde and Urquijo framed the problem of Basque as one having to do with its social distribution, in terms of the declining number of speakers, but especially, its absence from the domains of scientific thought, literature, and art. Basque, they stressed repeatedly, had to move from being a language of the rural areas and the "common folk," to become a language of the cities and the upper classes. What was becoming clear to the philologists and pedagogists at this time was that the social status of a language, more than the corpus per se, was the central factor determining usage, and that expanded usage was more essential to its survival in the modern world than grammatical regularity or imperfections. Consequently, the problems identified for study and reform become geared mainly to the question of usage (introducing new uses) and the social institutions which govern the reproduction of language practices (e.g. schools).

Once again, we find that the collection of statistical data on the population was considered to be a starting point for successful intervention into practices of language use. The Society's philologists were trenchant in their insistence that expositions on the spirit of the language, purification, and fanciful etymologies needed to be set aside in order to take up the serious business, begun by nineteenth-century dialectologists, of describing the social distribution of language practices.

It is necessary that each commune, on the one hand, and each form, each word, on the other, have its monograph, purely descriptive, done firsthand, and traced with all the observational rigor demanded by the natural sciences.[50]

This, however, proved to be a more difficult task than collecting physical characteristics, and the development of statistical linguistic profiles of the population had to wait until the sixties and seventies when incorporated into the census survey.

The interest in gathering statistics, emerging out of dialectology, is indicative of the attempt to look at language as a sociological phenomenon, once again at the level of the population, not just as an ideal system of rules as described by grammarians. This perspective is also revealed in the project of linguistic unification. The Basque language, at the time, had at least seven major dialects, some of which vary substantially from one another, and had no single standard variety or even orthographic conventions that were accepted by all writers.[51] Establishing a standard was considered to be the most pressing task of the Language Academy.

Ostensibly, unification is purely a question of corpus reform. Yet if we look at the debates over this problem in the publications of the academy, we find that the basic purpose of unification was to facilitate the introduction of Basque into new social spheres, especially education. It was basically a tactic of social intervention. For the modernizing men and women of the Basque Studies Society, the standardization of orthography, lexicon, and grammar seemed to be a matter of common sense. Sounding a lot like Meillet, Eleizalde pointed out that the maintenance of several literary varieties of Basque was simply too difficult, expensive, and confusing given the exigencies of modern printing presses and bureaucratic institutions. In discussing the pros and cons of various alternative standards the question which seemed to weigh the heaviest was not which one is more logical or linguistically perfect, but rather which one will be the most socially acceptable to the largest number of speakers, the easiest to learn, the least likely to provoke linguistic rivalries?

Whether for or against unification, the arguments over this issue reveal a growing perception of language as a social object. Intervention into the language was seen as having profound implications, either positive or negative, for the social dynamics of language use and transmission.

The task of language unification was never completed. In 1934, the president of the academy, Azkue, proposed a unified literary variety called *Gipuzkera Osotua*, based primarily on the Guipuzcoan dialect. This variety, however, was never officially adopted and the project of unification, like many of the other projects of the Basque Studies Society, remained uncompleted by the time the Civil War broke out in 1936. Understanding why this was so is important, but the failure of the attempt did not eliminate the strategy. It was becoming clear to language reformers that only those languages which are taught in the schools, used by government administrators, economic and social elites, read and developed in popular as well as erudite literature, would be the ones to survive in the modern world. This new perception of the interrelationship between language and social context has been developed with much greater specificity since the sixties, and is at the root of modern day demands for language planning.

Bringing the analogy between insurance and language planning full circle are the current efforts of language activists to spread a certain foresight with regard to language among the general population. The public display of statistics on language practices and popular lectures on the factors promoting language loss have been just some of the strategies used to encourage individuals to consider the social consequences of their personal language habits, and hopefully change them.[52]

In summary, I have argued that the notion of cultural identity as a subject for intervention and prophylaxis is central to the modern Basque ethnic movement, and that this notion emerges in the projects of the Basque Studies Society during the twenties and thirties. We have seen that, at the beginning of the century, the persistence of a Basque identity was tied up with questions of its biological health and particularity. In the course of the twentieth century, language has replaced race or biology as the primary target for intervention and management of Basque cultural identity, while biological health has become absorbed within the problem of social welfare. Though many Basques talk about having Basque features and continue to think of themselves as defined by their ancestry and surnames, the preservation of the language has become the key public symbol of the struggle for preservation of Basque cultural difference.

The problem of language revival provides the best illustration of how the organic metaphor of the social body is extended to the question of cultural identity. Language occupies a unique place, straddling the cultural and the social domains. In its earlier incarnation in the writing of romantic nationalists, language is an intangible aspect of culture—a sign of a unique world-view, a soul, a *geist*. This interpretation continues in the writings of nationalists. On the other hand, language is simultaneously being redefined as a social practice which obeys social and historical laws. Incorporated into the logic of a living social organism, language becomes susceptible to description in terms of pathologies, norms, and intervention. Indeed, the very process of restoring Basque to health today is called "normalization."[53]

The transformation in the vision and strategies of cultural revival which I am describing takes place during the historical intersection of nationalism and social welfare politics. The liberal discourse of individual or natural rights does not disappear. But alongside it emerges a new set of knowledges and practices aimed at describing the features of the social object—the Basque population—and the cultural object—Basque identity. We have seen a shared belief, whether in public hygiene, education, social insurance, or language, that social practices can be shaped through appropriate intervention, and that such intervention is deemed necessary for the maintenance of a healthy social and cultural body. In this transformation, social scientists and experts have become the truth tellers and diagnosticians of Basque identity and prophylaxis. Again, for reasons that remain to be studied, many of the proposed interventions were not successfully applied at the time. The vision and the strategy nevertheless survive and are central in determining the direction which cultural preservation takes in the post-Franco period.

Notes

1. Idoia Estornes Zubizarreta, *La Sociedad de Estudios Vascos. Aportación del Eusko-Ikaskuntza a la cultura vasca, 1918–1936* (San Sebastián: Eusko-Ikaskuntza, 1983), p. 98.
2. Santiago Roldán and José Luís García Delgado, *La formación de la sociedad capitalista en España, 1914–1922*, 2 volumes (Madrid: Confederación Española de Cajas de Ahorro, 1973); and Manuel González Portilla, "Los orígenes de la sociedad capitalista en el País Vasco. Transformaciones económicas y sociales en Vizcaya," *SAIOAK*, vol. 1 (1977), pp. 67–127.
3. William A. Douglass, "Introduction," in *Basque Politics: A Case Study in Ethnic Nationalism* (New York: Associated Faculty Press, and Reno: Basque Studies Program, 1985).
4. Robert Clark, *The Basques: The Franco Years and Beyond* (Reno: University of Nevada Press, 1979).
5. Juan Linz, "Early State-Building and Late Peripheral Nationalism against the State: The Case of Spain," in S. N. Eisenstadt and

Stein Rokkan, eds., *Building States and Nations: Analysis by Region* (London: Sage Press, 1973), pp. 33–116.
6. Antonio Elorza, *Ideologías del nacionalismo vasco, 1876–1937* (San Sebastián: L. Haranburu, 1978).
7. Jean-Claude Larronde, *El nacionalismo vasco: su orígen y su ideología en la obra de Sabino Arana-Goiri* (San Sebastián: Ediciones Vascas, 1977).
8. Marianne Heiberg, "Basques, Anti-Basques, and the Moral Community," in R. D. Grillo (ed.), *Anthropological Perspectives on Nation and State* (London: Academic Press, 1980), p. 53.
9. Cf. Beltza (Emilio López), *Nacionalismo vasco y clases sociales* (San Sebastián: Txertoa, 1976); Javier Corcuera, "Tradicionalismo y burgesía en la formulación del nacionalismo vasco. Lucha de clases y lucha nacional en Euskadi," *Materiales*, vol. 5 (1977), pp. 103–122; Francisco (Ortzi) Letamendia, *Historia de Euskadi. El nacionalismo vasco y ETA* (Barcelona: Ruedo Ibérico, 1977); and Marianne Heiberg and Manuel Escudero, "Sabino de Arana: la lógica del nacionalismo vasco," *Materiales*, vol. 5 (1977), pp. 87–101.
10. Cf. Jean-Claude Larronde, "El nacionalismo vasco..."; and Antonio Elorza, *Ideologías del nacionalismo vasco*.
11. Robert Clark, *The Basques...* ; and J. Javier Granja Pascual, "Leoncio de Urabayen y la Sociedad de Estudios Vascos," *Revista internacional de estudios vascos* (1985), pp. 353–384.
12. Luís de Eleizalde, "Metodología para la restauración del euzkera," *Primer Congreso de Estudios Vascos* (Oñate 1918), (Bilbao, 1919), pp. 428–439.
13. *Primer Congreso de Estudios Vascos*, p. 11.
14. Ibid., p. 20.
15. Robert Clark, *The Basques...* , p. 38.
16. Juan Pablo Fusi Aizpurua, "Prólogo," *Hermes 1917–1922*, vol. 9, reedition (Bilbao: Fundación Orbegozo, 1979).
17. Robert Wohl, *The Generation of 1914* (Cambridge, Mass.: Harvard University Press, 1979), p. 130.
18. Luís de Eleizalde, "Metodología para la restauración...," p. 431.
19. Leoncio Urabayen, "Un llamamiento a la riqueza que tiene corazón," *Boletín de la Sociedad de Estudios Vascos*, vol. 2 (1919), p. 22.
20. Given the disparity between Basque, a non-Indo-European language, and Spanish, Basque surnames are usually easily distinguished from Spanish names. The Basque Nationalist Party established that eight Basque surnames signified a true Basque, and that at least four were required for membership in the party.

21. Enrique Eguren, "Antropología," *Primer Congreso de Estudios Vascos* (Bilbao, 1919), p. 332.
22. A. Campión, cited in Jean-Claude Larronde, *El nacionalismo vasco...*, p. 122.
23. Enrique Eguren, "Antropología," p. 328.
24. Idoia Estornes Zubizarreta, *La Sociedad de Estudios Vascos*. . . .
25. *Primer Congreso de Estudios Vascos*, pp. 383–399.
26. Pedro Zufia, *Las escuelas de barriada en Vizcaya* (Bilbao: Imprenta Provincial de Vizcaya, 1930).
27. *Primer Congreso de Estudios Vascos*, pp. 397–398.
28. Leoncio Urabayen, "Enseñanzas especiales. Esbozo de un programa destinada a fomentar la cultura popular y las enseñanzas especiales en el País Vasco," *Tercer Congreso de Estudios Vascos* (Pamplona 1922) (San Sebastián: Eusko Ikaskuntza, 1923), p. 142.
29. Cited in J. Javier Granja Pascual, "Leoncio de Urabayen . . . ," p. 365.
30. Ibid., p. 364; and *Boletín de la Sociedad de Estudios Vascos* (1920), p. 19.
31. See Teresa del Valle, "Visión general de la antropología vasca," *Ethnica*, vol. 17 (1981), pp. 123–148; and Jesús Azcona, "Notas para una historia de la antropología vasca: Telesforo Aranzadi y José Miguel de Barandiarán," *Ethnica*, vol. 17, pp. 63–84, for critiques of how this rural focus in anthropology has contributed to an overly narrow understanding of Basque culture and society.
32. Manuel Chalbaud, "Estabilización de las clases sociales vascas," *Primer Congreso de Estudios Vascos*, p. 83.
33. Miguel Fernández Dans, "Casas de retiro y pensiones para la vejez," *Primer Congreso de Estudios Vascos*, p. 104.
34. Ibid., p. 105.
35. Cf. François Ewald, *L'Etat providence* (Paris: Grasset, 1986) for a fuller discussion of normalization effects of insurance.
36. *Segundo Congreso de Estudios Vascos (Pamplona, 1920), (San Sebastián: Eusko Ikaskuntza, 1920), p. 388.*
37. José de Orueta, "Conferencia—Resúmen," *Segundo Congreso de Estudios Vascos*, p. 276. [Emphasis added].
38. Ibid., p. 278.
39. José de Posse y Villelga, *La vida social en el País Vasco*. Lecciones pronunciadas en la VI Semana Social de Pamplona (Durango: Florentino de Elosu, 1914).
40. Luís Saiz, "Mutualidad de seguro agro-pecuario-forestal," *Primer Congreso de Estudios Vascos*, p. 281.
41. José de Posse y Villelga, *La vida social . . .* , p. 385.

42. Miguel Fernández Dans, "Casas de retiro . . . ," p. 107.
43. André Meillet, *Les langues dans l'Europe nouvelle*, second edition (Paris: Payot, 1928), p. 4.
44. The most famous of these is the Jesuit Larramendi's grammar *El imposible vencido. Arte de la lengua vascongada* (Salamanca, 1729), and his *Diccionario trilingüe del castellano, bascuence y latin* (San Sebastián, 1745).
45. Cf. Juan de Perochegui, *Orígen de la nación bascongada y de su lengua* [orig. 1760] (San Sebastián: Ediciones Vascas, 1978).
46. Luís Villasante, "Don Julio Urquijo y el problema de la unificación del euskera literario," *Anuario del seminario de filología vasca*, vol. 5 (1971), p. 43.
47. Idoia Estornes Zubizarreta, *La Sociedad de Estudios Vascos* . . . , p. 173.
48. See note 12.
49. Julio de Urquijo, "Lengua internacional y lenguas nacionales— El euskera lengua de civilización," *Revista internacional de estudios vascos*, vol. 10 (1919), pp. 164–180.
50. Julio de Urquijo, "Estado actual de los estudios relativos de la lengua vasca," *Primer Congreso de Estudios Vascos*, p. 425.
51. Various orthographies had been proposed, the most well known being that of Sabino Arana in 1896. It was later accepted by the Basque Academy in 1920.
52. Cf. Jacqueline Urla, "Ethnic Protest and Social Planning: A Look at Basque Language Revival," *Cultural Anthropology*, vol. 3, no. 4 (1988), pp. 379–394.
53. The meaning of normalization is somewhat ambiguous. It is occasionally used as a synonym for "normativization," or the creation of a standard of rules or norms for orthography, lexicon, and grammar. However, as used in the Basque language movement, normalization also refers broadly to the attempt to achieve a "normalized" social presence for Basque, and thus relies upon a preconceived notion of sociolinguistic *normalcy*.

GAC: Militant Carlist Activism, 1968-1972

by

Jeremy MacClancy

Every space has its boundaries; every political movement has its extremes, peripheral groups that highlight the concerns of the centre and throw its limits into relief—the edge defines the midpoint. That process of definition by location of the perimeter reveals the role of GAC (Grupos de Acción Carlistas) or Carlist Action Groups in modern Carlism. The reaction of the less combative Carlist leaders to the activities of this short-lived organization uncovers the tensions, contradictions, and shortcomings of Europe's oldest political party in the last years of Franco's regime. But GAC is more than just a metaphor for the Carlist Party in the early 1970s. It was, above all, a clutch of friends and acquaintances who, though sensitive to external pressures, made their own decisions about what operations to carry out and when to execute them. The GAC is both a historical symbol of opposition to the dictatorship and a subject in its own right. And in the following pages I discuss both aspects of this activist band.

If fieldwork is rarely easy, studying the recent history of a clandestine gang presents further problems of its own. Some members of the band are reticent about confessing to their past activities in case their comments attract police attention; some, wanting to make the memory of their endeavours shine, mix mild boasting with a strong sense of imagination; some are silent, hoping others will forget; others are suspiciously garrulous, trying to present an informal network of friends as though they were members of a highly structured organization; and always the secrecy of their past operations hinders systematic study. The investigator interviews as many participants as possible, cross-checks, and attempts to sieve some form of coherent account from his gathered mix of rumour, counterrumor, confession, and denunciation. In the midst of this mix it can be very difficult to hear the voice of someone who simply wishes to tell his story as well as he remembers it. Since it was such a loosely structured organization, with some members acting independently or deliberately not informing certain members of the group whom they considered too close to the party hierarchy of what they were planning to do, many GAC veterans have very different perceptions of what happened. So I cannot pretend to a "complete" picture of GAC detailing who did what, how much, and when. I am not even too sure what such a "finished" product would look like.

In the '50s and '60s Carlos Hugo, son of Don Javier de Borbón-Parma, the last pretender to the Spanish throne, and his associates transformed Carlism from an extreme Catholic reactionary movement still framed by the memory of its glorious feats, to a quasimodern political party. It had taken the authority and legitimacy of a hardworking, strong-minded populist prince to channel politically towards the left the discontent of Carlists who felt they had been deceived by their wartime companions. For, in a common phrase, the Carlists had won the war but lost the peace. Franco did not share the spoils of the victorious, and disgruntled Carlists entered the opposition to the dictatorship. They became the only group (unofficially) allowed to manifest its disagreement with the regime, since Franco could not afford to repress a popular movement whose rank and file had participated so memorably in the camp of the insurgents. The annual Carlist celebration at Montejurra, Navarra, became the only forum in the land for public criticism of the ruling order. Carlos Hugo, aided by his sisters and supported, above all, by the Carlist youth, gradually brought the party he had inherited closer to an explicitly socialist programme. Some older, right-wing Carlists did not follow this political evolution. They either left or were pushed out. Others accepted the move, at times reluctantly. Franco's tolerance was short-lived, however, as in December 1968 the entire Borbón-Parma family was expelled from Spain.

A few days after the expulsion, two thousand Carlists spontaneously demonstrated in the streets of Pamplona as they exited from a Mass celebrating the Day of Carlist Youth. Vexed by the expulsion of Carlos Hugo and shouting, "Franco traitor! Carlos Hugo freedom!" they advanced towards the civil government building. For the first time in many years, the demonstrators did not retreat when the Civil Guard pulled up in their vans. After half an hour of intense, close combat the Carlists dispersed, leaving fifteen of their fellows arrested and sixteen policemen wounded. The only remaining signs of the contest were bloodstains on the street, a litter of stones and police helmets, and some hurriedly painted graffiti against the expulsion signed in the name of "GAC."

GAC had formed shortly beforehand in the Act of Bidania, a meeting held in the Guipuzcoan village of that name. The few dozen young Carlists who had come to the gathering from all over Spain, but especially the four Basque provinces, wished to create a progressive wing within Carlism. Most had already militated in the Carlist student movement *Asociación Estudiantil Tradicionalista* (Traditionalist Student Association) or in the Carlist trade union *Movimiento Obrero Tradicionalista* (Traditionalist Worker's Movement), succeeded by *Frente Obrero Sindicalista* (Syndicalist Worker's Front). They wanted Basque autonomy and socialism—"Marxism" was then considered too strong a term. Many still associated it with the anarchism of the Civil War. According to Juan Félix Eriz, they unanimously approved a motion referring to the necessity to potentiate "the armed struggle,"[1] but others claim that this was only agreed upon later. Envious of ETA (which had not yet killed anyone) these foundermembers wished to create their own group. They saw the formation of GAC as a propagandistic act, as an organization which could respond more appropriately than the Carlist party to Franquist repression. To them, GAC would improve the image of Carlism by dramatically helping to rid it of its old reactionary associations.

GAC produced and distributed propaganda (GAC graffiti appeared on walls as far south as Seville) but the organization gained fame because an inner circle of about a dozen members formed an armed commando centred in Navarra.[2] In one of their first operations they attacked the Opus Dei University of Navarra and stole printing and photostating machinery which was used for the production of pamphlets. During the celebration of Montejurra in 1970 this core group of militants, wielding sticks and bludgeons, led the Carlist crowd in charging the police, overturning their jeeps, and then burning an enormous photo of Franco in front of the assembled multitude.

Two months later the progressive editor of *El Pensamiento Navarro*, Javier María Pascual, was sacked by his paper's directors— still faithful to the traditionalist line of Carlism. At first the commando thought of damaging the printworks, but it was finally decided to blow it up. Some members of the commando had already stolen from a military arsenal in Burgos half a ton of material: explosives, dynamite, *fulminantes* (percussion caps), and thirty kilos of *goma-2*. The operation, staged on August 23, was "very clean" (in the words of one participant). No one was hurt, no one was caught, and the equipment was destroyed.

Four months after that success, the commando decided to kidnap the chief of the American military base in Zaragoza while President Nixon was paying an official visit to Spain. The ransom was to have been the liberation of the members of ETA then undergoing trial in

Burgos—an event closely followed by the public. Just when the urban guerillas had completed their preparations, the American officer was unexpectedly transferred. Not to be outdone, two members of the band, Juan Querejeta and Carlos Catalan, tried to sabotage part of the base. After cutting their way through its wire fences, they laid several charges of plastic oxygen against the oil pipeline terminal and withdrew. But the next day none of the papers referred to the manifesto the commando had sent them claiming the action; only one mentioned (and then but briefly) that an explosion near the base had destroyed windows within a radius of three kilometres. The public was kept ignorant of the action.

Disappointed by this failure in getting its message across, the commando decided to implement an operation planned and prepared months before: an attack upon a television transmitter station on December 30 in order to superimpose a GAC communiqué over the televised image of Franco delivering his end-of-the-year speech. A member of GAC, however, arrested in the last week of December, revealed the plot. The operation failed, a policeman was wounded, and the guerillas were all caught. The informer fled to France and nothing more was heard of him until his corpse was found near the Swiss border.

The commando had lost much of its momentum as its leading, most active members were among those arrested during this failed operation. The next year, on the morning that Montejurra was celebrated, two remaining members of the group entered the offices of *Radio Requeté* in Pamplona, tied up the employees, and transmitted a message about the proposed federation of the peoples of Spain (an idea then being propounded by the Carlist party). Two months later, in a raid on the La Pamplonica sausage factory, two of the assailants were caught. The wounding of a female employee during the action, the daughter of a Carlist, caused GAC to lose much of its prestige within the party, and also produced an internal debate in the Congress of Carlist Youth that year. It was decided to set up a Marxist organization, *Fuerzas Activas Revolucionarias Carlistas* (Active Revolutionary Carlist Forces), which was later renamed *Movimiento Marxista-Leninista Uno de Mayo* (The May First Marxist-Leninist Movement). But neither of these organizations executed any operations; rather their members just engaged in debates.

The last operation involving a member of the Carlist commando was the raid in mid-October 1973 on a bank in the Pamplona suburb of La Rochapea by a young Carlist and two ex-members of ETA, who had left that organization in order to carry out "more military" actions. The aim of the robbery, viewed favorably by ETA, was to raise money to fund the kidnapping of Ullastres, Spanish ambassador to the Common Market in Brussels. The ransom was to have been the liberation of some imprisoned members of ETA and of the Carlist Commando. But the three guerillas were all caught and later sentenced to five years each.[3] GAC was now finished, for its members were either dead, in jail, in exile, or militating in other organizations, such as ETA.

The commando was informal and relatively unstructured. If Eriz's often intentionally hilarious account of the commando's manner of operating can be fully believed, then it is surprising that the group was not arrested as soon as it had formed. According to his telling of the tale, its members appear to have had little sense of the need for secrecy. The group often convened in the Colegio Mayor of Opus Dei (of which Juan Querejeta was then a member) in the mountains of Navarra. There they could pose as a collection of fervent Catholics engaged in a religious retreat. Decisions about operations were always made by unanimous agreement. There was no recognized leader, though GAC veterans characterize Querejeta and Massana as "almost the brains" of the gang. Massana, unlike the others who were in their early twenties, was already fifty. But he did have great experience in handling guns. The commando's scant resources came from running a short-lived music magazine, *Disco Press*, and the robbing of a few banks. But the raid on the Navarran Rural Savings Bank in Ulzama, for instance, only netted two million pesetas. And the bank manager of another branch, who—according to Eriz—rifled the till in order to give GAC money, was arrested.[4] Nor was the commando well armed. In the raid on the American base, the two guerillas were carrying a pistol and a machine gun that Querejeta's father had kept after the Civil War. The five who attacked the TV transmitter were only armed with a *nuevo largo* shotgun, a Remington repeater lent by a friend, a .775 rifle, and a parabellum pistol (which did not work).

Loosely-structured, underfinanced, and poorly-armed, the commando did, however, have the advantage of military assistance. These young Carlists benefited, as did the party on other occasions, from Carlists in the Spanish army. The raid on the Burgos arsenal was so successful because they had received inside information. According to Eriz, an officer from COES (an elite group within the army), who attended the inaugural meeting of GAC, volunteered to train young Carlists "ready for anything."[5] Carlos Catalan, a well-known member of the commando, claims that Carlists in the army supplied arms and instructed members of GAC; other members say that they knew nothing of such arrangements.

On December 22, 1968, the military governor of Navarra, General Joaquín de Bosch, was shown photos of the Carlist demonstration with Civil Guards spitting into red berets (an honoured symbol of Carlism), treading on widows of *requetés*, and kicking Carlist flags that had been carried in the war. He threatened the civil governor that he would take his soldiers into the streets if arrested Carlists were not released immediately. They were set free within two hours of their detention.

Members of GAC also made personal contacts with ETA, which was then a broad social movement, not just a terrorist organization. The commando gave ETA some of the explosives stolen from Burgos in exchange for a few modern arms and for training in how to make bombs. Juan Querejeta and his brother, Carlos, for instance, were instructed by Mikel "Makauben" Etxevarría Iztueta, a *famoso* of ETA. In the late '60s, ETA wanted to coordinate its units of action together with GAC in an integrated Basque National Front. But the attempt failed; the GAC commando, it seems, was too anarchic. However, several members of the Carlist commando did join ETA and some, realizing the party's lack of support for GAC, militated in both simultaneously. It is thought that some members of the Carlist commando used the name of GAC to recruit young Carlists into ETA.

Since the Civil War there had always been highly informal, purely activist groups who came from the ranks of Carlist workers, students, and anti-Facists. They combined the activist approach of the *requetés* (a tradition nourished within Carlism) with a progressive philosophy (in their opposition to the regime). There were always people secretly producing flysheets and pamphlets, and daubing walls with graffiti at night. In this context, GAC was simply an escalation of their activity. Before they did not have a name; now they did: "GAC." As one member of GAC confessed, he and his fellows had not yet fully developed their political personality; they were more influenced by their feelings than by their thoughts. Some GAC veterans recognize that certain members of the group were much more interested in operations than in ideology—they liked being men of action. Two members of the commando were fascinated, if not obsessed, by firearms.

Almost all these young activists had been brought up in Carlist homes decorated with photos and trappings of Carlist history. They had sat around the familial hearth (this, another tradition beloved of Carlism) listening to stories of the *requetés*' bravery in the face of battle told to them by their fathers or their widowed mothers. When the grandfather of Carlos Catalan was on his deathbed, he gave his fourteen-year-old grandchild the Carlist belongings of the family (rusting arms, yellowing documents, fading photos) to look after. Catalan promised he would continue the Carlist tradition of his hearth.

"GAC" was both organization and name, a term used by people for their own ends. To most members of GAC itself, the term signified the organization they had set up; the commando itself was separate and differently titled. The raids on the offices of *El Pensamiento* and the American base in Zaragoza were both carried out in the name of *Movimiento de Tres de Mayo*, (May 3rd Movement). The attack on the TV transmitter station was claimed in the name of the *Manifesto de las Fuerzas Democráticas* (The Democratic Forces' Manifest). The two young Carlists who took over *Radio Requeté* during the 1971 Montejurra celebration did not call themselves "GAC." Yet the term lives in Navarran popular memory because both Carlists and outsiders identifed the commando with GAC itself. Moreover the commando was so informal that some members acted independently and yet claimed their operation in the name of GAC. Carlos Catalan used the name GAC for the raid he and two friends carried out on Constructora Asturiana, a company owned by Carmen de Polo Franco, one of the late dictator's sisters. The money stolen, 3,300,000 pesetas, was used to pay the debts of a "critical wing" of the Carlist party, which had separated itself from the main organization the previous year, and to fund the publication of "Informe Montejurra '76," a dossier about the extreme right-wing killings of two Carlists during the annual pilgrimage to the mountain of Montejurra in May 1976.[6]

Generally, GAC is remembered positively because the commando did not kill anybody. When two militants of the ETA VI Assembly were caught robbing a bank in Galdacano, Vizcaya, in 1972, they at first said they were members of GAC because they thought they would receive better treatment. The original Carlist commando may not have accomplished very much because its members were caught so soon, but the name of GAC lives on. It is an easy label with which people can remember the extreme of Carlist activism in the late '60s and early '70s.

For its part, the Carlist leadership did not approve of GAC. It was against direct action, instead favouring the struggle of the masses. Pepe Zabala, secretary general of the party, had many verbal contests with members of GAC, whom he called "his students" because they had received political education in courses conducted by himself and other leading Carlists. When Juan Querejeta told Carlos Hugo and Zabala the day after the *Pensamiento* raid what he and the commando had done, they were both very shocked and completely opposed to that type of armed action. Carlos Hugo wanted Querejeta to go immediately and labour in Andalusia as a worker. But Querejeta would have none of that. The Carlist party put pressure on members of GAC, threatening to expel them if they did not desist. When five of the commando were arrested in the raid on the TV transmitter, the

Carlist leadership in Madrid failed to support them at all, despite the protests of José Angel Zubiaur and Auxilio Goñi, Carlist deputies for Navarra and Guipúzcoa, respectively, in the national *Cortes*. This pair of lawyers argued that despite their actions the youths were still Carlists and in need of legal aid, which they provided. But people within the party ranks, especially the youthful members, were sympathetic to GAC for it seemed a logical extension of Carlism's ever-increasing opposition to the regime.[7] Even María Teresa, the most militant of Carlos Hugo's sisters, called the TV transmitter raid "imprudent but rather amusing."[8] Also, leaders' condemnations of GAC were softened because the fathers of Juan Querejeta and of Mercedes Berazí (another member of the commando) were, respectively, the Carlist chief for the three Basque provinces and the chief for Vizcaya. Indeed the Carlist party could exploit indirectly the fact of GAC's existence for its own political purposes, for it showed that the political commitment of some party members went beyond mere rhetoric, helped dispel lingering doubts that the Carlists were still solidly traditionalists, and eased relations between the party and ETA. In these regards the work of GAC was successful.

In conclusion, both the Carlist party and GAC, in their different modes, maintained aspects of Carlist tradition: the members of both, of course, came from traditional Carlist backgrounds; both attempted to apply Carlist ideals of liberty, local autonomy, and social justice in a modern context; neither was highly organized nor properly financed. Carlos Hugo's brand of Carlism, committed to social change, stimulated people to examine their position in contemporary society. The Carlists of GAC carried his evolving political philosophy of "progressivism" and activism to a point where he could not venture. For Carlos Hugo and his collaborators wished to take the party towards the left, yet carry centre and centre-right Carlists with them as they went. This perhaps overextended social base became a major weakness of the party. Its leadership could not simultaneously support both armed left-wing activism and modified traditionalism. The Basque stronghold of the party effectively collapsed in the first five years of post-Franquist politics because increasing polarization between Basque nationalism and Spanish centralism left no political space for Carlist ideas of federalism. Just as ambitious politicians deserted Carlism for a wide variety of political parties, so ex-members of GAC entered the nationalist left wing of this political spectrum. GAC veterans still alive in Spain now militate in Herri Batasuna, Euskadiko Eskerra, or Eusko Alkatasuna. Separated by the political fragmentation characteristic of modern Spanish democracy, they are now only united by their common memory of informal unity in a single organization—

GAC. Even in their present division, they remain a symbol of their times.

Notes

This article is a first report of a wider study into postwar Carlism and Navarran politics in the last two decades. It is based on fieldwork conducted in Navarra from 1984 to 1987 and funded by an Economic and Social Research Council Postdoctoral Research Fellowship. The information in the first section comes from interviews, and Juan Félix Eriz, 1986; María Teresa de Borbón-Parma, 1979; José Carlos Clemente, *Historia del carlismo contemporáneo, 1935–1972* (Barcelona: Grijalbo, 1977); and *Montejurra* (a Carlist magazine published in Pamplona in the late 1960s). I have written nothing which is not already known by politically aware Navarrans who lived through the dying years of Franco's regime. Among the people who gave up their time to talk with me, I can mention José Fermín Arraiza, Carlos Catalan, Carlos Carnicero, Carlos Clemente, Julio Laita, José-Angel Perez-Nievas, Juan Querejeta, Federico Tajadura, and Pepe Zavala.

1. Juan Félix Eriz, *Yo he sido mediador de ETA: Mi larga andadura por un diálogo hacia la paz* (Madrid: Arnao, 1986), p. 84.
2. Though some GAC veterans claim that there were more commandos in other towns, such as Lérida, I have found no evidence of their operation. Some ex-members state that there were small groups of young Carlists in Burgos, Valencia, and Valladolid who would have been ready to act, but they never conducted operations because of the lack of organization.
3. *El diario de Navarra*, September 30, 1976, p. 23.
4. Juan Félix Eriz, *Yo he sido mediador de ETA...* , p. 106.
5. Ibid., p. 84.
6. *El diario de Navarra*, November 29, 1979.
7. Juan Félix Eriz, *Yo he sido mediador de ETA...* , p. 92. Carlists in villages, such as Cirauqui, Navarra, provided safe houses for members of the gang who had to go into hiding. According to Eriz, one employee of *El pensamiento* spontaneously showed the commando the best places for placing their bombs. His advice taken, he was then tied up.
8. María Teresa de Borbón-Parma, *La clarificación ideológica del partido* (Madrid: EASA, 1979), p. 110.

PART II: Social History: The Basque Country and Its Immigrant Diaspora

Aimery Picaud and the Basques: Selections from *The Pilgrim's Guide to Santiago de Compostela*

by

Rachel Bard

Introduction

Santiago de Compostela, in the northwest corner of the Iberian Peninsula, was a powerful magnet for the faithful from the ninth century until well into the Reformation. The pilgrimage to the tomb of Santiago (St. James)[1] reached a peak in the eleventh century, drawing travelers from everywhere in the Christian world. They ranged from the most devout for whom this was a supreme act of devotion, to sightseers, itinerant minstrels, adventurers, and profiteers. They came from Spain, Italy, Germany, Scandinavia, the British Isles and especially from France to pray at the saint's tomb. Because of the enormous numbers who undertook the difficult journey to the remote shrine, the pilgrimage to Santiago has no equal in the annals of Christianity.

No matter what road the pilgrims took, most were obliged to pass through the Pyrenees. This was the country of the Basques, those little-known mountain dwellers with their reputation for rapacity at worst and unfriendliness at best. Some travelers could avoid the peril by taking a sea route. Pilgrims from the British Isles could sail directly to Galicia. Others coming from the north could get around the mountains and their menace by following the coast south from Bayonne and along the Cantabrian shore to Galicia. But this route too had its drawbacks. The Normans were a coastal threat until the end of the tenth century, so for many the Pyrenees option seemed the lesser of two evils.[2] Still others came from the east to debark at Barcelona and make their way through Aragon to Castile, thence to Santiago. These too had piracy and bandits to fear; and the route through Aragon was so hazardous that many sought safe-conducts from its king.[3]

The whole journey, which might take months or years, was for most a once-in-a-lifetime experience. It was fraught with uncertainty and sometimes real danger. In time, hospices to minister to the pilgrims' health and welfare, and shrines and churches and cathedrals to encourage them on their spiritual journey, sprang up along the routes. So did entrepreneurs to profit from this parade of pilgrims. Practical guidance as to the perils and rewards and logistics of the journey was always in great demand. Finally, when the pilgrimage had been going on for more than two centuries, a written guide for the pilgrims appeared. Compiled and possibly written by a Poitevin cleric from Parthenay-le-Vieux in southwest France, Aimery (or Aymery) Picaud, it was the fifth and last book of a larger work, the *Liber Sancti Jacobi*, also known as the *Codex Calixtinus*. This was an anthology of materials relating to Santiago and the history of the pilgrimage route, dating from the first half of the twelfth century.

Book I of the *Liber Sancti Jacobi* is a collection of hymns, liturgies and sermons. Book II collects the miracles effected by Santiago. Book III relates Santiago's evangelical work in Spain and his eventual burial in Galicia. Book IV purports to be a history of Charlemagne's adventures in Spain, including his apocryphal visits to Santiago, written by Archbishop Turpin of Reims. Because of widespread doubt as to its authenticity, this book is commonly referred to as the "Pseudo-Turpin." The fifth and last book was the pilgrim's guide that is the subject of this study. In the seventeenth century, the monks at Compostela removed the doubtful chronicle ascribed to Turpin from the *Liber Sancti Jacobi* and renumbered the books, so that the *Guide* became Book IV.[4]

The original *Liber Sancti Jacobi* is in the archives of the Cathedral of Santiago de Compostela. This, and a copy in the archives of the Crown of Aragon in Barcelona, have been primary sources for all subsequent studies and translations. As for Book IV, the *Pilgrim's Guide* itself, most published versions of it have been fragmentary, with two notable exceptions: the complete text edited by P. F. Fita with J. Vinson in 1882, and the invaluable French translation by Jeanne Vielliard in 1938, revised in 1963.[5]

The guide is clearly a result of first-hand observation, and it is known that Aimery made the journey to Santiago, probably after 1132. He seems to have traveled with a Flemish lady, Dame Giberga, whose secretary or husband he may have been. Aimery was probably both editor (in the sense of the selector or acceptor of material for inclusion) and to a large extent author of the book. To lend it stature, he ascribed it to Pope Calixtus II; the Pope's name also appears, alone or with Aimery's, at the head of three of the eleven chapters. Though Calixtus was known to take great interest in Santiago de Compostela (he made it an archbishopric in 1120, and he favored its bishop, Diego Gelmirez), there is no evidence that he had any connection with the *Guide*. But he must have seemed to Aimery a perfect patron for his book, being a fellow countryman and suitably prominent, and having died in 1124, before the book appeared. Calixtus had been Count Guy of Burgundy and also had ties with Peninsular royalty; his brother, Count Raymond, was father of Alfonso VII of Leon and Castile.[6]

Whether Aimery really wrote the *Guide*, and if so, when, is still disputed. Many have addressed the question. Vielliard believed the author to be certainly French and probably Aimery when she wrote her 1938 study, and had not changed her mind by 1965.[7] King thinks Aimery journeyed to Santiago in 1120, and wrote or assembled the *Guide* by 1130.[8] Defourneaux concludes that Aimery was the author— for if he had been an editor, why were all the inclusions contemporary, with none of the previously existing works that would have been pertinent? And though some scholars believe the author to have been a Spaniard with considerable knowledge of things French, Defourneaux finds evidence to the contrary in the well-documented attribution of the hymns at the end of the *Guide* to various French churchmen: "It seems that only a French cleric with a good deal of culture could do this painstaking and skillful work of attribution and falsification."[9] Vázquez de Parga agrees that one person (Aimery) was responsible, but feels he may have been a collector rather than sole author. He dates the *Guide* after 1138 because it arrived at Santiago de Compostela with a cover letter (undoubtedly forged) from Innocent II, successor to Calixtus, to which were appended names of cardinals known to be in Innocent's curia that year.[10] Whitehill throws up his hands and calls it "apparently a fraud of the first order, a complicated mixture of invention and false attribution"—but a skillful one, intended to encourage the pilgrimage to Santiago. He agrees with Joseph Bedier that it was probably put together by the monks at Cluny, after Calixtus was safely dead and could not denounce the fraud.[11] However, Vielliard doubts the Cluny connection because none of the great cluniensian monasteries on the route are even mentioned.[12]

Whenever and by whomever the *Guide* was written, we are reasonably certain that about 1138 or shortly thereafter Aimery and Dame Giberga presented a copy of the complete *Liber Sancti Jacobi*, along with the spurious letter from Innocent II, to the Santiago church. After its period of popularity during the Middle Ages, the *Guide* did not exactly sink from sight. But it was chiefly known by ecclesiastics and historians. It was first published in its entirety in Paris in 1882, as previously noted. Ever since, it has been mined for insights on twelfth-century society, art, architecture, history, and geography. Much of its contents must be taken with a grain of salt; Aimery was hardly an unprejudiced observer. His enthusiasm for the people he met and the regions he passed through grew markedly less the farther he got from his home in Poitou, until he reached the absolute nadir in the Basque Country. Aimery's harsh views of the Navarrese and the Basques have not been accepted passively by the descendants of those he attacked. Arturo Campión, for example, says the "facts" in the *Guide*'s Chapter 7—the chapter most damning of the Basques—are in three categories: reliable, doubtful, and false. He charitably suggests that those in the first category were observed by Aimery personally, and that the misinformation was gathered from "enemies of the Basques."[13]

After crossing the Ebro River, Aimery found things a bit more to his liking and by the time he drew near to Santiago, he was able to say a few kind words about the Galicians.[14]

Despite the work's bias and age, it is still of interest to pilgrims and travelers along the famous route, who enjoy comparing Aimery's comments with their own impressions. For anyone concerned with medieval perceptions of the Basques, as well as of other people along the route, it is essential. It serves as a lively example of the "bad press" that Arturo Campión maintained the Basques had from the time of the Visigoths and Franks.[15] Somewhat earlier, for example, a St. Armand, who tried to convert the Basques in the seventh century, was reported to find them "ferocious, idolatrous, given to witchcraft, rapine, cheating."[16] Even the Muslims, bent on subduing the entire peninsula in the eighth century, declined to bother with the Basque Country, declaring the inhabitants to be barbarous and their land not worth occupying. About the time the *Guide* was written, a bishop from Oporto who had to go through Navarre disguised himself as a beggar to avoid "those shameless and cruel assassins, always eager to mistreat travelers, and whose language nobody understands."[17] Aimery's *Guide* did nothing to change these perceptions.

Santiago: the Legend and the Record

As for the cult of Santiago that was the excuse for the pilgrimage, a brief review of the legend and the verifiable history will provide background for perusal of the *Guide* itself.

The legend

Saint James the Greater (Santiago), one of the twelve apostles of Jesus, is said to have gone to Spain to preach and seek converts about A.D. 40. After returning to Jerusalem, he was beheaded by Herod Agrippa in A.D. 44. Two of his disciples rescued his body, placed it in a small boat, and, with miraculous aid, transported it to the Bay of Padrón in northwest Spain. After overcoming the opposition of the local pagan queen, Lupa, and after her conversion, they buried the martyr's body near the future site of the Cathedral of Compostela. For centuries, the saint's burial spot was lost and forgotten.

Early in the ninth century the grave was discovered by a man who was said to have been guided to its site in a field by a star and celestial music. (This is one explanation of the name Compostela, derived from *Campus Stellae*. Another is that the name came from the Latin *componere* (to bury) because this was the site of a former Roman cemetery.)[18] Soon, people from the region began to visit the holy site, possibly as early as the middle of the ninth century.[19]

As word of the holy shrine spread, so did reports of miracles effected by Santiago. One of the most famous was his intervention at the ninth-century Battle of Clavijo, where he aided the Christians in a wonderful victory over the Muslims.[20] Another pervasive story is of his emerging from the waves, with shells clinging to his garments, to rescue a warrior whose bolting horse had carried him into the ocean near Padrón. This is one of many tales accounting for the scallop shell as the pilgrims' symbol.[21]

The historical record

From medieval records, we know that in the ninth century Alfonso II of Asturias visited the shrine, declared Santiago the patron saint of the country and arranged for the building of a church and a monastery, and for the walling of the town to protect it from the Muslims.[22] The first written record of Santiago as a destination for pilgrims occurs in a Muslim chronicle, where it was alleged that Castilians were visiting the tomb in 844.[23]

By the eleventh century the pilgrimage was in full swing, rivaling those to Rome and Jerusalem and attracting up to two million travelers a year. Most of the pilgrims were filled with trepidation or at least curiosity about the quality and quantity of food and drink along the way, dangers to be expected (including hostility of the natives, especially the dreaded Basques), which sights were worth stopping or detouring for, and how long the journey would take.[24] So when Aimery's *Guide* appeared, it was welcomed.

Portions of the Guide *Relating to the Basque Country*

Of the eleven chapters of the *Guide*, the first seven have some pertinence to the Basque Country, and are translated on the following pages in their entirety. A few excerpts from Chapter 8 (describing saints' relics along the way, all outside the Basque Country) are translated. Chapters 9 and 10, concerned with the Cathedral and city of Santiago, are not translated.[25] Chapter 11, recommending proper procedure in treating pilgrims, is translated for its general interest.

The Pilgrim's Guide to Santiago de Compostela

Here begins the fourth book of the Apostle Santiago (Argument of the blessed Pope Calixtus)

If the curious reader seeks the truth in our works, let him open this book without hesitation or scruple; he is assured of finding it here, because the testimony of many people now living attests that what is written here is true.

Chapter I. The Roads to Santiago[26]
Chapter II. The Stages of the Route of Santiago
Chapter III. Names of the Cities and Towns on the Route
Chapter IV. The Three Good Hospices of this World
Chapter V. Names of the Road Tenders of Santiago
Chapter VI. Sources of Good and Bad Water along the Route
Chapter VII. Characteristics of the Countries and People along the Route
Chapter VIII. Holy Bodies of the Saints to Visit along the Route, and the Passion of St. Eutrope
Chapter IX. A Description of the City and the Church of Santiago
Chapter X. Apportionment of the Offerings at the Altar of Santiago[27]
Chapter XI. How to Receive the Pilgrims of Santiago

Chapter I. The Roads to Santiago

There are four routes which, leading to Santiago, come together at Puente la Reina, in Spanish territory; one of them passes through St. Gilles, Montpellier, Toulouse and Somport;[28] another, through le Puy, Conques, and Moissac;[29] another goes through Vézelay, Limoges and Perigueux;[30] still another goes by way of Tours, Poitiers, Saint Jean d'Angely, Saintes, and Bordeaux.[31]

The route that goes through Conques, the one through Limoges, and the one through Tours all meet at Ostabat, and after surmount-

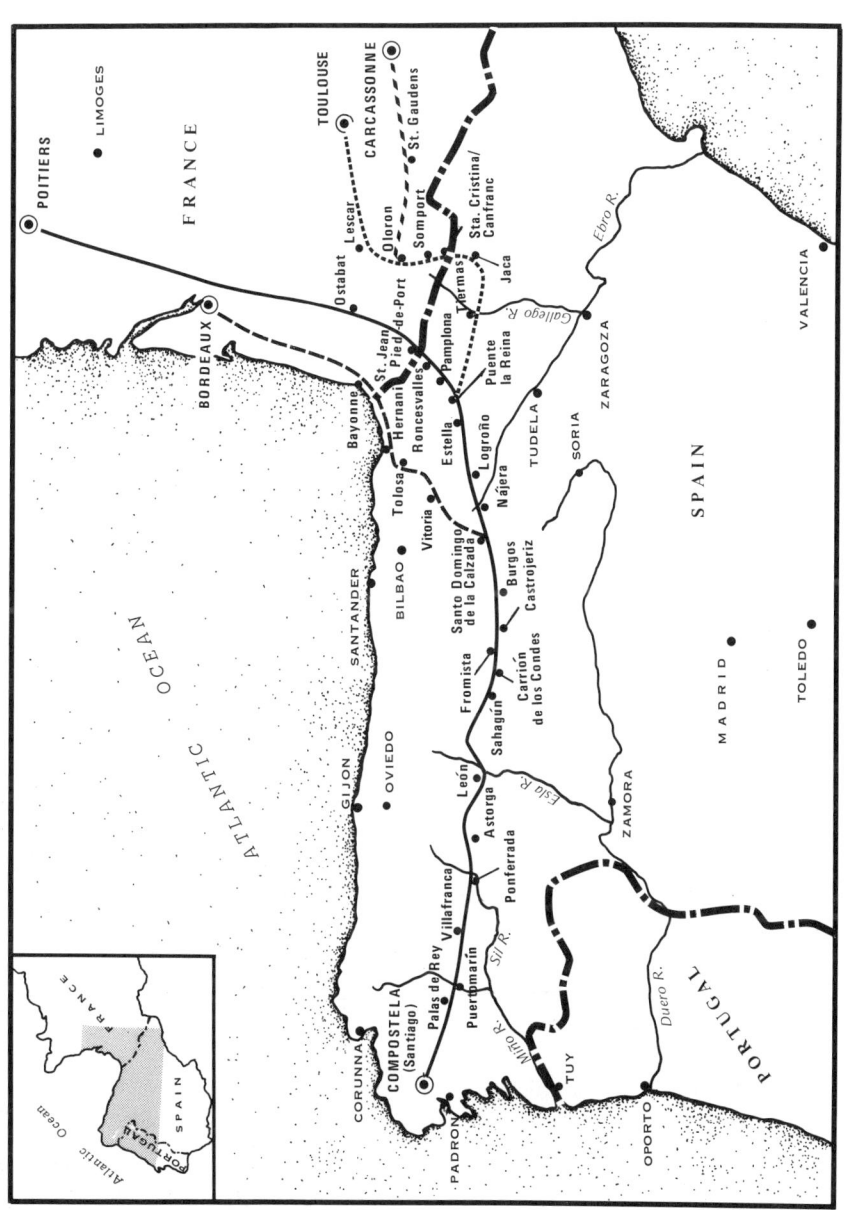

ROUTES TO COMPOSTELA (Santiago).

ing the Pass of Cize,[32] lead to Puente la Reina, where they join the route that comes by way of Somport; from there, one road leads to Santiago.

Chapter II. The Stages of the Road to Santiago, [by] Pope Calixtus[33]

From Somport to Puente la Reina there are three short stages: the first goes from Borce, a village situated at the foot of Somport, on the Gascon side, to Jaca; the second goes from Jaca to Monreal; the third, from Monreal to Puente la Reina.

From the Pass of Cize to Santiago, there are thirteen stages: the first goes from the village of St. Michel which is at the foot of the Pass of Cize, on the Gascon side, to Viscarret, and this stage is short;[34] the second, from Viscarret to Pamplona, is also a short one; the third goes from the city of Pamplona to Estella;[35] the fourth, from Estella to Nájera, is made on horseback;[36] the fifth, from Nájera to the city of Burgos, is also made on horseback; the sixth goes from Burgos to Fromista; the seventh from Fromista to Sahagún; the eighth goes from Sahagún to the city of León; the ninth from León to Rabanal; the tenth goes from Rabanal to Villafranca, at the mouth of the Valcarce, after crossing the Pass of Mt. Irago; the eleventh goes from Villafranca to Triacastela, crossing the Pass of Mt. Cebrero; the twelfth goes from Triacastela to Palas de Rey; and as for the thirteenth, which goes from Palas de Rey to Santiago, it is short.

Chapter III. Names of the Cities and Towns along the Road to Santiago

From Somport to Puente la Reina, these are the cities and towns to be found on the route of Santiago: first there is Borce, at the foot of the mountains on the Gascon side; then, after you pass over the crest of the mountain, you find the Hospice of Santa Cristina,[37] then Canfranc, then Jaca, then Osturit,[38] Tiermas, where the royal baths are (and where the waters are always hot), then Monreal; finally you reach Puente la Reina.

From the Pass of Cize, these are the most important towns to be found along the road to the basilica in Galicia: first, at the very foot of the mountain of Cize, on the Gascon side, there is the town of St. Michel; next, after passing over the crest of the mountain one arrives at the hospice of Roland, then the town of Roncesvalles; next you come to Viscarret, then Larrasoana, then the city of Pamplona, then Puente la Reina, then Estella where the bread is good, the wine excellent, meat and fish are abundant, and which overflows with the good things of life.

Next you go through Los Arcos, Logroño, Villaroya;[39] then you come to the city of Nájera; Santo Domingo de la Calzada, Redecilla, Belorado, Villafranca, the Mountains of Oca, Atapuerca, the city of Burgos, Tardajos, Hornillos del Camino, Castrojeriz, Itero, Fromista, Carrión (which is an industrious and prosperous city, rich in bread, wine and all sorts of good things); then there is Sahagún, where prosperity reigns; they say there is a meadow there where the sparkling lances of victorious warriors, planted there to glorify God, were long ago seen to sprout green leaves.[40]

Then come Mansilla and the city of León, residence of the king and court, filled with quantities of good things. Next, it's on to Orbigo, then the city of Astorga, then Rabanal (also called the Captive), then Monte Irago,[41] then Molina Seca, then Ponferrada, Cacabelos, Villafranca at the mouth of the Valcarce, then Castro Sarracenicum,[42] Villa Us, the Pass of Mt. Cebrero and the hospice at the summit of the mountain, then Linares, then Triacastela at the foot of this mountain in Galicia—where the pilgrims receive a stone which they carry with them to Castañola, to make the limestone to be used in construction of the apostolic basilica.[43]

Then it is the town of San Miguel, then Barbadelo, then the bridge over the Miño at Portomarin, then Sala Regina,[44] Palas de Rey, Libureiro, then Santiago de Boente, Castañola, Vilanova, Ferreiros, and finally Compostela, the most excellent city of the apostle, full of pleasures, guardian of the precious body of Santiago—and therefore recognized as the most fortunate and noble of all the cities of Spain.

And if I have rapidly enumerated all these cities and stages, it is so that the pilgrims who set out for Santiago may, being thus informed, provide for the expenses the journey will entail.[45]

Chapter IV. The Three Great Hospices of the World

For the sake of his poor, God has established three great sources of aid for them in this world: the hospice of Jerusalem, the hospice of Mont-Joux,[46] and the hospice of Santa Cristina at Somport. These hospices have been placed where they were necessary; these are the sacred places, the houses of God for the comfort of the saintly pilgrims, the repose of the indigent, the consolation of the sick, the salvation of the dead, aid to the living.

Those who built these blessed residences will inherit, without any doubt, whoever they are, the Kingdom of God.

Chapter V. Names of Some Who Have Worked on Road Upkeep on the Road to Santiago, [by] Aimery[47]

Here are the names of some *routiers*[48] who, in the time of Diego, archbishop of Santiago;[49] and of Alfonso, emperor of Spain and Galicia;[50] and of Pope Calixtus, repaired the road of Santiago, from Rabanal to the bridge over the Miño, for the love of God and of Santiago, before the year 1120,[51] during the reign of Alfonso of Aragon[52] and of Louis the Fat, king of the Gauls:[53]

Andre, Roger, Avit, Fortus, Arnauld, Etienne, Pierre,[54] who rebuilt the bridge over the Miño that had been destroyed by Queen Urraca.[55]

May the souls of these men and those who aided them repose in eternal peace!

Chapter VI. Good and Bad Rivers To Be Found on the Road to Santiago, by Pope Calixtus

These are the rivers that are found from the Pass of Cize and Somport to Santiago: from Somport, a healthful river called the Aragon descends, which waters Spain; from the Pass of Cize there flows a salubrious river which many call the Runa, and which goes through Pamplona. At Puente la Reina the Arga and the Runa run together. At a place called Lorca, to the east, runs a river known as the salty brook; there, guard against drinking from it or watering your horse; for this river kills.[56] Along its banks, while we were going to Santiago, we found two Navarrese seated and sharpening their knives; it was their custom to skin the pilgrims' mounts who drink of this water and then die. To our questions, they replied deceitfully that the water was good and potable; we then let our horses drink of it, and immediately two of them died, and these fellows flayed them on the spot.

The water of the River Ega, at Estella, is sweet, healthful, and excellent. The town called Los Arcos has a river with deadly water; and beyond Los Arcos, that is, between Los Arcos and the first hospice, runs a river that is fatal to horses and men who drink from it. Near a village called Turres, in Navarrese territory, runs another river which will kill horses and men who drink of it. From there, to a village called Covas, runs still another deadly river.

The great River Ebro runs through Logroño. Its water is good, and it abounds in fish. All the rivers from Estella to Logroño are dangerous for men and horses to drink, and their fish are poisonous to those who eat them, whether it is a case of the fish popularly called *barbeau* (barbel) or the one which the Poitevins call *alose* and the Italians *clipia* (shad) or the eel, or the tench, you should never eat them anywhere in Spain or Galicia because, beyond a doubt, you will either die soon after, or you will fall ill. If by chance someone eats them and does not become sick, it is because he is healthier than other people or perhaps he is acclimated by having lived long in the country. All the fish and beef and pork in all Spain and Galicia make strangers ill.

As for the rivers with sweet and healthful waters, this is how they are commonly called: the Pisuerga which passes through Itero del Castillo, the Carrión which flows through Carrión de los Condes, the Cea at Sahagún, the Esla at Mansilla, the Porma which is bridged by a great bridge between Mansilla and León, the Torío, which flows to León below the Camp of the Jews, the Bernesgua which passes near the same city on the other side, that is to say toward Astorga; the Sil which waters Ponferrada in a verdant valley, the Cua which passes through Cacabelos, the Burbia which runs into the Valcarce, the Miño which flows through Puertomarin; and a certain river that flows through a wooded area two miles from the city of Santiago. This place is called Lava-Mentula[57] because there, French pilgrims going to Santiago are in the habit, for love of the apostle, of washing themselves—not just partially, but cleansing the whole body of soil, after stripping off their garments.

The river of the Sar that flows between Monte del Gozo and the city of Santiago is held to be healthy; and also, the Sarela which flows from the other side of the city toward the west is likewise reputed to be healthy.

I have thus described these rivers so that pilgrims going to Santiago will be careful not to drink dangerous waters, and will be able to choose those which are safe for them and their animals.

Chapter VII. Names of the Countries that the Road to Santiago Goes Through, and the Character of their Inhabitants

Going to Santiago by the route of Toulouse, after having crossed the Garonne, one enters the Gascon country; and next, having surmounted the pass of Somport, one enters Aragon, and then comes to Navarre, and the bridge over the Arga and beyond.

But if one takes the route of the Pass of Cize, after Tours, one comes to the Poitevin country, fertile and pleasant and delightful. The Poitevins are vigorous people and good warriors, skilled at handling bows and arrows and lances of war, courageous at the battlefront, swift riders, elegant in their dress, handsome, witty, very generous, very hospitable.

Next you come to the land of St. Onge; from there, after crossing an inlet of the sea and the Garonne, you arrive in Bordelais country, where the wine is excellent, fish are abundant, but the language is rough. Those of St. Onge indeed have a coarse way of speaking, but that of the Bordelais is even worse.

Next come three tiring days of traveling through Les Landes of the Bordelais country.

This is a desolate region, with nothing to recommend it; no bread, or wine, or meat, or fish, or water, or springs; villages are rare on this sandy plain—which, however, has plenty of honey, millet, panicgrass, and swine.

If by chance you travel through Les Landes in summer, take care to protect your face from the enormous flies that swarm there, especially toward the south, and which are called wasps or gadflies; and if you do not watch your step carefully, you will plunge to the knees in the sea sands that are taking over the land.

After passing through this country one finds Gascony, rich in white bread and excellent red wine; it is clothed with forests and meadows, and has pure rivers and springs. The Gascons are empty-headed, talkative, mocking, debauched, drunkards, gluttonous, dressed in rags, and penniless; however, they are well trained in combat and remarkable for their hospitality to the poor. Seated around the fire, they habitually eat without a table and drink from the same cup. They eat a great deal, drink hard, and are poorly dressed; they are not ashamed about all going to bed together on a thin pallet of rotting straw, the servants along with the master and mistress.

Leaving this country, the route of Santiago crosses two rivers that flow hard by the village of Saint Jean de Sorde, one at the right, the other at the left;[58] the former is called a stream, the other a river; it is impossible to cross them any way but in a boat. Cursed be their boatmen! Indeed, though these rivers are not very wide, still these boatmen customarily demand a coin from everyone they transport to the other side—the poor as well as the rich; and for a horse, they scandalously extort four.

The boat is small, made of a single tree trunk, and can hardly carry the horses; when you get aboard, be careful not to fall in the water. You will do well to hold your horse by the bridle, behind you and in the water, outside the boat, and not to embark unless there are only a few passengers; for if the boat is overloaded, it soon capsizes.

Often, after receiving the money, the ferrymen take aboard such a large number of pilgrims that the boat turns over and the pilgrims are drowned; and then the boatmen wickedly rejoice after despoiling their bodies.

Next, in the vicinity of the Pass of Cize, is found the Basque Country, with the great city of Bayonne situated toward the north, on the sea. In this land they speak a barbarous language; the country is wooded, mountainous, lacking bread, wine, and food of all sorts; but one finds, in compensation, apples, cider,[59] and milk.

In this country there are evil toll collectors, notably near the Pass of Cize, in the town called Ostabat, at St. Jean and St. Michel Pied de Port; really, they should be sent to the devil. They greet the pilgrims with two or three sticks to extort an unjust tribute by force, and if some traveler refuses their demand and does not give them money, they beat him with their clubs and snatch the tax from him while abusing him and searching even in his breeches. They are ferocious people and the land they inhabit is also hostile, due to its forests and its wildness; the ferocity of the people's faces, likewise their barbarous way of talking, throw terror into the hearts of those who look on them. Although they properly should not exact a tax from anyone except merchants, they unjustly collect it from pilgrims and all other travelers. When the usual tax on some item should be, say, four or six sous, they demand eight or twelve—that is, double.

This is why we earnestly request that these toll-collectors, as well as the king of Aragon and the other rich men to whom they deliver money from this tribute, and all those in league with them: Raymond de Solis, Vivien d'Aigremont, the viscount of St. Michel, together with all their posterity to come, as well as the aforementioned ferrymen and Arnauld de Guinia with his posterity and likewise the other lords of the aforementioned waterways who unjustly receive from the ferrymen the price of the passage, and also the priests who, knowing this, still administer the Penitence and the Eucharist to them and celebrate divine office for them or receive them in the church— we earnestly request that all these men, until they make atonement by a long public penitence and moderate the tribute that they exact, be given a sentence of excommunication, published not only in the episcopal see of their own country, but also in the basilica of Santiago, in the presence of the pilgrims. And if it should happen that a prelate, whoever he may be, wishes through benevolence or self-interest to pardon them, may he be struck down with the sword of anathema.[60]

A public announcement must be made that these toll collectors may not under any circumstances exact tribute of any kind from the pilgrims, and that the boatmen must not charge double for the passage, but only one farthing if the traveler is rich; for a horse, one coin; and if the traveler is poor, nothing at all.[61]

And in addition, the ferrymen should be obliged to have large boats with plenty of room for men and their mounts.

In the Basque Country, the road to Santiago goes over a remarkable mountain called Port de Cize—perhaps because it is the gateway to Spain, perhaps because it is by way of this mountain that merchandise is transported from one country to the other.[62] To get across it, there are eight miles to ascend and as many to descend. This mountain is so high that it seems to reach the heavens; he who makes the ascent can well believe that he could stretch his hand up and touch the sky. From the summit one can see the Sea of Britain and the western sea,[63] and the frontiers of three countries: Castile, Aragon, and France. At the summit of the mountain is a site called the Cross of Charles because it was here that Charlemagne and his armies, while going to Spain, built a road with hatchets, pickaxes, mattocks, and other tools. And here, the first thing he did was to raise a symbolic cross to the Lord, and then kneel, turning toward Galicia, and address a prayer to God and Santiago. And still, pilgrims who arrive here are accustomed to bend the knee and pray, while turned toward the country of Santiago; and everyone plants his cross like a standard. You may see some thousand crosses hereabouts. This is because the place is the first station for prayer on the road to Santiago.

It was on this mountain, before Christianity had spread out through Spain, that the impious Navarrese and the Basques would not only rob the pilgrims going to Santiago, but would also "ride" them as if they were donkeys, and bring about their death.

Near this mountain toward the north is a valley called Val Carlos, where Charlemagne and his armies took refuge after the disastrous defeat at Roncesvalles. Many pilgrims to Santiago take this route, if they do not wish to climb the mountain.[64]

Next, descending from the peak, one finds the hospice and the church, in which is preserved the rock which Roland, that superhuman hero, split down the middle with three strokes of his sword. Next comes Roncesvalles, where long ago the great battle took place in which the king Marsile, Roland, and Olivier with 40,000 other warriors,[65] Christian and Saracen, met their death.[66]

After passing through this valley, one enters the Navarrese country, where there is no lack of bread, or wine, or milk, or cattle. The Navarrese and the Basques resemble each other and have the same characteristics in their ways of eating, dressing, and talking, but the Basques' faces are paler than those of the Navarrese.

The Navarrese wear garments that are black and short, stopping at the knee, in the Scottish style; they have shoes that they call *lavarcas*, made of an unfinished leather with the hair still on, which they attach around their feet with cords, but which cover only the soles of the feet, leaving the upper part bare. They wear dark-colored woolen cloaks, which reach to the elbow, fringed like a monk's robe, which they call *saies*.[67] These people are ill-clothed and their manner of eating and drinking is unpleasant; among the Navarrese, the whole household—servant and master and mistress—all eat together from the same pot, and with their hands at that!—without using any spoons; and they all drink from the same cup.[68] Watching them eat, you might imagine yourself observing ravenous dogs or pigs devouring their food; listening to their talk is like hearing dogs bark. Their language is completely barbarous. They call God, *Urcia*; the Mother of God, *Andrea Maria*; bread, *orgui*; wine, *ardum*; meat, *aragui*; fish, *araign*; a house, *echea*; the master of the house, *iaona*; the mistress, *andrea*; the church, *elicera*; the priest, *bela terra* (which means beautiful land); wheat, *gari*; water, *uric*; the king, *eregui*; Santiago, *Jaona domne Jacua*.[69]

They are a barbarous people, different from all others both in their customs and in their race; full of wickedness, swarthy, ugly-faced, debauched, perverse, perfidious, disloyal, corrupt, voluptuous, drunken, skilled at all kinds of violence, ferocious and savage, dishonest and false, impious and rude, cruel and quarrelsome, entirely uncultivated, fully instructed in every vice and iniquity. They are like the Gètes[70] and the Saracens in their malice, and are in every respect the enemies of our people of France. For a single penny, a Navarrese or a Basque will kill a Frenchman if he can. In certain regions of their country, in Vizcaya and Alava, when the Navarrese are in heat, the man displays to the woman and the woman to the man that which they ought to hide. The Navarrese fornicate scandalously with animals; they say a Navarrese man will put a chastity belt on his she-mule and his mare so that no one but himself may enjoy them. Women, as well as mules, are at the mercy of his debauchery.

This explains why all forewarned people condemn the Navarrese. However, they perform well on the battlefield, though they are not very good at assaulting fortified places; they pay their tithes regularly, and they are accustomed to making offerings to the church; every day, in fact, when he goes to church, the Navarrese offers bread, wine, wheat, or something else to God.

Wherever you see the Navarrese or the Basque, he is wearing a horn hung around his neck like a hunter, and he usually has in his hand two or three javelins, which he calls *auconas*.[71] And when he enters his house or is approaching it, he whistles like a kite, and when he is in his secret places or hiding alone to keep watch, and wishes to call his companions, either he imitates the hooting of an owl, or he howls like a wolf.

It is commonly said that the Basques have descended from the same race as the Scots because they resemble them in customs and traits. They say Julius Caesar sent three peoples to Spain: the Nubians,[72] the Scots, and the pusillanimous people of Cornwall,[73] to make war on the people of Spain because they had refused to pay him tribute; he ordered them to slay by the sword all the men, sparing only the women. These invaders came by sea, landed in this country and after demolishing their own ships, by fire and sword they laid waste the land from Barcelona to Zaragoza and from Bayonne to Mount Oca. They could go no farther because the Castilians united to drive them from their land. Having fled, they reached the mountains which are between Nájera, Pamplona, and Bayonne, along the sea in the lands of Vizcaya and Alava. Here they settled, building many fortresses and killing all the males. Taking the women by force, they had children by them who were later called Navarrese; thus is explained the interpretation of the name Navarrese as *non verus* (not true), for they were not the issue of a pure race or a legitimate stock. Or the Navarrese may have taken their name first from a city called Naddaver, which is in the country from which they came originally; this city was, in the earliest times, converted to the Lord by the preaching of the blessed Matthew, apostle and evangelist.

After this country one goes through the forest of Oca and toward Burgos, through Spanish territory, namely Castile and its countryside.[74] This is a wealthy land, with gold and silver; it produces plenty of forage and powerful horses; and bread, wine, meat, fish, milk, and honey are abundant. However, it has very few trees and it is peopled with wicked and vicious inhabitants.

Next, once one has passed through the country of León and the cols of Mt. Irago and Mt. Cebrero, one comes to Galicia. Here, the land is wooded, watered with rivers, well provided with meadows and orchards. The fruit is good and the springs are pure, but cities, villages, and cultivated fields are rare; wheaten bread and wine are in poor supply; but there are plenty of rye bread and cider, cattle and riding animals, milk and honey; the fish caught from the sea are enormous, but few in number;[75] and gold, silver, textiles, furs, and other rich goods are abundant there as well as splendid wares obtained from the Saracens.

The people of Galicia are, more than any of the other uncultured people of Spain, those who most nearly approximate our French in their customs, but they are said to be inclined to anger and wrangling.

Chapter VIII. Holy Bodies of the Saints along the Road to Santiago, which Pilgrims Should Visit

Translator's Note: None of the holy sites that pilgrims are advised to visit are in the Basque Country. Most are in France, including Arles, Toulouse, Puy, St. Leonard, Périgueux, Orléans,

Poitiers, Saintes, Blaye, and Bordeaux. Those in Spain are beyond the Basque Country, e.g., Nájera, Sahagún, León.

However, two have pertinence to Basque history: Toulouse, site of the Cathedral of St. Sernin, and Blaye, where Roland, the hero of Roncesvalles, was said to be buried.

St. Sernin, known in Spain as San Cernín or San Saturnino, bishop of Toulouse in the first century, is revered in Navarre for coming to Pamplona, where he converted Fermín. Fermín became first bishop of Pamplona and much later its patron saint.[76] The ancient church of San Saturnino in Pamplona bears witness to Sernin's role in bringing Christianity to the city.

Later back in Toulouse, Sernin suffered a horrible if glorious martyrdom. As Aimery recounts it, in Chapter VIII:

When passing along this route (Via Tolosana) one must go to venerate the holy body of the blessed Sernin, bishop and martyr, who, having been taken prisoner by the pagans and held in the capitol of Toulouse, was tied to fierce wild bulls, then pushed off the top of the capitol citadel and dragged a mile along the stone steps. His head was crushed, his brains burst out, and his body was broken asunder; with dignity he rendered up his soul to Christ. He was buried at a beautiful site near Toulouse, where the faithful built an immense basilica in his honor. The rule of St. Augustine is observed there, and God grants many indulgences to those who request them. His feast-day is November 29.[77]

Translator's Note: As for Blaye, Aimery's remarks on this city, located on the estuary of the Gironde, opposite Bordeaux, add a little to earlier references to the rout of Charlemagne's armies at Roncesvalles.

Next at Blaye, on the seashore, one should ask the protection of St. Romain; in his basilica also reposes the body of the blessed Roland, the martyr. Issue of a noble family, count in the retinue of Charlemagne, he was one of his twelve companions in arms and, impelled by the zeal of his faith, he went to Spain to expel the infidels. His strength was such that at Roncesvalles, they say, he split a boulder down the middle, top to bottom, with three strokes of his sword. The tale also goes that when he sounded his horn, the force of his blowing split it also down the middle. This ivory horn, thus cloven, is to be found at Bordeaux in the basilica of St. Seurin; and on the rock at Roncesvalles, a church was built. Later, having conquered kings and nations during many wars, wasted by hunger, cold, and excessive heat, wounded by violent blows, and flagellated continuously for the love of God, pierced by arrows and lance thrusts, this valorous martyr of Christ died, they say of thirst, in this valley of Roncesvalles. His blessed body was respectfully buried by his companions in the basilica of St. Romain in Blaye.[78]

Chapter XI. How to Receive the Pilgrims of Santiago

Pilgrims, whether poor or rich, whether returning from Santiago or on their way there, should be received with charity and respect by everyone; for whoever willingly receives them and gives them shelter has as guest not only Santiago but also our Lord himself—for he said in his gospel, "Who receiveth you, receiveth me." Many are those who have incurred the wrath of God because they were unwilling to receive the pilgrims of Santiago, or the poor.

At Nantua, a city between Geneva and Lyon, a weaver once refused bread to a pilgrim of Santiago who had asked for it; all at once, he saw his woven cloth collapse, ripped down the middle.

At Villeneuve, a poor pilgrim of Santiago spoke to a woman who was keeping some bread warm in the ashes, and asked for alms for the love of God and the blessed Santiago. She told him she had no bread, to which the pilgrim replied: "Would to God that your bread would change into stone!" The pilgrim left and was a long way off when the wicked woman went to get her bread out of the ashes— and found nothing but a round stone. Penitent, she immediately went in search of the pilgrim, but could not find him.

And one time at Poitiers, two stouthearted French pilgrims, returning penniless from Santiago, came to the house of Jean Gautier, near the church of St. Porchaire, and asked for lodging, for the love of God and Santiago; but found none. Later, a poor man took them into his newly built house on the same street, near St. Porchaire; and behold, by divine vengeance, that night a terrible fire broke out and quickly destroyed the whole street, beginning with the house where they had first asked for shelter and stopping just short of the one where they had been welcomed. Thousands of homes all around were burned, but the one where the servants of God had been received was spared, through his grace.

This is why everyone should realize that, rich or poor, the pilgrims of Santiago deserve hospitality and a sincere welcome.

Here ends the fourth book of the Apostle Santiago. Glory to him who wrote it, glory also to him who reads it.

It was the Church of Rome which first welcomed this book. One may find it now in many places, for example, in Rome, around Jerusalem, in France, Italy, Germany, Frisia and especially at Cluny.

Notes

1. The Spanish spelling of the saint's name, and of Spanish place names referred to in the *Guide*, will be used.
2. Elie Lambert, "Les routes des Pyrénées Atlantiques et leur emploi au cours des ages," *Pirineos*, vol. 7 (1951), pp. 335–382.
3. Jeanne Vielliard, "Pèlerins d'Espagne à la fin du moyen âge, ce que nous apprennent les sauf-conduits délivrés aux pèlerins par la chancellerie des rois d'Aragon, entre 1379 et 1422," in *Homenaje a Antonio Rubió*, vol. 2 (Barcelona, 1936), p. 267.
4. C. Meredith-Jones, ed., *Turpin, Archbishop of Rheims. Historia Karoli Magni et Rotholandi (ou Chronique du Pseudo-Turpin)* (Paris: Librairie E. Droz, 1936), p. 49.
5. For the bibliographic history of the *Guide*, see Jeanne Vielliard, ed. and trans., "Introduction," *Le guide du pèlerin de Saint-Jacques de Compostelle*, Third edition (Mâcon: I. Protat Frères, 1963), pp. v-xiii.
6. Walter Starkie, *The Road to Santiago: Pilgrims of St. James* (New York: Dutton, 1957), p. 39.
7. Jeanne Vielliard, "Le livre de Saint-Jacques et le Guide du Pèlerin," in Société des Amis de St.-Jacques-de-Compostelle, *Pèlerins et chemins de Saint-Jacques en France et en Europe du Xe siècle à nos jours* (Paris: 1965), p. 37.
8. Georgiana Goddard King, *The Way of St. James*, vol. 1 (New York: Putnam, 1920), p. 64.
9. Marceline Defourneaux, *Les français en Espagne aux XIe et XIIe siècles* (Paris: Presses Universitaires de France, 1949), pp. 80–102.
10. Luís Vázquez de Parga, José M. Lacarra and Juan Uría Ríu, *Las Perigrinaciones a Santiago de Compostela*, vol. 1 (Madrid: Consejo Superior de Investigaciones Científicas, 1948), pp. 174–175.
11. Walter Muir Whitehill, *Liber Sancti Jacobi. Codex Calixtinus* (Santiago de Compostela: Consejo Superior de Investigaciones Científicas, Instituto P. Sarmiento de Estudios Gallegos, 1944), p. xxviii.
12. Jeanne Vielliard, *Le guide du pèlerin...*, *Addenda*, note for p. xiii.
13. Eneko Mitxelena, *Viajeros extranjeros en Vasconia* (Buenos Aires: Editorial Vasca Ekin, 1942), p. 135.
14. Elie Lambert, "Le pèlerinage de Compostelle," in *Etudes d'histoire médiévales*, vol. 1 (Paris: Privat-Didier, 1957–1958), p. 36.
15. Eneko Mitxelena, *Viajeros extranjeros...*, p. 135.
16. Eugène Goyheneche, *Le pays basque* (Pau: Société Nouvelle d'Editions Régionales et de Diffusion, 1979), p. 94.

17. José Iribarren, "Bandidos y salteadores," *Príncipe de Viana*, vol. 3 (Pamplona: 1942), pp. 465–478.
18. Edwin Mullins, *The Pilgrimage to Santiago* (New York: Taplinger, 1974), p. 7.
19. T. D. Kendrick, *St. James in Spain* (Glasgow: University Press, 1960), pp. 13–21. Evidence of such an early visit to the site is found in a thirteenth-century Arab book cited by Luís Vázquez de Parga et al., *Las perigrinaciones...* , vol. 1, p. 35.
20. Ibid., p. 21.
21. For other explanations of the scallop shell, including the theory that it was a pagan amulet, see Luís Vázquez de Parga, et al. *Las perigrinaciones...* , vol. 1, pp. 129–132.
22. Walter Starkie, *The Road to Santiago...* , p. 22.
23. Luís Vázquez de Parga et al., *Las peregrinaciones...* , p. 35.
24. Regarding length of the trip, Aimery allows for thirteen stages (days' journeys) between the Pass of Cize near Roncesvalles and Santiago—a distance of about 500 miles. This leads one to believe the *Guide* was written for those wealthy enough to travel on horseback. Edwin Mullins, *The Pilgrimage...* , p. 118.
25. Vielliard lists several sources for partial or complete translations of these latter chapters, in French and English. Jeanne Vielliard, *Le guide du pèlerin...* , p. xi, note 2.
26. The reader will note that chapter headings listed here differ slightly from those given at the heads of the chapters themselves. This is in accordance with the original manuscript of the *Pilgrim's Guide*.
27. The heading at the chapter itself is "The number of canons of Santiago." The text first enumerates the number of canons, then explains how the weekly offering is to be divided among them and to other recipients.
28. Called the *Via Tolosana*, this was the usual route from Italy and Provence. Walter Starkie, *The Road to Santiago...* , pp. 81–82.
29. The *Via Podiensis*, traveled by Burgundians and Germans. Ibid.
30. The *Via Lemosina*. Ibid.
31. *Via Turonensis*, followed by pilgrims from England, Flanders, and Paris. Ibid.
32. The road over this pass, linking St. Jean Pied de Port on the French side of the Pyrenees with Roncesvalles (Roncevaux) on the Spanish side, followed the old Roman road that led from Bordeaux to Astorga. For more on Pyrenean routes, see Elie Lambert, "Les routes des Pyrénées...," *Pirineos*, vol. 7, pp. 335–382 and Eugène Goyheneche, *Le pays basque*, p. 100.
33. As noted in the Introduction, it is unlikely that Pope Calixtus was really the author.

34. Though the stages are described as "short," many were more than one day's journey even by horseback. This first stage from St. Michel to Viscarret was only about 35 km, but that from Estella to Nájera, for example, was 76 km, and that from Nájera to Burgos was 90 km. Luís Vázquez de Parga et al., *Las Perigrinaciones...*, vol. 2, p. 133.
35. This was part of the road Sancho the Great built from the Pyrenees to Nájera, after driving the Muslims out of the area between Logroño and Nájera. Defourneaux observes that this road building by Sancho may have been motivated by more than concern for the pilgrims' welfare. The influx of tourists and merchants was bound to have a civilizing effect on the sparsely populated regions the new route penetrated. Marceline Defourneaux, *Les français...*, p. 245. King agrees: "Small wonder that Kings of Navarre promoted the travel; it meant more to the mountain kingdom than the Union Pacific to the States a half century ago." Georgiana Goddard King, *The Way of St. James*, vol. 1, p. 100 and vol. 3 (New York: 1920), p. 420.
36. This was the last portion of Sancho's road. Formerly, pilgrims had to detour through Alava, for fear of the Muslims. Luís Vázquez de Parga et al., *Las peregrinaciones...*, vol. 2, p. 13.
37. Nothing remains of this hospice, once one of the most famous in Christendom. Walter Starkie, *The Road to Santiago...*, p. 126.
38. Or Astorito, now abandoned. Luís Vázquez de Parga et al., *Las peregrinaciones...*, vol. 1, p. 211.
39. Not the present Villaroya, which is to the southeast of the route; but there was another Villa rubea (Villaroya) near Logroño in the pilgrims' time—now nonexistent. Ibid., note 20.
40. The legend is recounted in the *Pseudo-Turpin* (the original Book IV of the *Liber Sancti Jacobi*).
41. The present Foncebadón is on the slope of Mt. Irago. There was probably a hospice there in 1103. Luís Vázquez de Parga et al., *Las peregrinaciones...*, vol. 2, pp. 280–281.
42. Vielliard translates this as Camp of the Saracens and links the site to an actual camp. King claims to have found the site of the camp. Georgiana Goddard King, *The Way of St. James*, vol. 2, p. 386. Uría believes the name comes from a medieval castle belonging to Sarracino, count of Astorga and el Bierzo. Luís Vázquez de Parga et al., *Las peregrinaciones...*, p. 307.
43. There were limestone quarries near Triacastela and none near Santiago. Each pilgrim brought a piece of limestone to Castañola (probably the present Castañeda), where there were kilns; the limestone was then transported by carts to Santiago. Thus the

pilgrims could play a direct part in building the basilica. Jeanne Vielliard, *Le guide du pèlerin*... , p. 9, note 4. Uría remarks that this pious exercise was more than symbolic, in view of the great numbers of pilgrims who could have brought their loads. Luís Vázquez de Parga et al., *Las peregrinaciones*... , p. 320.
44. Uría has been unable to identify this. Ibid., p. 340.
45. Vázquez de Parga points out that it would have been difficult for pilgrims to estimate their expenses, since the itinerary does not give exact distances between stops. Ibid., vol. 1, p. 212, note 21.
46. Vielliard explains that some have believed this referred to a hospice (Mons-Gaudii) at Compostela; but she is convinced it is the one founded in the tenth century by St. Bernard of Menthon for pilgrims to Rome, and that the three cited hospices correspond to the three great pilgrimages of Christianity: Jerusalem, Rome, and Santiago. Jeanne Vielliard, *Le guide du pèlerin*... , p. 10, note 1.
47. This is the only chapter ascribed solely to Aimery; Chapter IX (on the basilica and city of Santiago de Compostela) is attributed to Pope Calixtus and Aimery, jointly.
48. Vielliard translates the Latin *viator* as *routier*: not one strictly in charge of road maintenance, but rather a frequent traveler along the roads who helps to keep them in repair. Jeanne Vielliard, *Le guide du pèlerin*... , p. 11, note 5. King adds that many clergy were engaged in building roads and bridges and mending the ways in the Middle Ages, and were held in high repute for doing so. Georgiana Goddard King, *The Way of St. James*, vol. 1, p. 100.
49. Diego Gelmirez, bishop and then first archbishop of Compostela, died in 1139. Jeanne Vielliard, *Le guide du pèlerin*... , p. 11, note 6.
50. Alfonso VII, king of Galicia from 1112; emperor of León 1136–1157.
51. King believes that his citing the date 1120 makes that the probable date of his pilgrimage. Georgiana Goddard King, *The Way of St. James*, vol. 1, p. 72.
52. Alfonso I of Aragon (the Battler), reigned from 1104–1134.
53. Louis VII of France, reigned from 1108–1137.
54. Alfonso VII granted a privilege to this Pierre, also called Peregrino, in 1126, for his services in rebuilding the Bridge of Puerto Marin over the Miño. Jeanne Vielliard, *Le guide du pèlerin*... , p. 13, note 3.
55. A frequently embattled queen, daughter of Alfonso VI, she was married first to the Burgundian count Raymond, whom her father installed in Galicia. Raymond was usually at odds with his brother

Henry, ruler of Portugal, and Urraca did not stand idly by. Her second husband was Alfonso the Battler of Aragon, against whom she took the part of her son, Alfonso VII. Harold Livermore, *A History of Spain* (London: Allen and Unwin, 1958), pp. 108–111.

56. Lacarra testifies that the river (the Salado or Guesalaz) is indeed salty but not malignant. Luís Vázquez de Parga et al., *Las peregrinaciones...*, vol. 2, p. 130.
57. Now Lavacolla.
58. Vielliard says these are the Gave d'Oloron and the Gave de Pau. Jeanne Vielliard, *Le guide du pèlerin...*, p. 20, note 1.
59. The Latin manuscript reads *sicera*, a fermented drink like cider. Fita believed this was wrongly transcribed and should have read *cicera*—garbanzos (chick peas). P. Fidel Fita and Julien Vinson, *Le codex de Saint-Jacques de Compostelle*, (Paris, 1882). Vielliard, however, now holds with the original Latin, because the Basque Country does produce cider. Jeanne Vielliard, *Le guide du pèlerin...*, p. 21, note 2.
60. Not all the guilty parties castigated in this paragraph can be identified. The king of Aragon would have been Alfonso I the Battler (reigned from 1104–1134); Vielliard suggests that Raymond de Solis may be Raymond-Guillaume de Soule (1040–1062); however, his dates are in the century before Aimery is generally thought to have made the journey. The viscount of St. Michel was possibly the seigneur of St. Michel Pied de Port. Ibid., p. 23, notes 1 and 2. Despite the threat of excommunication, the toll collectors continued their unpopular practices at least until the end of the fifteenth century. J. García Mercadal, *España vista por los extranjeros*, vol. 1 (Madrid: Biblioteca Nueva, 1921), p. 114.
61. Few have defended the toll collectors against these charges, but Fausto Arocena says perhaps they felt they had to demand money from the pilgrims because many of the latter were carrying goods and trading clandestinely. E. Esparza, "Otra vez Aymeric Picaud" (review of *El país vasco visto desde fuera* by Fausto Arocena). *Príncipe de Viana*, vol. 11 (Pamplona: 1950), p. 355. Such "false" pilgrims, who simply went to sell goods, proliferated so much that, some centuries later, the entire pilgrimage was prohibited by the French rulers. Elie Lambert, "Le pèlerinage...," *Etudes d'histoire medievales* (Paris: Privat-Didier, 1957–58), p. 13.
62. The Pass of Ibañeta above Roncesvalles, alt. 1,280 m.
63. That is, the Atlantic. In this claim, Justo Garate sees evidence of Aimery's "excess of vista, which (also) made him see tremendous vices in the Basques." Justo Garate, "El nombre de Dios en

lengua vasca," *Príncipe de Viana*, vol. 19, (Pamplona: 1957), p. 145.
64. This is the route taken by the present main highway.
65. Vielliard and Meredith-Jones agree that Fita's translation of this as 140,000 men was erroneous. Jeanne Vielliard, *Le guide du pèlerin*..., p. 147. C. Meredith-Jones, ed., *Turpin, Archbishop of Rheims*....
66. Aimery appears to accept the French version of the legend popularized in the *Song of Roland*, which identifies those who in 778 attacked Charlemagne's armies as they made their way through the Pyrenees as Muslims. Later historians agreed that the attackers were Basques of Navarre.
67. From the Latin (taken from the Celtic) *sagum*, *saga*, which is found in Caesar, Titus Livius, and others. Jeanne Vielliard, *Le guide du pèlerin*..., p. 27, note 5.
68. Arturo Campión took exception to this criticism of the Basques for eating with their hands, pointing out that everybody did in those days. He suggests that Aimery's real displeasure was with the familiarity of masters and servants: "Navarre was a country of nobiliary institutions, but democratic customs, at least more than the country of the critic." In Eneko Mitxelena, *Viajeros extranjeros en Vasconia*, p. 140.
69. Julien Vinson, in his preface to the edition by Fita, gives a short study of this Basque vocabulary and refers to his two articles on the subject in the *Rêvue de linguistique*. Jeanne Vielliard, *Le guide du pèlerin*..., p. 29, note 1. Wentworth Webster's translations into Basque differ slightly from Vielliard's. Wentworth Webster, "The early Basque vocabulary," in Julien Vinson, "Les basques du XIIe siècle, leurs moeurs et leur langue," *Revue de linguistiques*, vol. 14 (Paris: 1881), pp. 121-122.
70. A barbaric people of ancient Thrace.
71. In Castilian, *azcona*, a missile weapon. Jeanne Vielliard, *Le guide du pèlerin*..., p. 31, note 1.
72. Wentworth Webster ascribes to Fita the translation of Nubians to "Numiani of Devonshire." In (Julien Vinson, "Les basques...," *Revue de linguistiques*, vol. 14, 1881, p. 123.)
73. The Latin epithet *caudatus* (cowardly, pusillanimous) was frequently applied to the English in the Middle Ages. Jeanne Vielliard, *Le guide du pèlerin*..., p. 31, note 2.
74. This could also be translated as Castile and Campos (province of Palencia). Ibid., p. 147, note for p. 33.
75. The Latin reads: *piscibusque marinis immanissimis et paucis abilis*, which some say may alternatively be translated as "one

finds some of the fish caught from the sea to be enormous, others very small." Jeanne Vielliard, *Le guide du pèlerin* . . . , p. 49.
76. Carlos Clavería, *Historia del reino de Navarra* (Pamplona: Editorial Gómez, 1971), p. 27.
77. Jeanne Vielliard, *Le guide du pèlerin* . . . , p. 49.
78. Ibid., pp. 79–81. Luís Vázquez de Parga et al., *Las perigrinaciones* . . . , vol. 2, p. 13.

Bilbao in the Economy of the Basque Country and Northwestern Europe during the Modern Era

by

Román Basurto

Geographic Factors in Bilbao's Commerce

Bilbao, according to T. Guiard's accurate characterization, was founded on iron, and its port was the principal center of trade for the iron and steel production of the seigneury of Vizcaya. Bilbao and its port were also Castille's export window for the wool derived from the flocks of Burgos, Segovia, and León, as well as those of Navarra.[1] At the same time, the extensive forests surrounding the city provided the necessary timber for naval construction to the shipyards located on the shores of the Nervión River, in Portugalete, Baracaldo, Abando, Deusto, and Bilbao itself.[2]

Thanks to these favorable economic geographical circumstances, Bilbao quickly managed to control a large part of the seigneury's commerce, converting it into a bridge between northern European ports and markets of the Iberian Peninsula. Viewed in external geostrategical terms, from the late Middle Ages and the early stages of the Modern Age, Bilbao constituted one of the links in the Burgos-Bruges axis which, in turn, was a part of the North Atlantic coastal maritime trade complex (the British Isles, southern Scandinavia, the North Sea, the Baltic, and the Cantabrian).[3] Viewed internally, Bilbao and its port, during the Middle Ages and the ancien régime, formed part of a unique and specific maritime ecosystem of the Basque Country.

This ecosystem encompassed four levels of activity which were clearly differentiated yet, at the same time, intimately related. There was a maritime zone characterized by considerable commerce, naval industry, and fishing activity. There was an interior agricultural zone.

A third zone was comprised of the uplands where cereal and forage crops were grown. Finally, there was the high mountain country with its pastoralism, charcoal manufacture, and mining.[4]

The small scale of the Basque Country and the abundance of both iron ore and timber explain why Basques have traditionally directed their energies toward the sea and metallurgy.[5]

Commerce in the Late Middle Ages

From the end of the thirteenth century, with aperture of the Straits of Gibraltar, a regular maritime route was established between Italy and Flanders which, while signaling the decline of the fairs of Champagne, fomented commercial ties between Mediterranean and Atlantic countries, with a concomitant development of navigation on the high seas.[6]

It is during this period that Basque mariners emerge as the provisioners of Gascogne wines and Vizcayan iron to northern European countries and transporters of yard goods which they obtained in English, Flemish, and Norman ports. When the first Italian mariners began to appear in the Mancha and the North Sea, the Basques were already well established in Atlantic commerce, notably in a heavy coastal trade which encompassed all French and Spanish ports.[7]

From the thirteenth century on, Basque products stand out in Europe's steel manufacturing. Beginning about the middle of that century we have documentation of Basque iron shipments in the port of Bruges. Throughout the fourteenth and fifteenth centuries, there is expansion of the European markets for Vizcayan and Guipuzcoan iron, which is imported through Atlantic, North Sea, and even Mediterranean ports.[8] Similarly, commissioners and owners of Basque vessels served as transporters of wool exports contracted by Burgos merchants.

Quickly there emerged parochial differences and a rivalry between the mercantile classes of Burgos and Vizcaya regarding the defense of their respective conflicting interests over jurisdiction of lading of ships' cargoes and their insurance. Despite an agreement between Bilbao and Burgos pacted in 1499,[9] their disputes continued until the eighteenth century. Such a lack of understanding between Bilboans and Burgalese did nothing more than harm both communities, given their mutual ties. Ultimately, the merchants of Burgos depended on Bilbao shipping, while Bilbao's shippers needed Burgos's business.[10]

From the fourteenth century, and principally in the fifteenth, significant quantities of fine Castillian wool were sent to Flanders and the Low Countries in general. Vizcayan ships loaded with wool and iron, while en route to Flanders, visited the French ports of Bayonne,

Bordeaux, and La Rochelle (under English dominion until the fifteenth century), where they took on wine. The voyage normally lasted one and one-half to two months. Frequently, the ships' captains were the owners of the merchandise they were transporting.

In Bruges they sold the iron and wool and purchased in the cloth fairs of Flanders a return cargo along with yard goods (camlets, linens, serge, etc.) provided to them by the Castillian and Vizcayan merchants established there, as well as by the Flemish merchants themselves.[11] The Basque merchants, and especially those from Bilbao, appear in the ports of Flanders from the middle of the fourteenth century, and plausibly had from that time representation in official Flemish circles. In 1494, the city of Bruges ceded them two houses, on which site they constructed a veritable palace called the *Proetorium Cantabricum*, eloquent proof of the importance of the Vizcayan nation in that city.[12]

In this same epoch, Basque seamen occupied a prominent place in the maritime industry, since they were hired by Italian businessmen and thereby became one of the principal motors of the Genoese economy in the fifteenth century.[13] In fact, it was the Basque seamen who introduced into the Mediterranean the large Nordic transport ship known as the *Kogge*, *Coque*, or *Coca*.[14]

In the transition from the Middle Ages to the Modern Age, it appeared that there was an auspicious future for the economic development of Bilbao. At the end of the fifteenth century, Bilbao was a commercial center in its full power, "a port endowed with the capacity to outfit, arm, and load vessels, with numerous seamen, expert pilots, industrial workers and shipyards, illustrious commerce, and copious fortunes."[15]

The Splendor and Decline of Bilbao at the Dawning of the Modern Age

At the beginning of the sixteenth century, the commercial importance of Bilbao was equal to that of Burgos as reflected in the concession of June 22, 1522, by royal decree issued in Seville by Queen Juana, and the founding of the Consulate, Exchange, tribunal for businessmen, and the University of Bilbao.[16] At about the same time, the Basque economy experienced a moment of prosperity, thanks to a series of favorable factors both of a structural and circumstantial nature.

Among the first of these is the fact that the maritime region of the Basque Country continued to be one of the steelmaking centers of Europe (along with Sweden and central Germany). Also, shipbuilding, which was intimately related to the metallurgical sector and which constituted the primary economic activity of the region, was stimulated by the growing demand for large vessels for the Indies fleets of both the Crown and the Andalusian merchants.[17] The best vessels on the American run were, in fact, those constructed in the Vizcayan shipyards.[18]

Among the factors that may be regarded as circumstantial, the discovery of the fishing banks of Terranova and the increase in the wool trade with northern Europe were particularly noteworthy.

Thanks to a decree issued by Charles V in 1529, Bilbao and San Sebastián, along with other Cantabrian ports (La Coruña, Bayonne, Avilés, and Laredo) and Mediterranean ones (Cartagena and Málaga), as well as Cádiz, were authorized as points of origin for trade with the Indies subject only to the condition that their ships put in at Seville on the return journey in order to declare their cargo. This freedom of commerce with America, conceded to Vizcayan and Guipuzcoan ports, was later constrained by other royal decrees on December 1 and 21, 1573. After that date, all of the vessels destined for America were obliged to sail together in the fleets leaving Seville or Cádiz.[19]

It seems that Basque merchants and mariners made scant use of the privilege of trading directly with America since, given the constant threat from corsairs in the Gulf of Biscay, it was safer and more profitable for them to participate in the official convoys to the Indies.[20]

Nevertheless, despite the good prospects that the sixteenth century seemingly offered for development of the Basque maritime economy, there would quickly appear a complex of contrary factors harmful to it. These included the successive wars that Spain fought in Europe (resulting in the loss of Flanders) and the shift of the axis of trade toward America.

The decline of the Vizcayan economy begins, seemingly, in the year 1575, a time which, according to F. Braudel, signals its eclipse. Basque participation in the American run evolves from being essential in the period 1520–1580 to becoming just one of many contributing forces by the eighteenth century.

Another cause of the Vizcayan decline is found in the progressive development of the maritime powers of northern Europe (England and Holland especially) that ultimately reduced northern Iberia to a position of dependency on them.[21] The evidence of this is seen in the gradual disappearance after 1569 of Vizcayan ships, loaded with wool and gold, on the Antwerp run, replaced by foreign vessels which on their return voyage took on salt, wine, and silver in Seville.[22] On the other hand, the progressive shift of the Spanish economy from the north to the south replaced the importance of the Cantabrian Atlantic with that of the American Atlantic.

The decline of the Basque littoral economy at the end of the sixteenth century anticipated by forty years the realignment of international economic relations.

The Growing Importance of the Wool Trade and the Evolution of Steelmaking at the End of the Seventeenth Century

By the second half of the seventeenth century, there began to appear in Segovia large-scale proprietors of sheep flocks who originated in Bilbao and who were also involved in the export trade.[23] This presence of Bilboan merchants in the very centers of wool buying must be explained as a concomitant of their attempt to salvage an active trading role in the final years of the seventeenth century,[24] when Bilbao could be considered as little more than a "colony of foreign industry."

The movement of the Bilboans to the buying centers seemingly had two beneficent effects: the elimination of a price monopoly on wool imposed by foreigners and a decline in the price of manufactured goods sent to Spain in exchange, as the number of autochthonous import merchants increased. Merino wool was purchased under a system in which the buyer advanced money to the producer prior to the shearing, at a lower price than that which the wool was worth when actually harvested.[25]

This type of *verlagsystem* involved the advanced payment of the wool production by the merchants, who were then able to decide upon the most propitious moment for its resale in the international marketplace. This system of international debt peonage was controlled by foreign traders or rich merchants who had access to European markets. The network of international merchants, which terminated in powerful financial groups in several northwestern European countries, reduced the local commercial class to a position of total dependency.[26]

Regarding the iron trade, beginning in the last third of the seventeenth century, there was an evident, notable development of Basque steelmaking, as reflected in the reiterated restrictions by the General Assembly of Vizcaya upon the exportation of iron ore. This increased activity continued, subject to short-lived circumstantial setbacks, until the last decade of the seventeenth century.

The continued growth of Basque iron ore production coincided, then, with a similar evolution experienced within this sector of the European economy throughout the Modern Age.[27] The sale of ore in this period reached high levels in European markets. Such a circumstance evidently benefited export traders, but not the owners or leasers of ironworks in the Basque Country who found it difficult to supply their foundries.[28]

The development of European steelmaking from the end of the sixteenth century, with the attendant appearance of the iron products of Liege primarily, and later of the Swedes, progressively undermined the export markets for Basque iron. To this factor should be added the other negative ones of the wars and piracy which also disrupted Vizcayan iron exports. Nevertheless, according to Guiard, the Vizcayan iron and steel business prospered throughout the seventeenth century. "The manufacture of iron and of steel was sustained in the Seigneury with ponderable estimation throughout the course of the seventeenth century, and there were spread about the territory a large number of forges, ironworks, hammers and foundries."[29]

In his *Averiguaciones de las Antiguedades de Cantabria*, published at the end of the seventeenth century (1689 and 1691), Henao provides a lively description of trade in Bilbao in that epoch which reflects considerable mercantile and industrial activity. Referring to the city's plaza, he notes, "From here, the estuary is filled with foreign ships, which bring and carry away merchandise, and that which they take most is wool and iron, with so many ships and with smaller craft as well that cross it, the estuary is like another settlement of people, moving upon the water. But why not if there are factories on it (and quite commonly there are) of galleons and other vessels because of the availability of planks, nails, rigging and other equipment, fabricated right there directly?"[30]

The Lack of Competitiveness of Basque Iron during the Second Half of the Eighteenth Century

Vizcayan iron, despite its excellent quality, encountered growing resistance in European markets after the middle of the sixteenth century and particularly beginning in the seventeenth due to increasing competition from steel metallurgy in Sweden and Liege. Swedish steelmaking, with its more advanced technology, was also favored with excellent and abundant iron-ore deposits, vast forests and waterways for hydraulic power. Consequently, Swedish iron would dominate European markets until the middle of the eighteenth century, at which time Russian iron produced from the steelworks installed in the Urals by Peter the Great begins to appear in the west.[31]

Similarly, the notable progress in this economic sector in England dating from the middle of the same century (due to the presence of coke coal for the founding and perfection of the puddling of cast iron into wrought iron in a reflecting oven), stimulated an impressive expansion of the English steelmaking industry after 1780. Beginning as early as 1760, this constituted a veritable industrial revolution of iron manufacturing.[32] Meanwhile, the price of iron produced in Basque foundries remained excessively high due to the costly vegetable charcoal that fueled them.

Given the inferior situation of the autochthonous iron industry with respect to foreign competition, it is not surprising that Basque officials solicited the government for protective tariffs and tax breaks.[33] Nevertheless, these measures were ineffective since, throughout the eighteenth century, the public bodies of Vizcaya and Guipúzcoa complained constantly that they were not being implemented.[34]

In 1766, the General Assembly (*Junta General*) attributed the decline of Vizcayan foundries to the introduction into the market of foreign iron, principally from the province of Liege and the kingdom of Sweden. The situation had become particularly grave since foreign iron was entering even through Bilbao and other Vizcayan ports,[35] as well as through Cádiz and Seville, ports where it was warehoused and then commingled with Basque iron. In 1777, the commissioner of the three Basque provinces met in Durango and agreed to establish an inspector in Cádiz whose mission it was to ensure that no foreign iron was shipped out to America.[36] While the presence of this official in Cádiz reduced embarcation of foreign steel for the Indies, he was unable to eliminate this contraband.

Furthermore, the Basque steel industry received another crippling blow with the Royal Order of July 29, 1779, which declared "foreign" all goods and products from Vizcaya and other "Exempt Provinces" as long as they refused to allow establishment of Spanish customs houses in their seaport. The charges that Basque iron would have to pay were stipulated in the tariff schedule of October 12, 1778, in addition to which it was subject to entry fees in the authorized ports of the Iberian Peninsula "in which case they were to be treated as if they were foreign."[37]

Given its inferior competitive situation with respect to the cheapest European iron, it seems that the solution for the Basque founding industry lay in improving manufacturing techniques, lowering of production costs and development of finishing processes that would provide completed metal products for the American colonial market as well as the interior peninsular one.

Given the excessive price of raw and semielaborated iron that was sent to America, as well as the high cost of New-World labor, it was preferable from an American viewpoint to buy foreign iron. This became one of the principal concerns of the Basque Society (*Sociedad Bascongada*), conscious of the inefficiency of Basque ironworks, which occasioned the loss of most of the economic benefit reported in the statistics of iron production. For this reason, the society proposed fostering finishing industries, those of *segunda labranza*, with the purpose of transforming iron into cutlery, hardware, castings (cauldrons for the army and navy), agricultural implements (picks, hoes, etc.), wire, and for the construction of cannons, anchors, bolts, etc. Paradoxically, since the late Middle Ages, other Europeans had been introducing such objects into the Basque market, made of iron first purchased there.

Another of the objects pursued by the Basque Society was that of improving the cost efficiency of the work force employed in the iron industry, "which, since it is the principal object of commerce of these two provinces, it can be said that the price of its first elaboration is the measurement of happiness in the country."[38] Unfortunately, such efforts met with little success. Proof of the interest in improving metallurgy is found, for example, in the hiring of French technicians to elaborate detailed studs by Josef Ynacio de Gallatebeitia, the Bilboan merchant who owned the frigate Achuri.[39] These were the possible avenues for improving traditional Basque steelmaking "with (its) many foundries and little fuel, with its expensive iron, and little demand for it, (so that) no one can foresee its progressive and durable fomentation."[40]

In the general assemblies held by the Royal Basque Society in Vergara in July of 1791, a project was presented which would establish a "Foundry Company for the perfection of the functions and elaboration of iron and establishment of new factories...."[41] Another fundamental objective posed by the company was the promotion and establishment of secondary manufacturers, seeking to provide anchors, hardware, and other necessary metal products.

In any event, and despite the infrastructural factors weighing negatively upon Basque eighteenth-century steel production, the collapse of Basque iron exports at the end of the century is attributable primarily to external factors. It is during the decade of the nineties when a succession of wars, first against France and then England, paralyzed the export trade in Basque iron products.[42]

The Negative Consequences of the Treaty of Utrecht
for the Basque Fishing Economy

During the Modern Age, Spain lacked sufficient production of salted fish or an alternative type of fish harvesting combining the two essential qualities of cost effectiveness and easy conservation and durability. These characteristics were essential, given the need to introduce the fish harvest into the interior of Castile, and given its consumption by Spanish families on the numerous feast days and days of abstention from meat dictated by the Spanish liturgical calendar.

It is also noteworthy that salt fish constituted practically the sole source of protein of the Spaniard of average means, given the relative lack of meat in the daily diet. Cod, due to its low price, was the preferred fish consumed by the lower classes.

The Iberian Peninsula constituted, from the beginning of the Modern Age, one of the best markets for codfish. This was particularly true of lightly salted, dried cod, the consumption rate of which was exceptionally high in Spain.[43] According to one sixteenth-century author, codfish was a food of peons,[44] and the English called it, deprecatively, "Poor John." The type of cod consumed in Spain, which was only partly salted, had the special names of "haberdine" or "merluche."[45]

At the same time, in the kingdom of Castile there were 120 days of abstention annually, since eating meat on Saturdays was prohibited, and sixty in Aragon and Navarra. The Navarrese political economist, Jerónimo de Ustáriz, calculated the consumption of codfish in the entire kingdom by taking an average of 130 days' annual abstention, multiplied by a daily intake of four ounces per family member in an average family of four, to arrive at an estimate of 6,000,000 ounces (a total of 375,000 quintals of codfish) with a monetary value of 2,437,000 pesos.[46]

The major portion of codfish imported into Spain after the Treaty of Utrecht was purchased from English traders who had found the commercial exploitation of the fishing banks of Terranova to be a veritable treasure trove. The renowned writer, Daniel Defoe, referred to " . . . that inexpressibly rich codbank of Newfoundland . . . which may be esteemed our mines of gold and silver."[47]

According to the estimates of the Bilboan economist, Nicolás de Arriquibar, the value of fish purchased from Great Britain and imported through the port of Bilbao came right after that of textiles imported from that country. This is startling, given the fact that textiles were the prime export items of the advanced nations of northwestern Europe, and were the principal source of the trade deficit of economically dependent countries such as Spain. According to Arriquibar's estimates, the value of the fish alone purchased from England was equivalent to all of Bilbao's imports from Holland, more than half the value of those from France, and much more than the total value of the combined imports in Bilbao from sources such as Portugal, Russia, Denmark, Flanders, and the port of Hamburg.[48]

Arriquibar, like his predecessor Ustáriz, was concerned with finding a solution to the dependency upon the importation of salted fish, which was actually aggravated after the Treaty of Utrecht. Ustáriz recommended that, insofar as the just petitions of Basques to obtain fishing rights in Terranova waters were ignored by the English, there should be a boycott of foreign fish imports in the kingdom, with outright prohibition of its consumption.

Under the Treaty of Utrecht (1713), France conceded to England sovereignty over Hudson Bay and Terranova. The French, henceforth, retained only the right to fish the banks surrounding the island.[49] The requests by the Marquis of Monteleón at the English court that Spanish subjects be allowed to continue operating in Canadian waters failed to bear fruit. Rather, the English included a clause in Article 15 of the Treaty of Utrecht which, while it theoretically recognized a Basque fishing right, resulted in a restrictive definition of it, based upon ambiguous wording in the final paragraph. The clause stated, "... and because on Spain's part it is insisted that to the Guipuzcoans and other subjects of His Catholic Majesty there pertains a certain right to fish at the island of Terranova, conscious (is) His British Majesty that to the Vizcayans and other peoples of Spain there are conserved undamaged *all of the privileges which with reason they make request.*"[50] Nevertheless, all subsequent attempts to obtain from English authorities permission for the Basque fishermen to continue to operate in their traditional Canadian fisheries proved to be in vain.[51]

The seigneury of Vizcaya and the province of Guipúzcoa did not fail, throughout the century, to press their claims and seek restoration of their lost fishing rights in international forums (the Congresses of Cambray (1721–1727), Soissons (1728), Aachen (1748)).[52] The Basques complained of what they regarded to be a usurpation, "... since through their Industry and the practice of the Nautical Art, merited from the immemorable past until now the renown as discoverers of the cod fishery, in the Seas of Terranova (of whose Possession all of the Nations, in times of Peace as well as in War, never deprived them (nor) of the custom of freely Fishing, drying and salting (the catch) in those Seas, represent once again to Your Majesty's superior and Royal intelligence that since celebration of the Peace of Utrecht in which the dominion over those Isles was conceded to the kingdoms of France and England, (the Basques) have been deprived not only of the Honor of their Discovery, but also of the convenience of providing this marvelous food to Your Majesty's subjects (and are excluded) entirely from being able to continue in this pursuit...."[53]

In 1718, the consulates (consulados) of San Sebastián and Bilbao sent a representative to the government requesting that it negotiate a peace treaty with England including the right to fish in Terranova, but to no avail.[54]

In a letter directed to King Phillip IV, the merchants of the villa of Bilbao and the city of San Sebastián, with regard to the celebration of the Congress of Cambray, complained not only of having been dispossessed by England of the honor of recognition that "Vizcayans" discovered "the cod fisheries in Terranova waters" and of the right to continue fishing in that region, but also to having been subjected to a regimen imposed by the English, " . . . in the price of codfish proportionate to their cupidity, and its provisioning being so indispensable to these kingdoms, it is easy to understand the pernicious consequences of Vizcayans no longer being able to continue in this fishing."[55]

Earlier, in 1712, the province of Guipúzcoa had sent its own representation to His Majesty to contend that England had been ceded "the liberty of this Province and use of the Ports of Terranova . . . in order to achieve the Peace."[56]

On July 30, 1728, the Diputation of the Province of Guipúzcoa met in the presence of don Manuel Ignacio de Aguirre, the king's secretary, to respond to a written order sent by the Marqués de la Paz, of the king's Council of State. In it, it was requested that the province research in the archives of the San Sebastián consulate certifications and acts that bore witness to the visitations of Guipuzcoan vessels that arrived in port with cargoes of codfish from Terranova. Such information was required so that Spanish plenipotentiaries at the Congress of Soisson, to be celebrated that year, could provide credence to the Basque claim for the right to operate in Terranova.

The province replied that no such disembarcation had been registered upon the return from Terranova since "the cargo of them was regarded to be a product of the Basque Country itself as happens at present with the ships employed in whaling."[57] Nevertheless, it was regarded opportune to apply a questionnaire among the Guipuzcoan mariners who had previously worked the Terranova run. This interesting exercise collected details and testimony from Guipuzcoan fishermen regarding their voyages to Terranova in the last years of the previous century.

With nostalgia, it was remembered that with the beginning of the eighteenth century (with a kind of golden age between 1680 and 1700), codfishing and whaling sustained a flourishing mariner class in both the seigneury of Vizcaya and the province of Guipúzcoa which, in addition to providing well for its families, provisioned His Majesty's navy. After that time, however, unemployment and poverty spread among the mariners, who found themselves obliged to become expatriates, offering their services to other powers "being they those who instructed the Dutch and the English in the fishing of cod, herring and whales, not to mention infinite others who, without leaving a trace behind, died in America."[58]

It can be said that the prohibition upon operating in Terranova supposed an authentic economic and social disaster for some localities in the Basque Country. Thus St. Jean de Luz and Ciboure declined rapidly, "misery spreading among the people and propagating emigration on a large scale."[59]

Also, for example, in an anonymous description of Lequeitio in the eighteenth century, it is said that the town was maintained by the "fishing of whales and cod and vineyards . . . " despite the fact that by this time maritime activity was reduced "due to the lack of fish and the existence of navies in which many people were involved."[60] During the century, the War of Succession in Austria (1744–1748) and the Seven Years' War (1756–1763) aggravated the situation that the Treaty of Utrecht created for Basque shipowners.

The Treaty of Paris in 1763 conceded to French Basques alone the right of fishing and drying fish on the French shore of the archipelago of the islands of St. Pierre and Miquelon.

Seemingly French Basque commerce in cod experienced a certain recovery after the American War of Independence, thanks to the franchises conceded in Bayonne.[61] On balance, however, Basque deep-water fishing, which had known such splendid successes, suffered an important reversal from which it would never recover. By the mideighteenth century, the art of fishing for whales and cod existed only in the memories of a few elderly fishermen.[62]

In this same period, in 1748, the province of Guipúzcoa lamented to the king that since the English had monopolized fishing in Terranova, the price of cod had gone up more than half, in addition to the notable damages suffered by Basque deep-water fishermen " . . . in your Lord's Ports there are no longer created the capable mariners that were involved in this navigation, and which used to be so useful to Your Majesty as crew in the Royal Naval Service."[63]

In the Assembly of the Royal Society of the Friends of the Country held in Vitoria in September of 1777, the necessity of restoring the two activities of whaling and cod fishing, of much transcendental importance to the economy of the Basque littoral, was reiterated.

In this fashion, it was thought to be possible not only to augment the maritime class itself, but also to provide the means of self-support to other towns as well, thereby seizing from foreigners the cod business and that in whale oil, whalebone, and sperm "with which they extract so much money from us."[64]

Logically, England was viewed as the cause of the decline of the Basque fishing industry.[65] Evidently, England had good reasons for refusing to let Spain participate in the benefits of the Canadian fisheries, despite the loss of income from ships' registries in the Americas and the slave trade.

There were two reasons for this failure of England to correspond to the Spanish concessions. On the one hand, there were obvious economic interests in maintaining an exclusive monopoly over the lucrative business of the sale of salted fish to the Catholic countries of the Mediterranean. On the other, there was the political reason that Terranova was considered to be the best seafaring school of the period.[66]

N.B.: A more complete and more detailed version of the ideas contained in this article may be found in my book, *Comercio y burguesía mercantil de Bilbao en la segunda mitad del siglo XVIII*. (Bilbao: Universidad del País Vasco/Euskal Herriko Unibertsitatea, 1983).

Notes

1. Teofilo Guiard, *Historia del Consulado y Casa de Contratación de la villa de Bilbao*, vol. 1 (reprinted, Bilbao: Editorial La Gran Enciclopedia Vasca, 1972), p. 76. In the opinion of J. Ortega Galindo (*Bilbao y su hinterland*, Bilbao, 1951), "the vital beginnings of the Villa are determined by its natural condition as the center of convergence of three rivers and an estuary. In this place, there was the necessity of permanent human settlement and goods, with the object of transferring them from the boat to the beasts of burden and vice versa."
2. T. Guiard, *La industria naval vizcaína* (Bilbao, 1917), pp. 12 and passim.
3. P. Chaunu, "Les routes espagnoles de l'Atlantique" in *Noveno coloquio internacional de historia marítima. Anuario de estudios americanos*, t. 25 (Sevilla, 1968), pp. 9, 103.
4. J. Caro Baroja, "La tradición técnica del pueblo vasco o una interpretación ecológica de su historia," *Vasconiana* (Madrid, 1975), p. 108. The Basque ecosystem is very similar to that of the Scottish highlands. Also, there is a good description of the different sectors of the traditional Basque economy in T. Lefebvre, *Les modes de vie dans les Pyrénées Atlantiques Orientales* (Paris, 1933), pp. 237-278.
5. J. Caro Baroja, *Los vascos* (Madrid, 1971), p. 195.
6. L. Suárez Fernández, *Navegación y comercio en el golfo de Vizcaya. Un estudio sobre la política marinera de la casa de Trastamara* (Madrid, 1959).
7. J. Heers, "Le commerce des basques en Méditerranée au XVe siècle (d'après les archives de Gênes)," *Bulletin hispanique*, vol. 7, 1955, p. 293.

8. J. Almunia, "Ferrerías en el País Vasco," *Real Sociedad Bascongada de Amigos del País Bicentenario de su fundación, 1765-1795* (Bilbao, 1967), pp. 112-121.
9. T. Guiard, *Historia del Consulado...*, pp. 11 and passim. While the Burgos merchants complained of the Vizcayan monopoly in wool transport (L. Suárez, *Navegación y comercio...*, p. 121) the latter accused the former of wanting to subject Bilbao's commerce to the jurisdiction of the consulate of Burgos (created in 1494, seventeen years before that of Bilbao) thereby monopolizing wool exportation and establishing unilaterally the charterings (M. Basas, *El comercio de Burgos en el siglo XVI* (Madrid, 1963), pp. 36-37).
10. T. Guiard, *Historia del Consulado...*, p. 15.
11. J. Finot, *Etude historique sur les relations commerciales entre la Flandre et l'Espagne au Moyen Age* (Paris, 1899), pp. 77, 93.
12. Ibid., pp. 284, 314.
13. J. Heers, "Le commerce des basques en Méditeranée...," *Bulletin hispanique*, vol. 7, 1955, pp. 292, 298, 302.
14. F. Braudel, *El Mediterráneo y el mundo mediterráneo en la época de Felipe II*, vol. 2 (Madrid, 1976), p. 183.
15. T. Guiard, *Historia del Consulado...*, p. 35.
16. Ibid., pp. 6-11.
17. F. Braudel, *Civilización material y capitalismo* (Barcelona, 1974), p. 297.
18. C. H. Haring, *Comercio y navegación entre España y las Indias en la época de los Habsburgos* (Mexico, 1939), p. 331. After 1593, Andalusian-built ships were prohibited on the American run, since they were constructed of green pine, a measure which favored construction in Cantabrian shipyards.

    The Casa de Contratación of Seville, from the early years of the sixteenth century, contracted for vessels and crewmen from the Cantabrian coast, and especially from Vizcaya and Guipúzcoa. Consequently, for this purpose, in 1505 the Casa de Contratación of Seville maintained a representative in Bilbao, Martín Sánchez de Zamudio. The state mandated, by means of constant decrees and privileges, the preparation of mariners and naval construction, indispensable elements in commerce with the Americas. Cf. P. Chaunu, *Seville et l'Atlantique (1500-1650)*, vol. 8 (Paris, 1949), pp. 250 and passim.
19. Ibid., pp. 18-19.
20. F. Braudel, *Civilización material...*, p. 350.
21. P. Chaunu, *Noveno coloquio internacional...*, t. 25, pp. 256-258.

22. H. Lapeyre, "El comercio de Bilbao en el siglo XVI," *Curso de conferencias sobre cuestiones históricas y actuales de la economía española, curso 1955-1956*, pp. 133-159. The number of sacks of wool exported through Santander destined for Flanders in the period 1558-1579 was 70,755, while those exported via Bilbao only totalled 6,556. There is not such a difference between Bilbao and Santander in the quantities sent to France in the same period: 10,587 compared to 27,785 respectively (M. Basas, *El comercio de Burgos...*, pp. 261-262). In the opinion of H. Lapeyre, the control of the wool trade, at least in the sixteenth century, was in the hands of the businessmen of the interior, making those merchants of Bilbao and Santander engaged in the trading mere supernumeraries of the former. Proof of this, according to him, was the scant attention paid to this branch of commerce by the General Assembly (*Juntas*) of Vizcaya, which focused its interest upon the commercialization of the seigneury's primary product: iron. M. Lapeyre, *El comercio exterior de Castilla a través de las aduanas de Felipe II*, "Estudios y documentos," no. 41 (Valladolid, 1981), p. 181.
23. A. García Sanz, *Desarrollo y crisis del antiguo régimen en Castilla la Vieja. Economía y sociedad en tierras de Segovia 1500-1804* (Madrid, 1977), p. 241, note 62.
24. L. M. Bilbao, "Crisis y reconstrucción de la economía vascongada en el siglo XVII," *Saioak*, vol. 1, no. 1, 1977, pp. 178-179.
25. P. Calatayud, *Tratado práctico sobre la compra y venta de las lanas merinas especialmente y otros géneros* (Madrid, 1757), p. 27.
26. I. Wallerstein, *El moderno sistema mundial. La agricultura capitalista y los orígenes de la economía-mundo europea en el siglo XVI* (Madrid, 1979), pp. 172-173, 269. Also V. Vázquez de Prada, *Lettres marchantes d'Anvers*, vol. 1 (Paris, 1959), p. 106.
27. J. Alcala Zamora y Queipo de Llano, "Producción de hierro y altos hornos de la España anterior a 1850," *Moneda y crédito* (Madrid, 1974), p. 151.
28. L. M. Bilbao, "Crisis y reconstrucción...," p. 164.
29. T. Guiard, *Historia del Consulado...*, pp. 527, 552.
30. G. Henao, *Averiguaciones de las antiguedades de Cantabria*, vol. 1, reedition (Tolosa, 1894), p. 190.
31. The first shipment of Russian iron sold in London dates from 1716. Nevertheless, by midcentury it was dominant in the London market, a time by which the production of Russian ingots had begun to surpass that of England, an advantage that would be maintained throughout the rest of the century. F. X. G. Coquin,

"Rusia: La iniciativa estatal y señorial," in P. León (ed.), *Inercias y revoluciones. Historia económica y social del mundo*, vol. 3 (Madrid, 1980), p. 42.

32. S. Lilly, "El progreso tecnológico y la revolución industrial, 1700-1914," *Historia económica de Europa*, vol. 3, *La revolución industrial* (bajo la dirección de C. M. Cipolla (Barcelona, 1979), pp. 205, 222).

33. By the Royal Decree of July 31, 1718, unelaborated iron of the Basque Country extracted outside the kingdom was exempted from payment of duties "in light of the fact that given the sterility of the Basque Country, iron is the only product of commerce." *A. H. N. Sección de hacienda. Ordenes generales de rentas*, vol. 3, folios 368-369. Vizcayan iron was also exempt from the admiralty duty, in accord with foral law number 9, a liberty confirmed by the Royal Decree of June 20, 1738, ("the Admiralty duty is not charged to the Iron of said Seigneury in the customs houses of land or sea") and by the Royal Order of March 4, 1741. (P. Fontecha Salazar, *Escudo de la más constante fée y lealtad de Vizcaya* [anonymous, no date], folio 35.) Vizcayan iron, as well as that from the mountains of Burgos, was equally exempt from the duties in the customs houses of Cartagena, Valencia, and Andalusia, though not from other accrued taxes (*A. H. N.*, vol. 13, folio 14). The seigneury of Vizcaya and the province of Guipúzcoa had managed to have removed certain royal provisions in the years 1619, 1621, 1627, and 1665, thereby prohibiting introduction into the kingdom of manufactured iron from Liege and other foreign states, under pain of disembowelment (Joseph Veitia Linage, *Norte de la contratación de las Indias Occidentales*, book 2, chapter 16, (first edition, Sevilla, 1672; reissued, Buenos Aires, 1945).

34. Proof of this is that the Royal Order of 1702 seems to have been ratified on May 28, 1776, requiring then that all iron products destined for America should bear the marks of their respective foundry owners in the kingdom.

35. *Junta General*, 18 julio de 1768, folio 100, verso.

36. *A. D. V. Sección de libros manuscritos. Veeduria de Cádiz*, folios 233-240.

37. *A. H. N., Sección de hacienda*, e. 23, folios 483-486.

38. *Extractos de las Juntas de la Real Sociedad Bascongada celebradas en la villa de Bilbao por setiembre de 1775*, pp. 55-56.

39. *A. H. P., Esno*. Antonio de Esnarrizaga, year 1782, protocol 3,464, folios 33-35.

40. *Informe presentado en 1789 por el teniente de Navío don Gerónimo Taberna a la Sociedad Bascongada*, resumido y

comentado por J. Almunia, "Ferrerías en el País Vasco," *Real Sociedad Bascongada...*, pp. 134–135.
41. *Extractos de las Juntas Generales celebradas en la villa de Vergara por julio de 1791*, pp. 36–41.
42. Nevertheless, in the middle years of the century, positive external and internal factors were at play which facilitated the export of Vizcayan siderurgical production. These included the increased targeting of the American colonial market which acquired greater importance as a substitute for the lost European ones and the increase in demand from the arsenals and shipyards of the navy.
43. A. R. Michell, "Las pesquerías europeas al comienzo de la Edad Moderna," *Historia económica de Europa de la Universidad de Cambridge*, vol. 5 (Madrid, 1981), p. 201.
44. F. Braudel, *Civilización material y capitalismo* (Barcelona, 1974), p. 169.
45. A. R. Michell, "Las pesquerías... ", p. 201.
46. Jerónimo de Ustáriz, *Theorica y práctica de comercio y de marina* (Madrid: Antonio Sanz, 1742), cap. 87, p. 277.
47. J. O. McLachlan, *Trade and Peace with Old Spain*, vol. 2 (New York, 1974), p. 7. According to S. Ricard, "Le commerce de la morue est infiniment précieux, Il occupe plus de 500 navires et procure à ceux qui la font des bénefices souvent considerables. Les anglois s'en étoient rendus les maistres et la possedoient presque sans concurrence avant la guerre actuelle. Ils ont retiré de trés grandes profits tout le temps qu'ils s'en ont été paisibles posseseurs," *Traité général du commerce*, vol. 1 (Amsterdam: Chez E. van Harrevelt, 1781), p. 47.
48. N. De Arriquibar, *Recreación política. Reflexión sobre el amigo de los hombres en su tratado de población considerado con respecto a nuestros intereses*, vol. 2 (Vitoria, 1779), Map 7, p. 164.
49. G. Zeller, *Histoire des rélations internationales. Les temps modernes, I. De Louis XIV à 1789* (Paris, 1972), p. 97.
50. The original text is as follows: "... And whereas it is insisted on the part of Spain, that certain rights of fishing at the island of Newfoundland belong to the Guipuzcoans, or other subjects of the Catholic King, her Britannic Majesty consents and agrees, that all such privileges as the Guipuzcoans and other people of Spain are able to make claim to by right, shall be allowed and preserved to them." Ch. G. Jenkinson, *A Collection of All Treaties of Peace, Alliance and Commerce between Great Britain and Other Powers from the Treaty Signed at Munster in 1648 to the Treaties Signed at Paris in 1783*, vol. 2 (London, 1785; reedition, 1968), p. 76, article 15.

The Marquis of Monteleón proposed that a paragraph be added to the Treaty of Utrecht that would state clearly the rights of Basques in the cod fisheries and whale hunting along the Canadian coasts. The text that he proposed was as follows: "The Guipuzcoans and other vassals of Your Royal Majesty will be maintained in their immemorial and free use they have enjoyed until now of navigating, commercializing and conducting whale and cod fishing in the New World even in time of war" (V. G. Palacio Atard, "Marqués de Monteleón en Londres (1716–1717))," *Anuario de estudios americanos*, vol. 1, 1944, p. 728.

51. Cf. M. Ciriquiain Gaiztarro, *Los vascos en la pesca de la ballena* (San Sebastián, 1961), pp. 318 and passim. "In reality such prohibition imposed upon Basque fishermen was singularly unjust, taking into account the fact that no country, until after the Treaty of Utrecht, had taken formal possession of those lands, which were only inhabited by the variegated, multinational ensemble of fishermen during the cod fishing season and the period devoted to the drying and salting of the cetacean. In the month of September of each year, the seafarers abandoned the coasts of Terranova, which then remained deserted until the beginning of the following spring." (V. G. Palacio Atard, *El tercer pacto de familia* (Madrid, 1945), p. 77).
52. Report sent by the seigneury of Vizcaya to don Joseph de Carvajal y Lancaster in 1748 with regard to the Conference of Aachen. *A. G. S., Secretaría de Estado*, leg. 7,011, no. 28.
53. Ibid.
54. In the Treaty of Madrid of 1721, a favorable positioning of Basque interests was achieved, but it never transcended being more than a mere diplomatic formulation devoid of practical consequences. The text stated that His Majesty the British king offered "to give of course his orders that the governors of the Island of Terranova and the adjacent ports and coasts should permit and put no obstacle in the way of Guipuzcoan and Vizcayan Spaniards involved in the fishing, fleshing and drying of codfish, of which they have been in immemorial possession." (Ciriquiain, *Los vascos en la pesca de la ballena*, p. 323. Also J. Carrera Pujal, *Historia de la economía española*, vol. 5 (Barcelona, 1943–1947), p. 29.
55. *A. G. S. Secretaría de Estado*, leg. 7,014, no. 10.
56. D. I. Egaña, *El guipuzcoano instruído en las reales cédulas, despachos y órdenes que ha venerado su madre la Provincia* (San Sebastián, 1780), p. 350.
57. *A. G. S. Secretaría de Estado*, leg. 7,014, no. 29. The analysis elaborated by the province of Guipúzcoa, of this important dossier, merits its own study, employing a critical perspective. One

would have to ascertain if the expeditions of Guipuzcoan cod fishermen to Terranova continued with regularity throughout the seventeenth century or, to the contrary, if by the beginning of this century there had been a decline in Basque fisheries and fishing ports. E. J. Hamilton, *War and Prices in Spain, 1651–1800* (New York, 1969), p. 177, places the decadence of Basque fisheries in the second half of the seventeenth century, after which time foreigners co-opted the provisioning of fish to the Spanish market. Selma Huxley Barkham situates the collapse of the Basque maritime economy earlier, in the last third of the sixteenth century, as a consequence of the state's massive levies of mariners for the "first Invincible Armada," Magellan's journey, the expeditions to the Azores of 1581–1583, and the final disaster of 1588. All of the foregoing was linked to the loss of the Flanders market. In her opinion, the ruining of the Basque maritime economy was an unintended consequence of Phillip II's policies. Although the Basque maritime economy experienced a certain recovery in the first years of the seventeenth century, it was, nevertheless, insufficient to enable Spanish Basques to maintain their dominant position in Terranova (contrary to what she states). Cf. Selma Huxley Barkham, "Guipuzcoan Shipping in 1571 with Particular Reference to the Decline of the Transatlantic Fishing Industry," William A. Douglass, Richard W. Etulain, and William H. Jacobsen, Jr. (eds.), *Anglo-American Contributions to Basque Studies: Essays in Honor of Jon Bilbao* (Reno: Desert Research Institute, 1977), p. 78.

58. *A. G. S. Secretaría de Estado*, leg. 7,014, no. 29.
59. L. Goyetche, *Saint-Jean-de-Luz historique et pittoresque* (Paris, 1883), pp. 152–155.
60. P. Aguado Bleye, *La villa de Lequeitio en el siglo XVIII* (Bilbao, 1921), p. 16.
61. Ch. de la Morandiere, *Histoire de la pêche française de la morue dans l'Amérique septentrionale*, vol. 2 (Paris, 1964), pp. 600–603.
62. "Whaling and deep-sea fishing appear in full vigor among the Basques in the hazy reaches of the Middle Ages. There is definite proof of their codfishing trips to Newfoundland by 1530 and whaling voyages off Greenland by 1622 *but in the mid-eighteenth century knowledge of either art remained chiefly in the mind of old and decrepit men,*" R. Dennis Hussey, *The Caracas Company 1728–1784. A Study in the History of Spanish Monopolistic Trade* (Cambridge, 1934), p. 170.
63. *A. G. S., Secretaría de Estado*, leg. 7,014, no. 27.

64. *Extractos de las Juntas celebradas por la Real Sociedad Bascongada de los Amigos del País*, Comisiones terceras de Industria y Comercio. Artículo 1, Pesca (Vitoria, 1777), p. 43.
65. Ibid., p. 44. "The causes of that which resulted in the decadence or, rather, the ruin of these branches of industry were the expropriation by England, by means of various peace treaties, of the Island of San Juan de Terranova, recognizing the great benefits that it afforded to the state, depriving absolutely the Spaniards of this commerce, and particularly to this country (the Basque area), whose people were innately endowed with this fishery."
66. H. A. Innis, "The Rise and Fall of the Spanish Fishery in Newfoundland," *Proceedings and Transactions of the Royal Society of Canada*, third series, vol. 25, section 2, 1931, p. 157.

An Estimate of Navarrese Migration in the Second Half of the Nineteenth Century (1879-1883)

by

Angel García-Sanz Marcotegui and Alejandro Arizcun Cela

In 1985 Professor Pérez Moreda[1] underscored the importance of Navarrese emigration during the Restoration and, at the same time, indicated the need to study the causes, regional origins, and destinations of the emigrants in question. The present article is a contribution to our knowledge of such processes during the quinquennium 1879-1883.

From the last decade of the eighteenth century to the middle of the nineteenth, Navarra, and all of the Basque Country in general, passed through a series of negative circumstances that inhibited its population growth compared with that of Spain as a whole. In fact, at particular times growth was stagnant or the population actually declined. This evolution may be seen in great detail in the censuses taken beginning in the second half of the eighteenth century. Navarra, which had 227,382 inhabitants in 1786, had 297,432 in 1857, which renders an annual growth rate of 0.49 percent. This is in contrast to the Spanish rate of 0.63 percent. As a consequence the percentage of Spain's national population constituted by the Navarrese declined from 2 to 1.9 percent over the period.

The causes of this slow growth were quite diverse, although interrelated. Bad harvests and wars, and the aftermaths of both, such as epidemics, at times of multiple illness; inadequate sanitation; emigration; etc. were the principal factors. We should remember that Navarra was a battleground for all of the wars of the period, and that epidemics such as typhus and cholera caused considerable mortality in several Navarrese regions.

After the First Carlist War the persistence of agriculture as the dominant economic activity, the weight of war damages, and new epidemics and conflicts all militated against demographic change from the Ancient Regime to a more modern one. The cholera epidemic of 1855 alone killed 12,000 people, or 4 percent of the population, and that of 1885 took another 3,261 lives.

In addition to all of these negative factors, there were certain internal characteristics of the population whose persistence helps to explain its weak growth. According to Livi Bacci the birth rates of the Basque Country and Navarra in 1787, 1797, and 1860 were below those of the Spanish national average, as were the marriage rates for persons between sixteen and twenty-five years of age and female nuptiality in general.[2]

In the second half of the nineteenth century there were fewer wars and epidemics than in the first half. The only war that affected Navarra directly was the Second Carlist campaign (whose demographic consequences remain unstudied). Similarly, the cholera epidemic of 1885 claimed fewer victims than did that of 1855. If to this we add that mortality rates, and particularly infant mortality, declined by the end of the century, we might expect to see the population increase at a greater rate between 1860 and 1900 than during the first half of the nineteenth century.

In fact, the annual natural increase in the population during this period was on the order of 0.60 percent (0.71 in the decade 1861–1870, 0.57 between 1878 and 1900, and 0.83 in the five-year period 1900–1905).[3] Nevertheless, the population totals remained practically static, as may be seen in Table One.

Table One: *Real Population Growth*

Year	Number of Inhabitants in Navarra	Percentage of Increase	Percentage of Increase in Spain
1797	227,382	—	—
1857	297,432	0.49	0.64
1900	307,669	0.08	0.43

Emigration provides the only logical explanation of this pronounced population stability in Navarra. In effect, between 1878 and 1887 real population growth in the province was minimal since the natural increase in the populace was offset by an annual emigration rate of 0.80 percent. Between 1888 and 1900 the emigration rate equalled four-fifths of the natural increase.

There is abundant, although incomplete and scattered, information regarding this exodus. It seems that emigration became common after the First Carlist War, stimulated by a law in 1843 which legalized departures to America. In fact, in 1852 the governor of Navarra disseminated a circular through the parish priests denouncing the massive exodus to America and the bishop of Pamplona, Severo Andriani, published his *Circular en que repruebe como inmoral el sistema de enganchar jóvenes de ambos sexos para conducirlos al Continente Americano bajo las seductoras promesas de una estable fortuna y un feliz porvenir*. ("Circular in which the System of Hoodwinking Persons of Both Sexes in Order to Conduct Them to the American Continent under the Seductive Promises of Establishing a Fortune and a Happy Future Is Demonstrated as Being Immoral.")

Clearly, the phenomenon attained considerable importance since, in 1888, the Provincial Council of Agriculture, Industry and Commerce warned that in mountainous areas emigration was so pronounced that some districts were experiencing a labor shortage.[4]

The perseverance of a farming economy, which in many respects was antiquated, prompted many Navarrese to seek employment outside their home area.[5] Consequently, in the *Estadística de la emigración e inmigración de España en el quinquenio 1891–1895* (page 75) it states that the Navarrese emigrated because of the effects of the recent civil war, the collapse of agriculture, the shortage of industry, and the overtures of the immigration agencies of Uruguay and the River Plate, among other causes.

The Commission of Social Reforms was concerned with the difficulties experienced by emigrants to America. In 1885 it publicized the misfortunes incurred by them, while noting that "the emigration (was) totally due to the fallacious promises made continually by the emissaries who go about the countryside." It seems that the commission was indifferent to the internal situation in the Navarrese peasantry as expressed in the reply that it received to its queries from Villamayor: ". . . in every town where there is the custom of harvesting wheat there are poor farm day laborers who live in ordinary circumstances. And to an even greater degree in those places where there is no such harvest there is an evident, horrible, antisocial, hellish, health destroying—I don't know what qualifier to give it—aspiration to exploit the sweat of the poor worker, to usury and debt."

Everything seems to indicate that the immigration agencies had an extensive network of "inveiglers" who took advantage of potential emigrants. In addition, the shipping companies advertised in Navarrese newspapers offering passage from Pasájes, Bilbao, and Bordeaux to Buenos Aires, Montevideo, Valparaiso, etc. "at extraordinarily cheap prices." The information that we possess regarding this is from the beginning of the following century, but it is plausible to imagine that there was a similar situation in the latter part of the nineteenth century. These shipping companies, like Chargeurs Reunis or The Pacific Steam Navigation Company, had their agents in Pamplona, Tolosa, etc. and some of them, like Domingo Apesteguía, worked for twenty-nine years at the profession. They offered fare reductions for entire families.[6]

Given its considerable social impact,[7] the emigration theme occurs in numerous literary contexts of the period.[8] To cite but one example which transcends the merely anecdotal, one might note the poem that received honorable mention in 1883, and which has the prosaic title "Emigración navarra a América, sus causas y consecuencias" (Navarrese Emigration to America. Its Causes and Consequences).

In light of the importance of the exodus, the Provincial Government (*Diputación Foral*) of Navarra and the bishops of Pamplona published numerous circulars designed to combat and contain emigration, by warning the population against the "hoodwinkers," but without much success.

For its part, the press paid considerable attention to the problem, devoting many articles to it. On November 29, 1885, the Madrid newspaper *El liberal* described the great multitude of emigrants leaving the train station of Pamplona for Bordeaux, as ingenuously confident of returning within a year with a large fortune.[9] *El anunciador ibérico* of Tudela referred to the proemigration propaganda campaign in Navarra and the large number of persons who were leaving the province. The newspaper noted, "if it continues in this manner the day will arrive when Navarra is left with a minuscule population."[10] The Carlist organ, *El pensamiento navarro*, noted on August 26, 1903, that there were 712 Navarrese in Cuba alone. It regularly pointed out the alarming proportions of the emigration phenomenon.[11] At the same time it occasionally informed its readers regarding departures from particular localities. For example, in its December 4, 1901, issue it noted that all the young men who had just turned eligible for military service in the town of Cáseda had emigrated to America; the October 14, 1905, issue said that seventeen young men from Navascués had done the same; when 100 young men from Pamplona failed to report for the draft it was attributed to emigration to America,[12] as had been the case two years earlier with another cohort of potential recruits.[13]

The Carlist newspaper at times petitioned the government to do something about this hemorrhaging,[14] but when this failed it directed its efforts at dissuading potential emigrants. In this regard it constantly published letters from different American countries in which the writers claimed that there was no employment there and painted a bleak picture of the circumstances of the emigrants.[15] In one of the letters the writer urged the Navarrese press to propagandize against emigration, noting that "anyone who is able to eat a piece of cornbread once a week should not (move) from the country (Navarra)."[16]

The efforts of *El pensamiento navarro* were condemned to failure given the lack of employment opportunity in Navarra. The canon Hilario Yaben underscored the inevitability of emigration since "it was an inevitable consequence of family organization in Navarra." For him, given his concern with social stability and the moral state of his countrymen, "emigration in Navarra is an unavoidable necessity. The (number of) families that work the land cannot be increased, because all the tillable soil is under cultivation."[17] To the contrary, other investigators deny that there is a direct relationship between inheritance system and emigration.[18]

To this point we have considered the importance of emigration in Navarra. Nevertheless, we do not have a precise understanding of the chronology of the evolution of the phenomenon, and there is a particular lack of studies of the regional origins of the emigrants. In this regard we have but a few theses, such as that of Idoate, which uses notary public protocols to document the departure of 1,415 emigrants from the Valley of Baztán between 1840 and 1880. Unfortunately, we do not have similar studies for other valleys that would facilitate comparisons.

For data regarding the profile of the emigrants our only recourses are the *Anuarios estadísticos de España* and the publications of the Instituto Geográfico y Estadístico. Their main drawback is that the information is incomplete, particularly in that it focuses exclusively upon internal migration to places such as Guipúzcoa, Madrid, and, notably, to Vizcaya in the Navarrese case. Other sources provide glimpses. For example, in 1898, according to one work, there were 4,087 Navarrese in Madrid.[19] At times the Institute provides information regarding departures from Spanish ports which, of course, omits a large portion of Navarrese and Guipuzcoans who left from Bordeaux. In other instances the disparities in the criteria employed when gathering the data make the results suggestive at best. Keeping this in mind, Table Two provides some indication of the magnitude of Navarrese emigration at particular points in time according to the *Anuario estadístico de España*.

Table Two: *Navarrese Emigration: Selected Years*

Year	Number of Emigrants
1860	637
1861	883
1880	802
1889	1,275
1890	461
1891–1895	1,669

Source: *Anuarios estadísticos de España*.

Fortunately, we have managed to discover more precise documentation, although it deals exclusively with overseas emigration, which permits us to study the unequal distribution in the incidence of emigration from distinct Navarrese municipalities during the quinquennium 1879–1883.

In 1883 the Comisión de Reformas Sociales (Social Reforms Commission) distributed a questionnaire in order to understand the circumstances of the working class, which contained a section (XXVII, questions 184–189) that elicited information on the following topics:

1. The annual number of persons emigrating by destination to Spanish overseas possessions, America, and other countries.

2. The number of returnees from the three above contexts, specifying if they were successful or not during their stay in other countries. This last question is answered infrequently and unreliably; consequently, we will exclude it from consideration.

Fortunately, in the Navarrese case a substantial number of municipalities replied. Indeed, 237 of the 269 town governments responded, representing 77.8 percent of the Navarrese population of the period. Excepting Pamplona and Tudela, which due to their size found it difficult to answer the questionnaire, all but a few responded, meaning that the sample is practically complete. Regarding the accuracy of the answers it is difficult to judge; however, in any event there is considerable internal coherence by region which speaks in its favor.

The real (*de hecho*)[20] population of Navarra at the end of the Second Carlist War was practically static, increasing but little from 294,000 inhabitants in 1877 to 304,051 in 1887. We have noted that this was due to economic privation which translated into emigration. The number of emigrants listed in the questionnaires cited above was 2,903 in the quinquennium,[21] with a net loss to emigration of 2,347 if returns are deducted from departures. This brute and net loss of persons represents for the period an annual average decline of 0.20 and 0.16 percent, respectively, with regard to the population of 1877.

This is a high rate if we compare it to the general statistics for Spain, in which the net loss to emigration is 0.08 percent annually for the period 1858–1870, and between 1878 and 1887 returns actually surpass departures by about the same rate. Navarra seems to have anticipated the subsequent "boom" in Spanish emigration, which reached 0.22 percent of the population annually between 1888 and 1897.[22] While Spain was recuperating some of the emigrants who had left in the years prior to the Second Carlist War, Navarra continued to send out a considerable number of persons, this despite difficulties in the American receiving areas which were victims of a depressed economic cycle.

The geographical origins of the emigrants are distributed unequally among the various zones of Navarra. In Map One we have opted for a regional (*comarcal*) division of the province which reflects variations in the organization of Navarrese agriculture. The difference between the municipality of Tudela, with its one emigrant, and the 454 of the Valley of Baztán underscores the disparity in emigration from region to region. In general terms we can say that as one moves northward within the province the rate of emigration increases. This is supported by Map Two, which reflects the emigration balances (all negative) of the different Navarrese regions.

Table Three provides the statistics that support this affirmation.

The two most northerly regions, the Humid Atlantic and the Pyrenean Valleys, stand out from all the rest with emigration balances that suggest a significant hemorrhaging of population. The Intermediary Zones and Pyrenean Foothills have departure rates that are a bit below the provincial average, while the Riverine Zones have small percentages, although still reflecting a negative balance. We should note that the Eastern Intermediary Zone is an exception to the general pattern in that its emigration rate is considerably greater than that of the Western Intermediary Zone and even slightly higher than that of the Pyrenean Foothills to the north.

With respect to the magnitude of returns the Eastern Riverine Zone is the most pronounced, approximating in this regard the Spanish national average. Conversely, the Pyrenean Foothills and the Eastern Intermediary Zone have extremely low percentages of returns. However, in the Eastern Riverine Zone the significance of the emigration rate and balance suffers from the extremely small volume of emigration in absolute terms, since only twenty-four persons emigrated and ten returned. The commission, in its report, noted that, "Of this emigration most went to our Spanish possessions, and this fact is more significant when we note that comparatively the emigration (from other regions) is considerably greater to other destinations in America."

At the beginning of this commentary we noted that the Navarrese population was practically stable between the 1877 and 1887 censuses, but that in regard to emigration it evolved differently in the various regions. Table Four reflects real growth (or decline) in the Navarrese population by regions.

Naturally, the evolution of the population seems more unequal if the municipality is selected as the geographic unit of study. Even so, in Map Two we can see the correlation between high emigration imbalances and the large number of municipalities experiencing population decline.

MAP 1: Division of Navarra by Regions.

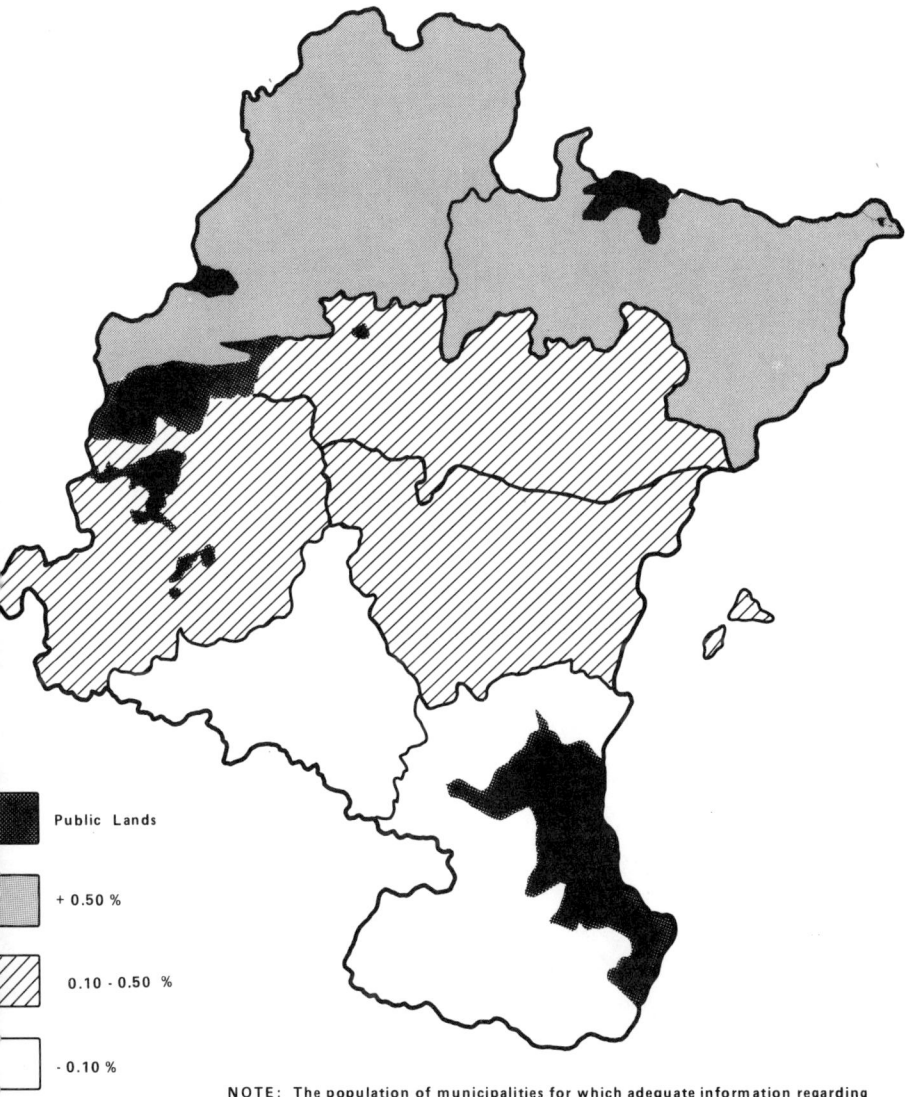

Public Lands

+ 0.50 %

0.10 - 0.50 %

- 0.10 %

NOTE: The population of municipalities for which adequate information regarding emigration is lacking have been excluded from consideration.

MAP 2: Average Annual Navarrese Emigration Rates to Foreign Destinations: 1879 to 1883. (Base Population in 1877).

Table Three: *Annual Rates of Emigration (1879–1883) and Numbers of Municipalities with Population Loss (1877–1887)*

Region	Annual Rate of Emigration	Balance (Emigration Less Organic Growth)	Returns as a Percentage of Departures	Number of Municipalities	Number of Municipalities with Population Loss
Humid Atlantic	0.57	0.41	27.9	51	35
Pyrenean Valleys	0.58	0.46	21.2	35	12
Pyrenean Foothills	0.17	0.16	9.1	38	12
Western Intermediary Zone	0.14	0.11	20.1	61	31
Eastern Intermediary Zone	0.22	0.21	6.9	40	15
Western Riverine Zone	0.04	0.03	17.0	16	2
Eastern Riverine Zone	0.01	0.01	47.7	28	2
totals				269	119

Table Four: *Real Population Movement in the Navarrese Regions: 1877-1887*

Region	Absolute Growth or Decline	Growth or Decline as a Percentage of the Population in 1877
Humid Atlantic	- 774	- 1.5
Pyrenean Valleys	+ 153	+ 0.9
Pyrenean Foothills	- 882	- 3.1
Western Intermediary Zone	+ 392	+ 0.9
Eastern Intermediary Zone	+ 2,162	+ 6.3
Western Riverine Zone	+ 1,375	+ 5.2
Eastern Riverine Zone	+ 4,454	+ 12.4

By itself Navarrese emigration abroad cannot explain the evolution of the population; indeed, as we shall see, it was not of particular quantitative importance during the years under consideration. Our present ignorance regarding natality and mortality in the Navarrese regions during the quinquennium under study precludes our making further observations concerning the natural movement of the population, but it is of interest to try to estimate the extent of Navarrese migration to other parts of Spain, which would then complement the figures for emigration abroad.

This estimate rests upon a supposition that should be made explicit—i.e., within Navarra there existed homogeneity among the different regions with regard to differences between birth and death rates, which between 1878 and 1884 was on the order of 0.8 percent.

We need not state that this supposition is very weak, but it allows us to construct an initial approximation of the problem. In such a situation it would seem advisable to limit our conclusions, which may be made based on the data in Table Five.

The tenuous conclusions that may be suggested are as follows:

—Although the flow of emigrants abroad was considerable, the movement of migrants to other parts of Spain was greater. In the first instance America was the favored destination while in the second it was Vizcaya. A dramatic example of the latter is provided by the municipality of Desojo from which six whole families had migrated to the Vizcayan town of Somorrostro in search of work.

—If emigration abroad was, comparatively speaking, considerable, departures as a whole are multiplied by 2.5 if we add migration to Spanish destinations. In combination the two

Table Five: *Estimate of Navarrese Migration to Other Parts of Spain: 1877–1887*

Region	Real Population Growth	Estimated Natural Population Increase	Estimated Migration Balance	Emigration* Abroad	Migration to the Rest of Spain
Humid Atlantic	-774	3,980	-4,754	-2,224	-2,530
Pyrenean Valleys	153	1,312	-1,159	- 752	- 407
Pyrenean Foothills	-882	2,258	-3,140	- 442	-2,698
Western Intermediary Zone	392	3,382	-2,990	- 462	-2,528
Eastern Intermediary Zone	2,162	2,694	- 532	- 698	+ 166
Western Riverine Zone	1,375	2,102	- 727	- 88	- 639
Eastern Riverine Zone	4,454	2,878	1,570	- 28	+ 1,604

* These figures are derived by doubling those for the period 1879–1883

movements explain Navarrese population stability for the period.

—In the Humid Atlantic region emigration abroad and internal migration were about equal in volume.

—In the Pyrenean Valleys and the Eastern Intermediary Zone emigration abroad dominated.

—In the Pyrenean Foothills and the Western Riverine Zones internal migration was far more pronounced than emigration abroad.

—In the Eastern Riverine Zone there is a net population gain due to in-migration from other parts of Spain and, one would suppose, Navarra as well.

Some general observations that we might make and which should be developed further regard:

—The comparatively large volume of Navarrese emigration in the period

—The correlation between geographical differences, evolution of the population, and emigration

—The major involvement in emigration of the northern part of the province, with certain differences in this regard between its two regions, the reasons for which we do not understand at present

—The more limited emigration from the Intermediary Zones which, nevertheless, is still greater than the national average

—The net population gain from in-migration in the Eastern Riverine Zone, which provides a population balance that is consonant with the Spanish national average.

Notes

1. Vicente Pérez Moreda, "Evolución de la población española desde finales del Antiguo Régimen," *Papeles de economía española*, vol. 20 (1984); and "Algunas reflexiones sobre la población navarra en los tiempos contemporáneos," *Congreso de historia de Navarra de los siglos XVIII, XIX y XX* (Pamplona: Príncipe de Viana, 1987).
2. Massimo Livi Bacci, "Fertility and Nuptiality Changes in Spain, Part I," *Population Studies*, vol. 12, no. 1 (1968), pp. 83–102; and "Fertility and Nuptiality Changes in Spain, Part II," *Population Studies*, vol. 12, no. 2 (1968), pp. 211–234.
3. Cf. Instituto Geográfico y Estadístico, *Movimiento de la población de España en el decenio de 1861 a 1870* (Madrid, 1877); Instituto Geográfico y Estadístico, *Reseña geográfica y estadística de España* (Madrid, 1912); and V. Pérez Moreda, "Algunas reflexiones . . . ," p. 9.
4. José Andrés-Gallego, *Historia contemporánea de Navarra* (Pamplona: Diario de Navarra, 1982), p. 52.
5. Domingo Gallego, *La producción agrícola y ganadera en el Alto Ebro desde mediados del siglo XIX a 1935*, Tesis doctoral leída en la Universidad Complutense de Madrid en 1986.
6. For additional information regarding the activities of shipping agents, see María Pilar Pildain Salazar, *Ir a América. La emigración vasca a América. Guipúzcoa, 1840–1880* (San Sebastián, 1984), pp. 54 and passim.
7. José Cola y Goiti, *La emigración vasco navarra* (Vitoria: Iturbe, 1886), passim.
8. Cf. the magazine *Euskara*, (San Sebastián), 1878–1883.
9. José Cola y Goiti, *La emigración . . .* , p. 161.
10. Cited in *El pensamiento navarro*, October 18, 1898.
11. Ibid., September 20, 1903, and November 3, 1906.
12. Ibid., June 26, 1908.
13. Ibid., November 30, 1906.
14. Ibid., January 27, 1901.
15. Ibid., June 14, 1899; January 31, 1903; January 1, 1904; July 29, 1906; October 2, 1906; March 12, 1907; August 30, 1907.
16. Ibid., January 1, 1904.
17. Hilario Yaben y Yaben, *Los contratos matrimoniales en Navarra y su influencia en estabilidad de la familia* (Madrid: Jaime Ratés, 1916), pp. 183–184.

18. Andrew Abelson, "Inheritance and Population Control in a Basque Valley (Baztán) before 1900," *Peasant Studies*, vol. 7, no. 1 (winter, 1978).
19. Angel Bahamonde Magro and Julián Toro Mérida, *Burguesía, especulación y cuestión social en el Madrid del siglo XIX* (Madrid: Editorial Siglo XXI, 1978), p. 260.
20. There is a distinction between *población de hecho*, or those present at the time that a census is taken, and *población de derecho*, or those with legal residence in a place but who are absent when censused.
21. We have excluded the statistics from Puente la Reina since they contain anomalies.
22. Vicente Pérez Moreda, "Evolución de la población . . . ," pp. 24, 33.

Factors in the Formation of the New-World Basque Emigrant Diaspora

by

William A. Douglass

At the outset I wish to note that my approach to the study of the Basque emigrant diaspora is likely to be more sociological and less historiographic than that of the trained historian. In part this stems from my professional perspective as an anthropologist; however, it also derives from the fact that I subscribe to the philosophy, stated most succinctly by Peter Laslett, that all good social science *and* history are ultimately an exercise in historical sociology.[1] I believe that this is particularly true when looking at a subject as complicated as patterns of human migration, a complexity that will become readily apparent in the course of this paper, since the proper study of migration requires a plethora of analytical axes. In the present work I will attempt to illustrate this point with examples drawn from the global Basque emigrant diaspora, while avoiding presenting a thumbnail synopsis of the argument *qua* historical account as found in *Amerikanuak: Basques in the New World*.[2] Rather, I will concentrate upon the theoretical concerns underlying and inspiring it.

We might begin by noting the importance of understanding the *structural givens* in both the Old-World sending areas and the New-World receiving ones. These assume many guises—including social, economic, political, demographic, and cultural forms. Furthermore, they are time specific and therefore constitute shifting or changing reality. It is this fact more than any other which places a premium upon detailed historiographic research if we are to understand the particulars of a given people's emigratory experience as opposed to general theoretical knowledge of the patterns of human migration. Furthermore, some of the factors remain constant, or at least conservative, providing certain *longue durée* patterns to the emigratory process while others are much more period specific. An example of the former from the Basque case would be the importance of the stem-family household, at least in rural contexts, and its propensity to produce disinherited *segundones* who are then prime candidates for emigration.[3] Viewed in such terms rural Basque society is potentially a veritable seedbed of emigrants and has been depicted as such.[4] Since we can discern a stem-family household in rural Basque society from at least the fifteenth century to the present, family structure would appear to provide one clear example of a *longue durée* factor.

Similarly, demographics within the context of the ecology of the Basque Country may provide another example, although, arguably, population trends have been more variable over the centuries than has family organization. This caveat notwithstanding, it would appear that for rural Basque society there were finite ecological limits upon the potential expansion of the agricultural economy, given the climate and topography, which made it impossible to accommodate population increase within the context of the traditional economy. This statement must, however, be tempered by a number of considerations. First, the traditional economy was never static. Through changes in technique, technology, and crops grown it expanded its population-carrying capacity. Second, the expansion of urban/industrial opportunity within the Basque Country meant that there was a viable alternative to overseas emigration for rural Basques. Interestingly, over time the Basque urban/industrial complex served both as a magnet for migrants from other areas of Iberia while providing some of its own candidates for overseas emigration. This latter dimension of Basque emigration has never been adequately studied or explained.

If we turn to another aspect of the Old-World structural features, the political factor, we find givens which are very time specific. Therefore, we might argue that during the sixteenth and seventeenth centuries access to the Spanish colonial enterprise proved attractive and stimulated Basque emigration. Indeed, Basques became handmaidens of the imperial enterprise and seemingly benefited more from it than other Iberian peoples. Conversely, in the nineteenth and twentieth centuries Iberian political developments (including the effects of the Napoleonic Campaigns, the First and Second Carlist Wars, and the Spanish Civil War) repulsed segments of the Old-World Basque population and created two new types of Basque emigrant to the New World—the politically disaffected and the actual political refugee.

It is necessary to consider the structural givens in the receiving areas as well. In this regard we might underscore the demographics of underpopulation in such places as North and South America and

Australia which created a political, economic, social, and cultural climate in which the phrase "to govern is to populate"[5] became the watchword. However, within this general pattern, which also assumes *longue durée* overtones, there was considerable periodic and episodic refinement. Hence, in Latin America prior to the New-World independence movements, emigration of Basques entailed a ruling class. Basques assumed key administrative posts within both the civil and ecclesiastical bureaucracies and were a prominent segment of the colonial mercantile class. After independence the majority of Basque emigrants constituted a settler, laborer class who entered the Americas with few resources and recourses.

As in the case of Old-World structural givens, it is critical to examine the historiography of changing circumstances in the receiving societies. Each receiving nation was prone to fine-tune its immigration policy, implementing changes which might either enhance or diminish the attractiveness of a given country to intending Basque emigrants at a particular point in time. Thus, nineteenth-century land laws in the United States, which made the vast public lands of the American West available to anyone on a first-come basis, stimulated the immigration of aspiring Basque sheepmen; conversely, twentieth-century changes, which limited access to public lands to U. S. citizens with substantial private landholdings, all but closed an era of Basque emigration to the United States. Similarly, the decision by Australia near the turn of the present century to recruit southern Europeans as canecutters for the Queensland sugar industry set in motion a series of circumstances that resulted in the establishment of a Basque-Australian colony. Conversely, mechanization of the Australian sugar industry in the mid-1960s all but terminated Basque emigration to that continent.

The substantive, geographic, and temporal examples could, of course, be multiplied. However, the foregoing should suffice to demonstrate the importance of considering the structural givens, and their variability over time, at both the sending and receiving ends of the emigratory process. In fact, we have just considered the essential features of the classic push-pull model that used to dominate the literature on human migration. That is, according to the model migration results when the perceived attractions of the potential destination outweigh the advantage of remaining *in situ* in the emigrant's homeland.

The push-pull model did, however, undergo refinement when the MacDonalds introduced the notion of *chain migration* in order to account for both the establishment and subsequent momentum of migratory trends.[6] In this view, migration responds not only to the macroanalytical imperatives considered earlier, such as social structural features, demographic patterns, and national legislation; rather, it is also a microprocess. That is, once established in the host country, each migrant becomes a potential link in an ongoing chain. He is a viable "contact" for future intending migrants who are likely to be kinsmen, fellow villagers, or at least acquaintances. Furthermore, he may become an active agent seeking to attract to his side other migrants of similar background. Once framed in such terms migration no longer transpires between macrounits such as Spain or Euskadi and Argentina or the United States. Rather, in the Basque case, for instance, it is better understood as the movement of people from Arneguy to Buffalo, Wyoming.[7] Similarly, the famed "Basque" emigration to Idaho becomes in fact "Vizcayan," or, more accurately, emigration from a small portion of coastal Vizcaya and the immediate interior between Guernica in the west and Markina in the east.[8]

Once having established the existence of the chain-migration process, it is important to realize that the links transpire between individuals. The content of these dyadic relations may differ substantially and may not be assumed a priori. That is, we have not exhausted the analytical possibilities by simply noting that an immigrant invokes kinship ties to join his cousin in the New World. Rather, the expectations and perceptions of both the emigrant and the cousin may differ substantially. To cite examples drawn from the Basque case, in the American West it is not uncommon for experienced Basque herders to note that they prefer working for Anglo employers rather than fellow Basques since the latter are more prone to exploit their countrymen. I encountered the same attitudes in Australia among some canecutters. Conversely, in both settings Basque ranchers and sugar-farm owners complained about distant kinsmen or friends of friends from the Basque Country who expected upon their arrival to be accorded not just a job but special treatment as "family." Such misunderstandings do not characterize the majority of cases of chain migration of kinsmen, fellow villagers, etc., but they do occur in varying degrees within a significant minority.

While the concept of chain migration has helped to clarify synchronic and/or short-term (i.e., over a few decades) migration patterns, the student of Basque emigration is confronted, at least in some parts of the world, with a diachronic manifestation of a similar process. By this I mean that in former Spanish colonial areas Basque emigration dates from nearly half a millennium ago. Consequently, in countries like Mexico, Venezuela, Cuba, Peru, Chile, Argentina, Uruguay, and the Philippines Basque emigration was played out over several centuries. At the same time it was not continuous and is best viewed as devolving in successive waves. While the processes of assimilation inevitably took their toll during the intervening periods, eroding Basque ethnic consciousness, particularly among the New-World-born descendants of the emigrants, it is also true that Basques demonstrated remarkable ethnic solidarity and hence staying power. Consequently, each new wave of Basque emigrants into a particular former Spanish colonial country encountered a certain Basque-American milieu and entered into an existing Basque ethnic category. Depending upon the country and whether dealing with fellow ethnics or outsiders, the preexisting ethnic charter provided both opportunities and constraints for the new Basque immigrants. In any event the options for the new arrivals were in part preconditioned in these "old Basque migration" contexts as opposed to "new Basque migration" ones such as Australia and the United States.

The point can be illustrated by noting that all Argentinians distinguish between Basques and Spaniards and considerable prestige attaches to the former identity. This cultural climate obviously influences the prospects of a newly arrived Basque immigrant in the South American nation. By way of contrast, in Australia and the United States the same immigrant is confronted with the question "What is a Basque?" when dealing with most non-Basques.

A related point concerns the connections of the successive waves and their descendants to one another as all seek to shape and influence what it means to be Basque. The products of the older waves and their New-World-born progeny are likely to be better established in the host society, and hence be in a dominant economic and political position vis-à-vis the newcomers. On the other hand, due to the inevitable effects of the assimilation process their Basqueness is likely to be more sentiment than substance. That is, they are likely to have a vague notion of ethnic pride framed, at least partly, in terms of family tradition. They likely speak no Basque and have little knowledge of or interest in current events in the Basque Country. Conversely, the newcomers are culturally very Basque, prone to be disdainful of their "Latinized" New-Wold-born fellow ethnics, and frustrated by the latter's ignorance of and disinterest in Old-World Basque issues.

There are contexts in which the two groups overlap. A prime example is in the founding of Basque clubs. In point of fact the New-World- and Old-World-born Basques in a particular area may cooperate in such enterprises, but also contest control of them. During the twentieth century the issue of Basque nationalism has been particularly abrasive and divisive for New-World Basque colonies. In some locales apolitical New-World Basques gained control of the club, while in others politicized Old-World-born Basques did so. Usually in such cases the vanquished simply withdraw and boycott the organization. However, in the case of both Mexico City and Buenos Aires each faction established rival clubs. Another variation on the theme is the creation of mutually antagonistic cliques within a single club. All of the foregoing possibilities are subject to modification over time, as the Basque community of a particular area continues to develop and evolve.

The push-pull model and chain-migration analysis exhaust the theoretical framework of much of the migration literature. That is to say, the common format of such studies is to view the immigrants in a particular setting and then to try to account for their coming by reconstructing (usually through secondary sources) their "Old-World background." Whether a study of the Italians of Chicago or the Japanese of Brazil, the format is essentially the same. Furthermore, the emphasis tends ultimately to be upon immigrant adaptation within the host society, rather than upon conditions in the sending areas. I would argue that the approach fails to address several extremely relevant issues in the migration process per se, and leads to one-dimensional treatments of it.

Of particular concern is the question of *alternative options* in the choice of destination. If in the push-pull model the emigrant eschews the option of remaining in his natal community in order to emigrate to destination X, to my mind it is equally important to understand why he rejected potential destinations Y and Z. In the Basque case, for example, we have already noted the longstanding tradition of Basque emigration to former Spanish colonial areas. In seeking to understand why Basques began to enter the United States in the midnineteenth century it is critical to know not only what was going on in the American West at the time but also the circumstances in Latin America and the Philippines. It is equally relevant to question why some rural Basques preferred Buenos Aires and Boise to Bilbao, Paris, and Madrid. In short, for the individual choosing a destination implies rejecting several others. Viewed as a collective phenomenon, Basque emigration is at times multidimensional and directed at several viable destinations simultaneously; at others it is much more narrowly defined and with fewer options. Again the issue can only be broached in terms of cross-national, comparative historiography. To frame the research in such terms is certainly much more demanding for the investigator. Yet, to my mind, it is the only way to avoid ad hoc, mechanistic explanations of the emigratory process. It is also the only means of insulating the analysis from conclusions based upon blatant ethnic stereotypy. For example, in the midnineteenth century in Argentina and in the twentieth-century American West to say "Basque" is to mean "sheepherder." The implication is that Basque emigrants herd sheep because of their Pyrenean background in sheep husbandry. The stereotype hides the fact that animal husbandry practices in the Argentine pampas and the American West differed markedly from their Pyrenean counterpart, and that few professional herders in the Basque Country entered the ranks of the emigrants. It also ignores the fact that in Australia to say "Basque" is to mean "canecutter" despite the fact that Australia is the leading sheep producer in the world!

Another dimension of the migratory process that has yet to receive adequate treatment might be termed the *migration dialectic*. Reference is to the fact that the individual's decision to emigrate has group consequences for both the sending and receiving areas. On the one hand the migrant becomes a bridge between them and serves as a conduit in a two-directional flow of resources, persons, and ideas. Regarding capital, for instance, the dowry system within rural Basque society provided many migrants with funds for their initial adaptation in New-World destinations. Regarding ideas and skills one need only note, for instance, that the Basque bakery emerges with regularity in such disparate locations as Buenos Aires, Santiago de Chile, San Francisco, and many small towns throughout the American West. The tradition found until recently throughout rural Euskadi of *casero* breadmaking no doubt provided many of these New-World Basque bakers with their initial experience. Conversely, there is the enormous impact upon Euskadi of emigrant remittances. One can argue that practically every village in the Basque Country has been affected to a greater or lesser degree by feedback of money, persons, and ideas from the overseas Basque diaspora. Caro Baroja documents, for instance, the influence of such forces in the Valle de Baztán during the eighteenth century.[9] Indeed, one of the least understood aspects of the migration process is the extent to which ties between the New World resulted in capital formation in rural Basque society which in turn capitalized, at least in part, the industrialization and urbanization of the Basque economy. One need only cite the many instances of men who herded sheep in the American West and then returned to Euskadi to redeem a mortgage on the family farm or buy a small business in their home community or an apartment in an urban area where they found a factory job. One might also note that emigrant savings in part financed twentieth-century modernization (to the extent that the term is relevant) of Basque agriculture. The internal plumbing, cement stable, silo, and machinery of many a Basque *baserria* were financed by money either sent from or brought back from the Americas.

There is, however, another dimension of the migragion dialectic that deserves consideration. I refer to the fact that there is a sense in which no migrant ever leaves or enters the same community as former or future ones. By this I mean that the departure of each emigrant effects a realignment of factors and forces in his home community as well as in his community of destination. Regarding the sending area a family loses a member, a neighborhood a neighbor, a parish a parishioner, a village a villager. There is, therefore, subtraction of human energy from the physical work force and spiritual energy from the community of fellows. At the same time there is one less demand upon the existing resource pool, which means that the economic opportunities of those remaining behind are redefined. The redefinition may be both negative and positive simultaneously, viewed from different perspectives within the system. For example, the departure of an active member of the labor force may mean that a particular *baserria* might have to reduce or eliminate its farm flock of sheep and rent out one of its fields to a neighbor. Conversely, the neighbor augments his resources, while from the standpoint of the village the communal pasturage to be distributed among participating households is increased.[10]

Similarly, the arrival of each new immigrant in the New World effects realignment of resources. If the immigrant enters an established immigrant/ethnic community he contributes to its critical mass. This can lead to both positive and negative outcomes. On the one hand, it undoubtedly contributes to the effectiveness of the ethnic collectivity *qua* social group. It is only by virtue of creating such critical masses that certain voluntary associations and ethnic institutions become feasible. Thus, the propensity of Basques to form clubs in places like Buenos Aires, Montevideo, Santiago de Chile, New York, San Francisco, Boise, Reno, etc. is predicated upon such concentrations. That there is the basis for a FEVA (Federación de Entidades Vasco-Argentinas) and a NABO (North American Basque Organizations, Inc.) in Argentina and the United States underscores the importance of those two destinations of Basque emigration as measured in sheer numerical terms. Conversely, the abortive attempts to found and sustain such clubs in places like Lima, Bogotá, Sydney, and Melbourne underscore the lack in such places of a critical mass of Basque immigrants, though all have some Basque immigration. The presence of such clubs obviously conditions the degree and rate of assimilation (or lack thereof) of Basque ethnics into the wider population. They therefore become critical elements, viewed over time, in attempting to understand the commonalities and differences between, say, Basque-Argentineans and Basque-Australians.

The critical mass concept may also allow us to understand the reactions, at times with negative overtones, of the wider host society to the immigrant group. Again, in the Basque case there are some spectacular instances in which immigrants were essentially too successful for local tastes. One might cite the sixteenth-century anti-

Basque riots in Potosí, the eighteenth-century ones in Caracas (against the economic hegemony of the Royal Guipuzcoan Company of Caracas), and the twentieth-century campaign against itinerant Basque sheepmen in the American West.[11] Such reactions tended to occur when Basque immigrants concentrated in a particular area. For example, in a sample of 1,068 Iberian-born persons in Mexico City in 1689 there were 162 from the Provincias Vascongadas and 56 from Navarra (or 20 percent of the total),[12] a ratio roughly four times that of the Basque/Navarrese population in Iberia.

Finally, it should be noted that the impact of the individual emigrant upon the host milieu varies greatly depending upon whether we are considering settled versus frontier contexts. In the latter instance, again using Basque examples, it is possible for a single individual to impact greatly the formation of both an immigrant subgroup and the wider society. Men like Pierre Luro in Argentina and Pedro Altube in the American West dazzled their contemporaries (Basque and non-Basque alike) and left an indelible imprint upon the histories of their respective areas (Argentina and the American West).[13]

Yet another critical refinement of the migratory process is what we might call *emigrant typology*. By this I mean that we must dissemble *the emigrant* into his various guises, and always against the background of the historical circumstances prevailing in both the Old and New Worlds at a particular point in time. Thus, there is the intending permanent settler who seeks a New-World future. He may be an unmarried individual or the head of an established family. The latter may emigrate alone, planning to establish himself in the New World, or he may travel to his destination accompanied by some or all of his family members. The emigrant may (as in the case of Basque officials within the civil and ecclesiastical administrations of the Spanish empire or the contract sheepherders of the American West and canecutters of Australia) assume a predetermined post within New-World society. Conversely, he may have precious little going for him by way of previous arrangements and be simply entrusting himself to chance as he embarks upon a new life. He may be a sojourner with his sights set firmly upon spending a few years abroad in order to return to Europe with the savings that will accord him socioeconomic mobility within Old-World Basque society.

Conditions in the receiving areas in part determine the nature of such emigration. Thus, Latin America has appealed to all strata of Old-World Basque society, since a familiarity with Spanish and Hispanic culture, and an existing group reputation in that part of the New World, eased their adaptation. A lawyer from Bilbao could practice his profession in Buenos Aires, whereas he could not do so in

Boise, Idaho. Similarly, American and Australian legislation and economic policy favored the entry of single Basque males (preferably from rural backgrounds). In short, one must differentiate between types of emigrants, and in doing so creates the grounds for speaking of Basque *emigrations* rather than a homogeneous migratory process.

Finally, mention should be made of the phenomena of *secondary migration* on the one hand and *return migration* on the other. Secondary migration refers to the fact that the migratory process is not limited to individuals who leave their natal villages for a particular destination where they then become either permanent settlers or sojourners before returning to Europe. Rather, some individuals migrate several times in their life, often to disparate destinations. Thus the Basque emigrant may first abandon his village to resettle in Bilbao before subsequently deciding to leave for an overseas destination. Many of the Basque sheepherders of the American West signed three or four contracts of three years' duration, returning to Europe for varying periods of time after the expiration of each. Nor does all Basque emigration necessarily originate in the Basque Country. In the midnineteenth century, when gold was discovered in California, the first Basque immigrants in the mining camps came from southern South America.[14] Similarly, in both the American West and Australia it is possible to discern secondary migration of sheepherders and canecutters to urban centers after an initial period of entry-level employment in the rural occupation identified with Basque ethnics. This secondary migration has created urban Basque colonies in the two nations that differ markedly from their rural counterparts.

Regarding the question of return migration it is important to note the propensity of Old-World Basques to retain an orientation to their homeland. This is particularly true of those who settled in non-Latin countries and may be attributed, at least in part, to the greater degree of difficulty for Basques to assimilate there compared with Hispanic countries. Of course, even in the Anglo settings Basque immigrants did adapt and changed their plans to return to Europe. These converts provided the basis for settled, permanent Basque-American and Basque-Australian communities.

At the same time, from throughout the Basque diaspora there has been a constant stream of returnees to the Basque Country. The feature of Old-World rural Basque social structure that allows an unmarried individual to remain in (or return to) his/her natal household means that any unmarried emigrant can retain the dream of ultimate reincorporation no matter how long the separation. Thus there are extreme cases of a bachelor uncle turning up after forty years' absence in the New World to resume residence in a household now headed by a nephew he has never met.

Another variation on this same theme is the unmarried or married emigrant who dreams of returning to the Basque Country for either an extended visit or to retire permanently. Upon arrival, however, many are quickly disillusioned by the reception. The notion that all Americans are rich causes many an emigrant's kinsmen to assume a thinly veiled predatory attitude toward their "American" relative. The Basque hotels of the American West are populated by elderly, bachelor ex-sheepherders, many of whom tried to retire in the Basque Country but lasted only a few months. They speak bitterly of the relatives who tried to take advantage of them.

Many returned emigrants are made uncomfortable by the changed reality of the Basque Country itself. That is, most leave in their youth and retain a frozen and idealized image of the Basque Country throughout their many years abroad. They return to a world in which automobiles have replaced oxcarts and the friends of their youth are aged or dead. After decades on the vast expanses of the Argentine pampas or the deserts of the American West, they find the scale of Basque geography tiny and restrictive. They also find that their act of emigration forever brands them in the local village as an *Amerikanua* or *Australianua*. While not quite outsiders, they are forever excluded from ever reassuming full membership in their natal community. They are therefore condemned to exist in a kind of social limbo. As one emigrant stated, "I lost my Basqueness without ever quite becoming an American." For others the trip home to the Basque Country leads to the realization that they have truly become Americanized. It is significant that the book that best expresses for Basque-Americans the nature of their collective experience is Robert Laxalt's *Sweet Promised Land*.[15] In the book Robert's father, Dominique, returns to his village only to discover that America, not Euskadi, has become for him *la dulce tierra prometida*. He returns to the American West, pleased with having visited his boyhood haunts, but knowing that it was his last trip to Europe since America is now truly his home.

I wish to conclude with a brief consideration of the current status of studies of Basque emigration and the emigrant diaspora. Certainly a few generalities are in order. Probably the most striking feature of the state of the art is the fact that we know relatively more about Basque emigration at the receiving rather than the sending end of the migratory process. This is particularly true when referring to the United States. In addition to the general framework provided by *Amerikanuak*..., and in McCall's "Basque-Americans and a Sequential Theory of Migration and Adaptation"[16] and Gachiteguy's *Les basques dans l'ouest américain*,[17] we have a plethora of theses detailing the history of individual Basque settlements. For Idaho these include Boise[18] and Shoshone.[19] For Nevada there is a dissertation on the Basques of Elko.[20] California has received the best coverage since theses have been written about the Basques of San Francisco,[21] Stockton,[22] Bakersfield,[23] and Chino.[24] There are also studies of the Basques of Salt Lake City, Utah;[25] Buffalo, Wyoming;[26] and Jordan Valley, Oregon.[27] Some of the studies are topical in nature as well, such as Sonia Eagle Diaz's study of Basque sports;[28] Sather's study of endogamy in Shoshone, Idaho;[29] Lane's study of the ecology of sheep transhumance;[30] Ruiz's analysis of legislation affecting Basque immigration;[31] Araujo's work on sheepherding and the disease echinococcosis;[32] and the work on Basque-American demographic patterns by Bilbao and Eguiluz[33] and Arrizabalaga.[34] Similarly, there have been dozens of published articles on various aspects of Basque settlement in the United States and three book-length biographies of Basque-Americans.[35] Finally, there is an annotated bibliography of Basque-American studies.[36]

At the same time there are many lacunae in the literature on North American Basques. While we do have a thesis on the Basques of Mexico City,[37] little is known of Basque activities in Central America and Canada. Regarding the latter we know that there is a group in the timber industry of British Columbia, that Basques herded sheep in the Canadian West, and that there were significant Basque maritime activities in the Miquelon and Port-aux-Basque areas of eastern Canada. In 1987 there was a Basque festival in the town of Trois Pistoles (Quebec), suggesting a Basque presence within the French Canadian experience. However, to my knowledge, none of these developments has received formal study as yet. Similarly, we still do not have a good analysis of the New York City port-of-entry Basque colony or the *pelotari*-based communities of New England and Florida. Few critical social institutions among the Basque-Americans have yet been documented (although recently there was an excellent thesis by Echeverría on the Basque hotels of California).[38] Sociolinguistic issues among the Basque-Americans beg for study, yet have attracted little attention to date.

The situation in South America is even more spotty. Aside from general works on the Basques of Argentina,[39] Uruguay,[40] Colombia,[41] and Cuba,[42] as well as Ispizua's work on the colonial elite,[43] we have little to guide us. The *Boletín del Instituto Americano de Estudios Vascos* occasionally publishes works on Basque-Americans, but these are generally biographical in nature, and deal with particular Basque personages. In short, we have little in the way of microanalytical historical sociology regarding the extremely important Basque communities of several South American countries.

Finally, Basque emigration to Australia and Asia remains relatively unstudied. I have completed a year of field research with Basques in Australia and plan to write a monograph about them. Jon Bilbao has studied Basques in the Philippines. However, both areas require considerable additional study. In short, studies of the Basque emigrant diaspora are flourishing but much remains to be done.

At the same time, to date there has been very little study of the causes and consequences of emigration in the Basque Country. Rather, the subject tends to appear in almost epiphenomenal fashion in other kinds of studies. Pierre Lhande's *L'émigration basque*[44] and *Amerikanuak: Basques in the New World*[45] are, to my knowledge, the only two general monographs on the subject of Basque emigration. It should be noted that neither of them employs primary data from Basque archives to determine the nature and magnitude of the emigration at particular periods. My work *Echalar and Murelaga: Opportunity and Rural Exodus in Two Spanish Basque Villages*[46] does use such information for the late nineteenth and twentieth centuries, but its scope is limited to two small communities. A somewhat more ambitious work is that of Pildain Salazar[47] which details emigration from Guipúzcoa to America between 1840 and 1870.

In short, the field of emigration studies in the Basque Country is grossly underdeveloped. Impressionistically, we know that emigration has impacted most of Euskalherria for several centuries and that there is a well-developed, worldwide Basque emigrant diaspora. At the same time it seems clear that emigration has affected particular communities and regions within the Basque Country differently. We have some idea of the movement of disinherited *segundones* out of rural Basque society, as well as an appreciation of the role of Basque explorers, administrators, and entrepreneurs in the Spanish colonial enterprise. However, we have practically no notion of the nature and extent of emigration from towns like Tolosa and Irún, or cities like Bilbao. Similarly, we are but dimly aware of the importance of feedback from the Basque emigrant diaspora to the European homeland. This fact is patently evident whether we consider that in one year (1793) of the eighteenth century 82 percent of the membership of the Basque Real Sociedad de los Amigos del País resided outside the Basque Country[48] or that in the twentieth century, in a sample of 842 persons from the village of Murelaga, Vizcaya, 25 percent had emigrated, and that their destinations embraced nine countries on four continents.[49]

The challenge is therefore clear. We need a combination of archival and oral historical studies at both the macro- and microstructural levels in the Basque Country if we are to gain a proper understanding of the processes of Basque emigration. Indeed, there is a sense of urgency regarding at least a part of the task. It may be argued that Basque emigration is currently in a period of quiescence. Restrictive immigration policies and/or economic crises in Latin America, the Philippines, Australia, Canada, and the United States have reduced Basque overseas emigration to a trickle. This is not to say that future conditions may not trigger renewed waves of Basque emigration. However, currently there is minimal feedback to Europe from the Basque diaspora. Those returnees who were involved in twentieth-century emigration, whether as bakers in Chile, sheepherders in Idaho, canecutters in Australia, businessmen in Mexico City, or *pelotaris* in Shanghai, are aging and dying. There is still time to record their impressions; a decade from now the pool of informants will be drastically reduced.

Notes

1. Peter Laslett, "The Character of Familial History, Its Limitations and the Conditions for Its Proper Pursuit," *Journal of Family History*, vol. 12, nos. 1-3 (1987), pp. 263-284.
2. William A. Douglass and Jon Bilbao, *Amerikanuak: Basques in the New World* (Reno: University of Nevada Press, 1975).
3. Louis Etcheverry, "L'expansion familiale considerée comme source de l'expansion coloniale: l'example des Basques," *Réforme sociale*, vol. 46 (1903), pp. 799-808.
4. William A. Douglass, "The Basque Peasantry: Closed or Open?" *Nord Nytt*, vol. 2 (1972), pp. 99-104.
5. Horacio Juan Cuccorese and José Panettieri, *Argentina, manual de historia económica y social*, vol. 1: *Argentina criolla* (Buenos Aires, 1971).
6. J. S. MacDonald and L. D. MacDonald, "Chain Migration, Ethic Neighbourhood Formation and Social Networks," *Social Research*, vol. 29, no. 4 (1962), pp. 433-448.
7. William A. Douglass and Jon Bilbao, *Amerikanuak...* , p. 335.
8. Ibid., pp. 330-333.
9. Julio Caro Baroja, *La hora navarra del siglo XVIII. Personas, familias, negocios e ideas* (Pamplona: Diputación Foral de Navarra, Institución Príncipe de Viana, 1969).
10. We do not develop these ideas specifically in *Amerikanuak*.... For some discussion of them in the Basque context cf. William A. Douglass, *Echalar and Murelaga, Opportunity and Rural Exodus in Two Spanish Basque Villages* (London: C. Hurst and Co., 1975). They are made more explicit in my analysis of emigration from a South Italian hill town (William A. Douglass, *Emigration in a South Italian Hill Town, An Anthropological*

History (New Brunswick, New Jersey: Rutgers University Press, 1984).
11. William A. Douglass and Jon Bilbao, *Amerikanuak*....
12. J. Ignacio Rubio Mañé, *Gente de España en la ciudad de México año de 1689. Introducción, recopilación y anotaciones* (Mexico City, 1969).
13. William A. Douglass and Jon Bilbao, *Amerikanuak*..., pp. 148–151; 256–258.
14. Ibid., pp. 203–204; 210–212.
15. Robert Laxalt, *Sweet Promised Land* (New York: Harper, 1957) and (Reno: University of Nevada Press, 1986).
16. Grant McCall, "Basque-Americans and a Sequential Theory of Migration and Adaptation," (master's thesis, Department of Anthropology, San Francisco State University, 1968).
17. Adrien Gachiteguy, *Les basques dans l'ouest américain* (Bordeaux: Ezkila, 1955).
18. John B. Edlefsen, "A Sociological Study of the Basques of Southwest Idaho," (Ph.D. dissertation, State College of Washington, Pullman, 1948); and Sister Flavia Maria McCullough, *The Basques in the Northwest* (San Francisco: R and E Associates, 1974).
19. Clifford Sather, "Marriage Patterns among the Basques of Shoshone, Idaho," (bachelor's thesis, Reed College, Portland, Oregon, 1961).
20. Richard Lane, "The Cultural Ecology of Sheep Nomadism: Northeastern Nevada 1870–1972," (Ph.D. dissertation, Department of Anthropology, Yale University, 1974).
21. Jean Francis Decroos, "The Long Journey: Assimilation and Ethnicity Maintenance among Urban Basques in Northern California," (Ph.D. dissertation, Department of Sociology, University of Oregon, 1979).
22. Carol Maria Pagliarulo, "Basques in Stockton: A Study of Assimilation," (master's thesis, College of the Pacific, Stockton, California, 1948).
23. John Allen Stafford, "Basque Ethnohistory in Kern County, California, 1872–1934 A.D.," (master's thesis, Sacramento State College, 1971).
24. Sonia Eagle Diaz, "Work and Play among the Basques of Southern California," (Ph.D. dissertation, Department of Anthropology, Purdue University, 1979).
25. Louise Dunn, "The Salt Lake City Basque Community: Atypical in the American West," (master's thesis, University of Utah, 1972).
26. Joseph Castelli, "Basques in the Western United States: A Functional Approach to Determination of Cultural Presence in the

Geographic Landscape," (Ph.D. dissertation, Department of Geography, University of Colorado, 1970).
27. Joseph H. Gaiser, "The Basques of the Jordan Valley Area, A Study in Social Process and Social Change," (Ph.D. dissertation, University of Southern California, 1944).
28. Sonia Eagle Diaz, "Work and Play...."
29. Clifford Sather, "Marriage Patterns...."
30. Richard Lane, "Cultural Ecology...."
31. Allura Nason Ruiz, "The Basques—Sheepmen of the West," (master's thesis, Department of History, University of Nevada-Reno, 1964).
32. Frank Patrick Araujo, "Basque Cultural Ecology and Echinococcosis in California," (Ph.D. dissertation, Department of Anthropology, University of California, Davis, 1974).
33. Iban Bilbao and Chantal de Eguiluz, *Vascos en el censo de población del oeste americano, 1900* (Vitoria-Gasteiz: Diputación Foral de Alava, n.d.); Iban Bilbao and Chantal de Eguiluz, *Matrimonios vascos en Idaho y Nevada, 1862–1941* (Vitoria-Gasteiz: Diputación Foral de Alava, 1983); Iban Bilbao and Chantal de Eguiluz, *Vascos en el censo de población de California, 1900* (Vitoria-Gasteiz: Diputación Foral de Alava, 1984).
34. Marie Pierre Arrizabalaga, "A Statistical Study of Basque Immigration into California, Nevada, Idaho and Wyoming between 1900 and 1910," (master's thesis, Department of History, University of Nevada-Reno, 1986).
35. Robert Laxalt, *Sweet Promised Land*, 1957; Louis Irigaray and Theodore Taylor, *A Shepherd Watches, A Shepherd Sings* (Garden City, New York: Doubleday and Co., 1977); Beltran Paris and William A. Douglass, *Beltran: Basque Sheepman of the American West* (Reno: University of Nevada Press, 1980).
36. William A. Douglass and Richard W. Etulain, *Basque Americans, A Guide to Information Sources* (Detroit: Gale Research Company, 1981).
37. Lorin R. Gaarder, "The Basques of Mexico: An Historical and Contemporary Portrait," (Ph.D. dissertation, Department of Anthropology, University of Utah, 1976).
38. Jerónima Echeverría, "A History of California's Basque Hotels," Ph.D. dissertation, Department of History, University of North Texas, Denton (1988).
39. José R. Uriarte, *Los baskos en la nación argentina* (Buenos Aires: La Baskonia, 1916).
40. Tomás Otaegui, *Los vascos en el Uruguay*, (Buenos Aires: Editorial Vasca Ekin, 1943).

41. Francisco de Abrisqueta, *Vascos en Colombia*, 2 vols. (Bogotá: Editorial Oveja Negra, 1985).
42. Jon Bilbao, *Vascos en Cuba* (Buenos Aires: Editorial Vasca Ekin, 1958).
43. Segundo de Ispizua, *Historia de los vascos en el descubrimiento, conquista y civilización de América*, 6 vols. (Bilbao, 1914-1919).
44. Pierre Lhande, *L'émigracion basque* (Paris: Nouvelle Librairie Nationale, 1910).
45. William A. Douglass and Jon Bilbao, *Amerikanuak*....
46. William A. Douglass, *Echalar and Murelaga*....
47. María Pilar Pildain Salazar, *Ir a América, la emigración vasca a América* (San Sebastián: Caja de Ahorros Municipal, 1984).
48. William A. Douglass and Jon Bilbao, *Amerikanuak*..., p. 109.
49. Ibid., pp. 5-6.

A Wanted Man: The Basque,
El Cojo Gómez, in Colombia

by

Kay Hummel

Helping Spain explore the New World, fifteenth-century Basque navigators were among the first non-Indians to tread the glistening shores of northwestern Colombia. This far corner of the Caribbean, containing the Gulf of Darien and the Isthmus of Panama, ensnared just a few of the first gold seekers and missionaries. Darien was a watery place and the empire builders did not linger in the Chocó, the region that became Colombia's most northwestern province. The great Pacific Ocean lay on the other side of its mountains and El Dorado always beckoned the conquistadors south into the unfolding South American continent. Over the centuries, Basques dispersed with Spain's osmotic flow into the Americas, gaining fame as cattlemen and sheepmen in the nations of the Río de la Plata and as astute entrepreneurs in ports and capitals from Mexico to Tierra del Fuego. Four hundred years were to pass before Colombia's Chocó again intrigued many outsiders, Basque or otherwise.

Not much changed in the Chocó over four centuries. Even today, northwestern Colombia still is not linked to Panama. The unfinished stretch of the Pan American Highway remains a fantasy road through the humid mountains and swamps of southern Panama and northwestern Colombia.

By the early twentieth century, North Americans did ram a canal through the Panamanian Isthmus and foreigners prospecting for gold, oil, and gum began to appear in the Chocó. Slowly, the Colombian government launched small colonies while talk of a road from the interior to the Pacific coast was prompted by the hunger for the Chocó's rich but inaccessible natural resources. The missionaries returned, too—Carmelite priests and brothers, many of them Basques from northern Spain, came seeking souls among the native tribes and black peasants of the Gulf of Uraba on the Chocó's Atlantic coast.

No hotels existed in the gulf town of Turbo where the Carmelites built a mission in 1918. These priests were privy to much frontier gossip, for they were Chocó's de facto innkeepers, hosting explorers who used Turbo as a springboard into the wilds of the Panamanian-Colombian borderlands. A variety of foreigners passed through the mission, some of them secreting out newfound riches, others stopping long enough to heap another jungle tale onto the pile of fact and fiction that made up the Chocó's current events.

Of all the stories the Carmelites heard, none equaled those told by a boisterous trader, Luís "El Cojo" Gómez Lekube. He conjured up adventures by the hour to willing listeners and, in turn, stories about Gómez Lekube became local legends. "This is the 'Cojo's' territory and he is the principal topic of conversation," wrote an American undercover agent investigating the Chocó in 1941. "At one time or another most of the men here have worked with him or for him, carrying in goods from the West Coast. Some hold him in awe, some hate him, most fear or respect him and practically all seem willing and anxious to serve him."[1]

With but a few years' sojourn in the Chocó, El Cojo Gómez became the biggest opportunist that backwater province had ever seen. Despite his loquacious habits, most people knew little of Gómez Lekube's background. Some thought him to be an expatriate Spaniard. The Carmelites, however, recognized him as a Basque, for he hailed from Vizcaya, one of the heartland provinces in the Basque Country of northern Spain. The priests seemed to understand the independent streak in their fellow Basque. His alternately brusque and warm behavior seldom surprised them.[2] But the Carmelite fathers, like all who got acquainted with Gómez, never quite knew which role he might be playing: outlaw wanted in Colombia and Panama, or patriot for the Basque cause when the forces of democracy and fascism were at war.

Luís Valentín Gómez Lekube was born February 14, 1901, in Guecho, Vizcaya, the eldest of three children. His father was an official with the Banco de Bilbao and frequently travelled abroad. His mother, Fermina de Lekube, died when her children were quite young. After a few years her husband remarried, and his new wife, Concepción Aramburu, added a fourth child, José Ramón, to the Gómez family.

At a tender age Luís tasted the world beyond Euzkadi, the Basque Country. He was only seven when the family moved to Buenos Aires. There his father opened a branch office for the Banco de Bilbao. The Argentine experience lasted just a year before the Gómez family returned to Vizcaya. Luís finished preparatory school with some difficulty, and his growing years were restless ones. Frequently he stayed with his mother's people, the Lekubes, in nearby Algorta.

Luís's father had plans for his unruly son. The young man had worked at various odd jobs around Algorta, but his father wanted him to enter the professions and ordered him to enroll in law school. However, Luís found law to be a tedious pastime. Romance and adventure occupied him while his disapproving relatives watched Luís fall in love with a Cuban actress. She was touring Spain with a theatrical company and could not remain with Luís Gómez Lekube. But that was no real hindrance. Luís simply let his love for the actress divert him from his dreary studies. He resolved to follow her and boarded a ship departing for Cuba.

The young man had an unexpectedly short stay in Havana. His angered father soon crossed the Atlantic to fetch the wayward Luís back to Bilbao. Father and son had their ultimate showdown. It ended with Luís breaking all ties with his family and his beloved in Cuba. He was sure he did not want to return to the Basque Country, but where could he escape his father's long grasp? Desperate, Luís caught the first ship out of Havana without bothering to ask its destination. He would never see his family again.

The steamer which Luís boarded put in at Cartagena, Colombia's historic port on the Caribbean. It was 1928. The young Basque landed penniless, but on the ship he had met a Colombian businessman who soon after gave Luís his first job as a salesman for the Singer Company.

Surprisingly, it did not take long for Luís Gómez Lekube to demonstrate that he was a serious entrepreneur. He had to survive. The rebellion against his father grew into an enduring capacity for hard work. Luís travelled from town to town, rapidly racking up commissions and making many valuable contacts. Luís developed a keen business sense. Fast-talking and with a true hustler's knack, he made the right deals more often than not. His friendships were deep and lasting, ones which he would count on in the future.

A young man in a hurry, Gómez Lekube did not hesitate even when it came to the question of marriage. While residing in Medellín, in 1929, he became friends with Manuel Angel, his future wife's cousin. Invited to the Angel family ranch in Antioquía one Sunday, Luís met Deyanira Angel and immediately fell in love with her. One month later they were married. Luís's persuasion and decisiveness served him well, for in Deyanira he found a wife of unswerving loyalty. She was beautiful and she was much like the Basque women of his homeland: practical and industrious. Deyanira may not have suspected how unusual her husband and her marriage would turn out to be, but she remained loyal through his long absences and unforeseen embarrassments. Receiving Luís's strange friends at all hours soon became habit, and Deyanira never lost her composure.

The thirties were a busy time for Luís and Deyanira. Keeping pace with foreign business expansion into Colombia, they led a mobile life dictated both by Luís's business pursuits and his whims. Their first son, Luís Andrés, was born in Venecia, Antioquía, in 1930 and their only daughter, Pilar, arrived while they were in Caldas (the province south of Antioquía) in 1934.

Luís Gómez Lekube could not abide idle moments.[3] Although he was doing well with the Singer Company, making more money in less time was his growing obsession. He quit the company in 1933 and began planning a new business venture. A trip to Colombia's northwest awakened him to the economic opportunities in the undeveloped reaches of the Chocó and southern Panama.

Panama's ports then bulged with foreigners and their wares. Japanese silks were plentiful and North American luxury items, such as perfumes and cigarettes, could be had at reasonable prices. In Colombia these goods were scarce and costly, being subject to heavy import duties. Other types of commerce had their attractions as well, particularly trade in precious metals. Chocóan peasants scraped platinum and gold from the rivers and sold them on black markets at twice the price paid by Colombia's national bank. Moreover, law and government were many miles distant from the no-man's-land of the Panama-Colombia border. Luís Gómez Lekube toted up these factors and decided it was time to go into smuggling. He had no doubt that he would become the best *contrabandista* in the Chocó's history, and he was not proved wrong.

Gómez moved to Turbo and briefly officiated as judge in the frontier town—reportedly named to this position through the influence of his powerful Antioquían friends from Medellín, the nearest big city. Luís also taught school in Turbo, and became acquainted with the locals and the Basque and Spanish Carmelite missionaries. But all this was preliminary. He spent most of his time learning the country, how to navigate its poorly charted inlets and how to traverse the densely vegetated topography of Chocó's mountains.

Gómez started his contraband business simply, first by buying a boat to travel back and forth between Colombia and Panama. He bought one of his more famous rigs, dubbed the *Snark*, from a retired U.S. admiral in Panama. In time the Basque came to own a larger boat, as well as many launches, canoes and a sailboat which he equipped with a machine gun. Water transport was an essential part of his operations, since less than 200 kilometers of paved roadway existed in the entire Chocó.[4] Calculated use of inland waterways usually proved far safer for Gómez than taking open roads or the well-travelled shipping lanes.

In Colón and other Panamanian ports the Basque bought silks, perfumes, canvas shoes, gunpowder and any special-order cargos he could obtain. Initially he sent the goods down the Caribbean side of the Darien peninsula to Turbo and other small villages near the Atrato River on the Gulf of Araba. He would ascend the Atrato, sometimes openly transporting his merchandise through the town of Riosucio. Next he hoisted the cargo onto mules and crossed the western cordillera of the Andes, descending to the remote Bay of Humboldt (locally called the Bay of Coredo) on the Pacific. One of Gómez's main Pacific depots was at the village of Curiche, from which his wares travelled down to Buenaventura, a large port over 300 kilometers to the south. Distribution of the contraband to the interior from Buenaventura was tricky, and Gómez relied on his wits and his contacts to deliver to clients in Medellín and Bogotá. Eventually, his Atlantic-side routes attracted too much official scrutiny so he restricted his operations more and more to the Pacific coast.

One of the smuggler's most involved transport schemes took him up the Atrato River to a point where he loaded contraband onto mule trains numbering as many as eighty animals. The muleteers cautiously picked their way through humid mountain peaks, 2,000 to 3,000 meters high, until reaching Urrao, a town close to the Chocó-Antioquía border. From Urrao, Gómez Lekube took several clandestine routes into Medellín, a hotbed of illegal commerce in the years preceding the Second World War. Medellín was close to the mines and was becoming Colombia's foremost industrial center, attracting legitimate businessmen and schemers alike. A 1941 Bogotá newspaper, commenting on the flourishing contraband in Antioquía, stated, "The reports thus far received indicate that Medellín has practically been converted into a free port."[5]

Bold and opinionated, Luís Gómez Lekube's demeanor did not conceal his success in his illegal pursuits. Although he could choose to be taciturn and secretive, the smuggler seldom passed up a chance to impress selected audiences with his stories and Horatio Alger talk. Many acquaintances recall the entertainment Gómez provided in idle village moments—detailing his adventures at sea, fights, and long, forced marches with the ability of an accomplished raconteur.

Besides verbal notoriety, the smuggler also had a physical trademark: he limped noticeably since his left leg was shorter than the right. He was called "El Cojo" Gómez, "the lame" Gómez. Not uncharacteristically, there was more than one story to explain his disability. Resulting either from a childhood accident or a later brawl, the limp added to his vivid personal appearance and contrasted sharply with his hardy demeanor. Despite the handicap, El Cojo waded miles through muddy streams and climbed Chocó's mountains on long trips. He delighted in his ability to overcome any obstacle, be it a bothersome limp or pursuing customs agents. He even refused to have surgery on the injured leg, although a Catalan doctor in Bogotá assured him that it could be repaired successfully. In appearance, El Cojo was a stout Basque, carrying some 190 pounds on his five-foot-five frame. There were noticeable scars about his neck and a stubborn glint in the dark eyes framed by his slightly graying black hair.[6]

What did El Cojo's contemporaries think of the Basque outlaw? One Basque priest who knew him in Turbo believed, "that in Luís Gómez Lekube's spirit, two compelling tendencies were at work: the aspiration for money and the aspiration for notoriety. He had the talent and preparation to have triumphed in life in an honest profession; but he preferred the adventures and hazards of smuggling because he hoped to make a lot of money in little time."[7]

El Cojo's children agree that their father was a risk-taking wanderer, but they also remember him as a practical philosopher. He lavished advice on them by quoting the golden rule and reciting French fables as moral lessons. He was not unlike a folk hero to them, explaining that smuggling was a "necessary" service while carefully pointing out that he did not trade in unacceptable items such as narcotics. His daughter, Pilar, tells stories of her father turning in "bad" *contrabandistas* to the authorities while protecting others, the "good" smugglers like himself.[8]

Perhaps the risk and fame of running contraband meant more to El Cojo than the actual profits he earned. Despite stories that he had become Colombia's biggest smuggler, he was not a rich man, according to several Basques in Bogotá. These Basques came to know El Cojo during the forties and recall that the outlaw had spare cash only intermittently. Mostly they remember him as a Basque pirate, personifying the independence they cherished in themselves. Probably the Basque who knew El Cojo Gómez best was a young exile from the Spanish Civil War, Francisco de Abrisqueta. He says that Gómez was generous to a fault, spending all his money on his family and native helpers. El Cojo lived simply and was ill at ease in big cities such as Bogotá. Abrisqueta adds, "He wasn't very cultured but he was wise and intelligent, an adventurer, a pure and complete *contrabandista.*"

Abrisqueta looked after the progress of the smuggler's adolescent son, Luisito, who was enrolled in a Bogotá school during his father's long absences. Luisito caused his share of mischief—a boy who apparently inherited his father's disdain of authority. Once he convinced another Basque teenager to run away to the Chocó to join his outlaw

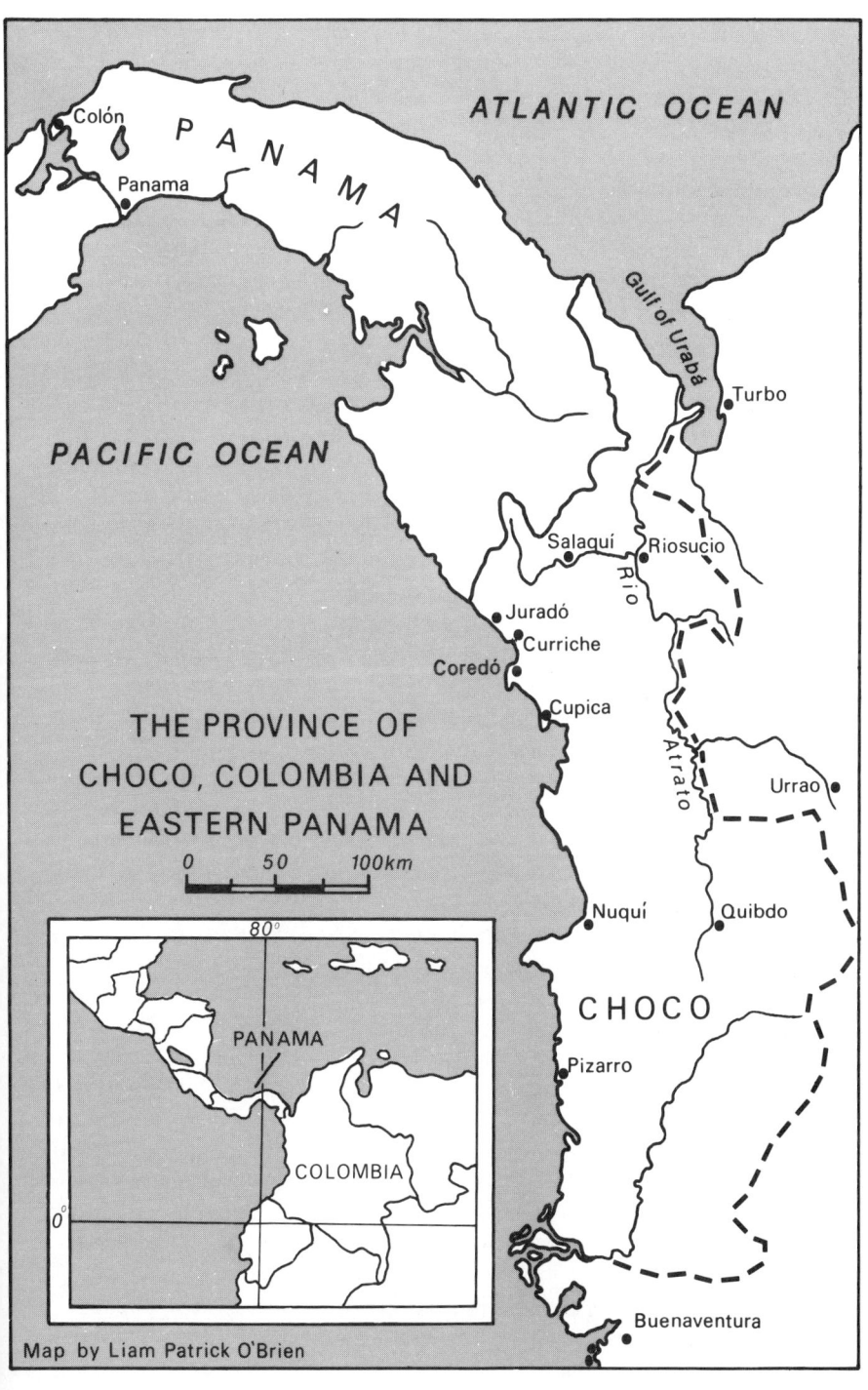

father. The pair was stopped only after covering many miles on a boat heading north on the Magdalena River. Luisito professed that he would rather work with his father than study and, by 1944, he was doing exactly that, having bolted school completely at age fourteen. Inherent in El Cojo's exploits were dangers posed by enemies he had made along the way. Not every deal could be managed smoothly. Nor were the "bad" *contrabandistas* the Basque exposed likely to forget his actions. El Cojo always carried a weapon, although it once proved to no avail when enemies ambushed him and slit his throat in Urrao. Somehow the bleeding was stopped. El Cojo's wife carried him by mule to a haven where a trusted doctor attended to him. The doctor was incredulous over his survival, as were the residents of Turbo upon El Cojo's return. Undaunted, he confided to one of the Basque priests how he had escaped death by tightly tucking his chin down over his neck, "all the while abusing his attackers with the strongest possible insults."

One of El Cojo's closest calls occurred at the mouth of the Atrato River during a boat chase near the town of Riosucio. Ten customs officials in a motorboat bore down on the smuggler and a helper in a rowboat. Yelling for his man to row harder, Gómez lit and hurled sticks of dynamite at the officers to gain some distance. He then directed a swift spray of machine-gun fire along his pursuer's water line, forcing them to swim to shore. He managed to slip home to Turbo, where he feigned all innocence under questioning. Details of this episode were common knowledge throughout the province, but every witness queried by officials seemingly knew nothing about it.

El Cojo's success did not rest solely upon his personal attributes, for he also needed to develop trustworthy relationships with the native peoples of the Chocó in order to maintain his supply of depots and cargo routes. Whether he bought or simply charmed them, the outlaw seldom lacked Indian and black helpers in nearly every village and port. His children remember the visits of Chocóan Indians to their Medellín home where the natives cooked and wove in the hallways until their father returned with presents for everyone.

Some people claimed to have worked for the smuggler just for the fun of it. Others identified with his ability to make money on the sly. El Cojo understood the marginality of life in the neglected Chocó, where prosperity could be measured by the number of pigs a person owned or by a single day's haul of fish.[9] People seemed to respond to his daring personality, so much so that one investigator reported:

> It is safe to say that more than eighty percent of the population of the Atrato Basin know him at least by reputation. Even those whom he has injured would take another chance on him

"El Cojo" with Cholo Indians, Colombia.

Luis Gómez Lekube in his yacht, the *Askatasuna*

and almost any of the negroes would feel honored to serve him. He has achieved fame as a romantic figure like Jesse James or Robin Hood. . . . It is well known that he comes and goes at will.[10]

By most locals at least, El Cojo Gómez seemingly was not judged by rigid standards of right and wrong. Back-country honor depended more on custom, on how a man dealt personally with his neighbors than on the precise legality of his livelihood. Hoodwinking the authorities only added to El Cojo's prestige in the eyes of many.

Nor were his supporters limited to the common man. On one occasion El Cojo donned women's clothing and walked out the front door of his Medellín home when the whole neighborhood swarmed with police who had come to arrest him. This narrow escape was only partly due to his own cunning, for El Cojo had been warned of the imminent raid by the very man who had ordered it, a Medellín detective. Such well-placed friends became fundamental factors in the smuggler's continuing success. In the late thirties, El Cojo temporarily moved his family to Panama City, also finding useful contacts there, including several American Canal Zone officials.

Unimpeded in his movements, the outlaw would be active in Colombia one week and turn up in Panama the next. Some policemen simply gave up trying to arrest him, since doing so might mean risking an officer's life in the Chocóan villages under El Cojo's control. In any event arrests may have been a futile exercise, given El Cojo's influence and connections. One colony administrator told an undercover agent: "The Cojo does no harm; he has his little business but is really not injurious to anyone."[11]

Attitudes toward the law, even in the remote Chocó, were not to remain so casual after world war erupted in 1939. Unexplained movements in the Panama Canal region began to worry the American authorities and plans for hemispheric intelligence coordination were drawn up.[12] U.S. military intelligence and the FBI began scrutinizing the pursuits of foreigners in the region, and El Cojo was not excluded from surveillance.

Late in 1940, Office of Naval Intelligence (ONI) personnel assigned to the American consulate in Medellín were the first to investigate Gómez, "reputedly the most outstanding as well as spectacular smuggler in Colombia." ONI found that El Cojo could purchase immunity from arrest and fines and that,

> Early in November 1940, an unusually large amount of contraband silks was confiscated, and GOMEZ being then in the vicinity, was immediately brought in for questioning. Definite evidence against him being nonprocurable, he was released, and

following his usual custom in such circumstances GOMEZ gave an interview to the Press, and claimed he was being illegally prosecuted. He also stated his offer to put at the disposal of the National Government his extensive knowledge of all the strategic points and regions of the Chocó, stating that he alone knew of two (2) almost perfect fields that could be used by airplanes: moreover, one (1) of them was within forty-five (45) minutes' flying time from the PANAMA CANAL.[13]

American authorities knew smuggling was widespread in the border region where Colombian and Panamanian military presences were nil. Suspecting that sabotage might come from any quarter, intelligence chiefs in Washington believed that as many as 1,000 Nazi agents might be operating in Colombia.[14] Before the war, Japanese and German agents in northern Colombia "were purchasing all the platinum they could lay their hands on," according to an FBI report to the Board of Economic Warfare.[15] Colombian Falange movements akin to those in Spain, a large German immigrant community, and German domination of Colombia's Scadta Airlines also worried American defense personnel.[16] But before Pearl Harbor made the United States an official belligerent, and as long as Colombia remained a neutral country, the United States could do little more than monitor political conditions and spy on suspicious individuals in Latin America.

In the spring of 1941, Naval Intelligence checked into El Cojo's affairs again, devoting much of a twenty-one-page report on the Gulf of Uraba region to the smuggler's misdeeds and associates. Posing as a mineral prospector, the ONI agent found much to dislike in the lifestyle of all Chocóan peoples, but was particularly distressed by Gómez's blatant contraband running. However, the agent found no real proof of Nazi activity in the Chocó. He concluded that El Cojo was then smuggling "only cheap Japanese silks" and that, "(h)e is an amiable personality and seems to have no political persuasion whatever, being interested only in his business. He gives the impression of a childish mind and his attitude toward life reminds one of a small boy." But the investigator cautioned that the bandit's immense influence might be misused: "His potential danger, however, is very great since he certainly could import arms, propaganda or even persons with a minimum of risk."[17]

But contrary to such early intelligence reports about him, political affairs had seized El Cojo's romantic imagination in a very special way during the late thirties. What the ONI agents and others had failed to appreciate was that El Cojo was a Basque, not merely a "Spanish" smuggler. Although apparently having broken all ties with his native land, the rebel began to receive news from exiled Basques and Spanish Republicans who immigrated to Colombia and Panama after their defeat by General Franco in the Spanish Civil War. Most importantly, El Cojo learned that his cousin from Algorta, José Antonio de Aguirre y Lekube, had been elected the first president of the Basque country when it gained its statute of autonomy from the Spanish parliament after the outbreak of the Spanish Civil War. El Cojo and José Antonio had been childhood playmates and Aguirre's mother had been especially kind to her nephew after his mother's death.

Now José Antonio de Aguirre was hiding in Belgium while Franco's Spain cultivated close ties with the emergent Axis powers. At the crossroads of the Americas, El Cojo learned of Franco's victory and dictatorial takeover. The outlaw Basque was outraged by the German bombing of the Basques' capital of Guernica and their loss of independence. Simultaneously, at home he saw a similar fascist menace spreading in conservative Colombian and Panamanian politics. El Cojo began teaching his children about their Basque heritage and, when his last child was born in 1938, he christened him Fermín Euzkadi—the first name for the boy's paternal Basque grandmother; the second from the Basque word for their homeland, meaning "land of the Euzkaldunak," the Basques. El Cojo also dubbed one of his motor launches the *Askatasuna*, the Basque word for liberty.

Gómez frequently visited Panama between 1938 and 1942, and there he made another patriotic gesture by sheltering two Basque orphans from the Spanish Civil War. One of these children was an adolescent, Victor Intxausti, who sometimes accompanied his benefactor on contraband excursions.

During his years in Panama City, El Cojo was reported to have a close friendship with a civil intelligence officer named "McIntire" in the Canal Zone.[18] Reputedly, the smuggler often discussed politics with McIntire and brought him interesting news from the Chocó. Their friendship perhaps explained the freedom from official harassment enjoyed by El Cojo. One unverified story about their relationship alleges that McIntire urged the Basque to participate in the overthrow of Panamanian President Arnulfo Arias in 1941.[19] With the Canal's defense a wartime priority, and given Arias' well-known fascist sympathies, the United States may have been eager to see a more pro-American leader in power. Arias had assumed office in 1940 after a disputed election, and American intelligence reports indicated that Washington viewed the antigringo Arias as a threat.[20] He had permitted rapid nationalization of Europeans, including many Axis citizens,[21] while refusing to cooperate with U.S. land acquisition and defense preparations.[22] Consequently, American officials looked the other way when Arias was deposed in a bloodless coup.[23] However, there is no definite evidence of El Cojo working as an American agent in the ousting of Arias.[24]

A few months after the Japanese attack on Pearl Harbor, Gómez sought out the Pacific Sector Commander-in-Chief of the Colombian Army and advised him that enemies could easily use the undefended northern Colombian coast for submarine reprovisioning and attacks on shipping lanes. Gaining an audience with General Delfín Torres Durán and other army officers, the Basque outlined in detail the features of the coastal inlets and rivers of the Chocó. He claimed that Colombia was not even "prepared to prepare for an immediate defense," and although a sovereign nation, she could request antiaircraft artillery, searchlights and technical help from the U.S. and also allow American planes to patrol over Colombian territory without prior permission.[25]

Whether worried about protecting his Chocóan domain during wartime trade interruptions or solely alarmed by the fascist threat to the Americas, El Cojo continued to promote himself and his defense theories. He gave the Civil Intelligence division of the Panama Canal Zone copies of his speech to the Colombian army and let it be known that he could help the Americans.

Apparently Gómez was in touch with American officials in the Canal Zone on an informal basis throughout most of the spring and summer of 1942. The real turning point in his wartime career occurred that fall, when his cousin, the exiled President Aguirre, toured eleven Latin American nations to foster support for the Allied war cause.

The previous year, Aguirre had escaped from behind Nazi lines in Europe. After an odyssey that took him from Berlin to South America, he accepted a professorship at Columbia University in New York.[26] His major preoccupation, however, was recruiting his exiled countrymen to work for the restoration of the Basque nation. He approached the United Nations, U.S. Vice-President Henry A. Wallace, and several U.S. State Department officials with a proposal of using loyal Basque exiles to propagandize in Catholic circles to counteract undemocratic elements in the Americas.[27] Aguirre was rebuffed by Secretary of State Cordell Hull and others who feared that U.S. involvement with any Spanish exile group would antagonize relations with Spain, possibly inducing overt cooperation between Franco and Hitler. Nonetheless, Aguirre departed for South America on what was billed as a university-sponsored speaking tour in the fall of 1942.[28]

The Basque leader met many of his exiled comrades in the Latin capitals. Some had been officials in his short-lived government. Aguirre and his dramatic escape story from occupied Europe inspired his fellow Basques. The exiled president did more than exhort his followers to guard against totalitarianism, however. During private visits of the

Latin American tour, Aguirre recruited his most trusted friends into a spy network to assist the United States and British intelligence services.

The State Department denied any role in sponsoring Aguirre's mission to South America, but in fact the trip had been arranged by Colonel William Donovan, head of the Office of Strategic Services (OSS). British intelligence had already used Aguirre's help in Washington, where he had persuaded a Basque janitor to help penetrate the Spanish embassy so that cipher books for decoding diplomatic communications could be copied. Similarly, the British, with Aguirre's influence, secretly obtained the ciphers from the Spanish embassy in Caracas.[29]

In Bogotá, Francisco de Abrisqueta responded to Aguirre's request for a Colombian spy network. He surveyed the known Basque population of Colombia and soon organized a group of ten to fifteen informants to report suspicious German, Japanese, or Spanish-Falangist activities. But for most of these Basques, collecting espionage was just a part-time affair of monitoring fascist propaganda.

Aguirre especially wanted to enlist his estranged cousin in the Basque spying operation. The isolated Chocó was strategically important to Allied shipping through the Panama Canal, and sightings of Axis vessels had occurred in both the Pacific and the Atlantic. Already between January and May of 1942, almost 400 Allied ships had been sunk between New York and the northern coast of South America.[30] Although the U.S. Caribbean Command quickly strengthened the defenses around the Panama Canal after Pearl Harbor, the potential for sabotage from adjacent nonbelligerent countries persisted.[31]

At President Aguirre's request, Abrisqueta soon located El Cojo in Panama. Late in 1942 they struck a deal. El Cojo agreed to become the Basque government's "Pacific Representative" in Colombia and demanded a $1,000 monthly salary as compensation for the contraband income he would forego while working as an informant. He tacitly agreed to stop smuggling if Colombia and Panama would drop all pending charges against him.[32] Abrisqueta secured the monies for El Cojo's services from the United States, but it is unlikely that the smuggler eschewed contraband completely, since his illegal profession did serve as his cover while poking around the Chocóan backcountry in search of Axis agents and their sympathizers.

Elated to have his expertise recognized, El Cojo plunged into the spy business. He prided himself on being a "local" informant. He laughed at some of the undercover methods used by the Americans and criticized the U.S. Navy's attempts at navigating Uraba's difficult coastal waters. Not shy in his opinions, he also criticized the Americans for their haughty behavior toward Colombians, warning that their superior attitudes would backfire by fomenting communism instead of democracy: "That in spite of the new American policy (Roosevelt's 'Good Neighbor' plan), Americans still abound who believe that they have descended from heaven to treat the natives with kicks, morally and materially."[33]

The Basque's espionage methods were as free-wheeling as his outspoken commentary. Frequently his prowling missions lasted for weeks or even months at a time. He occasionally used a radio to transmit information, but most of his reports were written. His daughter recalls that on his infrequent visits home, El Cojo would rush to the typewriter and remain seated there for hours until he had recapitulated the latest news from the Chocó. Some reports he sent to Abrisqueta in Bogotá, while others he brought to ONI officers in Balboa, Panama. Abrisqueta often had to condense El Cojo's lengthy letters before submitting the information to the FBI at the American embassy. Despite the "flowery style" of his reports, one ONI intelligence officer rated El Cojo as a "reliable informant" who is intimately familiar with the area he discusses.[34]

El Cojo was the only Basque working full-time as an informant, although Abrisqueta himself kept quite busy communicating with his contacts and reporting weekly to the U.S. embassy. Abrisqueta's spy network included several Basques (civilian and religious) working in other remote parts of Colombia, but none of these informants equalled the Basque outlaw in ferreting out subversive characters and trends. Abrisqueta recalls that El Cojo discovered several clandestine radio stations high in the Andean cordillera. Abrisqueta believes other information provided by El Cojo led to the sinking of a German submarine, the locating of a secret landing strip, and the arrest of Japanese agents fleeing north from Cali.

Intelligence documents obtained from the U.S. National Archives under a Freedom of Information request reveal other services rendered by El Cojo. In one report he claimed credit for the arrest of two Nazis by the Colombian National Police. But shortly afterwards these individuals were released, since they were able to bribe the police. "Just as I bought them when I was a smuggler, they (the Colombian police) can be bought with little money by any agent of the Axis," bemoaned El Cojo.[35]

On another occasion Gómez charged that a naturalized German, Karl Max Rausch, was a Nazi in the employ of the National Police of Antioquía. Rausch was impeding investigations of Nazi sabotage, according to El Cojo, and was a "carousing companion" of the American consul in Medellín.[36] The Basque also kept track of several other Germans. One was a manager of an Atrato River sugar mill, Reinhold Paschke, already known as an ardent Nazi and who had been dismissed as chief of naval construction at Colombia's Cartagena Naval Base.[37] El Cojo believed Paschke might be preparing a secret Atrato landing strip and managed to have him arrested. But the suspect was soon freed and returned to the Chocó, much to the smuggler's disgust. El Cojo wrote: "Now he has returned again and is laughing at the gringos and their intrigues. He insists on living in Sautata. The sugar mill is not operating but he has sixty hectares of flat land (how the Germans like flat land around the Canal!) sowed with rice."[38]

Perhaps things got a bit dull in the Chocó as the war went on. In succeeding months El Cojo uncovered fewer subversive activities, while his political commentary became more voluminous. The ineffectiveness of the Colombian Army and rising anti-American sentiments in Colombia were now his common themes. El Cojo may have become overzealous in his reports when hard spy news was scanty. And possibly he began inventing chicanery in order to maintain his role as purveyor of Chocóan intelligence.

In the spring of 1943 the Carmelite priests in Turbo were accused of using their mission bell tower to signal to enemy ships in the Gulf of Uraba. This charge caused such a ruckus that one priest had to travel to Bogotá to convince the U.S. embassy personnel that the Carmelites were innocent. The task of persuading U.S. authorities was complicated by the fact that the Carmelites were indeed a politically divided group. Some members were strong Basque nationalists, but others fervently supported Franco and embraced friendship with Hitler out of an almost primal fear of communism. The informant against the Carmelites was never identified, but at least one priest suspected that El Cojo was responsible. In no uncertain terms he told the smuggler that while it was true that some Carmelites were Francoists who believed in the triumph of the Axis, in no case had any missionary acted against U.S. interests.

Meanwhile, in Bogotá, Abrisqueta was unaware that the Carmelites had been falsely accused of anything, until one of the Basque priests in Turbo wrote him about the situation. He warned Abrisqueta:

> Truly, D. Luís (El Cojo) holds his tongue very little but I don't really know how far he's gone in his actions. Also, his reputation here is worsening and many Americans staying in our house have spoken very unfavorably of him. They attribute many false reports to him, and not only false ones, but unimaginable ones. They say he is already as good as fired from the intelligence service.[39]

After his run-in with the Carmelites, El Cojo's record as a patriotic spy is muddled. Unfortunately, all but one letter of his lengthy correspondence with Abrisqueta was destroyed; that letter, dated July 4,

1943, indicates El Cojo was continuing his espionage work normally, with no problems other than his usual shortfall in cash. Documents withheld by the Department of Justice for national security and privacy reasons also cast a cloud over the remainder of the Basque's spy career. Proof of his dismissal and reasons for it, if it did occur, are not available.[40]

The obtainable documents, however, paint contradictory pictures of the smuggler: "reliable" verbatim reports by a staunchly pro-American El Cojo stand in contrast to rumors in other reports that he was hauling broken-down amphibian plane parts or that he was suspected of smuggling Axis citizens into Columbia.[41] The flow of such wartime intelligence was immense. At least four different intelligence agencies operated in South America during those years.[42] Amidst a shadowy world of anonymous informants and turf-coveting intelligence services, a flamboyant hustler like El Cojo would have aroused many suspicions. Assessing the reliability of contradictory reports could not have been easy then; doing so forty years later is even more difficult.

To the Basques who knew him, it was unthinkable that El Cojo Gómez could be a double agent. He was as convinced as they that the Allies must triumph, followed perhaps by a liberation of Spain from Franco's dictatorial grip. He spoke for all Basque exiles when he pledged:

> We Basques are allies of the countries fighting totalitarianism. We are in a war with Franco and his damned falange just as we are against those who destroyed Guernica, the accursed Nazis. Because of this I am ready to do my utmost and if necessary, to spill my blood, to put an end to this curse on humanity.[43]

Did such Basque patriotism square with misleading the American authorities? Had El Cojo's personal safety required him to deliberately deceive, or did his fondness for trickery lead him astray?

Whatever the reason, after 1943 El Cojo Gómez no longer seemed to be a stellar informant for the United States. The last obtainable intelligence report concerning him originated from the U.S. embassy in Bogotá in the spring of 1944. The smuggler claimed that in the Caribbean port of Barranquilla a plot was brewing to overthrow the Panamanian government and that he, himself, was one of the conspirators! But a harsh evaluation followed this sensational report:

> The Naval Attaché agrees with the Military Attaché that "Cojo" Gómez is so notorious a smuggler and so inveterate a liar that his word is not to be relied upon. It is believed that whether or not there is any truth in his information, he is submitting it to

this embassy for the sole purpose of re-establishing himself in the good graces of the United States and Panamanian Governments, with a view to furthering his own personal interests.[44]

His spying on the wane, El Cojo turned to a legitimate business venture, one promising more money than he had ever dreamed possible. During the war he had discovered valuable stands of mahogany on the Chocó's Pacific coast. It was a rich find, stretching 250 kilometers from Panama to Bizolanao and extending eight kilometers inland at some points. An American friend from the Canal Zone examined the trees and advised Gómez to send samples to the United States. The appraisal was quite encouraging, but El Cojo knew he would need many workers and hefty capital to exploit the timber stand.

He went to friends in Medellín to secure initial funding for the mahogany harvesting. Several years earlier he had helped Pedro López Michelsen locate important chicle (gum) trees in the Chocó's steamy jungles. Now he convinced Pedro López and his father, Colombian President Alfonso López Pumarejo, to become his business partners. Two other wealthy Antioquíans, Pablo Echavarría and Gozalo Mejía, were brought into the deal as well. Through President López's influence, the partnership obtained an exclusive concession to log the Chocó mahogany reserves. Pedro López was the only partner other than El Cojo who personally participated in the business. López moved to Juradó but worked with the project for only a year, leaving the entire venture in the Basque's hands upon being named Colombian ambassador to France in 1945.

Logging mahogany for export in the roadless wilds of Chocó was not easy. El Cojo's skills and his backers' financial strength could not insure the mahogany deal against failure. El Cojo, his son Luisito, and their helpers toiled from sunrise to sunset, but their fortunes wavered. They stored the timber in piles secured with steel cables until it could be shipped to the Frederick Mahogany Company in the United States. Time and again the boats were delayed, and several shipments rotted on the beaches. Successive storms in the Chocó caused other losses. The partners were not recovering their investment as quickly as they hoped.

From the beginning, there was friction between El Cojo and two of his four associates, Pablo Echavarría and Gozalo Mejía. Apparently the Medellín businessmen became distrustful of the fast-talking Basque. Finally, they split the partnership, with Mejía and Echavarría taking the mahogany stands near Juradó while the Lópezes and Gómez Lekube kept the other half of the concession in the Coredó area.

It was in the summer of 1946 that the two Antioquíans decided to liquidate all their remaining mahogany in Juradó. Inexplicably, most of their wood rotted during the following months. Mejía and Echavarría, according to El Cojo's son, placed the blame on his father. In October they sent three black natives to close down their operations in the Chocó. Little was known about Concepción Ospina, Gustavo Ovalle, and Jeremías Aspriela except that they were reputedly the "three best *bugas* (blacks) around." These men sought out Gómez and suddenly events became deadly serious.

As with his spying career, the story of El Cojo's last adventure has several versions. Sketchy newspaper accounts written days later unequivocally charge that Luís El Cojo Gómez murdered the three black men at sea. One article described the panic in Coredó when the clothing of the dead men and pieces of their dynamited boat floated onto the village beaches. Claiming that the pirate Gómez was prepared to murder the entire village, the story says he extracted the peasants' silence, "when he came to them asking if they had heard any detonations the night before, to which the *campesinos*, foreseeing what could happen to them, flatly answered no."[45]

Reportedly the murder of the three men occurred on October 31. Young Luís was captured in Juradó while his father fell prisoner in Nuqui, some twenty-three days after the alleged homicide. El Cojo was taken to Juradó on November 28. The villagers formed a mob seeking revenge as the outlaw was marched down the beach. A young man raced through the angry crowd and broke through the men guarding the Basque prisoner. With a swift stroke, the youth plunged a dagger into El Cojo's chest (some say, on the right side, where lay the bandit's heart). Luís Gómez Lekube fell to the sands and died within minutes.

The Colombian newspapers reporting these events were not particularly impartial, nor did their reporters actually witness the tragedies. The articles speculate on El Cojo's guilt in dramatic tones, even referring to a letter the rebel supposedly wrote, bragging of the triple murders to a friend. One article also claimed that on the night of his death, the natives of Juradó guarded El Cojo's body out of fear that he would spring back to life.[46]

The only living witness to most of the events, El Cojo's son, tells the story this way: the mahogany exports were causing enough headaches for the Gómezes that autumn when the disgruntled Medellín partners sent a "thug" to the Chocó. Luís admits that a serious disagreement already existed, and none of the parties was blameless. The hired bully in turn sent the three men, Ospina, Ovalle and Aspriela, to pick a fight with El Cojo Gómez.

On October 31, the three *bugas* surprised Luís and his father on the open sea near Coredó. Both parties were heavily armed. El Cojo and Luís fled full throttle to the north, returning the fire of their attackers. The two Basques reached a large rock outcropping and hid behind it until the pursuing boat came around the other side. For an hour they exchanged fire. In the end, the three black men were dead and El Cojo and Luís crept into Coredó under darkness. They knew that shedding the blood of three local men, even in self-defense, would incite an unforgivable frontier wrath.

Luís and his father felt trapped. Too many years of El Cojo's misdeeds were piled upon the lonesome Chocó beaches. Luís says his father wanted to find authorities who would at least listen to his side of the story. El Cojo headed south for Buenaventura and left his son in one of their supply huts, high on a pinnacle above Coredó. For three nights the frightened teenager defended himself from the angry villagers who unsuccessfully tried to scale the cliff and kill him. Finally, on the fourth day, someone sent a surrender note up to Luís and he agreed to give himself up: "I felt all gone, done in."[47]

From Coredó, Luís was marched to Curiche and then to Juradó a few days later. His captors treated him harshly, chaining his arms and legs to the walls of a crude bamboo hut that passed for a jail in Juradó.

Luís does not know how El Cojo was finally captured. He believes his father voluntarily went to the authorities after hearing a rumor that his son had been shot. Newspaper accounts differ. One story reports that El Cojo talked a retired army officer into accompanying him to Juradó to load gasoline. A later version stated that he was captured in Nuqui, after which a sizable investigatory team and El Cojo's lawyer arrived. When the whole group departed for Juradó, "El Cojo had a horrible fainting spell, falling into a pitiful spiritual prostration."[48] El Cojo, guarded by several policemen, reached Juradó on November 28. At last Luís was set free, but before he ever saw his father a sudden hush engulfed the mob on the beach. El Cojo had been stabbed. They told Luís that his father was dead at the other end of the shore. Luís lunged for a weapon and tried to run to the spot where his father had fallen, but his jailers quickly overpowered him and tied him up again.

Fifteen days later Luís was led out of the bamboo hut. The officers shoved him into a motorboat and chained his arms to the steering device. The authorities dumped his father's putrefying body into the craft, boarded themselves, and ordered the terrorized boy to navigate the launch out of Juradó. In the days since El Cojo's murder, the officers had been unable to depart Juradó because the port's tricky entrances defied their navigational skills. Normally, all boats anchored outside in open sea and cargoes were hauled in by Indian fishing canoes. The men had no recourse but to rely on the son of the dead smuggler in order to depart.

Luís maneuvered the launch out of Juradó on a high tide and turned south for Buenaventura. Soon his jailers ordered him to stop and bury his father on a desolate beach near Nuqui. They resumed the trip and when Luís stepped onto the Buenaventura pier, a crowd greeted him with cries of "pirate" and "murderer." Next he was taken inland and incarcerated in the juvenile section of the Cali jail. Nearly three months elapsed before his mother and several Basques from Bogotá could procure a judge's order to free him. All charges against him were dropped.

A blur of talk, but little action, followed El Cojo's murder; some family members believed that journalists and officials involved were bribed. They charged that the "hired gun" of the Medellín partners had conveniently disappeared. Frustrated and feeling powerless, the family wanted to clear El Cojo's name but did not know how to proceed. A year later, El Cojo's saga remained compelling—in Buenos Aires and Bogotá a newspaper account on the first anniversary of Gómez Lekube's death chronicled his heroics as a Basque freedom fighter whose "final gesture of rebellion" ended in an "unjust death."[49]

Meanwhile, El Cojo's widow had to convince her husband's outraged brother to remain in Spain. Deyanira believed revenge could not be found in the tangle of legends surrounding her husband's life and death. For his son, Luís, justice also seemed illusory. Luís felt that there had been fault "on all sides," and getting even would restore neither his father's life nor the carefree time they had shared in the wilds of the Chocó.

Businessman, outlaw, Basque patriot and spy—these were many colorful hats El Cojo Gómez proudly wore in Colombia. The final toss of each hat sometimes careened uncertainly, but the boldness of their wearer was never in dispute. Pedro López remembers his Basque friend thus:

> He related many adventures to me but I'm not sure all of it was true, for he had a great imagination. In any case, he made an epoch, he was feared and loved at the same time, and his worth was put to the test on more than one occasion.... He was a generous person, of good heart with his friends, but a terrible enemy, as he so demonstrated, never vacillating before anyone to defend himself and that which he believed and considered just.[50]

In the Chocó, El Cojo had irreverently defined right and wrong in his own terms. Accepting life as a dare, he was a larger-than-life figure in a frontier society until he transgressed its code of ethics for the last time.

While he left his children penniless, Luís Gómez Lekube impressed upon them the greatness of their Basque heritage and taught them that honor was individually earned. Even his youngest son, Fermín Euzkadi, barely seven years old when El Cojo died, was imbued with his father's passion for adventure. In 1968 he made the trip from Panama to Turbo by launch, then trekked alone through the Chocó's jungles. His purpose was to retrace the steps of a Basque rebel, the father he had scarcely known. Along this arduous route, the son met old people of all races who had known and loved El Cojo. These friends helped Euzkadi along his way, providing him with supplies and with tearful remembrances of how his Basque father had blustered about the same land over thirty years earlier.

Notes

1. National Archives and Records Service (hereafter, "NARS"), RG 38, Records of the Office of the Chief of Naval Operations, Serial R-278-41, "Supplementary Report from Ground Investigator Concerning Various Persons Residing in the Gulf of Uraba Region, Colombia," September 8, 1941, p. 10.
2. Interviews and several contemporaneous letters provided information about Gómez Lekube's personality. In addition, a four-page fictional account of a "typical" encounter with the outlaw appears as "Aparece el Cojo Gómez" in Juan Antonio Irazusta's book, *Amarga es la vida* (original in Basque). Irazusta spent time with Carmelite priests and other Basques who knew Gómez and also interviewed Luís Gómez Angel after his father's death.
3. See note 2.
4. Contraloría General de la República, *Geografía económica de Colombia, Tomo VI, Chocó* (Bogotá, 1943), pp. 522–523.
5. *El Tiempo*, Bogotá, January 29, 1941.
6. Many informants described El Cojo Gómez and several photographs of the smuggler were obtained. Another description appears in NARS, RG 38, Serial R-278-41, September 8, 1941, p. 13.
7. Letter to Francisco de Abrisqueta from Carmelite priest (name withheld) who knew Luís Gómez Lekube in Turbo, May 7, 1979.
8. El Cojo's justification for smuggling echoes what another Basque wrote about the widespread Basque smuggling in the Pyrenees of Spain and France: "Para el vasco el contrabando no es sino una inocente acción. Un obispo, y dicen que el hecho es verídico,

al evacuar una consulta de un contrabandista muy escrupuloso por cierto, le habría explicado que el pecado de contrabando no existe, sino en los actos de corrupción del encargado de vigilar las fronteras. En conclusión, no puede haber pecado si no hay corrupción. Y no habiendo por las autoridades decisión en ese sentido, ley o *bando*, no puede haber *contra*bando." M. Iriart, *Cosarios y colonizadores vascos* (Buenos Aires: Editorial Vasca Ekin, 1945), p. 45.
9. Ibid.
10. NARS, RG 38, Serial R-278-41, September 8, 1941, p. 14.
11. Ibid., p. 13.
12. In 1940, the Joint Committee on Intelligence Services, including top State Department, War Department, Navy and FBI officials began meeting to coordinate intelligence matters as the probability of U.S. involvement in world war increased. NARS, RG 165, Records of the War Dept. General and Special Staffs, contains the records of these meetings. Also see Rhodri Jeffreys-Jones, *American Espionage, from Secret Service to CIA* (New York: The Free Press, 1977), pp. 133-145.
13. NARS, RG 38 Serial 194-1940, "Activities of Luís ('El Cojo'— trans. 'the Crippled One') Gómez, Reputed Most Outstanding Smuggler in Colombia," November 27, 1940.
14. NARS, RG 165, "Conference between Representatives of State Dept., Military Intelligence Division of War Dept., Naval Intelligence and the Federal Bureau of Investigation on July 16, 1940."
15. NARS, RG 226, Records of the Office of Strategic Services (OSS), 23455, "Development of Platinum and the Activities of the Compañía Minera Chocó Pacífico, S.A., in the Republic of Colombia."
16. Spruille Branden, *Diplomats and Demagogues* (New Rochelle, New York: Arlington House, 1971).
17. NARS, RG 38, Serial R-278-41, September 8, 1941, p. 14.
18. Those interviewed recalled that El Cojo's greatest Canal Zone friend was a "Governor McIntire." However, records of the Panama Canal Company show C. S. Ridley as governor in the late thirties while a C. A. McIlvaine was his executive secretary. *Panama Canal Record*, vol. 31. Possible confusion of English surnames by Spanish-speaking informants may prevent proper identification of this individual. A similar last name ("McDaniel") appears on intelligence reports El Cojo Gómez submitted to the Office of Naval Intelligence Civil Intelligence Division in Balboa, Panama—J. M. McDaniel, Jr., Lt. Cmdr., USNR, apparently took information from the smuggler on a number of occasions.
19. Two of El Cojo's children are convinced that their father planned but did not physically participate in the ouster of President Arias.

They say that the friendship between their father and "McIntire" was such that El Cojo was one of the few people allowed to visit the American in the hospital when he later died of cancer. Other contemporaneous informants could not verify El Cojo's involvement in the coup, but they do recall that the smuggler was very happy to see Arias removed from office.

20. NARS, RG 226, 6108, Office of Naval Intelligence (ONI), 15th Naval Dist., "Panama: Political Forces, Political Parties," August 18, 1941. NARS, RG 59, Records of the Dept. of State, "The Establishment of the de la Guardia Government in Panama," R & A 147, Latin American Section, November 17, 1941.
21. NARS 226, 23202, "Survey of Panama," War Dept., 1942.
22. NARS, RG 226, 13320, "Subversive Activities in Panama and Vicinity," December 1941.
23. NARS, RG 59 (Diplomatic Branch), 819.01/90, Wilson to Sec. of State, Oct. 9, 1941. Walter LaFeber, *The Panama Canal* (New York: Oxford Univ. Press, 1978), pp. 97–98.
24. A Basque priest then working in Chocó recalled that El Cojo Gómez was traveling in Uraba when Arias was overthrown in October 1941. El Cojo was extremely anti-Arias and confided to the priest that "he would have taken Sr. Arias prisoner if he had had the necessary help." Letter of P. T. Larrazabal, O.O.D. to Kay Hummel, Sept. 27, 1977. My Freedom of Information Act appeal for intelligence materials on El Cojo Gómez thus far has recovered no data involving the smuggler in the demise of Arias. However, on law-enforcement (privacy) and national security grounds, many pages of El Cojo's file have been withheld by the U.S. Department of Justice.
25. NARS, RG 226, 17018, ONI Serial 51–42, 15th Naval Dist., "Colombia, Political Forces, War-Making Powers," February 25, 1942.
26. José Antonio de Aguirre y Lekube, *Escape Via Berlin* (New York: The Macmillan Co., 1945).
27. NARS, FDR Library, Wallace Papers, Wallace to Welles and attachments, Container No. 117, 1942. NARS, Diplomatic Branch, 810.404/27, 810.00/91, 810.00/92, January 1942.
28. NARS, RG 59, 852.01, 707, Donovan to Hull, July 3, 1942; Hull to Donovan, July 8, 1942. Federal Bureau of Investigation (FBI), Bureau File 100–101074–9x3, José Antonio de Aguirre, Report of Special Agent, San Antonio, Texas, August 12, 1942.
29. H. Montgomery Hyde, *Room 3603* (New York: Farrar, Strauss & Co., 1962), pp. 216–217.

   By using Aguirre's help, it appears that Donovan of the OSS was disregarding an intelligence coordination agreement that had put the FBI in charge of all intelligence for the Americas while the OSS was to concentrate its efforts in Europe, Africa and Asia. Aguirre's Basque spy network apparently worked with the OSS, FBI, and British Intelligence in Latin America, but at the time of his 1942 trip, the network's precise relationship to these agencies was not well defined. The U.S. embassy in Caracas reported in October 1942 that Aguirre had talked with the legal attachés (FBI agents) there and "stated that although his mission ostensibly was one of rapprochement with university leaders in the Republics visited it had a larger object, i.e., proper preparation of the organization as a whole for closer cooperation with the American and British in intelligence matters. He added that while he would prefer to work solely with Americans he felt obligated for various reasons to assist the British also, but he said that before departing on the present trip he had been in touch with Secretary Stimson and Col. Donovan, and he hoped that it might prove possible to work out a unified system for handling intelligence information." NARS, RG 59, 852.01/726, "Visit to Venezuela of Basque President José Antonio de Agurrre," October 10, 1942.

Aguirre also tried to recruit Basque sailors as spies on Spanish ships with the aim of passing information to both British and American intelligence. ONI, Social 01299316, May 7, 1943; and ONI, Naval Attaché, Caracas, Serial 109–43, April 20, 1943.

30. Carlos Rangel, *Del buen salvaje al buen revolucionario* (Caracas: Monte Avila Editores, 1977), p. 99.
31. U.S. Adjutant General's Office, Historical Section, "History of the Panama Canal Department," 4 vols., unpublished manuscript, Dept. of the Army, Office of the Chief of Military History, Washington, D.C., 1947. NARS RG 226, 10976, "Situation in Colombia."
32. El Cojo's daughter also believes that her father made yet another demand of U.S. officials—that his "black sheep" brother, Juan Gómez Lekube, be returned to Spain after his arrest for alleged fascist activities in England. Reputedly this request was granted. Upon learning of El Cojo's violent death in 1946, Juan wanted to come to Colombia to seek revenge for his brother but Deyanira (El Cojo's widow) convinced Juan that it was futile to get involved. Juan Gómez Lekube died in Barcelona in the late sixties. Another complication arises concerning El Cojo's half brother, José Ramón Gómez Aramburu. He came to live in Panama City, and one intelligence report lists José's home as El Cojo's Panama headquarters. El Cojo reportedly smuggled José Ramón into Colombia. On one occasion, he had the Subdirector of Foreigners in Medellín draw up false papers for him in November 1940 (NARS, RG 38, Serial 194–40, November 27, 1940). No other evidence

concerning José Ramón and the extent of his involvement in El Cojo's smuggling has been obtained. He is believed to be still residing in Panama.
33. NARS, RG 38, Serial 193–43, 15th Naval Dist., "Panama-Colombia, Political Forces, Foreign Penetration," November 13, 1943.
34. Ibid.
35. Ibid.
36. NARS, RG 38, Serial 148–43, 15th Naval Dist., "Colombia, Political Forces, Foreign Penetration," September 28, 1943.
37. NARS, RG 38, Serial R-239–43, Naval Attaché, Bogotá, "Reinhold Paschke," June 11, 1943.
38. NARS, RG 38, Serial 148–43, September 28, 1943.
39. Letter to Francisco de Abrisqueta from Fr. T. Larrazabal, Turbo, Colombia, May 24, 1943.
40. To avoid any possible political problems, Francisco de Abrisqueta destroyed all copies of his correspondence with El Cojo (except for the July 4, 1943, letter). In addition to examining available wartime records at the National Archives, the author made a Freedom of Information Act (FOIA) request to the FBI and other agencies in 1979 to obtain intelligence documents relating to El Cojo, President Aguirre, and Abrisqueta. Although the FBI and CIA provided some documents, many pages were either sanitized or were withheld in their entirety.
41. FBI, Bureau File 62–62736–400, Censorship Daily Report 6537, October 8, 1942. NARS, RG 226, 15645, Hoover to Donovan, "Activities in the Turbo-Uraba Region of Colombia," April 30, 1942.
42. Between 1941 and 1943, ONI had seventy posts in Latin America. But Naval Intelligence had to share intelligence responsibilities with the army's Military Intelligence Division (MID) and with the FBI under a jurisdictional plan instituted by President Roosevelt. Overlapping functions and other miscues plagued these agencies. A merger with the OSS never did occur, although it was discussed. In addition, British Intelligence (BSC) was very active in South America. R. Jeffreys-Jones, *American Espionage* . . . , 1977. "Office of Naval Intelligence, U.S. Naval Administration in World War II, Office of the Chief of Naval Operations, Office of Naval Intelligence," 4 vols., unpublished, Naval History Division, Washington, D.C., n.d.
43. "Un vasco, cojo y contrabandista que luchó contra los Nazis en el Chocó," *El Espectador*, Bogotá, Jan. 21, 1984.
44. NARS, RG 38, Serial R-135–44, Naval Attaché, Bogotá, "Luís V. ('el Cojo') Gómez, Notorious Smuggler, Informs of Plot," May 30, 1944.

45. "El pueblo asesinó en Jurado al pirata Gómez de Lecube (sic)," *El Tiempo*, Bogotá, December 6, 1946.
46. Ibid. Another article detailing the affair appeared in *El Tiempo*: "A los 23 días fue descubierto horrendo asesinato en la Intendencía del Chocó," November 24, 1946; "El Cojo Gómez, famoso contrabandista, asesinado a puñal por un niño de 16 años," *El Diario*, Bogotá, December 3, 1946.
47. Luís Gómez Lekube (son), interview with author, Medellín, Colombia, August 1977.
48. "El pueblo asesinó... ," *El Tiempo*, December 6, 1946.
49. "Un vasco... ," *El Espectador*, January 21, 1948. This article first appeared in a Buenos Aires newspaper and may have been written by a Basque there who had knowledge of El Cojo's drama.
50. Letter of Pedro López Michelsen to Kay Hummel, August 1977.

California's Basque Hotels and Their *Hoteleros*

by

Jerónima Echeverría

In the early 1850s, when the first "Argentine Basques" set foot on California soil in search of gold, they brought with them a knowledge of open-range herding and a social institution they called *ostatua* (inn or hotel). Hopeful miners arrived with dreams of wealth and, in many cases, of a triumphant return to South America or *Euskal herria* (the Basque Country). They did not consciously intend to establish the Basque hotels or boardinghouses, nor the sheep industry that the hotels supported so well; yet the two became intertwined and eventually made their mark in western American history.

As a result of the gold rush, California became the major port of entry for Basques, and the state is believed to be the site of the first Basque hotels in North America.[1] The Golden State also continues to host the largest Basque population of the fifty United States and the greatest number of currently functioning hotels.[2] Of the 119 Basque hotels and boardinghouses that have been part of California's history, eleven still function in some capacity.[3] They can be found in Fresno, Los Banos, Bakersfield, Chino, and San Francisco. Of the eleven, one is an "old style," all-Basque boardinghouse; three no longer take in new boarders; one offers rooms to both Basques and non-Basques; and the remainder reserve their rooms for Basques while relying upon their restaurant revenues for their livelihood.

The earliest evidence of Basques in the hotel business in North America is found in the mission town of San Juan Bautista, California.[4] There, in the early 1850s, a Basque named Julian Ursua owned and operated a hotel that fronted on the old town plaza. Ursua sold the building to an Italian, Angelo Zanetta, who had recently married María Laborda, a French Basque from Bayonne. On 24 June 1856, the Zanettas reopened the Hotel Plaza and, under their management, it became a major center for travelers, local ranchers, and businessmen. Available hotel registers dated 1863 through 1866 indicate that local Basque ranchers stopped at the Plaza as well. Juan Indart, Juan Echeverri, and Juan Mendizabel of the Rancho San Luíz Gonzaga, and Esteben Lugea of Rancho Quien Sabe, Claro Echeveria, Ramón Chevarria, Julian Ursua of San Juan Bautista, and José Aurrecochea of Burns Creek were among them.[5]

While it is true that there were Basque ownership and clientele at the Plaza Hotel in the 1850s and 1860s, it did not cater exclusively to Basques as did later California *ostatuak*. The Plaza was not the first Basque hotel in North America, but is best considered the forerunner or precursor of later *ostatuak*. From 1850 through the 1880s, other pioneer Basques established way stations similar to the Plaza along major wagon and railway lines. In the early 1860s, for example, John and Mary Indart built a two-room adobe on the Sentinella Ranch in Merced County. One family descendant refers to the adobe as "a small hotel" which accommodated travelers, sheepmen, and gold seekers.[6] In 1874, about sixty miles to the west, Juan Etcheverry built another small hotel with a large livery stable in Tres Pinos and, in February of 1884, about thirty miles south, John Iribarne announced the opening of his Chester Hotel.[7]

Also among the earliest California Basque outposts were Juan Miguel Aguirre's hotel in San Francisco and the French Hotel in San Juan Capistrano, owned by Domingo Oyharzabal and Juan Salaberri. Like the others, these two establishments were opened in the first decades of Basque hotelkeeping, between 1850 and 1880. Unlike the others, however, the Aguirre and French hotels enjoyed a longevity which carried them into the twentieth century.

Juan Miguel and Martina Aguirre booked passage for San Francisco from Montevideo on *Le Bon Pere* in 1849 and, after their arrival, Juan Miguel began a water transport service. The success of his business led him to invest in local real estate and, eventually, to construct the city's first handball court at 2 Dupont Circle as well as its first Basque hotel at 1312 Powell Street in 1866.[8] The Aguirre Hotel greeted Basques for almost forty years before it was destroyed in 1906 by the famed San Francisco earthquake and fire. It is quite likely that Aguirre's establishment deserves the designation of first Basque Hotel in North America, since it was probably the earliest to cater mainly to immigrating Basques while serving as a regional center for local Basque-Americans.[9]

While Aguirre, Etcheverry, and Iribarne were operating Basque hotels in northern and central California, another was about to open in the sleepy southern California town of San Juan Capistrano. There, in February of 1878, across from the old, fenced-in mission, Domingo

Oyharzabal and his partner Juan Salaberri purchased two of the town's original adobe buildings. The partners immediately converted the Casa Manuel García into a hotel, calling it the French Hotel, and made the Yorba Adobe next door their home.[10] Given that the French Hotel was San Juan's first hostelry, it is unlikely that its clientele was exclusively Basque. In fact, a non-Basque guest named Clifton Johnson left our earliest eyewitness description of it, reporting that his room was a "rather bare and shabby apartment with a bed that had two boxes under it to prop up the slats."[11] Like the Plaza, Tres Pinos, and Chester hotels, the French Hotel operated within one block of a major stage route.

From the opening of the Plaza Hotel in 1856 to the years when Oyharzabal and Salaberri formed their partnership in San Juan Capistrano, a new social institution had claimed its place in the American West. Not surprisingly, the California of "boom and bust" was its first home. The Basque *ostatua* emerged as a result of increased Basque immigration and was often directly related to the sheep industry. In the 1870s and 1880s, for example, many San Joaquin Valley Basques took their first jobs with the Miller and Lux ranches in Merced, Madera, Kern, and Fresno counties.[12] Shortly thereafter, Basque hotels began appearing in those counties in small and relatively isolated towns like White's Bridge, Huron, Mendota, and Firebaugh.[13]

Completion of the transcontinental rail system in 1869 and the Basque dominance of the expanding sheep industry were two additional factors that led to the marked increase of Basque immigration around the turn of the century. In addition, the years between 1890 and 1930 reveal a change in the basic migratory pattern of Basques within the United States.[14] Whereas the tide had originated in San Francisco and moved east during and after the gold-rush years, it became a powerful east-to-west flow in the 1890s. Years of peak Basque migration also marked the beginning of a Basque exodus from California to the Great Basin states and lasted until the 1930s, when the effects of national origins immigrant quota legislation were felt throughout the American West. As would be expected, such migratory trends had a direct impact upon the longevity of Basque hotels.

Recent immigration studies indicate interesting trends among Basques who arrived in New York in the five-year period from 1897 to 1902. Of the 636 names in the population studied, 86 percent were male and 77 percent single.[15] Although of varied ages, 65 percent of the men ranged between sixteen and thirty years of age and 464 of the 636 were Spanish Basques. A clear pattern emerges: most Basque immigrants during this period were young, unmarried males from Spain. While there is little evidence regarding the migratory pattern in subsequent decades, it is likely that the majority of *Euskaldunak* arriving in the United States before 1910 continued to be unmarried males. Such a pattern substantiates the thesis that, in the absence of family, the *ostatua* was the major social institution for Basques in the New World at the turn of the century.

In addition to the *ostatuak* that had opened earlier as rural outposts and small transportation centers, concentrations of Basque immigrants began forming in small neighborhoods within San Francisco and Los Angeles before the turn of the century. Each of the "Basque towns" featured clusters of *ostatuak* within geographically compact areas. At times, as many as five hotels were located within a two- or three-block distance. Where California's Basque hotels from 1850 through 1880 had tended to be isolated resting spots for travelers, sheepmen, and miners, the "Basque towns" that emerged in these two coastal towns became social centers for the regional American Basque communities and also led to the expansion of *ostatuak* to outlying areas.

Despite numerous parallels, the patterns of growth and development in California's first two "Basque towns" differed slightly. San Francisco's first hotel, owned by Juan Miguel Aguirre, was critical to newly arrived Basques and to their northern California employers. For nearly three decades, the Aguirre hotel served as the only San Francisco *ostatua* of record, until the 1890s when others appeared in the Powell Street neighborhood. In Los Angeles, on the other hand, by 1880 there was a group of hotels at the intersection of Alameda and Aliso streets. By 1940, however, southern California Basques had dispersed and Los Angeles's "Basque town" was defunct, whereas San Francisco continues to host one boardinghouse and a few Basque restaurants today. Therefore, while Los Angeles's "Basque town" was the more concentrated during its peak years of 1890 through 1910, its northern counterpart enjoyed longevity.

As Marie-Pierre Arrizabalaga demonstrated in her statistical study, southern California and Los Angeles County experienced large increases in numbers of Basque residents from 1860 through 1880.[16] This steady increase in the local Basque population caused Martín Biscailuz, editor of the Basque-language newpaper *Escualdun Gazeta*, to estimate that over 2,000 Basques were living in Los Angeles in 1886.[17] While subsequent census records repudiate the claim, there certainly were enough Basques in the area to support numerous *ostatuak*. Between 1872 and 1890, local directories listed twelve separate Basque lodging houses and hotels and, in the following decade, an additional thirteen were cited.[18] Finally, in the decade between 1910 and 1920, boardinghouses known as Mayo's, Sempere's, Olasso's, Urruty's, and Bengochea's could all be found within a city block of the Oyamburu and Victoria Basque hotels.[19]

The years between 1920 and 1930 mark the final chapter of the "Basque town" neighborhood in Los Angeles. The construction of an electric train line down Aliso Street introduced new cultures to the old neighborhood. Intensifying transportation systems criss-crossed the area, older buildings were torn down for the widening of roads, and other ethnic groups, such as the Chinese and Japanese, began living in the old, insular neighborhood.[20] Eventually, the death knell was sounded when the construction of the Union Rail Station caused further demolition in the neighborhood.

Unfortunately, less is known about San Francisco's Basque neighborhood in the years between 1860 and 1900 than that of Los Angeles. The earthquake and subsequent fires of 1906 are largely responsible for the gap in the record, as many collections of municipal and county archives were destroyed. Nonetheless, city and county directories indicate that San Francisco had a well-established "Basque town" by the 1890s. By 1896, for example, the first two Basque hotels on Powell Street were joined by hotels de France, des Alpes, de Basse Pyrenees, Europa, and New Pyrenees.[21]

San Francisco's early "Basque town" shared some characteristics with that of Los Angeles. In both cases, clusters of *ostatuak* sprang up and formed a nucleus for surrounding communities. Both became regional centers for the wider Basque population, and both contributed to the development of newer communities in their hinterlands. While the Basque neighborhood in Los Angeles subsided and collapsed by the Second World War, San Francisco's "Basque town" expanded to the present. Perhaps the nature of urban development in the Los Angeles metropolitan area was the most important "push" factor for southern California Basques to relocate in surrounding areas, while Basques in San Francisco were able to adapt to urban growth by taking "town jobs" as gardeners, janitors, bakers, and laundry workers.[22] In Los Angeles, on the other hand, Basques were often directly tied to sheep raising, wool production, or other agricultural endeavors.

Although the Basque population in Los Angeles declined in the twentieth century, it served as a training ground for those who would become hotelkeepers in Bakersfield, as well as for *hoteleros* who made their way to Tehachapi, Santa Barbara, Chino, and Puente. For example, Jean Burubeltz managed the Ballade House in Los Angeles before moving to Bakersfield to operate the Iberia Hotel in 1906.[23] Perhaps the best example of a *hotelero* or *hotelera* moving from one Basque colony to another is that of Hortense Anchordoquy, who ran a small boardinghouse near the Santa Barbara train station in the late 1920s, moved to the old Borderre French Hotel near De La Guerra Plaza in 1931, relocated to Los Angeles in 1932 with her husband Francisco Ciaurritz to find hotel work, and then began managing the Tehachapi Hotel in 1936.[24]

What the *ostatuak* of Bakersfield, Santa Barbara, and southern California have in common is similar roots—that is, many of their founders could be traced to the "Basque town" neighborhood of Los Angeles. The *ostatuak* were "spin-offs" of an earlier day but, beyond that, they differ. Bakersfield's and Santa Barbara's Basque colonies had developed by the twentieth century and had formed "Basque towns" of their own, one with a San Joaquin Valley agricultural base, the other with a coastal-town flavor. To the south, Chino and Puente's hotels matured differently. Thirty and forty years after their cousins had developed in Santa Barbara and Bakersfield, the towns of Chino and Puente produced three Basque hotels that catered to an urban, southern-California lifestyle, in a time when comparatively few Basques were immigrating to the United States. Puente's Valley and Puente hotels opened in 1930 and 1939 respectively and were both defunct by 1948. Chino's Centro Vasco, on the other hand, has been operating continuously since 1940 when Jean Baptiste and Grace Robidart had it built.[25]

To the north, however, several colonies of Basques clustered in the central and northern San Joaquin Valley. That valley had provided ample territory for sheep raising and, when the industry declined, many Basques turned to other forms of ranching and farming. Towns like Fresno, Merced, Los Banos, Bakersfield, and Stockton, all in the San Joaquin Valley, provided the setting for many *ostatuak* in the late nineteenth and twentieth centuries. In the decades since 1893, when the nearly century-old Noriega Hotel opened its doors as the Iberia Hotel, Bakersfield has hosted five Basque hotels. Of the five, only the Noriega still functions as a Basque boardinghouse, serving family-style meals punctually at lunch and dinner hours with the ring of the bell that hangs above the bar. The old Pyrenees Hotel has been open since 1901, but only serves restaurant-style meals, while the d'Europe, Metropole, and Amestoy closed decades ago.

Approximately forty miles southeast of Bakersfield, up in the foothills of the Sierra Nevadas, is the small town of Tehachapi. Nestled in a gorge 4,000 feet above Bakersfield, the town was founded in the summer of 1876, when the Southern Pacific Railway finally surmounted the difficulties of the steep grade and reached the little valley at its summit. In the two decades after its foundation, the small town swelled with the influx of miners and stockmen. By 1895, Tehachapi had its first two Basque hotels—the Piute Hotel owned by Goyehen and Young and John Pierre Martinto's Basse Pyrenees. These were followed by Jean Esponda's Basko Hotel, the Cesmat, the Franco-American, the Juanita, and Tehachapi hotels.[26] In 1952, however, the remaining *ostatuak* were destroyed by a powerful earthquake, as was much of Tehachapi.

In 1897, just four years after Bakersfield Basques christened the Noriega Hotel and two years after the Piute opened in Tehachapi, Fresno Basques celebrated their first *ostatua*. Founded by Martín Iribarren and John Bidegaray, the Bascongado led the way for founding of eleven more Fresno *ostatuak* in ensuing decades. The old Frechou House on Tulare Street, the Ballazes' Vitoria Hotel, the Esains' Hotel Basque, and the Lugea brothers' Hotel de Spanio are among those remembered fondly by Fresno's earliest Basques. Today the Santa Fe, Yturri, and Basque hotels continue the Fresno tradition in Basque hotelkeeping.

Though rarely discussed today, at one time Stockton had one of the largest and most rapidly expanding "Basque towns" in the San Joaquin Valley. There, between 1907 and 1970, some nineteen Basque hotels served local *Euskaldunak*, their families, and visiting valley sheepmen. Among the more popular was the Hotel California on San Joaquin Street. Operated by Alfonso and Fermín Alustiza, one of the rare father and son partnerships in Basque hotelkeeping, the California operated between 1924 and 1969.[27] Another Stockton *ostatua* with remarkable longevity was the Hotel Central, owned by the Artozqui family for over four decades, from 1916 to 1960.

Of the 119 *ostatuak* in California's history between 1856 and 1988, approximately 40 percent were located in the San Joaquin Valley towns of Stockton, Los Banos, Merced, Bakersfield, and Fresno; 21 percent were found in Los Angeles; and 19 percent in San Francisco. Table One presents a list of California towns with *ostatuak* by geographical area and suggests that the hotels and boardinghouses formed clusters within Basque colonies throughout the state.[28] Also, note that twelve communities having only one or two hotels or boardinghouses are listed. In some cases, as in San Diego, Bishop, or McKittrick, only a single advertisement could be found for each, and the establishments may have operated for no longer than a single year.

Nor does the table reflect the longevity of individual *ostatuak*, such as the Noriega in Bakersfield, which approaches its centennial in 1993.

Thus far, little has been said to define the *ostatuak*. Hotelkeepers frequently called their establishments boardinghouses or hotels, many using both terms interchangeably. Given that few Basques dwell upon the hotels in their personal recollections, the claim that the *ostatuak* were the *Amerikanuak*'s major social institution may seem bold. But the Basque hotel may best be considered an "invisible institution,"

Table One: *Geographical Groupings of California* Ostatuak

Date of Establishment through Last *Ostatuak*	Community, County or Town	Number of *Ostatuak*	
1856-1890	Merced & San Benito Counties	4	(3%)
1866-1988	San Francisco	23	(19%)
1878-1903	San Juan Capistrano	1	(1%)
1878-1939	Los Angeles	24	(21%)
1886-1899	West Fresno County	4	(3%)
1893	San Diego	1	(1%)
1893	San Jose	1	(1%)
1893-1988	Bakersfield	5	(4%)
1893	Bishop	1	(1%)
1895-1952	Tehachapi	7	(5%)
1897-1988	Fresno	11	(8%)
1899-1935	Santa Barbara	6	(5%)
1907-1970	Stockton	19	(16%)
1914-1988	Los Banos	2	(2%)
1920s	Sacramento	2	(2%)
1920	Alturas	1	(1%)
1924	McKittrick	1	(1%)
1929-1955	Merced	1	(1%)
1930-1988	Susanville	2	(2%)
1930-1948	Puente	2	(2%)
1940-1988	Chino	1	(1%)
1856-1988		119	(100%)

especially to Basques themselves. In the dozen interviews collected from early Orange County Basques at the Cal State Fullerton Oral History Collection, for example, over half mention staying at Basque hotels upon their arrival in California, yet not one mentions a hotel by name.[29] Perhaps the *ostatuak* were so thoroughly integrated into Basque-American society that even the *Amerikanuak* were unlikely to distinguish them from their everyday life, as is the case with an invisible institution.

On the other hand, most Basque-Americans have been eager to describe the helpfulness of the *hoteleros* upon their arrival in the United States. In California, as throughout the West, initial contacts with *hoteleros* are frequently remembered for a lifetime. In some instances, *hoteleros* arranged employment for herders, before sending for people in the old country. If a Basque did not have a job upon arrival, the hotelkeeper was likely to search for work for him in the community, on a neighboring ranch, or with a sheep outfit in the area. In the meantime, the *hotelero* might extend liberal credit, room, and board in exchange for the newcomer's future business and eventual repayment.

Once the traveler arrived at his final California train depot, say in Tres Pinos, Bakersfield, Fresno, or Los Banos, he had only to gaze across the street to find the Basque hotel recommended to him by an *Euskalduna* at his preceding stop. At the hotel, he was likely to find a long, rectangular, two-story wooden building, possibly with a semi-enclosed handball court adjacent to one of the long exterior hotel walls. There may have been chicken pens, a few livestock, a livery, and a vegetable garden in the empty lots alongside and behind the building as well. Inside, he would have first encountered a bar, card room, and dining area, with noises emanating from the kitchen located at the back of the building. Upstairs, there would have been small, sparsely furnished guest rooms with either single beds or dormitory-style bunks.

The hotel offered a number of conveniences that helped the newcomer cope with the unfamiliar. Since about one-half the shepherds were laid off in the winter season, many herders used the hotels as their winter base. Whether they were on the range or in residence, they used the *ostatuak* as their permanent mailing address and as a storage facility for their Sunday suit and extra gear. Many a hotel set a room aside for storing bedrolls, suits, camp gear, dated mail, and personal papers. Moreover, if a herder were injured on the job and needed to recuperate, his boss was likely to send him to the nearest Basque hotel for care. And, finally, upon retirement many elderly herders made the hotels their home.

In addition to being the herder's home away from home for the immigrants, the *ostatuak* served other important functions for the local Basque-American families. As hotel owners began sending for Basque serving girls to work in their hotels, the *ostatuak* became a primary setting for young, unmarried Basques to meet. So frequently did Basques meet their future spouses at the hotels that the *ostatuak* have been described as "marriage mills." In addition, wives living on remote ranches would come to stay at the hotels during the last months of their pregnancies and frequently gave birth there. Not uncommonly, outlying Basque ranchers sent their children to the hotels to board during the school year. Moreover, special events such as wedding parties, family celebrations, dances, and wakes often took place in the hotels. And, where local Catholic churches were absent, hotel dining rooms may have provided the settings for baptisms, marriages, and funerals.

Sunday was the day to visit the local hotel. Basques from distant ranches packed up their families and, depending upon available transportation, made their way to a favored *ostatua*. There they were likely to share a Sunday meal, watch handball matches, play a few rounds of *mus*, sing folk songs and dance. For many hotelkeepers, Sunday was both dreaded and anticipated, for it was the most profitable day of the week and yet required the most intense work. As one *hotelera* stated, "Sunday was our toughest day."[30]

Generally speaking, Basque-Americans remember the *ostatuak* fondly. When interviewed, Basques are likely to speak of the people they met at the hotels and the relationships they formed there. Occasionally, a Basque couple will discuss their lifelong friendship with other newlyweds they met while honeymooning at an *ostatua*. Nevada Basques developed a special term for the relationship, calling their couple-friends *urtekoak* (those married in the same year). They also reported celebrating anniversaries and special events together throughout their lives.[31]

Although most Basques have reacted positively to the *ostatuak*, a few have also been willing to discuss some negative aspects of hotel life. For example, one individual suggested that the hotels could also be a "prison" that limited job possibilities for the newcomer and delayed his or her mastery of English. He remembered a few examples where some elderly Basques who had come to the United States seeking their fortunes as herders had been unable to amass savings. Upon retirement, these herders had neither the finances nor the will to return to *Euskal herria* as planned. Because they had depended upon the hotels for their social and employment contacts for decades, and spoke only Basque, their choice of residence upon retirement or unemployment was limited to the most familiar hotel. There they lived out their days in relative solitude, taking odd jobs whenever possible. In so many words, the hotel had made their transition to the New World easier while at the same time limiting their ability to become part of it.[32]

Hotelkeeping could be difficult for the families running the hotels as well. In one interview, a *hotelera* stated that in the hotels "there was no room for weakness" and that the daily demands of cleaning, cooking, and serving interfered with the family's desire to be together. Another *hotelera* complained that during the years she and her husband operated a hotel, they never got away together. In addition, a child of a hotelkeeper reported that "we kids never wanted to run a hotel. . . . your front room was always a bar."[33]

In some locations, hotelkeeping was not highly regarded among local Basques. From about 1890 through 1920 in Stockton, for example, such a period occurred when *hoteleros* were thought to have less status than local ranchers and stockmen.[34] The anti-*hotelero* sentiment among Stockton's Basques at first suggests the Old-World distinction between *baserritarak* (people of the farmsteads) and *kaleterrak* (people of the street or townships).[35] But the preference for agricultural occupations among Basques throughout the American West also reflects the comparatively limited demand for *ostatuak*. In 1900, 66.4 percent of all Basque-Americans in California, Nevada, Idaho, and Wyoming were involved in some form of agriculture, while only 6.6 percent worked in hotels. Ten years later, Basques in agricultural occupations numbered 2,037, which was more than six times the number employed in hotels.[36]

One Old-World characteristic that played a more certain part in the development of Basque hotels in the West is that of first-neighbor, or *lenbizikoatia*, assistance. While the practice of aiding one's neighbor is not unique to Basques, the highly systematic first-neighbor tradition among Old-World Basques is well documented.[37] Modified manifestations of *lenbizikoatia* among New-World Basques have also been apparent among hotelkeepers. One notable example occurred in Bakersfield on 6 November 1979, when the staff at Noriega's hotel awaited the large party attending the funeral services for Dr. Clerou, a French-American physician who had cared for many Bakersfield Basques. Just before the one hundred and fifty guests arrived, Noriega's Louis Elizalde had a fatal heart attack. Word of Louie's death raced through the neighborhood and when the news reached Mayie Maitia at the Wool Growers, she left her restaurant in order to manage the dinner party on behalf of the Elizalde family. Once things were in order and everyone had been served, Mayie slipped unnoticed out the back kitchen door, diagonally through the adjacent lot and alley to her own business. In a more practical instance of *lenbizikoatia*, Amelie Sorhondo welcomed Catherine Goyenetche into San Francisco's "Basque town" with advice and assistance in exterminating troublesome roaches. Whether pragmatic or selfless in nature, hotelkeepers transfered the spirit of *lenbizikoatia* to the New World and readily helped one another in difficult times.

While Basques in the United States could recognize elements of Old-World culture at the hotels, there neither is nor was any establishment exactly like the *ostatuak* of the American West in *Euskal herria*. In the Old-World village, local taverns provide the gathering place for locals to visit and exchange daily news, while the corresponding setting has frequently been the *ostatua* in the New World. In the latter case, the Basque-American encountered a larger facility in which he could reside, eat, play handball, dance, or play cards.

The hotelkeeping couple was often called upon to represent both the Old and New Worlds, and their ability to do so was crucial to the success of their *ostatua*. For the newly arrived Basque the *hoteleros* served as interpreters of American culture. For the New-World Basque and his children they provided a sense of Old-World heritage. In essence, the hotelkeeper couple had to win the trust of the Old-World Basques while accommodating the demands of the younger generations as well.

Very rarely was a hotelkeeper alone able to manage an *ostatua*. More often, a husband-and-wife team operated the hotels with the occasional assistance of other family members. Traditionally, he ran the bar from morning until closing while she supervised the preparation of noon and evening meals, the serving girls who waited tables, and the cleaning girls who maintained the rooms. If business was good and there was ample demand, hotelkeepers were able to hire additional bartenders, serving and cleaning girls, and cooks. If the couple could not afford to hire additional help, the two did the work themselves. Also, hotelkeepers rarely advertised to fill job openings since they preferred verbal recommendations.

Whenever possible, hotelkeepers found it advantageous to avoid problems before they might occur. For example, renting rooms exclusively to Basques served to diminish potential problems in dealing with "outsiders." *Hoteleros* and their regular boarders generally policed the hotels themselves. In one instance, when a herder attempted to bend house rules, boarders reported to the *hotelera* that "old Dave in room twelve" had just taken a lady upstairs. Immediately, she scaled the stairs, pounded on the door, three boarders at her side and room key in hand, and insisted that the visitor leave, threatening that she was about to enter and escort her to the front door herself. As can be imagined, this direct approach toward misdemeanors embarrassed a few customers, but curtailed potentially troublesome situations in the future.

One area where internal policing was less effective regarded payment. Hotelkeepers reported that collecting money from an itinerant herder was occasionally a problem. When a potential boarder requested a room, he was assigned one and asked how long he intended to stay. During "signing in," the exchange of money was rare, as was an official record of the visit. The understanding was that the customer would pay upon departure or, if his stay were to exceed seven days, he would either pay at the end of the week or at an arranged time.

Hotelkeepers knew, however, that during "hard times" they might absorb the loss until a herder or sheepman could earn enough to repay his debt. If a herder who stayed at the hotel left without paying, or making some arrangement to pay in the future, he was likely to face the threat of ostracism from the local community. Certainly, he would not be welcomed back at the same hotel and, if the Basque community was small enough, others would come to know him as unreliable or dishonest. Being "known" in such a fashion would damage his likelihood of securing work in the area.

Generally speaking, an Old-World Basque male and an American-born Basque female constitute the "perfect" hotelkeeping couple.[38] Among the eleven *hoteleros* interviewed by Jean Decroos, nine were born in *Euskal herria* and a majority had married New-World Basques.[39] With this combination, the first-generation client could share common Old-World concerns with the hotelkeeper in his native *Euskera*, but turn to the *hotelera* when he needed assistance with New-World dilemmas. She was generally the more familiar with "American ways" and could serve as translator, escort, and adviser.

Preliminary reports suggest that, when compared with the *hotelero*, the *hoteleras* had more demanding schedules and did more than their fair share of the work around the *ostatuak*. While the informant population is primarily female, and potentially biased, there is no reason for doubting the claim. Moreover, one early resident of "Basque town," Los Angeles, reported that women who worked the hotels there were virtually slaves, performing the large variety of tasks needed to keep the enterprise going. Daily work hours began around six in the morning and lasted until the last customers were served, with breaks and/or free afternoons granted during occasional lulls in the hotel's routine.

Such rigorous daily schedules undoubtedly contributed to the hotel operators' relatively brief tenure in business. In fact, *hoteleros* rarely remained in operation beyond fifteen or twenty years, if that long. In Stockton, for example, only two of the thirty-five families in hotelkeeping remained over fifteen years.[40] The strain of the daily morning-to-night work hours in part explains the short term of hotel ownership. In addition, *ostatuak* rarely passed successfully to second-generation family members. One exception, however, was Alustiza's California Hotel in Stockton. In that case, father and son together operated the business until Fermín retired and Alfonso stepped in as sole proprietor. In other examples, however, second-generation hotelkeepers were too far removed from the Old-World village, the sheep camps, and the language to earn a herder's trust.

One might wonder how large a Basque colony was needed to support a hotel or group of hotels. For example, in 1900 Bakersfield had a population of 213 Basques and hosted four hotels.[41] In 1917, Stockton had "twenty core Basque families and a large floating population of single Basque men" that supported four large *ostatuak* with adjoining handball courts.[42] In both instances, the "floating populations" must have augmented business greatly, as the potential for "regular" customers from the local Basque population seems limited. In fact, the survival of *ostatuak* may have been more dependent upon business generated from traveling sheepmen than locals.

One observer has suggested that "front" and "back" behavior is an important aspect of social groupings found in Basque hotels and boardinghouses.[43] A non-Basque at a hotel might be engaged in conversation up to a point. Conversation beyond that point is reserved for those who are familiar with one another, speak Basque, or are Basque. For the few non-Basque hotelkeepers interviewed in this study, evidence of "front" and "back" behavior among Basques and other *hoteleros* has been painfully evident. In two instances, the lack of full acceptance within the Basque colony has been uncomfortable and threatened business. In one case, the embittered hotelkeeper felt forced to encourage non-Basque clients, and has done so fairly successfully.

In addition to supervising and orchestrating the complex front-back, insider-outsider functions that transpired within the *ostatuak*, *hoteleros* also had to be aware of the hotel network or system throughout the United States, and especially in the western states. A Bakersfield Basque vacationing in a San Francisco *ostatua*, for example, would return home with assessments of the hotel, the service, and the hotelkeeper. Because their business was dependent upon referrals to and from other hotels, the hotelkeeper had to be well informed regarding services available elsewhere and sensitive to the greater network of hotels.

Complex familial affiliations throughout the hotel network also facilitated the referral system among *ostatuak*. For example, *hotelera* Anselma Ballaz Amestoy of Bakersfield and *hotelero* Tomás Ballaz of Fresno were sister and brother, Bakersfield's Jean Elizalde and Jean Burubeltz of Bakersfield and Los Angeles were nephew and uncle, and Jean Pierre Martinto of Tehachapi's Basse Pyrenees was uncle to Lyda Esain of the Basque Hotel in Fresno. Family ties also existed in Los Angeles's "Basque town," where the Errecas, Ballades, and Burubeltzes were all related by marriage. In Bakersfield, two of the Maitia brothers and their wives were involved with ownership of the Basque Cafe, the Amestoy Hotel, and the Wool Growers Restaurant.

Complementing word of mouth, advertising was a second major means for *hoteleros* to attract clientele. During the 1890s, business card-size advertisements frequently appeared in the issues of *California-ko Euskal Herria* and *Escualdun Gazeta*. In addition, East Bakersfield directories from 1899 through 1915 indicate that all local hotelkeepers competed for business with advertising. The general rule has been, however, that *hoteleros* have limited "outside" advertising in general publications and purchased advertisement space in specialized newspapers, such as *Voice of the Basques*, in the 1970s, and specific annual Basque picnic bulletins. Finally, it seems that the *ostatuak* can be classified based upon function. For example, José Miguel Aguirre's early San Francisco hotel was most likely a transit hotel, whose primary function was to house sojourners for brief periods, accommodate their intended travel plans, and send them on their way in hopes that they might return again in the distant future. Because transit hotels, by definition, moved people in and out of their doors rapidly, they may have indirectly contributed to the development of *ostatuak* in surrounding areas. Hotels generated as offshoots of Los Angeles's "Basque town," such as those in Chino, Bakersfield, and Puente, could be called spin-off hotels. Another type would be the regional Basque hotel. For example, many San Francisco hotels served as vacation and honeymoon spots for California and Nevada Basques. Hotels that had less potent drawing power, but still attracted Basques from neighboring counties, such as those in Stockton, Fresno, and Bakersfield, might be distinguished as district hotels.

In addition to the transit, spin-off, regional, and district hotels, a fifth type might be called the local hotel. Serving the needs of local herders and their families, these hotels were small-scale centers found at the county and town levels. Puente, Merced, Los Banos, and Alturas have all hosted such local hotels. An irony of the local hotel's existence is that, while its survival has been dependent upon those in rural or agricultural occupations, it has been most successfully located in small urban centers. The small town or rural *ostatuak* of Firebaugh, Mendota, Huron, and McKittrick, for example, disappeared decades ago.

Certainly, many *ostatuak* fall into overlapping categories. For example, the Ogden hotels in Utah served as the regional center for Great Basin Basques, yet they were also transit hotels situated near major railways. Likewise, both regional and local hotels might be found in "Basque towns." Categorization of types of Basque *ostatuak* is useful but should not be regarded as rigid or exclusive. The final type of Basque *ostatuak* would be the tourist hotel, which depends upon non-Basque clientele for survival.

The decline of the traditional *ostatuak* in recent decades has been accompanied by the emergence of the tourist hotel. As opposed to the traditional Basque boardinghouse, these hotels offer room and board to Basques and non-Basques, or rent rooms without board. They tend to employ non-Basques who often dress in Basque costume, decorate their interiors more than traditional hotels, offer a menu which includes non-Basque dishes, accept all major credit cards, and advertise in local media. Such establishments are a step or two removed from the traditional *ostatuak* and, in many cases, represent a gradual evolution from a Basque hotel to a restaurant with a Basque theme.

Where *Amerikanuak* are familiar with "Basque towns," one might encounter a distinction between the Basque boardinghouse and Basque hotel. While the terms are still used interchangeably, "Basque towns" occasionally have had boardinghouses completely closed to "outsiders" or non-Basques. If a Basque ever discusses the difference between boardinghouses and hotels, the major criteria for the distinction seems to be based upon who is being served there. The only California example of a boardinghouse which is off limits to non-Basques today is Jean and Amelie Sorhondo's place in San Francisco.

In California, the disappearance of the boardinghouses and devolution from hotel to restaurant has been obvious. Basque hotels in Los Angeles, Stockton, Merced, Tehachapi, McKittrick, Alturas, Puente, and Santa Barbara have disappeared; and in Los Banos, Chino, Susanville, parts of San Francisco, Bakersfield, and Fresno, hotels have either closed their doors to boarders or severely limited the number of new residents. Instead, they encourage their restaurant businesses, catering to both non-Basques and Basques. In San Francisco and Bakersfield, the construction of clubhouses or cultural centers has, in some ways, replaced the old downtown *ostatuak*.

As the central and crucial gathering place for both American and European Basques over the past century, the *ostatua* has clearly served as an important social institution. In the first five or six decades of Basque migration to the United States, when young herders arrived unmarried to seek their fortunes and return to *Euskal herria*, the hotels served as the immigrant's job placement agency, his extended family, and primary source of assistance. Without question, the *ostatua* was the group's major social institution in those early decades. As more and more Basques arrived and began raising their own families, however, the central role of the hotel shifted somewhat to provide a focal point for the Basque-American community as well.

Whether as a home away from home for the immigrant herder or a social institution for an established Basque colony, the *ostatua* depended upon the presence of a Basque ethnic population. Recently, the Basque herder is an increasingly rare figure on the western ranges. Of the 742 herders under contract to the Western Range Association in 1976, 58 percent were from Latin America. Only 106, or one in six, were culturally Basque. A decade earlier there were twice as many herders and fully 95 percent were Basque.[44] The lack of herders impacts the ethnic awareness of the Basque-American population as well, since it deprives it of its prime source of Old-World cultural influence with which to countermand, if only in part, the assimilation pressure from the wider American society. One might therefore predict that unless there is renewed immigration of Old-World Basque herders, which is highly unlikely, the *ostatuak* will be gone by the twenty-first century or will have evolved into the tourist version which parodies rather than continues the Basque hotelkeeping tradition of the American West. To the memory of the *ostatuak*, *Amerikanuak* and their descendants bid a fond farewell.

Notes

1. Douglass and Bilbao note an earlier presence of Basque-owned bars, hotels, and boardinghouses in the Río de la Plata region by 1842. William A. Douglass and Jon Bilbao, *Amerikanuak: Basques in the New World* (Reno: University of Nevada Press, 1975), pp. 151–160.
2. U. S. Census, Department of Commerce, Bureau of the Census, *Ancestry of Population by State, 1980* (Washington: Government Printing Office, 1983), pp. 51–56.
3. Jerónima Echeverría, "*California-ko Ostatuak*: A History of California's Basque Hotels" (Ph.D. dissertation, University of North Texas, Denton, 1988), pp. 235–238. Contents of this article are based upon this research project.
4. "Basque Beginnings in California," Talbott Papers. Private Collection, Los Banos, California; Joseph Arburua, "Rancho Panocha de San Juan y los Carrizalitos" (Manuscript, University of Nevada-Reno, Basque Studies Collection, 1970); and Izaac Mylar, *Early Days at the Mission San Juan Bautista* (Watsonville, California: Valley Publishers and San Juan Historical Society, 1970) are three excellent sources that deal with the Plaza Hotel in San Juan Bautista.
5. "History of San Juan Bautista, Panoche, Los Banos," Talbott Papers. Surnames are presented here exactly as Zanetta recorded them, despite probable misspellings.
6. Mrs. M. Indart, interview with Ralph Milliken, San Juan Bautista, California, 5 February 1933, Ralph Milliken Papers, Milliken Museum, Los Banos, California.
7. Mr. L. Larios, interview with Ralph Milliken, Hollister, California, undated. Ralph Milliken Papers; and Fannie Yturriarte McCullough, interview with Elena Talbott, Hollister, California, 25 September 1972. Talbott Papers.
8. Rockwell R. Hunt, *California and Californians*, vol. 3 (Chicago: Lewis Publishing Company, 1932), pp. 121–122.
9. Accounts describing the Aguirre Hotel can be found in Anne B. Fisher, *The Salinas: Upside-Down River* (New York: Farrar and

Rinehart, 1945), pp. 208-233; Joseph Arburua, "Rancho Panocha," p. 17; and William A. Douglass and Jon Bilbao, *Amerikanuak...*, p. 377.
10. U. S. Department of the Interior, National Register of Historic Places Inventory Nomination Form, 2. Oyharzabal French Hotel File. City Hall, San Juan Capistrano, California. Also, Samuel Armor, *History of Orange County, California* (Los Angeles: Historic Record Company, 1921), p. 1644.
11. Descriptions from Johnson are cited in National Registry Application, Oyharzabal French Hotel File.
12. Mary Grace Paquette, *Basques to Bakersfield* (Bakersfield: Kern County Historical Society, 1982), pp. 1-3, 81; and Sodie Arbios, *Memories of My Life: an Oral History of a California Sheepman* (Stockton: Techni-Graphics Printing, 1980), pp. 22-25.
13. Charles W. Clough and William B. Secrest, Jr., *Fresno County—the Pioneer Years: From the Beginnings to 1900* (Fresno: Panorama West Books, 1985), pp. 256, 262; Paul E. Vandor, *History of Fresno County* (Los Angeles: Historic Record Company, 1919), p. 1927; and "Mouren Farm Company of Huron," *Fresno Bee*, 28 August 1981, p. C4.
14. Craig Campbell, "The Basque-American Ethnic Area: Geographical Perspectives on Migration, Population and Settlement," *Journal of Basque Studies*, vol. 6 (1985), pp. 83-89.
15. Iban Bilbao and Chantal de Eguiluz, *Diáspora vasca*, vol. 1: *Vascos llegados al puerto de Nueva York, 1897-1902* (Vitoria-Gasteiz: Diputación Foral de Alava, 1981).
16. Marie-Pierre Arrizabalaga, "A Stastical Study of Basque Immigration into California, Nevada, Idaho, and Wyoming between 1900 and 1910" (Master's thesis, University of Nevada-Reno, 1986), pp. 36-38.
17. William A. Douglass and Jon Bilbao, *Amerikanuak...*, p. 336.
18. Jerónima Echeverría, "*California-ko Ostatuak...*," pp. 68, 75.
19. Ibid., p. 84; and Dominic Sorçabal, interview with the author, Huntington Beach, California, 1 May 1987.
20. Karen J. Weitze, "Aliso Historical Report," Office of Environmental Planning, Department of Transportation, Sacramento, California, January 1980, p. 13.
21. Jerónima Echeverría, "*California-ko Ostatuak...*," pp. 84-86.
22. Jean Francis Decroos, *The Long Journey: Social Integration and Ethnicity Maintenance among Urban Basques in the San Francisco Bay Region* (New York: Associated Faculty Press and Reno: Basque Studies Program, 1983), pp. 42-43.
23. Mariana Etcheverria, personal correspondence, Paquette Papers, Private Collection, Sonora, California.

24. Mary Grace Paquette, *Basques to Bakersfield*, pp. 57-58; and José Campos, interview with author, Santa Barbara, California, 4 June 1987.
25. Juliette Robidart Campos, interview with author, Caruthers, California, 23 April 1987.
26. Jerónima Echeverría, "*California-ko Ostatuak*...," pp. 113-118, 236, 242.
27. Steve Ybarrola, a native of Stockton, has compiled an exhaustive list of hotels in Stockton's "Basque town" and generously shared it with the author. Ybarrola Papers, Private Collection, Providence, Rhode Island.
28. Compilation from Jerónima Echeverría, "*California-ko Ostatuak*...," pp. 236-244. Percentages are rounded to nearest whole numbers.
29. Early Orange County Pioneers Oral History Collection, California State University at Fullerton, California.
30. Catherine Inda Goyenetche, interview with author, San Francisco, California, 13 May 1987.
31. Gretchen Holbert, interview with author, Gardnerville, Nevada, 20 May 1987.
32. Anonymous. Interview with the author.
33. Anonymous. Interviews with the author.
34. Elena Celayeta Talbott, interview with author, Los Banos, California, 8 May 1987; and Pete Iroz, interview with author, 11 June 1987, Stockton, California.
35. Marianne Heiberg, "Inside the Moral Community: Politics of a Basque Village," *Basque Politics: A Case Study in Ethnic Nationalism*, William A. Douglass (ed.) (New York: Associated Faculty Press and Reno: Basque Studies Program, 1985), pp. 285-308.
36. Marie-Pierre Arrizabalaga, "A Statistical Study...," p. 126.
37. Sandra Ott, *Circle of Mountains: A Basque Sheepherding Community* (Oxford: Clarendon Press, 1981) is an excellent example.
38. The perfect-couple concept is presented in William A. Douglass, "Home is a Hotel," *American West*, vol. 17 (July/August 1980), p. 31; William A. Douglass and John Bilbao, *Amerikanuak*, p. 379; and Jean Francis Decroos, *The Long Journey*..., pp. 44-47.
39. Jean Francis Decroos, *The Long Journey*..., p. 45.
40. Jerónima Echeverría, "*California-ko Ostatuak*...," pp. 158-160.
41. Marie-Pierre Arrizabalaga, "A Statistical Study...," p. 11.
42. Sheldon Davis, "Stockton Citizens from the Pyrenees Mountains," *Stockton Record*, Talbott Papers, Los Banos, California.

43. Douglas G. Hale, "Quasi-Groups and Boundary Maintenance in a Basque Hotel," student paper, University of Montana, undated, Basque Studies Collection, University of Nevada-Reno Library.
44. William A. Douglass, "The Vanishing Basque Sheepherder," *American West*, vol. 17, p. 61. Of the 433 Latin Americans, there were 271 Peruvians, 161 Mexicans, and one Columbian.

The Overland: The Last Basque Hotel

by

Gretchen Osa

Ongi Etorri proclaims the sign above the entrance to the dining room of the Overland Hotel in Gardnerville, Nevada: a hearty "welcome" to four generations of Basques, Basque-Americans, and other guests. Regulars here are still greeted by name and a firm handshake. "Lon' tine no see," chuckles Eusebio Cenoz, the owner-bartender from Navarra, as he offers up his specialty, the "picon punch"—a tasty but lethal mixture of amer picon liqueur, brandy, soda, and grenadine punctuated by a lemon twist, a curling exclamation of fellowship. From the bar one proceeds carefully (Speed Limit: two picons per hour), Gibson-girl glass in hand, into the cozy European dining room decorated like a family parlor with souvenirs, photos, and paintings of *Euskalherria*, the Basque Country.

At dusk Eusebio switches on the 50s-style, electric image of a giant martini glass on Main Street and Elvira, his Guipuzcoan wife, stirs the huge cauldron of soup expectantly. Sometimes he forgets the neon sign and she chides him, but it doesn't matter. The Overland does not advertise; the regulars know the way and one assumes that the hungry straggler will find the front door.

The dining room is full by 6:15. The warmth of bodies close together permeates the place—picon punches all around! Two of the four slots begin to spin, jangle, and roll. Someone slips fifty cents for three plays into the old juke box: *Ama Ezkondu*, *On the Road Again*, and *Bésame Mucho* alternate with the sound of laughter. Marcelino, a permanent boarder, characteristically slams the back screen door, red bandanna in place about his leathered neck, and shuffles in taking his place at the bar where the wooden rail curves around towards the TV with its evening news that he regards but never contemplates. There is no fuss made about the children scattering poker chips (red-white-blue) across the floor in joyous abandon.

No one arrives late, for reservations are not taken, and there is no set closing time. Everyone who enters belongs to this warm lap of a place—a place where they know your name and your heartaches, whether you prefer vanilla or spumoni ice cream, and how you like your coffee.

There are no laminated menus here, no endless lists of omelettes and burgers. The fresh-stock-vegetable soup, basket of French bread, and labelless bottle of burgundy, the heart of the meal, appear before you get a chance to reconsider or even consider. This is egalitarian fare in which the steaks, lamb chops, chicken, and prawns are *prix fixe*, and the heavy platters shared. You may eat one bowl of soup or five, depending upon your inclination. The bread basket is bottomless and you can pick up your lamb chops with your fingers with no compunction. Add to this propitious beginning a tossed, green-garden salad, oiled with a secret, garlic-base dressing; french fries cut from red, new potatoes; the ubiquitous *lapikua*, or Basque stew; garbanzos with pork ribs; tongue in tomato sauce; salt cod and potatoes; lamb shanks and pimientos; paella; ravioli or homemade spaghetti, and you have a feast. As an exclamation mark to the hearty meal, Renée Presto, Mari-Angeles Pérez, or Debbi Borda, who together have served for over twenty years at the Overland, bring on the ice cream or sheep's-milk cheese, coffee, and the optional after-dinner drink, *sol y sombra*: a curious concoction of clear anisette and amber cognac, thus the moniker "sun and shade"—a drink as singular and contradictory as the Basque himself.

For over a hundred years the Basque hotels in Nevada and the West have offered up such sun and shade to the boarder, the traveler, the diner, the reveler, and the man simply *leku barik*, "without a place." The "sun" is that of light and warmth: the bare bulb glaring its white eye over the *mus* match (a game of Basque poker) at a barroom table, the steamy atmosphere of the ivy-festooned kitchen, heart and hearth of the hotel, whence endless cauldrons of homemade soups and stews waft their opulent aromas to the expectant, salivating diners.

There is also shade and shelter here from the glare of life. At the bar the talk is loud, raucous, back-slapping, the banter of old friends and new enemies with open wounds. On TV the prize fight drones on as the not-so-latest issue of *El País*, its airmail-weight paper badly frayed by the fingerings of many hands, is passed around. On feast days there are the frenetic strains of an accordion as it punctuates the Dionysian dizziness of *jotas*, polkas, and *paso dobles*. The old songs are still sung in a cappella harmony, by a few.

In the corner, beneath the map of Spain, there is an over-stuffed chair where a boarder or a straggler can still find peace nursing a pernod while nodding off from time to time. There are long Saturday afternoons filled with late autumn light where a man can warm his old bones by the window and wonder about life and the *sombra* of death. And at four, *merienda* or tea time, he can claim the stepladder stool in the kitchen and sip hot *café con leche*, nibbling biscuits with Reynalda or Vidal, who understand a man's private silence.

Tonight at the Overland the restaurant is full. Here is the usual vacation assortment of retired Californians, wind surfers, construction workers, and a birthday party in the back for one of the Borda clan. At their regular table number seven sit the elderly Yerington couple, retired now from farming, who peer like children into the familiar kitchen as their soup is served. They are happy tonight with the shared secret that the cloves of fresh garlic they have brought their old friends will stud their own lamb chops. The farmer nudges his life's companion as the husky worker in front of them at number six praises the fresh garlic and the succulent chops to his girlfriend while pondering aloud, "Do ya think they'd sell us a bottle of this here wine?"

Nectarines, peaches, melons, and cucumbers, fat and August-ready, decorate the clean counters of the kitchen where Elvira rushes to and fro, apron-frocked and smiling, a light sweat on her forehead. She barks out orders to Vidal, the dishwasher, who is not electric but Mexican, and then, like an assassin, hacks the New York steaks with a cleaver. She glances happily at the fresh fruit and vegetables; yesterday the Ugaldes were in, with wet kisses and hugs all around and a quick greeting in mixed Spanish, Basque, and broken English, while they dropped armfuls of cornucopiaed goodwill upon the counters before going in to dinner.

Upstairs Marcelino's room is clean, lemon-scented. It is minimal, almost threadbare by modern standards: no air conditioning, no plastic in-room coffee, no Magic Fingers, no TV. The bathroom down the hall is immaculate and sun-washed. There is a deep, claw-footed tub, and fluffy towels were set out by Mari-Angeles just this morning. His toothbrush hangs by the sink next to Fermín's. He uses his young workman friend's toothpaste without thinking, determined to keep his teeth in his head for another year or so (toothless heads make ugly corpses.) He will rest a few hours and eat dinner later. His place will be saved. Perhaps someone will be up for a game of *mus*, or there'll be *flan*, egg custard, for dessert!

Seven-thirty p.m.: like clockwork, which is curious since he wears no watch, Marcelino descends the steep stairs. As he makes his way down to the dining room the massive oak bannister creaks beneath the combined weight of eighty years, his and the hotel's—all the weary, sliding hands upon its surface remembered for a moment, the smoothed recesses of each wooden stair imprinted with countless footprints.

He sits down, favoring his bad hip, and María brings him his soup and bread. A teetotaler, he drinks no wine. A confirmed misogynist, he grumbles half-heartedly at the small affections of the women who call him *abuelo* and *buru zuri*, "old white head." He eats alone tonight; he has lost his companions, every one (left to die among women and *Amerikanuak*): Old Gregorio, who bussed dishes for his keep right to the end; Martín, the self-made millionaire whose room has been repainted since he passed on two summers ago (all his things moved out, *Alaxe!* "Like that!" *Ze escándalo*!), Mateo, the young bartender who sometimes shares the old herder's table, is only there on weekends. He's working on a master's degree at the nearby university (*Zelako bullshita ori*!). And, worse than bad, he got married last summer (*Andra gaistoak!* "Roguish, conniving women!").

Yet in his heart he knows it is the women who comfort his last days; the women of the hotels down in the valleys who made his survival possible in the early years. A man without a woman could get "sheeped," *soraturik*, go stark, raving mad with so much loneliness, so many sheep, so much snow. It was the town, with its open bar and simple, clean room, which made the wilderness days possible. It was the hotel which had kept the men going in bygone days ... and now.

The robust immigrant women who manned, or rather "womaned," the hotels are gone, but their daughters, nieces and granddaughters remember. One laughingly recalls the honeymoon bell downstairs in the bar which was allegedly attached to a deep, wide bed in room number seven upstairs, the stories about it as long and twisted as the cord running down through the floor from the iron bedpost. Another woman recalls the corpse of Paz Mendi together in a casket with her stillborn twins: cold, young, and waxen as she lay in state in the hotel parlor. One woman still complains about the Borda boys down the street who terrorized the alley behind the long string of Basque hotels in Gardnerville. Because she was a girl they sabotaged her chances of learning handball against the back wall of the Eastfork, and she never forgave them. A woman who grew up "on the other side of the tracks" in a Basque hotel in Reno remembers the cleaning of rooms on Saturday, the sound of the trains, the *pangingi* games in the alley below, Chinese and Greek voices mixed with Basque and Italian.

An Elko woman talks freely about her father's speakeasy in the basement of their hotel, where wondrous sights were to be seen through a child-fashioned peephole: a drunken priest, a Basque wake complete with corpse, a raid by the "prohibes," poker games, fist fights, whiskey, and phonograph music. She comments that although her father, like most of his generation, was a card-carrying Republican to his dying day, he was also an early promoter of social welfare: a whole bottle of moonshine was thoughtfully left in the pocket of an old overcoat hanging on a hook in the downstairs "john" expressly for the destitute and sad of heart.

A central Nevada woman remembers the day her father rousted some troublemakers from his bar with a .45, and an even more intimidating diatribe of Basque and Spanish cusswords. Her neighbor recalls a great uncle who had a dancing black dog and once threatened to "shoot pleny dead" the public health sanitarian who merely suggested that he install separate bathrooms for "the womens and the mens to pees!"

There are stories of whole chickens hanging beak down in the bathroom of one hotel during the hot summers, of a Basque woman of dubious honor who lost her bustle jumping out a second-story window during a raging fire, of the annual *txarri boda*, literally "pig wedding," at which swine were slaughtered with great ceremony in anticipation of sausage-making and ham-curing. All the women remember wash day, the hit parade, and ice boxes; running errands for the non-English speaking herders and that precious nickel passed from large hand to small; the dances where a girl might get away with a sip of beer; and Sundays when one's best clothes were pressed for Mass. *Aie ama!* they sigh collectively, telling their individual tales. "Oh! How times have changed!"

Gone now are the spartan, thunder-mugged rooms with a communal bathroom down the hall; gone, the long "family-style" tables with their familiar, red-checkered oil cloths, the art deco water pitchers, and the toothpicks in emptied Tabasco Sauce bottles; gone, the accordion music, the *jotas* and the waltzes, the bedrolls stacked up in the hall, bundles of foreign letters kept in the safe; long past, the trips to the coal bin or the woodpile, to the garden or to the pantry where the future was stacked securely in predestined quantities of pasta, potatoes, and jewel-colored preserves.

Gone forever is the Chinese laundry across the alley whence the linen sheets and pillow cases, towels, aprons, and sanitary cloths came back in tight, immaculate bundles pressed like magic; the fish market, the ice house, the lumberyards, and the skating rinks—all gone. The faded lines of the handball courts are barely visible on the crumbling walls of the old hotels. No one dances now in the geranium-filled courtyards lined with dancers, mops, buckets, and brooms. No dancers spill out onto the street on Independence Day or San Fermín. They are feeble and arthritic, if not deceased; they now rub their joints reflectively in unison, lingering over steaming cups of coffee royals at the funeral feasts of the departed. The Basque sheepherder of the American West is gone. Like the cowboy he has become an anachronism, a rugged icon of the Old West and the last frontier. In the summer of 1987 a film crew from *Euskal Telebista*, the Basque television station, traveled to Nevada to do a segment on this lonely hero for a continuing documentary entitled, "Basques of the World." After many telephone calls, plane rides, and sagebrush-studded, dusty journeys over miles and miles of dirt roads they left without finding a single Basque sheepherder. One lone Peruvian, a small crew of Mexicans, and a stuttering Spaniard of indeterminate origin were the spoils of their noble quest. Among their Basque trophies, much to their surprise, was a congressman, a vice-president of Harrah's, a celebrated writer, a presidential candidate, millionaires, and owners of grand hotel casinos.

The rugged men of the hills are gone but their sons, nephews, and grandsons remember. One of the prominent Basque-Americans interviewed for the documentary still had his father's rifle; another recited a *bertso*, an impromptu, troubador-like verse in Basque which he had learned around a high desert campfire. Another wistfully told the old stories of frozen jaws, howling coyotes, low provisions, and blizzards in the Sierra Nevadas. They spoke of the gentian solitude of a sunset on the Black Rock Desert, the rainbow flash of trout in the Truckee, the rarefied air of the Rubies and the oasis lap of Carson Valley. And they all spoke of the hotels. . . .

The hotels, however, were a mixed blessing to the independent herder. This woman-tended haven was both solace and confinement to him, fellowship blended with the loss of absolute freedom. Like the sailor come home to a landlocked village, the herder entered the hotel conditionally, determined to leave. The hotels would be there, red-bricked sentinels of a new order, awaiting his return.

The Overland in Elko, the Star, the Telescope, the Nevada, the Amistad, the Commercial, the Morning Star, Jack Creek Bar, Dinner Station, the Winnemucca, the Overland in Winnemucca, the Martin, the Busch, the Paradise, Gastañaga's, McDermitt Bar, the Santa Fe, the Toscano, the Silver Club, the Colonnade, the Ely Hotel, the Eastfork, the French, Currie Bar, the J & T, and the Overland in Gardnerville were all the bastions of Nevada's sheepherder culture.

There are those who say that like Marcelino, the lone ex-herder who lives upstairs at the Overland, the hotels have outlived their purpose. They are nothing more than glorified, ethnic steakhouses. But if you sit quietly, reverently watchful, as the rays of sunlight and warmth filter their way down upon the *mus* table; if you sit sipping a *vermut español* listening to *Jotas Vascas*, C4 on the jukebox, waiting for Elvira to call you to the dining room; if you listen carefully you'll hear them, feel them, know their collective story as if all the hearts and minds, dreams and heartaches of those who have passed through these doors had ionized into sunlight and breath beckoning, welcoming, whispering . . . *Ongi Etorri*.

About the Contributors

Elena Arana Williams, a native of the Basque Country, received her M.A. in folklore from the University of Pennsylvania. She continues to pursue her interest in Basque traditional narrative. She resides in Villanova, Pennsylvania.

Alejandro Arizcun Cela is a professor of modern history at the University of the Basque Country and vice-president of the Instituto Navarro de Historia Económica y Social "Gerónimo de Ustáriz" (Pamplona). He is the author of *Economía y sociedad en un valle pirenaico de antiguo régimen, Baztán, 1600-1841* (Pamplona, 1988) and *Series navarras de precios de cereales, 1600-1841* (Madrid, 1989).

Jesús Azcona is a professor of social anthropology at the University of the Basque Country. His publications include *Etnia y nacionalismo vasco. Una aproximación desde la antropología* (Barcelona, 1982) and *Para comprender la antropología*, 2 volumes (Estella, 1987 and 1988).

Rachel Bard is a writer, editor, and teacher in the Tacoma, Washington, area. She is the author of *Navarra: The Durable Kingdom* (Reno, 1982) and is currently researching the life of Berengaria of Navarre for a biography.

Román Basurto is a history professor at the University of the Basque Country. He is the author of *Comercio y burguesía mercantil de Bilbao en la segunda mitad del siglo XVIII* (Lejona, 1983) and *Guecho: La evolución de los modos de vida de una anteiglesia de Vizcaya* (Getxo, 1989).

Teresa del Valle is a professor of social anthropology at the University of the Basque Country and vice-president of the European Association for Social Anthropology (EASA). Among her numerous publications are *Mujer vasca. Imagen y realidad* (Barcelona, 1985) and *Korrika: Rituales de la lengua en el espacio* (Barcelona, 1988).

William A. Douglass, anthropologist, is coordinator of the Basque Studies Program, University of Nevada-Reno. His works include *Death in Murelaga: Social Significance of Funerary Ritual in a Spanish Basque Village* (Seattle, 1969) and *Echalar and Murelaga: Opportunity and Rural Exodus in Two Spanish Basque Villages* (London, 1975).

Jerónima Echeverría is an assistant professor in the Department of History, California State University at Fresno. She recently completed her doctoral dissertation entitled "*California-ko Ostatuak*:

A History of California's Basque Hotels" (1988) at the University of North Texas. She is currently working on a book regarding the history of Basque boardinghouses in the United States.

Roslyn Frank is a professor and acting chair of the Department of Spanish and Portuguese at the University of Iowa. She is the author of *En torno a un mito: El euskara y el indoeuropeo* (San Sebastián, 1980) and "De los orígenes del euskera: fábulas integristas y separatistas," *Journal of Basque Studies in America*, vol. 4 (1985), pp. 45–77.

Angel García-Sanz Marcotegui is a professor of modern history at the University of the Basque Country and president of the Instituto Navarro de Historia Económica y Social "Gerónimo de Ustáriz" (Pamplona). His several publications include *Demografía y sociedad de la barranca de Navarra* (Pamplona, 1985) and *Republicanos navarros* (Pamplona, 1985).

Kay Hummel was awarded the Samuel Arnold Fellowship for foreign independent study upon her graduation from Brown University in 1976. She spent the following year in Colombia researching its colony of Basque immigrants. She lives in Boise, Idaho, and has coauthored a sourcebook and atlas entitled *Oregon Indians* (Oregon Historical Society, 1983).

Jeremy MacClancy is a senior associate member of St. Antony's College, Oxford University. He is the author of *To Kill a Bird with Two Stones: A Short History of Vanuatu*, ([Vanuatu], 1981).

M. E. R. Nicholson is an anthropologist, an instructor for Emeritus College of the Marin Community College District, and an adjunct professor with the Basque Studies Program of the University of Nevada-Reno. Her published articles include "The Basque Notary, an Intercultural Mediator," *International Journal of the Sociology of Law*, vol. 15 (1987), pp. 85–103, and "Change without Conflict: A Case Study of Legal Change in Tanzania," *Law and Society Review*, vol. 7 (1973), pp. 747–766.

Gretchen Osa is a secondary schoolteacher of Spanish in Gardnerville, Nevada. The daughter of a Basque hotelkeeper, she has recently concluded a study of Nevada's Basque hotels funded by the Nevada Humanities Committee.

Jacqueline Urla recently obtained her doctorate in cultural anthropology from the University of California at Berkeley. She is the author of "Ethnic Protest and Social Planning: A Look at Basque Language Revival," *Cultural Anthropology*, vol. 3, no. 4 (1988), pp. 379–394. She was recently awarded a postdoctoral fellowship at Rutgers University where she will be writing a book on the historical construction of Basque identity.

Other Titles in the
Basque Studies Program Occasional Papers Series:

no. 1: *The Long Journey: Social Integration and Ethnic Maintenance among Urban Basques in the San Francisco Bay Region*,
by Jean Francis Decroos (1983)

no. 2: *Basque Politics: A Case Study in Ethnic Nationalism*,
edited by William A. Douglass (1985)

no. 3: *Arriaga, the Forgotten Genius: The Short Life of a Basque Composer*,
by Barbara Rosen (1989)

Available from:
The Basque Studies Program
University of Nevada
Reno, NV 89557